CAMBRIDGE STUDIES
IN ENGLISH LEGAL HISTORY

Edited by
D. E. C. YALE
Fellow of Christ's College
and Reader in English Legal History at the University of Cambridge

THE HIGH COURT OF DELEGATES

BY

G. I. O. DUNCAN

Lecturer in Law in the University of Bristol

CAMBRIDGE

AT THE UNIVERSITY PRESS

1971

Published by the Syndics of the Cambridge University Press
Bentley House, 200 Euston Road, London N.W.1 2DB
American Branch: 32 East 57th Street, New York, N.Y.10022

Library of Congress Catalogue Card Number: 73-138376

ISBN: 0 521 08024 X

Printed in Great Britain
at the University Printing House, Cambridge
(Brooke Crutchley, University Printer)

CONTENTS

PREFACE

This book owes its origin to research undertaken for a doctorate in philosophy of Cambridge University and in its present form is based upon the dissertation tendered for that purpose. The Court of Delegates was chosen as a subject because the civil law in England, although a fascinating bypath of legal history, has been little explored until recently. Today, happily the position is changing; this volume may, with due deference, take its place alongside the work of R. G. Marsden, over half a century ago, on the Court of Admiralty, and more recently of G. D. Squibb, Q.C. on the Court of Chivalry. A new study of the Court of Admiralty is now being undertaken at Cambridge, and when this is completed, most of the secular civil law courts in this country will have been thoroughly examined.

One lesson which the research student learns early in his career is that the records he is examining will answer only some of the questions so insistently put to them, and it is for this reason that so much space has been devoted to procedure. It had been intended to consider the development of legal doctrine by the court, and the influence of those common law judges who acted as delegates would have made this a fascinating study; but the archives have hidden their secrets behind a door to which the present author can find no key, and it is clear that no key, in fact, exists. However, it is hoped that the chapters on procedure will be of some use and interest; the records are particularly rich in procedural material and this, as far as is known, is the first book in which a detailed account of the subject has been illustrated by reference to the workings of a particular court.

Scholarly research yields its own pleasures; none gives more satisfaction than the acknowledgment of those whose advice or encouragement has helped in bringing the work to fruition. I am deeply endebted to Mr M. J. Pritchard, Fellow of Gonville and Caius College, Cambridge, who first suggested the subject to me and whose tireless patience as a research supervisor saved me from many errors. My grateful thanks are also due to Mr D. E. C. Yale, Fellow of Christ's College, Cambridge, and to Mr G. D. Squibb, Q.C., who acted as examiners of my research dissertation and made a number of most helpful suggestions, and to Mr K. C. McGuffie, the Admiralty Registrar, who was kind enough to read the dissertation and who made valuable comments on Admiralty practice. Finally, a particular debt of gratitude is owed to the staff at the Ashridge Repository of the Public Record Office; by their unfailing helpfulness and courtesy they did everything in their power to lighten the sometimes uncongenial task of examining the original sources.

G.I.O.D.

PRINCIPAL ABBREVIATIONS

Ad. & E.	Adolphus and Ellis's Reports, 1834–40
Atk.	Atkyn's Reports, 1736–55
B.	Baron of the Court of Exchequer
C.	Justinian's *Codex*
Carth.	Carthew's Reports, 1686–1701
Co. Inst.	Coke's Institutes
C.P.R.	*Calendar of Patent Rolls*
Cro. Eliz.	Croke's Reports *temp.* Elizabeth I, 1582–1603
C.S.P.D.	*Calendar of State Papers, Domestic*
Cur. Mil.	Curia Militaris
D.	Justinian's *Digest*
DEL (followed by class list number)	Records of the Court of Delegates
D.N.B.	*Dictionary of National Biography*
Dy.	Dyer's Reports, 1513–82
Eccl. Courts Rep. (1831–2)	*Practice and Jurisdiction of the Ecclesiastical Courts in England and Wales.* R. Com. Rep., 1831–2
E.H.R.	*English Historical Review*
F.E.L.	J. T. Law, *Forms of Ecclesiastical Law*
Hagg. Ecc.	Haggard's Ecclesiastical Reports, 1827–33
H.C.C.	G. D. Squibb, *High Court of Chivalry*
H.E.L.	W. S. Holdsworth, *History of English Law*
H.M.C. (followed by MS reference)	Calendar of the Historical Manuscripts Commission
J.	Justice
Jones, T.	T. Jones's Reports, 1667–85
K.B.	Court of King's Bench
L. & P. Hen. VIII	*Calendar for Letters and Papers, Foreign and Domestic, Henry VIII*
Lit.	Littleton's Reports, 1626–32
L.Q.R.	*Law Quarterly Review*
L.R.P.C.	Law Reports, Privy Council, 1866–75
Mod.	Modern Reports, 1669–1732

Moo. K.B.	Moore's King's Bench Reports, 1519–1621
Mos.	Moseley's Reports, 1726–31
Nott. Chan. Cas.	Lord Nottingham's Chancery Cases, 1673–82
O.J.	T. Oughton, *Ordo Judiciorum*
P. (preceded by date)	Law Reports, Probate, Divorce and Admiralty Division
P.R.O.	Public Record Office
P.Wms.	Peere William's Reports, 1695–1735
Raym. T.	Sir T. Raymond's Reports, 1660–84
Ridg. Ir. T.	Ridgeway, Lapp and Schoales's Irish Term Reports, 1793–5
R.R.	*Return of all Appeals in Causes of Doctrine or Discipline made to the High Court of Delegates*
Sel. Cas. Chan.	Reports of Select Cases in Chancery by a Gentleman of the Temple, 1724–33
Shower	Shower's Reports, House of Lords, 1694–99
S.P. Car. II.	State Papers, Domestic, Charles II
S.P. Eliz. I.	State Papers, Domestic, Elizabeth I
St. Tr.	State Trials
Swans.	Swanston's Reports, 1818–19
Vern.	Vernon's Reports, 1681–1719
Ves. J.	Vesey Junior's Reports, 1789–1817

TABLE OF CASES

If a case has been cited more than once in the text, there may be variations in the spelling of proper names, the mode of citation and the date (if the references have been taken from different documents); such cases are reproduced in the table below in the form which they took in the first citation. For the citation of civilian cases in the form '*X* v. *Y*' rather than '*X* c. *Y*' see *H.C.C.*, p. xix.

TABLE OF STATUTES

The earlier Acts are cited from the *Statutes at Large*.

CHAPTER I

THE COURT OF DELEGATES—AN HISTORICAL SURVEY

It may be plausibly argued that the structure and workings of a court are best investigated by analysis under various heads, so that separate consideraton is given to jurisdiction, procedure, the judiciary and so forth. When this method is employed, the reader is provided with detailed information about those various aspects of the court which are most likely to be of use and interest to him. But an investigation which is purely analytical has one serious defect; the history of the court as a whole is obscured and its development as a single judicial unit is never made clear. The function of this chapter is to avoid this danger by providing a brief historical survey of the Court of Delegates with particular reference to the statutes which affected it and their background, and to the influence upon it of periods such as the Interregnum. In order to do this successfully, it is necessary to consider first the origin of civil law appeals in this country (in both secular and ecclesiastical causes) and then to give some account of the statutory reforms imposed upon ecclesiastical appeals at the Reformation; only when this has been done can the final emergence of a single Court of Delegates with appellate jurisdiction over civil law matters be properly understood.

From the earliest days of the civil law in England, appeal was possible from the courts which administered it;[1] in this they no doubt modelled themselves upon Roman law, in which the right of appeal was widely admitted.[2] But in this early period one cannot speak of the Court of Delegates, if by this expression is meant a tribunal with jurisdiction over all civil law appeals; as will be shown, such a body did not emerge until the civil law in this country had entered upon its decline.[3] There was, in fact, no permanent court for such business; an appellant would petition

[1] The courts of Cambridge University seem to provide the only exception to this rule; see pp. 40–2 *post*.

[2] W. W. Buckland, *A Text Book of Roman Law* (Cambridge, 1950), p. 670.

[3] See pp. 17–19 *post*.

the appropriate authority and judges-delegate were then appointed, whose jurisdiction to try the appeal did not extend beyond the limits of that single cause.[1]

Authority over these appeals was divided. From the secular courts, petitions were directed to the king and the delegates appointed to hear them were his representatives; from the courts of the Church, however, appeals might go to the Holy See, until the Reformation. The right of the Crown to deal with secular appeals seems never to have been questioned and this business was conducted without comment,[2] but the propriety of appeals to Rome has been controverted and requires further consideration.

A number of the older writers give some account of the origin and growth of appeals to Rome and these accounts are in substantial agreement.[3] Such appeals are thought to have begun in the reign of King Stephen (1135–54) at the instigation of Henri de Blois, Bishop of Winchester and Papal legate. Attempts to appeal had been made before this, however, for in the reign of Henry I (1100–1135) the Pope had complained that the King of England would allow no appeals to be made to him and even earlier, in the time of William Rufus (1087–1100), the bishops and barons had told Anselm, who wished to appeal to Rome, that this could not be done without the king's consent.

From their very beginning, such appeals were widely regarded with disfavour and a further check was provided by the Constitutions of Clarendon,[4] which laid it down that the course of appeals should run from the archdeacon to the bishop, from the bishop to the archbishop of the province and then to the king, while there was to be no right of further appeal without royal consent. In the Parliament of Northampton these constitutions were renewed, but later attempts were made to evade the rule as to appeals and certain persons were imprisoned for this reason in the reign of the first

[1] It is likely that this practice is also borrowed from Roman law; in the late Empire, appeals to the emperor were dealt with in the same way (*C.* 7. 62. 32).

[2] There is little evidence in print about the early practice of the secular courts; for the Court of Admiralty see R. G. Marsden (ed.), *Select Pleas in the Court of Admiralty* (London, 1894), vol. 1, p. lxxix; for the Court of Chivalry, G. D. Squibb, *The High Court of Chivalry* (London, 1959), p. 221; nothing has been found for the Courts of Oxford University.

[3] The account which follows is based upon R. Burn, *Ecclesiastical Law* (London, 1781), vol. 1, pp. 52–3 and W. Blackstone, *Commentaries on the Laws of England* (London, 1800), vol. 3, pp. 66–7.

[4] Constitutions of Clarendon, 1164 (ch. 8).

three Edwards.[1] But the custom of appealing to Rome became too well established to destroy and it was not until the reign of Henry VIII and the decisive break with the Holy See that they came to an end.

This account of the matter by the older text-book writers may well have appealed to the patriotism of their readers (as no doubt it was intended to do) and it has all the plausibility of the partially true. But a more recent study of the subject suggests that it requires correction in some important respects.[2]

There now seems to be little substance in the proposition that appeals to Rome were 'vigorously withstood by the nation'[3] or 'were always looked upon by the English nation...with an evil eye'.[4] The advantages of Papal jurisdiction were not recognized by the Continent alone,[5] and as Mrs Cheney says 'it was inevitable that those who could not obtain redress of grievances in their own province or diocese should wish to take their case to the court of appeal recognized by every ecclesiastical court in the West.'[6] Moreover, litigation is not brought before a court unless the parties (or at least one of them) wish it to be heard there. The number of causes tried by way of appeal by the end of the twelfth century shows that Papal justice was popular early in England.[7]

It is true that the early development of appeals to Rome is correctly associated with that period of Stephen's reign when Henri de Blois, Bishop of Winchester, was Papal legate. Henry of Huntington (an almost contemporary writer) spoke of 'new appeals' in connection with the council of London in 1151 and these he attributed to the machinations (as he saw it) of the legate.[8] Another

[1] The position is thus stated in Burn, *Ecclesiastical Law*, vol. 1, p. 53, although the authorities he cites do not seem to support him.

[2] What follows is based upon M. Cheney, 'The Compromise of Avranches of 1172 and the Spread of Canon Law in England', *Eng. Hist. Rev.*, lvi (1941), pp. 177–97.

[3] Burn, *Ecclesiastical Law*, vol. 1, p. 52.

[4] Blackstone, *Commentaries*, vol. 3, p. 66.

[5] Thus, in the reign of Stephen, the English church of its own volition reiterated the rule (expressed in *Decretum*, C, II, XVII, qu. IV, c. 29, *si quis suadente*) that only the Pope could absolve a man who had struck a priest.

[6] Cheney, *E.H.R.*, vol. lvi, p. 178.

[7] The records investigated in the course of 'a rapid search' by Mrs Cheney attribute sixty or seventy each to Gilbert Foliot, Bartholomew of Exeter, and Roger of Worcester; many more may have been tried by these and other judges.

[8] 'In Anglia namqe appellationes in usu non erant, donec eas Henricus Wintoniensis, dum legatus esset, malo suo crudeliter intrusit.' (T. Arnold (ed.), *Historia Anglorum* (London, 1879), p. 282).

historian, Gervase of Canterbury, stated that the succession of Theobald as legate was marked by 'appellationes antea inauditae'. But it is now clear that writers such as Burn and Blackstone were wrong in stating that there were no appeals to the Pope before the appointment of Henri de Blois as legate. As early as the episcopate of Urban of Llandaff (1107–33/4) suits were taken to Rome in connection with the land and rights of the see,[1] and these disputes were referred to English judges delegated by the Pope.[2]

Perhaps Mrs Cheney makes too much of the fact that all the litigation taken to Rome by Bishop Urban had to do with the boundaries of his see. The solution of such a question of fact, she suggests, could hardly be arrived at without delegation and so the fact that the cause was taken to Rome at all (which must have meant that Urban envisaged delegation being used) implies that the idea of appeals to Rome, to be dealt with by delegation, 'had already become fairly well established'.[3] It is unlikely, however, that such an established course of delegated appeals would have grown up without canonical regulation, and no canons are to be found on this subject earlier than the decretals of Alexander III who was Pope towards the end of the twelfth century.[4] The most that can safely be said is that there were isolated appeals from a much earlier period but probably no settled practice until Alexander's pontificate.

Again, it is true in a sense to say that Henry II 'resumed and maintained' his grandfather's claim to control appeals,[5] for this is established by numerous letters addressed to the king concerning appeals, which make it clear that his consent had been obtained. But this cannot be taken as evidence that such appeals were objectionable to the Crown (which is what Burn and Blackstone imply) for the very number of such letters shows that appeals were common; they 'came to Rome from England as soon as from other countries, and judges-delegate were appointed to adjudicate in England at precisely the period when delegations first became common elsewhere, that is, in the pontificate of Innocent II'.[6]

[1] J. G. Evans (ed.), *Liber Llandavensis* (Oxford, 1893), pp. 30–67 and 87–94.

[2] Jaffe-Wattenbach (ed.), *Regesta Pontificum Romanorum*, no. 7511.

[3] Cheney, *E.H.R.*, vol. lvi, p. 179.

[4] Z. B. Van Espen, *Jus Ecclesiasticum Universum* (Cologne, 1729), bk. 3, pt. 5, tit. 2, ch. 3.

[5] Burn, *Ecclesiastical Law*, vol. 1, p. 53.

[6] Cheney, *E.H.R.*, vol. lvi, p. 180.

The final misunderstanding of the older writers has to do with the Compromise of Avranches.[1] This is represented as a triumph for the pro-Papal party, who wrang from a reluctant king the concession of a free right of appeal to Rome. Modern research, however, with a greater familiarity with the circumstances surrounding the Compromise, has reached a rather different conclusion. No doubt in Henry's eyes a reconciliation with Rome was desirable enough, but his conduct of the negotiations was far from that of a man prepared to make any concession to achieve it; 'he had refused to meet the first legates, and had held up negotiations for more than six months while he settled the affairs of Ireland; the legates waited in Normandy from before Christmas [of 1172] till after Easter, and Henry only returned finally because he feared political trouble in his French dominions.'[2]

The true significance of this settlement, in short, can be understood only by setting it in a broader context than that provided by Henry's squabbles with the Pope; 'appeals to Rome had already become an integral part of the organization of the Church, and a peace which refused to allow them would have been as unthinkable as a peace which did not recognize the Pope as head of the English church'.[3]

The Compromise of Avranches, then, did no more than confirm a rule already well established, that litigants before the courts of the Church in England might take appeals to the Holy See, and this state of affairs continued, without significant popular objection or legislative interference, for several centuries.[4] When the secular civil law courts established themselves, they used a course of appeal within this country which was very similar,[5] and an observer of the legal scene in the early sixteenth century would have found a

[1] i.e. the agreement by which Henry II was reconciled to the Church following Becket's murder; see H. M. Gwatkin and others (eds.), *Cambridge Medieval History* (Cambridge, 1911–36), vol. 5, p. 566.

[2] Cheney, *E.H.R.*, vol. lvi, p. 196.

[3] *Ibid.*

[4] The exaggeration by some writers of public objection to such appeals has already been referred to; see pp. 2–3 *ante*. Of the various Acts which were intended to regulate relations with Rome in the Middle Ages, only the two Statutes of Praemunire (27 Edw. III, St. 1, c. 1 and 16 Ric. II, c. 5) touched upon appeals and their scope was far narrower than has sometimes been suggested; Holdsworth has shown that they were not intended to apply to those ecclesiastical causes over which the secular courts claimed no jurisdiction (Sir William Holdsworth, *A History of English Law* (London, 1903–66), vol. 1, p. 586).

[5] See p. 2 *ante*.

settled practice for all civil law appeals; in secular matters, a petition was presented to the Crown, which would appoint delegates to hear the cause, while appeals from the ecclesiastical courts went to the Holy See, which would normally dispose of them in the same way.

This ordered pattern was disturbed and then destroyed by the Reformation. The right of appeal to Rome from decisions of ecclesiastical courts in England was abolished by Henry VIII and this event, together with the complex developments which affected ecclesiastical appeals in the following three reigns, marks the second stage in the gradual development of a single Court of Delegates.

The change began with two statutes,[1] the first of which was provoked by the final crisis in the domestic circumstances of Henry himself. The fact may be briefly told.[2] Henry had become enamoured of Anne Boleyn and was determined to marry her. His wife, Catherine of Aragon, refused to facilitate the marriage by entering a religious house and an annulment was planned, the evidence for which was accumulated in a leisurely fashion. Early in 1533, however, the need for expedition became apparent; Anne was with child by Henry and by January he knew it. It was essential for the plans he had in mind regarding his succession that the child should be legitimate, and this end could be achieved only by a declaration of nullity given in England itself, for in November of the previous year the Pope had warned Henry that any attempt to separate himself from Catherine on his own authority would result in his excommunication. It was essential, moreover, that there should be no possibility of appeal out of the country from an English decree, as Catherine had made it abundantly clear that she would not be deprived of her rights without a struggle. This made it necessary that Parliament should be induced to declare invalid all appeals to Rome in matrimonial causes.

Henry acted quickly and it was soon widely rumoured that legislation relating to his divorce would be brought before the Commons. The Bill, when it was brought in, had no easy passage. The fears that were expressed concerning its possible effects had more to do with commerce than religion; the Pope, it was argued, could persuade Christian princes to regard the kingdom as

[1] 24 Hen. VIII, c. 12 and 25 Hen. VIII, c. 19.

[2] The following account is based on H. A. L. Fisher, *The History of England from the Accession of Henry VII to the Death of Henry VIII (1485–1547)* (London, 1906), ch. 12 and A. F. Pollard, *Henry VIII* (London, 1951), ch. 11.

schismatical and interrupt the course of trade.[1] But these considerations and others like them the king's adherents brushed aside, arguing that Henry's bold example would soon persuade other princes to act in like manner.[2] In the end, the Bill passed into law, and its successful passage is probably due partly to Henry's astuteness in making no other demands upon Parliament at the time and partly to the masterly handling of the Commons by Thomas Cromwell, a figure already formidable.[3]

The Act deserves careful consideration, partly for its intrinsic importance and partly because its preamble has been widely misunderstood. This portion of it, which is long and typically florid in the style of the period, sets out Henry's views on the constitutional relationship between the spiritual and temporal powers of the state, a view said to be derived (with convenient vagueness) from 'divers sundry old authentick Histories and Chronicles'. England is declared to be a body politic consisting of the Spirituality and Temporality. The Body Spiritual, whose learning is highly praised, is declared to be fully capable of deciding spiritual questions 'without the intermeddling of any exterior Person or Persons'.[4] The various statutes already passed with the

[1] The effect of an interdict upon the wool trade with Flanders was particularly feared, as so many people depended upon it that its interruption 'would create a horrible rebellion, and more than civil war'. (*Calendar of Letters and Papers, Foreign and Domestic*, Henry VIII, 1533, p. 128; a despatch of Chapuys to the Emperor Charles V).

[2] Purely religious objections were countered by the (false) statement that the Pope had withdrawn his objections to the divorce (Fisher, *The History of England* (*1485–1547*), p. 318).

[3] Sir George Throkmorton, in a letter to Henry VIII written several years after the passing of the Act, referred to a conversation he had had with Sir Thomas Dyngley about Parliamentary business, in which the Act of Appeals had been mentioned. Dyngley had expressed his surprise that the Act had passed so readily, to which Throkmorton replied 'it was no wonder as few would displease my Lord Privy Seal'. (*L. & P. Hen. VIII*, 1537, p. 332). Cromwell had much to do with the arrangements for the divorce (see *L. & P. Hen. VIII*, 1533, pp. 205, 212, 219, 230, 231) and Throkmorton's letter suggests that he may have been responsible for seeing the Bill through Parliament.

[4] It is this passage, in particular, which has been misinterpreted; the flamboyant eulogy of clerical learning which it contains has been used by some writers as a basis for the theory that the preamble was intended to regulate the relationship between Church and State and to make the clergy the only fit judges in spiritual causes (see the extravagant conclusions drawn by Bishop Gibson in his *Codex Juris Ecclesiastici Anglicani* (London, 1713), vol. 1, pp. xx–xxii). Enough has been said already about the circumstances surrounding the Act to show that its sole aim was to establish the independence of the ecclesiastical courts in this country from Papal control, as a means of solving the domestic

end of hindering appeals to Rome are referred to, and the physical inconveniences of such appeals are dilated on.

The substance of the Act begins with the latter part of section 2. Certain spiritual causes are specified (those relating to testamentary and matrimonial matters, and to tithes, oblations and obventions); no appeal outside the realm is to be allowed in respect of these causes and provision is made to prevent the execution of excommunications from Rome which might result from appeals there.[1] The Act went on (in ss. 5–8) to establish a course of appeals within the realm. Causes might begin before the court of the archdeacon, bishop or archbishop,[2] and fifteen days were allowed to appeal to the higher tribunal.[3] If a cause reached a court of an archbishop (whether English or Irish)[4] it was 'there to be definitively and finally ordered, decreed, and adjudged, according to Justice, without any other Appellation or Provocation[5] to any other

problems with which the King was confronted. The difficulties involved in a clash of jurisdiction between secular and religious courts can hardly have been in the draftsman's mind and contemporary evidence suggests that the solution of this problem in the years following 1533 was very different from that advanced by Gibson. See G. C. Brodrick and W. H. Fremantle, *A Collection of the Judgments of the Judicial Committee of the Privy Council* (London, 1865), pp. xxx–xxxv, where the matter is fully discussed.

[1] The act contained no saving of Papal jurisdiction in respect of appeals already sent to Rome but not yet determined, as did the Elizabethan statute which revived it (1 Eliz. I, c. 1). Indeed, it is specifically stated that the Act is to apply to appeals 'already commenced, moved, depending, being [or] happening' (s. 2).

[2] The language of these sections is rather confusing and it may be as well to set out the provisions in greater detail. Four possible starting points for an action were envisaged, and the course of appeal was to depend upon which of them was chosen: (i) the archdeacon (or his official) of a bishop to that bishop and from him to the archbishop; (ii) a bishop (or his commissary) to the archbishop; (iii) the archdeacon (or his commissary) of an archbishop to the Court of Audience or Arches and thence to the archbishop; (iv) the archbishop; in this case there was no appeal. The curious provision made for the archdeacon of an archbishop is probably to be explained by the special privileges of such archdeacons, one of which appears to have been exemption from the appellate jurisdiction of their archbishop's Consistory Court, so that appeals went directly from the archdeacon's court to the highest court of the archbishop (and not first to the Consistory Court, as was the case with a bishop's archdeacon). See B. L. Woodcock, *Medieval Ecclesiastical Courts in the Diocese of Canterbury* (Oxford, 1952), p. 13.

[3] The civil and canon law allowed only ten days for an appeal to be lodged (J. Ayliffe, *Parergon Juris Canonici Anglicani* (London, 1734), p. 80 and authorities there cited).

[4] The provision making the archbishop's court the last resort applied to Ireland also, for the Act declared that the rules established for the archbishops of Canterbury and York should be 'so likewise [for] all other Archbishops in other the King's Dominions, as the Case by Order of Justice shall require.' (s. 6).

[5] The terms are not synonymous; see Ayliffe, *Parergon*, p. 72.

Person or Persons, Court or Courts'.[1] There were special provisions if the appeal 'shall or may touch the King, his Heirs or Successors'.[2]

In the event, the Act never had to be invoked for its prime purpose—the frustration of any attempt by Catherine to appeal to Rome. The Queen took her stand upon the assumption that all of Cranmer's proceedings were without authority, so that there was no valid sentence from which an appeal could lie.[3] But the Act had as well a more general application, and the authorities acted energetically to see that its provisions were made public and acted upon. The Council ordered that the statute was to be proclaimed throughout the kingdom and that the full text was to be printed and set up on every church door,[4] while in the following year an information was laid by James Bacon, a London brewer, against John Dakins, the commissary of the Dean and Chapter of St Paul's, and others, for having taken an appeal to Rome contrary to the terms of the statute, and having obtained from the Pope an instrument directed to the Prior of St Mary Spytell at Shoreditch for the annulling of a sentence given in a matrimonial cause to which Bacon was a party.[5]

[1] Despite the decisive nature of the language in these sections, it is doubtful whether the Act would have had the effect of preventing reconsideration of the decisions of archbishops' courts. A subsequent hearing, analogous to a commission of review, would probably have been allowed, for the very similar language of 25 Hen. VIII, c. 19 and 8 Eliz. 1, c. 5 was understood by the courts to permit of such reviews (see pp. 62–6 & 67–9 *post.*)

[2] s. 9. In such a case, the ultimate court of appeal was the Upper House of Convocation in the province where the cause began (and not, as Blackstone suggested, a tribunal consisting of 'all the bishops of the realm, assembled in the upper house of Convocation' (Blackstone, *Commentaries*, vol. 3, p. 67)). It was held in a Privy Council judgment that this provision was abrogated by 25 Henry VIII, c. 19, as ss. 3 and 4 of that Act required that all ecclesiastical appeals should be directed to the king in Chancery (*Gorham* v. *Bishop of Exeter* (1850); in Brodrick and Fremantle, *A Collections of the Judgments of the Privy Council*, p. 65, it is stated that the case was reported by Moore, but it has proved impossible to identify the passage in the report in which this argument occurs).

[3] Brodrick and Fremantle, *A Collection of the Judgments of the Privy Council*, p. xxxviii.

[4] *L. & P. Hen. VIII, 1533*, p. 600. The king went to great trouble to have his anti-Papal legislation advertised and an earlier draft of the memorandum just cited contained additional articles to this end. The Mayor and others of the City of London were to 'liberally speak at their boards, and teach their servants that the Pope...has no jurisdiction here. Also...the nobility should bruit the same, wherever they go' (*ibid.*).

[5] *Ibid.* p. 600. This is the only example discovered of a deliberate attempt to evade the Act.

As an independent provision for a course of appeal in a limited number of causes, the Act had only a brief life, for a statute was passed in the following year to regulate appeals which applied to all spiritual causes and which altered, in some important respects, the earlier provisions.[1] Two factors, however, gave it a continuing importance. Firstly, it fixed the course of appeal which was incorporated (with only one significant alteration)[2] in the Second Act of Appeals, for the latter provided (at s. 3) that appeals in all ecclesiastical causes were to be made with reference to the course laid down in the former statute.[3] Secondly, it made an important reform of the civil and canon law rule regulating the time allowed for appeals,[4] by extending this period from ten to fifteen days.[5]

The provisions of the First Act of Appeals must have seemed startling enough, but the country was soon to discover that it was only a first stage in that movement towards reform upon which the king was now bent and which he was impelled to prosecute with fresh vigour by the refusal of the peremptory terms for a compromise with Rome which he had offered later in 1533. By December of that year the Council was making plans of a revolutionary nature and in the middle of January following, Parliament assembled to sanction those measures which marked the final

[1] 25 Hen. VIII, c. 19. [2] See p. 11 *post*.

[3] Thus both Acts had to be repealed by Mary (1 & 2 Ph. & M., c. 8, ss. 6 & 8) and revived by Elizabeth (1 Eliz. I, c. 1, ss. 4 & 6). The precise relationship between them was still troubling the courts as late as 1850 (*Gorham* v. *Bishop of Exeter* (1850); see note 2 on p. 9 *ante*).

[4] See Ayliffe, *Parergon*, p. 88.

[5] 24 Hen. VIII, c. 12 attracted a little case law, which must be noted. It was held in one case (cited as *Anon.* in C. Viner, *A General Abridgment of Law and Equity* (Aldershot, n.d.), vol. 17, p. 252 and as *Heath* v. *Atworth* in Dyer (1564–5), 240) that an appeal was good if made in terms to the archbishop of the province, even if it was also made to a particular court of the archibishop (e.g. to the Archbishop of Canterbury in his Prerogative Court). The Act allowed appeals only to the archbishop and not to a named archiepiscopal court, but the judges were prepared to regard the words naming the court as superfluous and void, so that the residue (which merely named the archbishop) was sufficient to make the appeal valid.

In *Lee's Case* (1690), Carthew 169, the King's Bench ruled that no appeal would lie to the Archbishop of Canterbury from the Dean of the Arches (who had suspended Lee from practising as a proctor), on the ground that the dean was the archbishop's deputy and there could be no appeal which lay, in effect, from the archbishop to the archbishop. The Act was not cited in the course of argument or judgment but, as Carthew observed, a consideration of it would have shown that such an appeal was not impossible, for s. 7 provided for an appeal from the Court of Audience or Arches to the archbishop (when the cause had begun before the archdeacon of an archbishop or his commissary).

breach with Rome. The scheme of legislation was thorough and complete. First fruits were no longer to be paid to the Bishop of Rome, English bishops and archbishops need not be invested by him and the right of the Crown to nominate bishops by means of the *congé d'élire* was given statutory confirmation.[1] All dispensations and licences from the Pope were prohibited, as was the payment of Peter-pence.[2] By no means the least among these acts was 25 Henry VIII, c. 19, by which all recourse to Rome was prohibited and new provision made for ecclesiastical appeals.

After certain provisions for the proposed reform of canon law,[3] the statute turned to appeals in ecclesiastical causes, which it regulated in far more complete a manner than the First Act of Appeals. From Easter of 1534, no appeals were to be made to Rome out of the king's dominions and this rule was to apply, not merely to the limited number of causes specified in the First Act but to all ecclesiastical 'Causes or Matters happening to be in Contention, and having their Commencement and Beginning in any of the Courts within this Realm, or within any of the King's Dominions, of what Nature, Condition or Quality soever they be of'.[4] The course of appeal laid down in the First Act of Appeals was to be followed but one important extension was made to its provisions; if there was 'lack of justice' in any archbishop's court, the aggrieved party was to have the right to appeal to the king in Chancery, whereupon a commission would be issued under the Great Seal to persons who would hear and determine the cause and whose judgement should be 'good and effectual, and also definitive'.[5] It was further provided that 'no further Appeals [are] to be had or made from the said Commissioners for the same'.[6] The penalty of *Praemunire* was invoked against anyone who attempted to appeal to Rome in defiance of the statute and against the 'Aiders, Counsellors and Abettors' of such persons.[7]

The remainder of the statute provided for appeals from decisions by the heads of various bodies corporate, such as abbeys, priories, monasteries and so forth, which had previously been exempt from ordinary jurisdiction and had enjoyed a right of appeal direct to Rome. Here also appeal was to lie to royal delegates in the manner

[1] Embodied in 25 Henry VIII, c. 20.

[2] *Ibid.* c. 21.

[3] ss. 1 and 2. See pp. 12–14 *post.* [4] s. 3. [5] s. 4.

[6] s. 4. In fact, this provision was interpreted as allowing further consideration of a cause by way of review; see pp. 62–6 *post.* [7] s. 5.

provided by the earlier part of the Act. Care was taken to see that the destruction of Papal authority over exempt houses should not increase the jurisdiction of local bishops or archbishops, for the Act provided that they were to have no greater right to intermeddle with such appeals than they had enjoyed before.[1]

The statute also made provision, as has been mentioned, for the reform of the canon law, and the fate of this attempted reform must now be briefly considered, as its success would have produced significant alterations in the structure of the court and would have made the whole system of appeals in civilian causes very different from what, in fact, it became.

The reforms which have been already discussed were clearly aimed at the complete extirpation of Papal authority in this country and it seemed to Archbishop Cranmer manifestly anomalous that the old code of canon law, sanctioned by Rome and often extolling the authority of the Roman See in extravagant language,[2] should still remain in force in this country and be studied here. The king required no urging to show his independence of the laws as well as the authority of the Holy See, and the first part of the Second Act of Appeals set this reform in train. Henry was given power during his life time to nominate thirty-two persons (of whom half were to be clerical, and half laymen drawn from both Houses of Parliament) who were to examine the existing code and draw up a new one.[3] The commissioners were eventually chosen and set to work,[4] and in due course they produced a reformed code of canon law which required nothing but Henry's formal ratification to become binding. A letter was actually drawn up for this

[1] s. 6.

[2] For examples, see J. Strype, *Memorials of Thomas Cranmer* (Oxford, 1848), vol. 1, p. 294.

[3] 25 Henry VIII, c. 19, s. 2. The language used in the section suggests that their sole function was to examine the laws then in force and decide which of them were to be preserved, but the form eventually taken by the *Reformatio Legum Ecclesiasticarum* makes it clear that the commissioners interpreted their function much more widely, and the preface to the edition of 1571 speaks of their drawing up 'novae leges' (E. Cardwell (ed.) *The Reformation of the Ecclesiastical Laws* (Oxford, 1850), p. xxiv). In fact, many of the provisions of the new code were revolutionary; see R. C. Mortimer, *Western Canon Law* (London, 1953), p. 61.

[4] Two other statutes (27 Hen. VIII, c. 15 and 35 Hen. VIII, c. 16) were passed with the same import as 25 Hen. VIII, c. 19, s. 2, and it may have been several years after 1533 that the work was begun; it seems impossible to fix the time more precisely, although Strype suggests that the commissioners were at least nominated before 1544 (*Memorials of Thomas Cranmer*, vol. 1, p. 295).

purpose,[1] but for some reason it was never signed and the whole problem of canon law reform was carried over into the next reign. Under Edward VI, Cranmer again applied himself to the matter; new commissions were issued,[2] the earlier code was revised and it was again brought to the point where nothing was required to give it binding force but the king's ratification. But once more success eluded Cranmer; Edward died with the code still unratified,[3] and the Marian reaction lasted long enough to destroy any hope of the reform's being taken up after her death. One final attempt to revive it was made under Elizabeth, but it failed,[4] and the *Reformatio Legum Ecclesiasticarum* passed into history.

Although it never achieved the force of law, the provisions of the reformed code relating to appeals deserve brief consideration here. The sixty-one chapters of the title *De Appellationibus* purported to regulate every aspect of the matter and in chapter XI an *ordo*, or course of appeal, was established. From archdeacons, deans and others below episcopal rank and having ecclesiastical jurisdiction, a litigant might proceed to the bishop, from the bishop to the archbishop and from the archbishop to the king. At that point, the cause might be heard by one of two tribunals; if it was a weighty matter, it would go to a provincial council, but if it was of lesser importance it would be heard by a court consisting of three or four bishops.[5] Further appeal was forbidden.[6]

These provisions, had they become law, would have established a final court of appeal different in several significant ways from the Court of Delegates. Two matters in particular call for comment. Firstly, the highest appellate tribunal for almost all ecclesiastical causes would have had none but episcopal judges,[7] whereas the Act

[1] *Ibid.*, App. XXXIV. [2] Under the terms of 3 & 4 Edw. VI, c. 11.

[3] The most likely explanation of this is that the three-year period provided by the Act of 1549 (during which royal ratification alone would have sufficed to make the code binding) had expired and Parliamentary consent was now necessary. (Cardwell, *Reformation of Ecclesiastical Laws*, p. ix). [4] *Ibid.*, pp. iii–iv.

[5] It is difficult to tell whether or not the code envisaged a permanent judicial bench; there is an ambiguity in the Latin text, which merely states that the appeal was to be heard 'a tribus quatuorve episcopis, a nobis ad id constituendis'.

[6] 'Quibus rationibus cum res fuerit definita et judicata, per appellationem amplius cognosci non poterit' (ch. XI). The interpretation by the courts of 25 Hen. VIII, c. 19 and 8 Eliz. I, c. 5 (see pp. 62–6 & 67–9 *post*) suggests that this provision, had it passed into law, might not have been held to prohibit reviews.

[7] It is likely that a provincial council would have been far too cumbersome for any but occasional use.

25 Henry VIII, c. 19 did not require judges of ecclesiastical appeals to be qualified in any way and only two commissions have been found among the records of the Court of Delegates in which bishops alone were named.[1] Gibson plausibly suggested that the Act was deliberately drafted in this form to offset the influence of the episcopate, the sincerity of whose adherence to sound Reformation principles was then in some doubt,[2] and it may well be that the choice of none but bishops for the final court of appeal in ecclesiastical causes, which the compilers of the new code proposed to erect, resulted from the misguided belief during Edward VI's reign that the position had permanently altered. Be that as it may, it is clear that the influence of such a tribunal upon ecclesiastical law would have been drastic in periods of conservative reaction (e.g. when the power of Laud was at its height).[3]

The exclusively clerical nature of the judicial bench proposed for the appellate court in the *Reformatio Legum Ecclesiasticarum* would have had one other important result. Only ecclesiastical causes would have been heard before it and litigants appealing from the Court of Admiralty and other civilian tribunals could never have had recourse to it; as a result, the later union of clerical and secular business within the confines of a single appellate court would never have occurred. Secular appeals, it is true, might later have been amalgamated for reasons of administrative convenience, but there is no certainty of this and it is at least possible that the older arrangements would have been adhered to; the appointment *ad hoc* not only of judges but also of clerical officials, whose jurisdiction lapsed with the cause, so that it was no one's concern to preserve the records of that cause. For this reason alone, modern scholarship may be thankful that the proposals of the Edwardian reformers were never put into effect.

Discussion of the *Reformatio Legum Ecclesiasticarum* leads the narrative of the ecclesiastical Delegates' history into the reign of Edward VI, for it was in the closing year of that monarch's life that the last abortive attempt to give the new code validity was made. In fact, no statute passed in that reign affected appeals from the church courts and, although not a single document from that period survives among the records now preserved in the Public

[1] See p. 178 *post*. [2] Gibson, *Codex*, vol. I, p. xxi.

[3] For further reflections on this theme, see Brodrick and Fremantle, *A Collection of the Judgments of the Privy Council*, pp. xvii–xviii.

Record Office, it may be reasonably assumed that the Delegates were active. Their jurisdiction may have been limited, however, by the use of commissions in ecclesiastical affairs, an innovation of some importance which will be more closely considered a little later.[1]

The accession of Mary, an ardent Catholic and supporter of Papal supremacy, resulted in a temporary reversion to the older practice for church appeals. The troubles which marked the beginning of her reign were no doubt the reason why no immediate action was taken to restore the situation as it had been, and for the first eighteen months the existing arrangements seem to have continued undisturbed. The queen was crowned on 1 October 1553, but the legislation which gave legal effect to the Marian reaction was not brought into Parliament until after her marriage and the arrival of Cardinal Pole as legate in November of the following year. A little later, the necessary Bill was introduced into Parliament.[2] It was a long enactment of some fifty-five sections and it restored the power of the Roman See as comprehensively as the earlier statutes of Henry VIII had destroyed it, repealing the whole series of 'Articles and Provisions made against the See Apostolick of *Rome*, since the twentieth Year of King *Henry* the Eighth'. Among the Acts repealed were 24 Hen. VIII, c. 12 and 25 Hen. VIII, c. 19.[3]

It might have been argued that some decisions of the royal judges-delegate already given in spiritual matters could have been set aside for want of jurisdiction, since they had been given by laymen.[4] The Marian Act re-established the rule that only spiritual persons had the right to give judgment in spiritual causes, but the validity of judgments already given was confirmed; Cardinal Pole's dispensation made special provision for delegated as well as ordinary jurisdiction and the whole dispensation was incorporated into the statute and confirmed by Parliament.[5]

[1] R. G. Usher regarded the letters patent issued under Edward VI in 1549 as the beginning of the High Commission (*The Rise and Fall of the High Commission* (Oxford, 1913), pp. 21–2).

[2] 1 & 2 Ph. & M., c. 8.

[3] In ss. 6 and 8 respectively.

[4] The earliest surviving records of these Delegates (an Act Book for the years 1538–45) makes it clear that laymen were acting as judges by this time; thus Sir Thomas Moyle, Speaker of the House of Commons, acted as a commissioner in *Breirton* v. *Bradshaw and others* (1545), DEL 4/1/447. The statute 37 Hen. VIII, c. 17, passed in 1545, had allowed lay judges to sit in the ecclesiastical courts.

[5] 1 & 2 Ph. & M., c. 8, s. 33. Paragraph XVI of the dispensation made provision in the following terms for sentences delivered in ecclesiastical causes by lay

The way was now open for appeals to Rome on the old pattern and such evidence as is available confirms that such appeals occurred. The Elizabethan Act which restored royal authority over ecclesiastical causes had to make special provision for two appeals to Rome which were pending at the time when the statute was passed.[1]

One other event of significance in the history of appeals from church courts occurred under Mary; the consolidation of the High Commission. The substance and form of the letters patent which conferred authority upon the commissioners for causes ecclesiastical had fluctuated under the previous reign, but the commisssion issued in 1557 provided a pattern from which there was no significant deviation thereafter and the commissioners began to play an ever-increasing part in their chosen field.[2] The effect of the High Commission upon the ecclesiastical Delegates was of singular importance, for it probably succeeded in drawing away from the regular episcopal courts (and thus from the Delegates, who constituted the ultimate court of appeal from those tribunals) many causes which would otherwise have come before them. Causes of doctrine and discipline (the jurisdictional field which the High Commission had made peculiarly its own) were, it seems, especially affected, and it has been suggested that their almost complete absence from the Delegates' records before 1641 is to be explained by the activities of the rival body.[3] The success of the High Commission is to be explained partly by its superior procedure and

judges (including judges delegate): 'Ac omnes processus in quibusvis instantiis coram quibusvis Judicibus, tam ordinarijs quam delegatis, etiam laicis, super materijs spiritualibus habitos et formatos, et sententias super eis latas licet nulliter et de facto, quoad nullitatem ex defectu jurisdictionis praefato tantum insurgentem, sanamus, illosque et illas authoritate Apostolica confirmamus.'

[1] 1 Eliz. I, c. 1, ss. 39–43. The arrangement made was surprisingly liberal. It was enacted that any decision given by the Roman tribunal in those two causes should be binding upon the English courts, provided that sentence was given not later than sixty days after the current session of Parliament ended. If the appeals had not been sentenced at Rome by then, they might be prosecuted within this country.

[2] Usher, *The Rise and Fall of the High Commission*, pp. 23–5.

[3] *Ibid.*, pp. 311–12. Rothery, it is true, included in his return forty-five causes of this nature heard by the Delegates between 1533 and 1640 (*Return of All Appeals in Causes of Doctrine or Discipline made to the High Court of Delegates.* H.C. Return, pp. 2–17; 1867–8, LVII, 108–23), but he admitted that many of these were only marginally concerned with doctrine and discipline (*R.R.*, p. ix).

relative swiftness and partly by the fact that its decisions, once given, were very unlikely to be questioned.[1]

Mary's reforms, although extensive, were short-lived. Papal supremacy (including the right to appeal to Rome) died with her, and upon Elizabeth's accession a religious settlement was made which proved permanent; on this sure foundation the ecclesiastical delegates were re-established. The supremacy Bill, brought into Elizabeth's first Parliament, restored her father's handiwork as thoroughly as Mary's legislation had destroyed it. Its aim was 'to restore to the Crown the ancient Jurisdiction over the Estate Ecclesiastical and Spiritual, and [to abolish] all Foreign Powers repugnant to the same';[2] as a part of this restoration, 24 Hen. VIII, c. 12 and 25 Hen. VIII, c. 19 were both revived.[3]

Few documents survive to illustrate the workings of civil law appeals (whether ecclesiastical or lay) during Elizabeth's reign, but the period is an important one, because by its end it is possible for the first time to speak with some certainty of a single Court of Delegates. During her reign (and possibly before it)[4] the various administrative machines which dealt with civil law appeals had begun to merge into one and by her death in 1603 this process was far advanced, if not already complete.

The precise date when this amalgamation occurred cannot be given on the basis of evidence now available, but the termini within which the change took place can be stated with some precision. A single court cannot have existed before 1533, because until then there were two separate founts of authority for civil law appeals—the king and the Pope. It is equally clear that by

[1] In strict law, it is wrong to say that decisions of the High Commission were final and irreversible, as Usher suggests (*The Rise and Fall of the High Commission*, p. 312). In his *Institutes of the Laws of England* (London, 1671), pt. 4, p. 341, Coke makes it clear that a review could always be granted upon general principles, even if the letters patent under which the commissioners were acting did not themselves provide for such reviews (as they sometimes did; see T. Rymer and R. Sanderson, *Foedera* (London, 1704–35), vol. 17, p. 212); moreover, the records of the Delegates contain references to one cause appealed from the High Commission (*R.R.*, p. iv). Such reviews were so rarely granted, however (none has been positively identified in the course of this investigation apart from the one referred to above), that the decisions of the High Commission might properly be regarded as final in practice. The matter is more fully discussed at pp. 36–40 *post*).

[2] 1 Eliz. I, c. 1.

[3] By ss. 4 and 6 of the Elizabethan Act respectively.

[4] See footnote 1, p. 18 *post*.

the early seventeenth century, there was a single administrative machine—and in a very real sense a single court—for all appeals, both ecclesiastical and lay.[1]

The evidence for this proposition is extensive. A single set of Act Books contain references to both lay and clerical business and the entries are arranged without any attempt to distinguish between different categories of litigation.[2] All this business is dealt with by a single set of officials, there being no distinction drawn between registrars for ecclesiastical causes, registrars for Admiralty causes and so on. Finally, the Delegates who tried the appeals did not sit at different times and places to deal with secular and clerical business, as was the practice of the separate courts of first instance.[3]

The reason for this amalgamation is nowhere explained but may be plausibly conjectured. The explanation may well lie in considerations of administrative convenience. From the beginnings of civil law appeals in this country, all the civilian courts were governed by substantially the same procedure, and their appeals were managed in exactly the same way, by the appointment of *ad hoc* judges. One serious drawback to this system was the absence of continuing administrative machinery; there seem to have been no permanent records in which an account of all the appeals could be set down and no permanent officials (registrars, clerks and the like) who could be made responsible for the care of the documents and the conduct of judicial business. This was clearly inconvenient but as long as the lay courts and the church courts acknowledged

[1] There may have been such a court at some time between 1533 and 1554 as this (like the period following Elizabeth's accession) was a time when all the civil law courts looked to the one head. However, not enough documentary evidence survives for the period before *c.* 1600 to make a firm conclusion possible.

[2] e.g. folio 18 of the second surviving Delegates' Act Book contains entries for *Hamner* v. *Reade* (1601), DEL 4/2/18 (an ecclesiastical cause) and *Waltham and others* v. *Rawley and others* (1601), DEL 4/2/18 (an Admiralty cause). It should be observed that the only causes which can be positively identified in these records came from the church courts and the Court of Admiralty. Evidence for the minor civil law tribunals (the Court of Chivalry and the Courts of Oxford University) is wanting until the series of Repertory Books begins in 1619; the earliest appeal recorded there from the Court of Chivalry is *Harris* v. *Leake* (1625), DEL 8/70/pt. 1/19 while from Oxford the earliest recorded appeal is *Loggins* v. *Nayton* (1623), DEL 8/70/pt. 1/12. It must be remembered, however, that these courts never sent much business to the Delegates; once the appellate arrangements for the Court of Admiralty and the ecclesiastical courts had merged, it is unlikely that the other courts would have remained outside the new system for long.

[3] T. Oughton, *Ordo Judiciorum* (London, 1738), tit. II.

different masters, no union of their appellate systems was likely. The Act of 1533 removed this impediment and the manifold advantages of passing all the business through a single administrative machine must have become apparent before long; that such a machine should have come into existence within seventy years was probably inevitable.

From the early seventeenth century, then, one is entitled for the first time to speak of the Court of Delegates and not merely of Delegates appointed to try civil law appeals of one sort or another; to the history of this court the remainder of this chapter is devoted.

Little need be said of the court's progress in the first four decades of the seventeenth century. This period is not entirely without interest, however, as sufficient records have survived from this time to make possible a close study of its operations.[1] From these it is clear that the court had established a settled procedure and was dealing with a fairly large volume of business.[2] No legislation was passed affecting the court directly, and had it not been for the upheaval of the Civil War it may well have continued to function in relative obscurity throughout the whole of that century.

Such an ordered existence was not to be, however, and when the struggle between king and Parliament broke out, the Delegates were caught up in it. They continued to sit in London until 1643, but the king's withdrawal to Oxford in that year resulted in the establishment of rival courts and for a period there were two tribunals claiming the name and performing the functions of the Court of Delegates.[3] Little information survives about the Oxford Delegates, but one of their sittings (probably the first) is entered in the Act Book for 1642–47.[4] On 19 April 1643, the Delegates sat 'in Cancella Boreali infra Ecclesiam parochialem beate Marie Virginis infra Academiam Oxonie', the judges present being the Earl of Dorset (the Lord Chamberlain), Lord Cottington, Sir Edward Nicholas and Dr Egidius Sweit; John Oughton, the usual

[1] The Act Books run in an almost unbroken series from 1601 to 1650 and are invaluable for a study of procedure. There are also fairly complete files of sentences and a number of bills of costs. It is to be regretted that almost no cause papers survive from this period.

[2] In the years 1620, 1630 and 1640, thirty-seven, sixty-eight and one hundred and nine commissions were issued respectively.

[3] It was not the only civilian tribunal which followed the king. It is clear from *Greaves* v. *Babington* (1646), DEL 4/18/121 that sessions of the Prerogative Court were held at Oxford and that the records of that court were brought up from London.

[4] DEL 4/18/34.

deputy registrar, was in attendance. Commissions were presented in two actions, both, apparently, appeals by the Spanish Crown from judgments of the High Court of Admiralty; both causes were adjourned to 15 June, to the Consistory within the House of Convocation at Oxford.

This brief entry is the only reference to sittings at Oxford, and if further business was conducted during the king's stay there the records of it have not come down to us. Throughout the whole of this period, a court under Parliamentary control held sessions in London, and it is to these that the entries in the Act Book for 1642–7 largely relate. These entries are of some interest, as many of them throw light on the difficulties which litigation during the Civil War involved.[1] Some of these stemmed directly from the king's withdrawal; thus in *Lake* v. *Lake*[2] the appellant's proctor protested that he had been unable to obtain transmission of the process from the Prerogative Court, as the seal of that court had been removed to Oxford and the process could not issue without it, while the record of *Hayward* v. *Tufton*[3] makes it clear that litigants who tried to obtain new commissions about this time were similarly frustrated, as the Keeper of the Great Seal had taken it to Oxford towards the end of May 1642 and the new seal authorized by Parliament was not available until January of the following year. Most of the difficulties, however, resulted from the confused state of the country; decrees of the court could not be served upon the parties against whom they were directed,[4] commissions for the examination of witnesses could not be executed[5] and parties living in the country were sometimes unable to communicate with their legal advisers in London.[6] Perhaps the most serious impediment

[1] As was to be expected, the number of commissions issued over this period dropped sharply. There was a continuous decline from one hundred and nine in 1640 to eighteen in 1644, but by 1650 the number had risen to fifty-two.

[2] (1643), DEL 4/18/38.

[3] (1644), DEL 4/18/70.

[4] e.g. *Themilthorp and King* v. *Themilthorp* (1642), DEL 4/18/33; a mandate directed against the respondent was to have been executed at Henley in Oxfordshire, but 'racione militie in dictis partibus geste' it had not been returned.

[5] e.g. *Mathewes* v. *Ernely* (1646), DEL 4/18/126; a commission *ad partes* decreed by the Court had lapsed because fighting was taking place in the area where it should have been expedited.

[6] e.g. *Perkins and Swan* v. *Scott* (1649), DEL 4/19/139; the appellants explained their apparent desertion of their appeal by declaring that over the period in dispute they had lived at Kingston-upon-Hull and 'ratione belli intestivi in hoc Regno Anglie et presertim in partibus praedictis commoti' they had been unable either to come to London themselves or to send letters there.

to the smooth working of the court was the shortage of judges and this difficulty is vividly illustrated by an allegation of the appellant in *Hayward* v. *Tufton*.[1] In the commission granted to him, the two common law judges on the quorum had been Sir Robert Berkeley of the King's Bench, and Sir Francis Crawley of the Common Pleas but they had been in prison or engaged on business which made it impossible for them to attend the court. Of the civilian judges, Sir Henry Marten had died, while his condelegates, Drs Wood and Heath, had withdrawn from the business of the Court and could not now be found.[2] This problem seems to have been recurrent and as late as 1646 it resulted in the cancellation of entire sessions.[3]

The coming of peace and the establishment of the Commonwealth brought great changes in the structure and workings of the English courts and the Court of Delegates, although it survived, was affected by them. The tribunals which had hitherto sent their appeals to the king in Chancery or in Council were much altered. The ecclesiastical courts were deprived of much of their authority,[4] and their jurisdiction either lapsed or was transferred elsewhere,[5] while the Court of Chivalry was suspended and later replaced by a Parliamentary committee.[6] The university courts apparently remained untouched.[7] The most important of the

[1] (1644), DEL 4/18/70.

[2] The absence of advocates and proctors was also a source of complaint; e.g. *Hayward* v. *Tufton* (1644), DEL 4/18/70.

[3] The number of sessions in the Michaelmas term 1646 was reduced to four and a memorandum in the Act Book explains that the hearings were diminished 'ob defectum competentis numeri Dominorum Delegatorum Regiorum' (DEL 4/18/121). Two sessions were omitted from the following Hilary term for the same reason (DEL 4/18/131).

[4] By 16 Car. I, c. 11 (repealed at the Restoration by 13 Car. II, st. 1, c. 12). It should be noted that the Prerogative Court (whose jurisdiction was confined to testamentary matters) was preserved during the lifetime of Sir Nathaniel Brent, who became its judge in 1644 (C. H. Firth and R. S. Rait, *Acts and Ordinances of the Interregnum* (London, 1911), vol. 1, pp. 564–6). Upon his death, other arrangements were made for testamentary business; see p. 22 (note 4) *post*.

[5] Thus adultery and fornication were converted into crimes (the former becoming a felony) to be dealt with by the secular courts (*ibid.*, vol. 2, pp. 387–9). Probate and administration of wills were provided for as described in note 4 above, while legacies were to be sued for at common law (*ibid.*, vol. 2, p. 959).

[6] *H.C.C.*, pp. 66–7 and 68–72; Firth and Rait, *Acts and Ordinances*, vol. 1, pp. 838–9.

[7] The Ordinance of 1 May 1647 (*ibid.*, vol. 1, pp. 925–7) which set up a committee whose members were to act as visitors for the University of Oxford and its colleges, specifically saved the rights of the chancellor, and three appeals came to the Delegates from Oxford during the Interregnum.

surviving civilian jurisdictions was undoubtedly the Court of Admiralty; this was regarded with some favour and the 'Ordinance for setling the Jurisdiction of the Court of Admiralty' of 12 April 1648[1] in substance confirmed the compromise, by no means unfavourable to that tribunal, which had been made in 1632–3 between the civilians and the common lawyers.[2]

The Court of Delegates continued to be employed as an appellate body despite the restrictions in the number of courts from which business could now come to it. What provision was intended for appeals from the committee which handled chivalry causes, it is difficult to say; appeals from this jurisdiction were never common,[3] and it is possible that none arose during the Interregnum. It is certain that none went to the Court of Delegates, for throughout that period it heard causes from only three tribunals—the Prerogative Court,[4] the Court of Admiralty and the Courts of Oxford University. The function of the Delegates had never been purely appellate, however, and during the Commonwealth its original jurisdiction was widely invoked. The right of the court to hear causes at first instance was extended by ordinance, and it heard many more of such causes than was customary; some of these, it seems, were matrimonial disputes which would formerly have begun in the ecclesiastical courts.[5]

The reforming spirit of the Interregnum did not leave the Delegates untouched and a number of changes in the structure and workings of the court deserve consideration. The Act of 17 April 1649 restored an appellate jurisdiction in prize to the Court of Delegates and at the same time took certain steps to accelerate its procedure when such causes were heard.[6] The period of fifteen days allowed for an appeal from the *judex a quo* was preserved, but the later stages of procedure were now subjected to similar limitations, which had not existed before. The appellant

[1] *Ibid.*, vol. 1, pp. 1120–1. This ordinance was to last three years, but several later enactments were passed to extend it.

[2] *C.S.P.D.*, 1631–3, pp. 427, 516, 519, 527, 539–40.

[3] There were only seven from 1625 to 1739 (*R.R.*, p. xxiv).

[4] From 1653, when Sir Nathaniel Brent died, until the Restoration this court was replaced by a committee of twenty persons, the members of which were to act as 'Judges for the Probate of Wills, and granting of Administrations' (Firth and Rait, *Acts and Ordinances*, vol. 2, pp. 702–3) but, throughout the whole of this period, the Delegates' records still refer to it as the Prerogative Court.

[5] For a full account of the court's original jurisdiction, see pp. 42–50 *post.*

[6] Firth and Rait, *Acts and Ordinances*, vol. 2, pp. 66–75.

was required to present the commission to at least two of the judges-delegate within two days of obtaining it and to apply for an inhibition and monition for process at the time of presentation, while within six days of presentation the libel and instrument of appeal were to be exhibited. Failure to comply with this time-table was to be treated by the Delegates as desertion of the appeal, which was then to be remitted back to the Court of Admiralty. The later stages of procedure were to be equally prompt; if no new matter was pleaded within six days after transmission of process, the Delegates were to conclude the cause and assign it for sentence, while if admissible new matter was tendered, the Act required that 'some certain short term' should be allowed *ad proponendum omnia*, and no more than 'a competent time' for proof, after which the Court was to proceed to publication, conclusion and sentence 'without any other or farther stop or removal whatsoever'.

Interesting changes also occurred during this period in the structure of the Court. Although full commissions[1] or commissions embracing judges of the common law as well as civilians were occasionally issued before 1650, most causes were heard by a bench of five civilians. In the following ten years, however, only twenty-four commissions were of the latter kind, and none of these was introduced later than May 1652; beyond that date, they all included common law judges. It is clear that about this time a deliberate policy was initiated of issuing only mixed commissions. The most probable explanation of this change is the political unreliability of civilians,[2] although the reforming temper of the period must not be overlooked, and the Cromwellian government may well have believed that the court would work more efficiently (and perhaps more speedily) if the judges of Westminster Hall were always represented on it.

Two other changes occurred in the personnel of the court over this period. One is a considerable increase in the size of the average commission. Until 1650, a commission issued to civilians only would normally comprise five members and a commission to

[1] This term was usually confined to a commission in which four groups, bishops, peers, civilians and common law judges were represented; see *ex parte Hellier* (1754), 3 Atkyns 798.

[2] *H.E.L.*, vol. 5, pp. 17–18. There was, of course, a respectable number of civilians on the Parliamentary side; see W. Senior, *Doctors' Commons and the Old Court of Admiralty* (London, 1922), pp. 92–3.

civilians and common law judges eight members; the number might be greater if the commission was of adjuncts or review,[1] but in the period 1640–50 there were only ten causes decided by more than fifteen judges. During the Interregnum, the position was very different and commissions issued to more than twenty Delegates were by no means uncommon.[2]

The second change is a widening in the classes of persons chosen. Before 1650, Delegates were rarely selected outside the ranks of civilians (and on occasions, common law judges, bishops and peers); when, as sometimes happened, other persons were nominated, the choice was governed by considerations which are readily intelligible. Thus serjeants-at-law occur from time to time, but they had long been used to perform judicial functions, while superior clergy, such as deans, seem to have been employed on occasions in place of bishops. From the beginning of the Interregnum, however, there appears to have been a much broader choice of Delegates and, although one is certain to find civilians and (after 1652) common law judges on the bench, there were many others who were never employed in this capacity except during this period. The newcomers were, as might be expected, persons likely to be well disposed to the government. Thus the City of London was well-represented, the Recorder of London and various aldermen sitting from time to time,[3] and the names of army officers not infrequently recur.[4]

It may be thought that these reforms must have had a significant effect upon the working of the court, but too much should not be made of them. Prospective judges-delegate may have been reluctant to accept appointment to commissions unless the responsibility for exercising judicial office during the Interregnum could be shared among a large group,[5] but it is clear from the

[1] For an explanation of these terms, see p. 83 and p. 62 *post*.

[2] Some commissions were very much larger than this: e.g. *Lane* v. *Pavey* (1653), DEL 8/71/pt. 1/65 (thirty-nine judges); *Lady Blount* v. *Blunt and others* (1653), DEL 8/71/pt. 1/66 (forty-four judges).

[3] e.g. *Lane* v. *Pavey* (1653), *supra*.

[4] Men such as Lambert, Desborough, Harrison, Danvers and Marten sat on occasions and Cromwell himself was included in one commission (*Davenport* v. *Lucy and others* (1652), DEL 8/71/pt. 1/59; he is described as 'Lord Generall of England').

[5] This cautious attitude was common at the time; 'In the anxious avoidance of individual responsibility, no one man... accepted office other than membership in committees' (*C.S.P.D.*, 1649–50, p. vii).

Assignation Books that the number of persons sitting, both to conduct the formal stages of the trial and to give sentence, was not significantly higher than before. Similar considerations apply to the recruiting of judges outside the conventional categories; it appears that persons without legal qualifications were usually to be found on special commissions only, and they were rarely involved in the ordinary appellate work of the court. The invariable inclusion of common law judges on commissions was the only reform in the composition of the bench during the Interregnum which had a lasting effect. There was a reaction after the Restoration, but this was soon followed by a reversion to the former practice and soon after *c.* 1700 civilians were never allowed to sit alone.[1]

In addition to the changes mentioned above, there was a noticeable decline in the amount of business coming before the court at this time. The average number of causes heard annually in the years 1631–40 (the last normal decade before the outbreak of the Civil War) was seventy-seven, but in the period 1650–9 the number dropped to only thirty-five. Almost the only tribunals which sent up appeals during this period were the Court of Admiralty and the Prerogative Court and these figures serve as a demonstration of the extent to which the Delegates had relied before upon the other heads of civilian (and especially ecclesiastical) jurisdiction for business.[2]

The restoration of Charles II in 1660 brought an inevitable reaction and most of the courts which had been abolished were restored to the exercise of their former jurisdiction; as a part of this process, the old hierarchy of civilian courts, with the Delegates at its head, was carefully reconstructed. The ecclesiastical

[1] See p. 180 *post.*

[2] There is some evidence that Charles II during his exile sanctioned the conduct of maritime litigation by commissions of delegacy, at least in causes where the subject matter of the dispute had come within the jurisdiction of a friendly power. One such cause arose in 1649 when a Dutch ship in which a Scotsman had shipped goods was seized by three Irish frigates sailing under royalist commissions of war, and taken to Dunkirk where most of the cargo was confiscated without judicial proceedings. The owner of the goods petitioned the king, then in exile in Holland, and a commission was issued to two judges-delegate in Brussels, who heard the cause at first instance and gave sentence in 1650 (the sentence being ratified by Charles shortly after). The validity of these proceedings, and in particular the effect of the Act of Oblivion upon them, was the subject of a reference to Sir Leoline Jenkins in 1678 (W. Wynne, *Life of Sir Leoline Jenkins* (London, 1724), vol. 2, pp. 787–90).

tribunals were formally reinstated to their full authority by statute,[1] the Court of Admiralty and the Court of the Chancellor of Oxford continued their uninterrupted life and the Court of Chivalry needed no formal Act to revive it, as it had merely ceased to sit in 1640. As the Court of Delegates had continued to function during the Interregnum, it required nothing but confirmation of the validity of its proceedings over that period; this was provided by 12 Car. II, c. 12, which ratified all judicial proceedings from 1 May 1642.[2]

There followed a long period of well over one hundred years when the Delegates sat and did business without legislative interference or marked procedural change, and when no event occurred concerning the court which is worthy of remark.[3] But as early as the Restoration, if not before, a number of factors began to operate which were destined to have a profound effect upon all the civilian tribunals; these factors must now be considered, as they provide a context against which the eventual abolition of the Delegates is more readily understood.

Even in the sixteenth century, the civilians were under attack by Westminster Hall and by the end of the century following their decline was far advanced.[4] The tribunals of the Church, which formed the largest and most important group of courts in which the civilians practised, saw their jurisdiction dwindling on every side. In certain testamentary matters (such as the administration of estates) they were so hampered by the common law courts that a transfer of this business to the Chancery was inevitable.[5] Their jurisdiction over defamation, although it lingered on until the last decade of the eighteenth century, had been practically extinguished by common law interference very much earlier.[6] Their right to punish heresy and offences against morality was circumscribed by statute,[7] and by the end of the seventeenth

[1] 13 Car. II, st. 1, c. 12, which repealed 16 Car. I, c. 11 (apart from the section relating to the Court of High Commission).

[2] The Delegates were expressly named in s. 1. of that Act.

[3] Its workings were of course affected, as were those of other tribunals sitting in London, by such events as the Plague and the Great Fire. These are discussed at pp. 206–8 *post*.

[4] For early incursions by the common lawyers, see Senior, *Doctors' Commons*, pp. 67–9.

[5] *H.E.L.*, vol. 3, pp. 557–8 and 594–5.

[6] *Ibid.*, vol. 5, pp. 205–6 and authorities there cited.

[7] *Ibid.*, vol 1, pp. 618 and 620.

century, the only jurisdiction which the common law made no attempt to usurp was that which embraced matrimonial causes and matters entirely ecclesiastical.

The other courts which sent appeals to the Delegates were in no better plight. Coke's attack on the Court of Admiralty earlier in the century and the effect of the Great Rebellion resulted in the transfer of much business from the practitioners there to their rivals at Westminster Hall.[1] The Court of Chivalry had succeeded in rebutting attempts by common lawyers to practise before it,[2] but underwent continual attacks upon its jurisdiction over defamatory words and the amount of business coming before it had dwindled away to nothing by 1737.[3] No information appears to be in print relating to the Courts of Oxford University, but this jurisdiction may also have been involved in the prevailing decline.[4]

By the beginning of the nineteenth century, the need for radical reform of the whole judicial system had become apparent, and most of the tribunals where justice was administered were subjected to critical scrutiny by a series of commissions.[5] For the courts of law and equity, reform and (eventually) amalgamation were found appropriate, but for those tribunals administering the civil law, a sterner remedy was devised.[6] It was in the second decade of the century that detailed investigations began and in 1824 a report was issued on the structure and workings of several civilian courts, including the Court of Delegates.[7] Its scope was narrow, and while it suggested several reforms of relatively minor

[1] *Ibid.*, vol. 1, pp. 553–4 and 556–8. [2] *H.C.C.*, pp. 133–4.

[3] *Ibid.* p. 117.

[4] Of the twelve appeals from this court recorded in the Repertory Books from 1619 to 1789, nine were heard before 1700.

[5] The process was summed up by Sydney Smith in a characteristic epigram: 'The whole of creation has been put into commission and handed over to barristers of seven years' standing.'

[6] Dissatisfaction with the ecclesiastical courts seems to have been fairly general at that time. There survives among the cause papers in *Knight* v. *Jones* (1821) DEL 8/79, a letter in which a litigant expressed himself in emphatic language on the subject: 'I am just returned from the Landaff Court where I am again harassed and which Court is here the terror of all and the ruin of many—it is really lamentable and distressing to see how the unfortunate Persons who are brought into this iniquitous place are served—you have seen a little of it and something of the nature of its proceedings but not a tenth of the overbearing and very disgraceful conduct of the Old Man who is placed there for the purpose of *administering Justice.*'

[7] *The Courts of Admiralty, Delegates, and Appeals for Prizes.* R. Com. Rep.; 1824 (240) IX, 75.

matters (such as fees) it seemed generally satisfied with the court and no drastic changes were proposed. Within a few years, however, the ambit of these and other investigations of particular courts was found to have been too restricted,[1] and in 1832 commissioners appointed to enquire into the practice and jurisdiction of all the ecclesiastical courts in England and Wales submitted a comprehensive survey of the entire subject.[2]

Shortly before this, the attention of Parliament had been attracted towards the Court of Delegates by the curious case of *Clark and Clark* v. *Dew*.[3] This was a testamentary cause, turning upon the allegation that the testator was insane. The proceedings in the Prerogative Court lasted four years and were ended by a judgment of Sir John Nicholls against the will, in which the doctrine of partial insanity was extensively explored. An appeal was then made to the Court of Delegates, which confirmed the original sentence almost two years after that sentence had been given; a later application for a commission of review was refused. The cause was before the courts for almost seven years, the costs amounted to over £10,000 and one of the unsuccessful parties was imprisoned in the Fleet by order of the Delegates. He presented a petition to the House of Commons in which he requested 'such enquiries... as may lead to a thorough change, not only in the constitution of the Ecclesiastical Court, but that of the Court of Judges Delegate, and place the power thereof respectively within such limits as may be consistent with the laws and constitution of this realm; and generally to reform, regulate, and improve the proceedings, and correct the practice of those Courts.'[4] A petition was also presented to the House of Lords.[5]

The whole of these proceedings displayed the ecclesiastical courts (and especially the Court of Delegates) in far from their happiest aspect and it is significant that shortly after the commissioners charged with an investigation of these tribunals began their

[1] The courts of the Archbishop of Canterbury had been the subject of a report in 1823 (R. Com. Rep.; 1823 (462) VII, 27) and those of the Bishop of London in 1824 (R. Com. Rep.; 1824 (43) IX, 25).

[2] *Practice and Jurisdiction of the Ecclesiastical Courts in England and Wales.* R. Com. Rep.; 1831–32 (199) XXIV, 1.

[3] (1826), DEL 7/12. The proceedings at first instance were apparently not reported, but there is an account of certain matters dealt with after remission in 1 Hagg. Ecc., 311 (*sub nomine Dew* v. *Clark and Clark*).

[4] The Petition of J. Clark.

[5] Hansard, *Parliamentary Debates* (N.S.), vol. 22, cols. 1307–8.

work, they were requested by the Lord Chancellor to report 'specially and immediately' on the Court of Delegates and in particular to consider the possibility of transferring its jurisdiction to the Privy Council. In a special report, bearing date 25 January 1831, they set out the results of their enquiry.[1]

The special report is a short document, as its authors contented themselves with enumerating the defects of the court (as they saw them) and the corresponding advantages of the Privy Council as a successor to its jurisdiction. It shows signs of having been hastily composed and some of the objections taken to the court's structure and workings suggest an imperfect understanding of the evidence. Thus there is no reason to imagine that the absence of a permanent judiciary affected 'the uniformity of decision'[2] (and the argument would in any case apply with equal force to the Privy Council itself), while the suggestion that the use of separate commissions made it impossible to promulgate general rules of practice is not born out by the records.[3] Other objections, however, were more valid. The petition and commission required for each cause undoubtedly involved litigants in expense which could have been avoided had a permanent body such as the Privy Council enjoyed the jurisdiction, while the procedural rules of the council were such that commissions of adjuncts or review could have been dispensed with, and the costs of such commissions avoided.[4] The fact that practising advocates acted as Delegates was an especial defect in the court's structure and the special report drew attention to the danger of allowing judges to give decisions which might affect causes in which they were engaged as practitioners.[5] Most serious of all, perhaps, was the doubtful competence of the civilian judges;[6] although most commissions achieved a reasonable balance between junior and senior advocates,[7] a majority of those attending for informations and sentence were usually juniors,[8] while even the

[1] *Eccl. Courts Rep.* (1831–2), pp. 5–8. [2] *Ibid.*, p. 6.

[3] See the Standing Orders of 1703 and 1706 (p. 199 *post*) and the *Monitiones Generales* (pp. 197–8 *post*). [4] *Eccl. Courts Rep.* (1831–2), p. 7.

[5] *Ibid.*, p. 6. [6] *Ibid.*, p. 6, pp. 159–60. [7] See p. 186 *post.*

[8] This is revealed by a survey of causes selected from the Repertory Books at five-yearly intervals; the relevant entries in the Act Books or Assignation Books were then examined (to discover which of the civilian Delegates appointed for these causes attended sittings of the court), and the seniority of these civilians was established by reference to the list of advocates in E. Nys, *Le Droit Romain, le Droit des Gens et le Collège des Docteurs en Droit Civil* (Brussels, 1910), pp. 139–55.

seniors were often those who had obtained the least practice in the courts.[1] The report concluded that the structure of the Court was 'essentially defective' and recommended that the jurisdiction should be transferred to the Privy Council.[2]

There seems little reason to doubt that the recommendation was a wise one. It may be true that the Court of Delegates had no irremediable defects, but those which had accumulated and to which the report directed attention could hardly be left unredressed. Most, if not all, of them could have been cured by the creation of a permanent bench, but the opportunity of carrying out such a reform in the seventeenth century had been lost.[3] Now it was too late, for to have taken such a step in 1832 would merely have been to duplicate the Privy Council; there would have been two tribunals with substantially the same judicial personnel and with an appellate jurisdiction in ecclesiastical causes.[4] Such an arrangement would have run counter to the whole trend of the nineteenth-century reforms, which were directed towards decreasing the number of jurisdictions. The only obvious alternative to the Privy Council was the House of Lords, but the structure and workings of that body can hardly have recommended it as a successor to the Court of Delegates.[5] In the light of these considerations the choice of the Privy Council seems not only reasonable but inevitable.

The commissioners' recommendation was accepted by the government and in due course embodied in legislation;[6] the necessary Bill was introduced into the House of Lords on 5 July 1832. The Lord Chancellor in his speech did little more than repeat the arguments of the special report and there was little debate.[7] The Bill recited the provisions of 25 Hen. VIII, c. 19 and of 8 Eliz. I, c. 5 and went on to repeal the whole of the latter Act and so much of the former as gave power to appeal to the king in

[1] This point was taken by Lord Brougham in his reform speech of 1828 (*H.E.L.*, vol. 13, pp. 297–8).

[2] *Eccl. Courts Rep.*, (1831–2), p. 7.

[3] See pp. 188–90 *post*.

[4] The Privy Council already enjoyed such a jurisdiction in respect of ecclesiastical appeals from the overseas possessions of the Crown (*Eccl. Courts Rep.* (1831–2), p. 7).

[5] The suggestion was put forward in the course of evidence before the commissioners (*ibid.*, p. 160).

[6] 2 & 3 Will. IV, c. 92.

[7] Hansard, *Parliamentary Debates* (Third Series), vol. 14, cols. 78 and 259–60.

Chancery. Any person who could formerly have appealed to the king in Chancery under the repealed Acts might now appeal to the king in Council, and any such appeal was to be heard and determined as it would have been had the rescinded statutes remained in force. Decisions of the Privy Council were to have the same standing as those of the Court of Delegates (except that reviews of them were prohibited). In the course of his speech the Lord Chancellor promised that adequate provisions would be made for the council to discharge its appellate functions, and in the following year a further Act was passed to this end.[1] It constituted the Judicial Committee of the Privy Council and regulated its jurisdiction and procedure in some detail; it also provided that all appeals to the king in Council were to be referred to that committee.[2] It is this tribunal which enjoys today most of the appellate jurisdiction of the Court of Delegates.[3]

[1] 3 & 4 Will. IV, c. 41. The constitution of the Privy Council (like that of the House of Lords at this time) made it unsatisfactory for the discharge of judicial business. Lord Brougham, in his reform speech of 1828, spoke scathingly of the retired colonial governors and junior Lords of the Admiralty who did most of the work, with almost no professional assistance (*H.E.L.*, vol. 13, p. 298).

[2] Formal reference is no longer necessary. See 7 & 8 Vic., c. 69, s. 9; 8 Edw. VII, c. 51, s. 5; Statutory Rules and Orders, 1909, No. 1228.

[3] 3 & 4 Vic., c. 86 confirmed the right of the Judicial Committee to hear appeals in ecclesiastical causes. Appeals from the Court of Chivalry may also come before the committee (*H.C.C.*, pp. 223–4), and the same is true of appeals from the University Courts of Oxford (H.S. Giffard (Earl of Halsbury) and others, *Laws of England*, (London, 1907–17), vol. 9, p. 29). The Court of Admiralty sent its appeals to the committee until 1875 when the Admiralty jurisdiction was transferred to the High Court by 36 & 37 Vic., c. 66; from that date, marine appeals have gone to the Court of Appeal and thence to the House of Lords (*H.E.L.*, vol. 1, pp. 518 and 638–44).

CHAPTER II

JURISDICTION

The jurisdiction of an appellate court requires consideration under two main heads; it is necessary to enumerate both the courts from which appeals came and the nature of the business which these courts sent up. In the present case it also seems desirable to discuss separately certain aspects of the Delegates' jurisdiction which were either controverted or in some way unusual; their right to hear appeals from the High Commission and from the university courts may serve as an example of the former category and their original jurisdiction of the latter. Finally, the relationship between the Delegates and the House of Lords, which has been a matter somewhat misunderstood, may conveniently be examined here, although it is not in strictness relevant.

JURISDICTION – GENERAL CONSIDERATIONS

The appellate jurisdiction of the Delegates, both statutory and non-statutory, derived from four sources; the ecclesiastical courts, the Court of Admiralty, the university courts and the Court of Chivalry. Of these, the first had by far the most complex structure, being organized by diocese and by province. Every archdeacon within a diocese had the right to hold a court with a limited jurisdiction, from which appeal lay to the consistory court of the bishop. This tribunal had a general jurisdiction in ecclesiastical causes and most litigation began there; an appeal lay to the provincial courts of the archbishop. Both provinces had several such courts. In the southern province the most important was the Court of Arches, which acted as the court of appeal from all the consistory courts of the province and also enjoyed an original jurisdiction in all ecclesiastical causes.[1] There was also a Court of Audience, which exercised a concurrent jurisdiction of somewhat uncertain extent with the Court of Arches, and a Prerogative Court which took cognizance only of testamentary causes. From all these provincial tribunals, appeal lay to the Delegates.[2] Lying outside this hierarchy

[1] This brought the Court of Arches into competition with the consistory courts and its instance jurisdiction was partially restrained (*H.E.L.*, vol. 1, p. 601).

[2] The structure of the courts was the same in the northern province.

were the courts of the peculiars exempt from episcopal and archi-episcopal control, which had the right to send appeals direct to the Delegates,[1] and the High Commission whose decisions might, it seems, be subject to review by them.[2] The most important marine tribunal was the Court of Admiralty which originally heard both instance and prize causes, although the latter became the province of a separate court and subject to a separate course of appeal;[3] it also took cognizance of appeals from inferior Admiralty courts, both in this country and in the dominions beyond the seas.[4] The universities of Oxford and Cambridge each had their own courts, and appeals might rise within them from inferior to higher tribunals.[5] Finally, there was the Court of Chivalry, which throughout the whole of its active life sent appeals to the Delegates.

The nature of the business which these tribunals sent on appeal to the Court of Delegates requires little consideration here, as the jurisdiction of the various bodies which administered the civil law in England is fully discussed in the printed authorities.[6] However, certain information relating to the amount of appellate business available to the Delegates and its distribution among the various jurisdictions may be obtained from the Repertory Books, and a survey at ten-year intervals follows.[7]

[1] *H.E.L.*, vol. 1, p. 600; 25 Hen. VIII, c. 19, s. 6.

[2] See pp. 36–40 *post*.

[3] See pp. 79–80 *post*.

[4] *R.R.*, p. xxiv; in such causes there might be a further appeal from the Court of Admiralty to the Delegates; e.g. *Wroughton and others* v. *Spencer Mann* (1786), DEL 8/73/pt. 3/53, which began in the Vice-Admiralty Court of East Florida.

The Cinque Ports were a special case; their Admiralty jurisdiction was completely exempt from the control of the Court of Admiralty and their appeals were sent to the Delegates. An attempt was made in *Stock* v. *Cullen* (1676–7), Jones T. 66, to deny this right of appeal but without success; the action was compromised before judgment was given and, although the problem was later referred to Sir Leoline Jenkins and Dr Wiseman, who gave an emphatic opinion that causes could not pass from the Cinque Ports to the Delegates (Wynne, *Life of Sir Leoline Jenkins*, vol. 2, p. 782), at least two such appeals were later entertained (*Lang* v. *Nelson and others* (1697), DEL 8/72/pt. 2/61; *Grand* v. *Benson and others* (1709), DEL 8/73/pt. 1/26).

[5] The precise extent of the Delegates' jurisdiction in University causes is disputed; see pp. 40–2 *post*.

[6] For the ecclesiastical courts, see *H.E.L.*, vol. 1, pp. 614–32; for the Court of Admiralty, *ibid.*, pp. 548–68; for the university courts, *ibid.*, pp. 167–9 and 171–5; for the Court of Chivalry, *H.C.C.*, pp. 1–28 and 138–61.

[7] This survey is necessarily confined to the period embraced by the Repertory Books themselves, i.e. 1619–1789. A mark of interrogation indicates that the provenance of the cause cannot be more precisely stated.

Year	Audience	Arches	Pre-rogative	Admiralty	Miscellaneous	Total
1619	13	15	9	1	St Peter ad vincula, York Exch., D. & Ch. of Windsor	41
1629	5	17	12	8	5 Ports Prerogat. C. of Ireland (3) York Con. (2)	49
1639	13	45	28	24	5 Ports Lincoln? York Con. (3) York? (3) Armagh	119
1649	—	—	33	13	—	46
1659	—	—	27	6	Oxford	34
1669	—	16	16	—	special c.	33
1679	—	7	13	2	York? (3) Ireland?	26
1689	—	4	13	2	York? (3) special c.	23
1699	—	1	6	2	Ireland? Bridgnorth D. & Ch. of Windsor	12
1709	—	7	4	2	Ireland? (2) York? (2) 5 Ports	18
1719	—	4	1	1	York? (2) Ireland? (2)	10
1729	—	8	10	—	Prerog. C. of Ireland Ireland? York Con.	21
1739	—	8	5	2	Ireland	16
1749	—	1	5	—	York? (3) Ireland?	10
1759	—	—	1	—	Dorchester Ireland?	3
1769	—	1	5	1	Ireland?	8
1779	—	1	3	2	—	6

Despite the limitations of these figures, it seems that certain tentative conclusions may be drawn from them. It is clear that for the whole of the period for which information is available the court was mainly concerned with appeals in ecclesiastical causes. The amount of secular business attracted to it was never considerable;

most of it came from the Court of Admiralty, the most important of the secular tribunals, but even this body never contributed more than one-third of the causes begun in any one year (and usually far fewer).[1] The form in which the information is presented in the Repertory Books makes it impossible to provide a detailed analysis of the ecclesiastical business, but the available evidence suggests that the greatest part of it was testamentary.[2] Only a few causes seem to have come from Ireland, although Rothery suggests the contrary;[3] this is probably to be explained partly by the trouble and expense involved in taking an Irish appeal to England and partly by the fact that appeal from the Irish Court of Delegates was by review.[4] The steady falling off in the number of appeals which began after the Restoration and gained momentum during the eighteenth century illustrates the decline of all the civilian courts over this period.

It remains to consider briefly certain limitations upon the appellate jurisdiction of the Court of Delegates, deriving from the general law governing civilian appeals, or from restrictions imposed by the common law courts. About the former, little need be said here; the civil law placed few limitations upon appeals and the matter is fully discussed elsewhere.[5] The restrictions of Westminster Hall were more formidable; the jealousy which the common lawyers felt for the civilians extended to the Delegates and whenever the latter attempted an improper assumption of jurisdiction, a prohibition might issue.[6] The Delegates might themselves on occasions refuse to entertain a cause, on the grounds that it appertained to the common law;[7] in such cases, no doubt, they merely anticipated interference.

[1] The ratio of ecclesiastical to Admiralty appeals may well have been different in the sixteenth century, when the Court of Admiralty entered upon its most flourishing period, but the relevant documentary evidence no longer survives.

[2] The whole of the jurisdiction of the Prerogative Court was of this character and it seems that some of the causes heard by the Courts of Arches and Audience were testamentary.

[3] *R.R.*, p. xxiv.

[4] See *Goodwin* v. *Giesler* (1794), Ridg. Ir. T., 371. For the difficulty of obtaining reviews, see pp. 62–74 *post.*

[5] See pp. 54–9 *post.*

[6] The attitude of the common lawyers is well brought out by the direction of Richardson and Jones JJ.K.B. to Sir John Lambe, who had brought certain litigation into the Court of Delegates which related to a matter being tried in the King's Bench (*C.S.P.D.*, 1625–49, p. 423).

[7] e.g. *Bishop of Kildare* v. *Archbishop of Dublin* (1710), DEL 6/33/5; the court ruled that the cause concerned a royal donative and was thus properly triable at common law.

THE COURT OF DELEGATES AND THE HIGH COMMISSION

For the greater part of its life the Court of Delegates was the only ecclesiastical tribunal in England which derived its authority from commissions of the Crown, but for a period ending in 1641 it shared this distinction with one other body, the royal commissioners for causes ecclesiastical. This link apart, they had much else in common; they both employed the procedure of the civil law, they both had ecclesiastical business as their primary concern, and, as Usher has shown, the same persons were often to be found exercising jurisdiction under both types of commission.[1] The relationship between the two courts has never yet been investigated and rests very largely upon a basis of conjecture; to find the truth of the matter may not be easy, as the destruction (apparently deliberate) of many of the High Commission's records has left its history dark, while very few documents survive in the Delegates' archives before the first decade of the seventeenth century. Some tentative attempt may be made, however, to throw some light upon two specific problems: the relationship between the High Commission and the Court of Delegates in the hierarchy of appeal and the effect of the operations of the former tribunal upon the latter.

The theory of their relationship is clear enough and the received view of the matter is given by Coke.[2] From a decision of the High Commission no appeal lay as of right, but a commission of review might be applied for,[3] and this was available whether or not the Letters Patent from which the High Commissioners derived their authority provided for it in terms. The view that decisions of the High Commission were irreversible is thus an erroneous one,[4] the mistake probably resulting from the fact that clauses in commissions expressly allowing for the possibility of review were apparently rare.[5] Despite this, it is clear that reviews, although they

[1] Usher, *The Rise and Fall of the High Commission*, p. 311.

[2] 4 Inst., p. 341.

[3] This was available only as a matter of grace; see pp. 62–6 *post*. The proposition that a review might lie was established in *Bird* v. *Smith* (1606–7), Moo. K.B. 781.

[4] See Usher, *The Rise and Fall of the High Commission*, p. 312; W. H. Frere, *The English Church in the Reigns of Elizabeth and James I (1558–1625)* (London, 1904), p. 354; p. 17 *ante*.

[5] For an example, see the Letters Patent in Rymer, *Foedera*, vol. 17, p. 212.

could be granted, were of very infrequent occurrence,[1] and Usher is undoubtedly correct in substance when he describes a decree of the High Commission as that desideratum of the seventeenth century litigant, 'a decision which could not be reversed'.[2]

Coke's account of the matter goes no further than the statement of it above, but, despite the authority attaching to any of his pronouncements, there is reason to believe that it represents an over-simplification of the true position. The Court of Delegates, acting under a commission which gave the necessary authority, could, it seems, review decisions of the High Commissioners, but an appeal from the Commissioners to the Delegates was not the only means by which the two tribunals might be brought into contact; if a cause passed on appeal from, say, a diocesan court to the Court of Arches and thence to the Delegates, could the High Commission intervene at that point and reverse the Delegates' decision? The assumption upon which Coke's view is apparently based (that the High Commission, like the Court of Delegates, had a settled place in the judicial hierarchy of appeal) should have made such intervention impossible, but this view of the relationship between the commission and the other ecclesiastical tribunals does not seem to be tenable in the light of recent research. Usher has shown that the 'appellate' jurisdiction of the High Commission was of a curious order; the commissioners recognized no formal right of appeal to their authority, but they were prepared, when they saw fit, to try *ab initio* causes which had already been tried by an ecclesiastical court and to ignore entirely the earlier proceedings.[3] It also seems possible that the diocesan courts sometimes refused to recognize decisions of the High

[1] The only example which has been positively identified is *Cowpland* v. *Senhouse and others* (1630), *R.R.*, p. 14 (no. 34). *The Bishop of Exeter and others* v. *Withers* (1611), *R.R.*, p. 7 (no. 16) was not a review of a decision of the High Commission but of an earlier judgment of the Court of Delegates itself. In his *Catalogue of Processes in the Registry of the High Court of Delegates, from 1609 to 1823* (London, 1823), p. 1, J. Addams refers to the papers in *Wild* v. *Ackson* (1638), DEL 1/3 as an appeal from the High Commission; in fact they are a return of commissioners *ad partes* who had examined certain witnesses by order of that tribunal and their inclusion among the Delegates' records is accidental. It is possible that *The Earl of Hertford* v. *Lord Mounteagle* (1605), DEL 4/3/86 was an appeal from the High Commission, as the cause is described in the entry given above as coming from 'honorandi domini Comissionarij in prima instancia huius cause'.

[2] Usher, *The Rise and Fall of the High Commission*, p. 312.

[3] *Ibid.*, pp. 96–8.

Commission in causes which they themselves had sentenced; thus it appears that a formal place in the order of appeal was neither claimed by the High Commission nor conceded by its rivals.

In the face of this confusion it is not easy to find an apt description for the relationship between the High Commission and other tribunals exercising spiritual jurisdiction, but it seems true to say that the commissioners had a right of 'intervention' in respect of any cause which fell within that jurisdiction, even if that cause was already pending before another ecclesiastical court or had been sentenced there.[1] That there was a free exercise of the right to intervene in the affairs of diocesan courts is clear enough, but it is by no means certain that the Delegates were subject to similar interference. If Usher's view of the matter is correct, however, there seems no reason why they should not have been, if a litigant against whom they had given judgment could complain of some miscarriage of justice for which the Delegates were responsible. Only one cause has been discovered bearing upon the matter, but it suggests that intervention by the High Commission did in fact occur. In *the Bishop of Exeter and others* v. *Withers*[2] the party supplicate[3] was a vicar choral of Exeter Cathedral against whom an action for deprivation had been brought by the bishop and members of the chapter. The litigation finally came to the Delegates who reversed the decision of the lower courts and confirmed Withers in his position; after their judgment had been given, however, proceedings were begun against him before the High Commission, which again deprived him. A commission of review was then obtained by the bishop and his colleagues in an attempt to reverse the earlier decision of the Delegates, but Withers refused to plead and judgment was eventually given against him. The interest of the cause lies in the reason for Withers' refusal to plead, which was based on his belief that a decision of the Delegates

[1] Usher suggests that this interference was probably subject to certain limitations, and some weighty reason would have to be advanced such as 'lack of jurisdiction, inability to enforce the sentence in the lower court...or the failure of the ecclesiastical judge to investigate the facts thoroughly' before the commissioners would take cognizance of a cause (*ibid.*, pp. 98–9). It also seems necessary to assume that intervention was not possible when the Delegates had reviewed and reversed a decision of the High Commission itself, as such intervention would have made nonsense of the granting of the review.

[2] (1610), DEL 4/5/188.

[3] For this term, see p. 75 *post*.

would avail him nothing in the face of deprivation by the High Commission.[1]

Too much weight cannot be attached to this single cause, and when interpreting it the possibility must be kept in mind that the proceedings before the Delegates and the High Commission were based upon different facts. If, however, (as is likely) the facts were the same, the cause is an example of an intervention by the High Commission to reverse a judgment of the Court of Delegates, and the unsuccessful litigant at least had no doubts as to which decision would prevail. Nevertheless, the cause is an isolated one and in all likelihood the relationship between the two tribunals was never precisely worked out, because situations of the kind which arose in this cause did not occur frequently enough to produce a line of clarifying judgments.[2]

It remains to consider the effects of the High Commission's operations upon the Court of Delegates, the chief of which, it has been suggested, was the attraction of almost all doctrinal and disciplinary causes from the regular ecclesiastical courts (with the Court of Delegates at their head) to the commissioners.[3] That this is a plausible (and almost certainly a correct) statement of the position need not be doubted, for the High Commissioners could probably provide a remedy which was quicker and cheaper than that of the tribunals with which they competed.[4] But the warning must be given that it remains an assumption and no more, and that statements such as 'there were practically no appeals on doctrine or discipline to the delegates, previous to 1660'[5] are not supported by available evidence. The only records which can with certainty

[1] 'casu quo domini Judicantes huius Curie Sententiam eorum diffinitivam pro parte et in favorem sui prefati Roberti Withers et confirmacionem Sententie diffinitive sive finalis decreti per dominos Judicantes delegatos antedictos lati et promulgati (prout eos utique iusticia mediante facturos sperat) legerint et promulgaverint, ipse tamen prefatus Robertus Withers nullum commodum aut utilitatem exinde capere neque ad locum unius vicariorum Choralium predictum restitui eodemque gaudere poterit (Sententia diffinitiva per dominos Commissionarios ad causas ecclesiasticas predicta lata in suo robore et vigore remanente)'.

[2] The most probable reason for this is that intervention by the High Commission occurred in most causes before the litigation reached the Court of Delegates. In *the Bishop of Exeter and others* v. *Withers* (1610), DEL 4/5/188, it is likely that the High Commissioners would have deprived Withers at an earlier stage of proceedings, had not both the court of first instance and the Court of Arches found against him.

[3] Usher, *The Rise and Fall of the High Commission*, pp. 311–2.

[4] *Ibid.*, p. 312.

[5] *Ibid.*, p. 311.

be attributed to the ecclesiastical Delegates, and which survive from the first fifty odd years during which their tribunal co-existed with the High Commission, are two bundles of sentences; these documents are far too meagre to act as a solid basis for any generalization. For the next forty years, the surviving documents of the Court of Delegates are more substantial in point of bulk, but they also are too succinctly written, for the most part, to make possible any firm identification of doctrinal and disciplinary causes.[1] Only the discovery of more informative material can convert a strong presumption into a certainty.

APPEALS FROM THE UNIVERSITY COURTS[2]

The Universities of Oxford and Cambridge have long maintained their own courts and these applied (until the nineteenth century) the rules of the civil law.[3] Although the contrary might be expected, the appellate system followed by each University seems always to have been different and the course of appeal within each requires separate consideration.

There is general agreement about the workings of the courts at Oxford. A cause began in the Court of the Chancellor,[4] from which an appeal lay to the Court of Congregation and from that tribunal to the Court of Convocation.[5] It seems that from the earliest times (at least in secular matters) it was possible to appeal from a decision of the latter body by petition to the king in Chancery,[6] who would appoint delegates to consider it.[7] After the ecclesiastical Delegates

[1] See the comments of Rothery in *R.R.*, pp. xv–xvi; the present writer can amply confirm their truth.

[2] For a general account of these courts, see J. Williams, *The Law of the Universities* (London, 1910), pp. 89–100; *H.E.L.*, vol. 1, pp. 165–76.

[3] The Oxford courts were given statutory permission to follow common law procedure in 1854 (17 & 18 Vict., c. 81, s. 45); the Act did not apply to Cambridge, but it has been suggested that since the last decade of the nineteenth century the courts of both universities may apply common law procedure (Williams, *op. cit.*, p. 90).

[4] This is described by Holdsworth as 'by far the most important' of the Oxford courts, but there were others; the Court of the Steward, the Court of the Coroner and the Court of the Clerks of the Market (*H.E.L.*, vol. 1, pp. 169–71).

[5] T. Wood, *An Institute of the Laws of England* (London, 1772), p. 521.

[6] Before the Reformation, presumably, appeals from Oxford in ecclesiastical matters went to the Pope, as from any other English court with a spiritual jurisdiction.

[7] Such an appeal lay only if the three courts which had already heard the cause were not in agreement; if they had all reached the same decision, no further appeal was possible (Blackstone, *Commentaries*, vol. 3, p. 85). In *H.E.L.*, vol. 1,

were created in 1533, petitions in all causes, both clerical and lay, were directed to the king, and once a single Court of Delegates had come into existence, appeals from Oxford must have started to come before it.

In the surviving records of the Delegates twelve appeals from Oxford are referred to, the earliest being heard in 1623; nine of these appeals were made in the seventeenth century and three in the eighteenth. Most of them are clearly described in the Repertory Books as coming from the House of Convocation, but some of the entries suggest a different provenance for certain of the causes; thus *Loggins* v. *Nayton*[1] is entered as an appeal from the Commissary of the Chancellor, and *Milles* v. *Byrd*[2] as an appeal from the vice-chancellor or his deputy, while *Keblewhite* v. *Falkes*[3] is designated merely as 'Oxon'. It is possible that in some causes, of which these are examples, it was permitted to proceed *per saltum* to the Delegates from the court of first instance within the university, without previous recourse to the Houses of Congregation and Convocation.

The right of appeal of which litigants could avail themselves in the Cambridge courts is rather more uncertain, and information coming to light in the course of this investigation suggests that it was narrower than is commonly believed. Within the university itself, the course of appeal differed from that prevailing at Oxford. The judges at first instance were the chancellor or vice-chancellor (or in certain cases the chancellor's commissary); causes which began before the commissary might proceed on appeal to the chancellor or vice-chancellor and thence to the Senate, while the latter body also served as a court of appeal for litigation which the chancellor or vice-chancellor heard at first instance.[4] All this is clearly established, but it is the possibility of appeal from a decision of the Senate which has been a cause of uncertainty in the past. Most authorities state flatly that an appeal lay from Cambridge to the Delegates: thus Wood, in his description of the system of appeal prevailing at Oxford, explained that a litigant dissatisfied with a decision of the Convocation there could present

p. 170, Holdsworth also cites A. Duck, *De Usu et Authoritate Juris Civilis Romanorum*, bk. 2, ch. 8, pt. 3, tit. 30, but neither the Leyden edition of 1654 nor the London edition of 1689 supports his citation.

[1] (1623), DEL 8/70/pt. 1/12. [2] (1653), DEL 8/71/pt. 1/66.

[3] (1656), DEL 8/71/pt. 1/75.

[4] *H.E.L.*, vol. 1, p. 175; Williams, *The Law of the Universities*, p. 97.

a petition to the King in Chancery and judges delegate would then be appointed to consider the matter. He then passed to Cambridge, and declared that 'the Appeal is of this Nature' there.[1] Later authorities were rather more cautious but they too, for the most part, were of opinion that both universities managed their appeals in the same manner; Palmer, after stating that an appeal lay to the Delegates from Oxford, continued 'the Case is understood to be the same at Cambridge',[2] while Halsbury held that the transfer of jurisdiction from the Delegates to the Privy Council in 1832 'probably' included these appeals.[3]

Although the authority in favour of this view is weighty, it is not universally accepted;[4] it seems to have been arrived at by way of analogy from the Oxford practice rather than by a study of available records and the material surviving in the Delegates' archives lends it no support. The Repertory Books contain entries for every appeal which came before the Delegates from 1619 to 1789, but there is not a single reference to a cause from Cambridge over the whole of that period; moreover, no process embracing a Cambridge appeal has survived and among the Cause Papers, all of which have been examined, no document relating to such an appeal has been found. The absence of any documentary evidence is significant and it seems a reasonable conclusion that no appeal lay.[5]

ORIGINAL JURISDICTION

The Court of Delegates was erected as an appellate tribunal and most of its business was of this character. It had in addition, however, an important original jurisdiction which fell under

[1] Wood, *An Institute of the Laws of England*, p. 521.

[2] J. Palmer, *The Practice in the House of Lords on Appeals etc.* (London, 1830), p. 3.

[3] Earl of Halsbury, *Laws of England*, vol. 9, p. 29. The latest authority to express the same view is H. E. Peek and C. P. Hall, *The Archives of the University of Cambridge* (Cambridge, 1962), p. 50.

[4] Holdsworth stated (*H.E.L.*, vol. 1, p. 175) that no appeal lay from the Senate, but the principal authority for this statement is Halsbury, *Laws of England*, vol. 9, p. 150, which does no more than set out the course of appeal within the university and is silent as to appeals outside it. In the light of Halsbury's statement on the subject (referred to in footnote 3, above) the passage on which Holdsworth relies does not seem to establish his point. Holdsworth also cites Williams, *The Law of the Universities*, p. 97; this author merely declares, without comment or authority, that no appeal lies outside Cambridge.

[5] A detailed study of the records of the Cambridge courts (which does not seem to have been undertaken) would no doubt throw further light upon the matter.

various heads, the commonest being the retention of the principal cause when an appeal *a gravamine* came before it. It is proposed to discuss first retention and then other examples of original jurisdiction.

(i) *Retention of the Principal Cause*

In the civil law, an appeal might be made either *a causa principali* or *a gravamine*;[1] in the former case, the appellant objected to the decision of the *judex a quo* on the merits of the whole cause, while in the latter his objection was directed against some interlocutory decision of that judge in the course of the hearing (e.g. the rejection of a witness). If an appeal *a gravamine* came before the Delegates they might give a decision which would be remitted to the lower court and the *judex a quo* would continue his hearing of the principal cause, but in certain circumstances the Delegates would 'retain the principal cause', i.e. take it out of the hands of the lower court and themselves give judgment on it.[2]

It seems likely that this form of original jurisdiction was inherent in appellate tribunals operating within the civilian system, an hypothesis suggested by two considerations: (i) the jurisdiction was conferred upon the Delegates neither by the commissions under which they acted nor by statute; (ii) it was exercised by other appellate tribunals. The usual form of commission contained no specific reference to retention,[3] while the statutes which regulated appeals to Delegates conferred no such authority.[4] That other appellate tribunals within the civilian system could retain a principal cause is made clear by causes such as *Bowerman* v. *Fust*[5] in which Bowerman, objecting to the admission of certain pleadings tendered by Fust in the Commissary Court of Winchester, appealed to the Court of Arches, which retained the principal cause after deciding the grievance in Fust's favour.

[1] *O.J.* CCLXXVI.

[2] The practice is still followed on occasions by the Privy Council when hearing appeals in ecclesiastical causes; e.g. *Voysey* v. *Noble* (1870), L.R. 3 P.C. 357 at 365.

[3] In *Lambell* v. *Lambell, Lambell intervening* (*in the principal cause*) (1646), DEL 4/18/120, the court decreed retention 'iuxta tenorem Comissionis Regie Delegacionis' but this is the only example of a right to retain conferred by commission which has been found in the course of this investigation. No reason was assigned in the relevant act for the unusual form of the decree.

[4] Thus 25 Hen. VIII, c. 19, s. 4 merely says that the ecclesiastical Delegates were to 'determine every such Appeal, with the Causes and all Circumstances concerning the same.'

[5] (1789), DEL 8/73/pt. 3/64.

In the early part of the court's life, the practice regulating retention was somewhat fluid. The Delegates would often dispose of the grievance before retaining the principal cause (if retention were decided on); it was by no means uncommon, however, to decree retention long before judgment on the grievance was given and proceedings in both causes could then continue side by side.[1] By the latter half of the eighteenth century, however, it was customary for retention to depend upon the decision of the court in the grievance; if the Delegates found for the appellant in the grievance the principal cause was usually retained, whereas if they found for the respondent it was for the most part left in the hands of the *judex a quo*.[2]

If retention were decreed, the Delegates began to hear the principal cause from the point to which the judge of the court below had taken it; thus if only some of the witnesses had been examined before retention, the Delegates would direct that the depositions of the rest be taken and would in due course order publication of all the evidence not yet published.[3] The judges who heard the principal cause were the same as those previously appointed to hear the grievance and no new commission was issued.[4]

The decision of the Delegates to retain a principal cause was an important one, as it could have significant effects upon the interests of the parties to the litigation. One result of retention was that the cause might be brought to a much quicker conclusion than

[1] If this happened, considerations of logic required that the court should reach a decision in the grievance before deciding the principal cause, and the usual decree for retention embodied this requirement: e.g. *Angell* v. *Townson* (1608), DEL 4/4/143; the court retained the principal cause 'ita quod non finiatur causa principalis nisi prius discusso gravamine'. Provided that this rule was adhered to, decisions in both causes might be given on the same day: e.g. *Holt* v. *Savage* (*in the grievance*); *Holt* v. *Savage* (*in the principal cause*) (1614), DEL 4/6/255.

[2] Rothery's exposition of the practice governing retention (*R.R.*, p. xi) should be regarded with some reserve. His statement of the rules suggests that the decision to retain was always made after judgment in the grievance had been given, but this, as has been shown above, was by no means always true. Also inaccurate is the statement of practice given in *Savile* v. *Savile* (cited in *Matthews* v. *Warner* (1798), 4 Ves. J. 186 at 202) that whenever an appeal came to the Delegates on a grievance it was the custom to take possession of the whole cause.

[3] e.g. *Codrington* v. *Rodman* (*in the principal cause*) (1619), DEL 4/7/316.

[4] No entries have been found in the Act Books or Assignation Books relating to the presentation of new commissions for the principal cause, although presentation of the original commission for the grievance is always described.

would otherwise have been possible. The effect of decreeing it before a decision was given on the grievance was, as has been seen, that grievance and principal cause might be heard together and judgment in both might be given on the same day; had there been no retention, however, the Delegates' judgment on the grievance would have been sent back to the lower court, which would then have continued its hearing in the principal cause and given a judgment in it, possibly some considerable time later. Still more important, perhaps, was the effect of retention upon the parties' subsequent right of appeal. Without it, the decision of the *judex a quo* in the principal cause was one from which an appeal would lie to the Delegates as of right, but if the principal cause were retained, the Delegates gave a decision in it from which there was no appeal (except by way of a commission of review, which was granted only rarely, and as a matter of grace, not of right).[1]

(ii) *Special Commissions*[2]

It must sometimes have happened that persons involved in litigation, which fell within the competence of the ordinary ecclesiastical courts, were anxious, for one reason or another, that their business should not pass through such courts in the usual way, but should be dealt with extraordinarily. The Court of Delegates may well have seemed the most suitable tribunal for such causes; it stood at the apex of the civilian hierarchy, its judges were chosen anew for each cause (thus offering an important litigant some prospect of influencing the choice)[3] and precise limits could be set to a hearing by the terms of the commission from which the Delegates derived their authority.[4]

As a result, a convention seems to have grown up that certain business could be initiated before the Delegates at first instance,

[1] On one occasion, this point was raised in argument before Lord Nottingham in an application for a review (D.E.C. Yale (ed.), *Lord Nottingham's Chancery Cases* (London, 1961), vol. 2, p. 733). He did not take it up specifically in his judgment, but presumably it may have influenced him to grant a review. For reviews, see pp. 62–79 *post*.

[2] This section excludes the period of the Interregnum, when the original jurisdiction was somewhat enlarged; see pp. 46–50 *post*.

[3] For an example of the exercise of such influence, see *the Countess of Essex* v. *the Earl of Essex* (1613), 2 St. Tr. 786 at 816–17; two judges were added to the commission in the course of the hearing in the hope that they would provide a majority for the plaintiff.

[4] see *the Countess of Essex* v. *the Earl of Essex* (1613), *supra*, at 818, where Archbishop Abbot comments on certain clauses introduced into the commission of adjuncts for the purpose of assisting the plaintiff's cause.

although the circumstances justifying their direct intervention were never precisely defined. Oughton appears to be the only text-book writer to comment on this jurisdiction, and he does no more than remark that such commissions might be decreed 'in Complementum Justitiae', giving as examples causes in which an archbishop was concerned or the like.[1] Only twelve causes can be identified with some certainty from the records, as being of this character, and, as Oughton suggests, they make it clear that these special commissions were most frequently employed to despatch judicial business in which the primates were involved, as in six of these causes the Archbishop of Canterbury or York is a party. The causes seem to have little else in common; one was matrimonial, two (and perhaps three) related to episcopal dilapidations, one arose from a visitation of the Chapel Royal at Windsor and the others cannot be identified with any certainty.

This jurisdiction was apparently invoked by petition, and the procedure is well illustrated by an unsuccessful application in 1670.[2] A Mr. Pierrepoint, the nephew of the Marquess of Dorchester, had been lured into an alehouse and had, while in liquor, been married to a minister's daughter according to the rites of the Book of Common Prayer. He had put in a petition for an 'extraordinary Commission' to dissolve the marriage, directed either to the king or to the Lord Keeper; the latter had referred it to Sir Giles Sweit, Dean of the Arches and Sir Leoline Jenkins, Judge of the Prerogative Court, requesting them to hear counsels' argument 'touching the Legality and Conveniency of granting such a Commission' and to give him their opinions on it. They reported that they had heard the petitioner's counsel but were not satisfied that a commission could properly be allowed him, as the litigation, in their opinion, should pass through the usual courts.

(iii) *Original Jurisdiction during the Interregnum*

To the forms of original jurisdiction exercised by the Delegates and described above, there was added during the Commonwealth a statutory power to proceed at first instance in a limited class of matrimonial matters.[3] The Act under which the court was em-

[1] *O.J.*, CCCII/2/e/vi.

[2] Wynne, *Life of Sir Leoline Jenkins*, vol. 2, pp. 723–4.

[3] An Act enabling the Lords Commissioners for Custody of the Great Seal of England to issue Commissions of Delegates in Cases of Pretended Marriages. 10 January 1652 (Firth and Rait, *Acts and Ordinances*, vol. 2, pp. 496–7).

powered to proceed was intended to remedy the mischief resulting from the abductions and forced marriages of young women, offences which the disturbed conditions of the Civil War and its aftermath may well have made common, and which existing legislation was perhaps not adequate to repress.[1] The event which was the immediate cause of the legislation was the abduction of a certain Jane Puckering, a baronet's daughter who, it was alleged, had been carried away to Flanders by one Joseph Walsh and others; after briefly rehearsing the facts of the case, the statute enacted:

That the Lords Commissioners for the Great Seal of England for the time being...are hereby Enabled to grant one or more Commissions under the Great Seal, to such discreet and able persons as they shall think fit; which said Commissioners, or any three or more of them, shall have full Power and Authority to send out Summons to convene the said Joseph Walsh, and such others as they shall finde meet, before them, at the suit of the said Jane Puckering.

They were then to go into the matter and 'as the Right in that case shall require' to annul and make void the marriage if the facts justified it.

This was apparently felt to be an effective remedy for other cases of a like nature, and the Act went on to provide that similar commissions might be issued in the future:

And be it further enacted, that if any woman hath been or shall be by force seized on or carried away against her will, or hath or shall have words wrested from her either in this nation or beyond the seas, whereupon a marriage with any person is or shall be pretended, in all such cases, upon complaint made to the Lords Commissioners for the Great Seal of England for the time being, on behalf of such woman, the said Lords Commissioners shall and may, and are hereby authorized and required to grant like commissions to such discreet and able persons as they shall think fit to appoint, to send out summons, and convene the persons before them: and whether the defendants appear, or withdraw themselves, and stand in contempt, to proceed and admit the libels, allegations and proofs upon oath upon the merits of the cause upon behalf of such woman; and to hear and definitively determine the said matter, either for the affirming

[1] The statutes 3 Hen. VII, c. 2 (The Penalty of carrying a Woman away against her will that hath lands or Goods) and 39 Eliz. I, c. 9 (He that taketh away a Woman against her will that hath Lands or Goods, or is Heir Apparent to her Ancestors, shall lost his Clergy) were apparently the principal statutory provisions already in force. They were expressly saved by the Interregnum Act now under consideration, as was 'any other Act or Law now in being for the punishment of such... offenders'.

or the annulling and making void the said pretended marriage, as the right in that case shall require, and to give their final sentence and judgment thereupon.

It is unfortunate that few of the surviving records of the court relate to litigation conducted under the Act,[1] but the little evidence remaining suggests that these causes followed the same general pattern. A typical instance is *Burnett* v. *Webb and others*.[2] Sarah Burnett was the daughter of a gentleman of Norwich. She was possessed of considerable means which were coveted by Webb 'a Crooked person and but an Apprentice and a Servant of a small estate'. With the aid of confederates he gained influence over her, giving her 'Caraway Comfitts and Marmalett' and showing her a document drawn up by a fortune-teller which declared that she was to be his wife. She was prevailed upon, against her will, to enter a church and go through a form of marriage with Webb, but she took the first opportunity of protesting that all this was done without her consent. The court declared the marriage null and void.

Twenty special commissions, empowering the Delegates to exercise original jurisdiction, were issued during the Interregnum.[3] Some of these were certainly heard under the Act,[4] but others can have had no connection with it, for *Norton* v. *Moggs*,[5] as appears from some depositions surviving in that cause, was an action based upon bigamy, while *Pittman* v. *Pittman*[6] was brought by a wife against a husband for a decree of nullity on the ground of impotence. Causes such as these lie outside the clearly circumscribed limits of the Act and they can only be explained as examples of that rather vaguely defined original jurisdiction which, as has been

[1] The procedural steps taken in these causes are set out in the Assignation Books but the entries are too succinct to be of much value. One of the surviving Deposition Books (DEL 3/5) consists very largely of evidence taken in these causes and a number of sentences (in some of which a detailed statement of the facts is set out) also relate to them.

[2] (1652), DEL 5/15/23.

[3] DEL 8/71/pt. 1/49–89 *passim*. The last of these commissions (f. 89) was issued in July 1660, shortly after the Restoration, but at a time when the ecclesiastical courts had clearly not been restored and the judicial machinery of the Interregnum was still functioning.

[4] The evidence of sentences or depositions makes it clear that causes such as *Barlow* v. *Wogan and others* (1652), DEL 5/15/no. illegible; *Waterland* v. *Pindar and others* (1653), DEL 5/15/32 and *Wissen* v. *Futter* (1651), DEL 5/15/9 are of this character.

[5] (1656), DEL 3/17/unfoliated.

[6] (1660), DEL 8/1/2.

seen,[1] the Delegates possessed and which had on occasions been exercised in matrimonial causes.[2]

During the Interregnum there were, in fact, two channels available through which matrimonial litigation might pass. The first of these was the Court of Delegates itself, for the decay of the ecclesiastical courts had left it as the only survivor among those tribunals with any jurisdiction (whether original or appellate) in matrimonial matters. Advantage was apparently taken of precedents such as *the Countess of Essex* v. *the Earl of Essex*[3] to pass conventional business of such nature (e.g. petitions for decrees of nullity) through the Court of Delegates and it is no doubt because of the longstanding connection of the Delegates with such litigation that the special matrimonial jurisdiction of the Act of 1652 was conferred upon them.[4]

In addition, some matrimonial business during the Interregnum was handled by Justices of the Peace at Quarter Sessions. It was apparently a part of government policy to bring marriage as far as possible within the secular sphere, and to this end an Act was passed in 1653 which provided for the solemnization of marriage by justices as the only lawful form;[5] it also provided that jurisdiction over some matrimonial disputes should be given to Quarter Sessions.[6]

Some material can be found to illustrate the workings of this legislation,[7] but what is uncertain is the precise way in which matrimonial litigation was shared between the Delegates and the justices. The Act of 1653 is silent on the matter,[8] but bearing in mind that the justices were without legal training, it seems a

[1] See pp. 45–6 *ante*.

[2] e.g. *the Countess of Essex* v. *the Earl of Essex* (1613), 2 St. Tr. 786.

[3] *Supra*.

[4] See pp. 46–8 *ante*.

[5] See Firth and Rait, *Acts and Ordinances*, vol. 2, pp. 715–18.

[6] *Ibid.*, p. 718.

[7] A typical case is quoted by F. A. Inderwick in his study of the period (*The Interregnum* (London, 1891), p. 44); Quarter Sessions declared to be null and void a marriage between Anthony Lowther, son and heir of Robert Lowther, deceased, and Bridget, daughter of James Fleetwood D.D., on the ground that Anthony was not of an age to contract a valid marriage. See also J. C. Jeaffreson (ed.) *Middlesex County Records* (London, 1889–92), vol. 3, p. 264.

[8] It conferred jurisdiction upon justices in Quarter Sessions, or upon 'such other persons...as the Parliament shall hereafter appoint'. This may indicate an intention formally to confer similar powers upon the Delegates, but no later legislation can be found which makes any such provision, and the Delegates' authority to handle ordinary matrimonial litigation seems to have depended solely upon their original jurisdiction, which existed before the Interregnum.

reasonable conjecture that they were confined to causes involving no great difficulty, while those that raised complex points of law went to the more experienced tribunal.[1]

The composition of the special commissions issued to the Delegates during the Interregnum and the procedure involved in their execution set them a little apart from the ordinary appellate business of the court. They were much larger than usual and much more varied, with a substantial admixture of common law judges and laymen. A typical example is *Burnett* v. *Webb and others*;[2] forty-one commissioners were appointed, comprising ten common law judges (including all three chief justices), a member of the Council of State, three judges of the Admiralty, seven other civilians, two serjeants-at-law, the attorney-general, the solicitor-general, the Attorney of the Duchy of Lancaster, the Recorder of London and several army officers and laymen. Another commission of the same nature included Cromwell himself.[3] While it is true that most commissions of delegacy issued during the Interregnum were more broadly based than before, none were as large or as varied in their membership as these; it is, perhaps, a tribute to the importance of this litigation in the eyes of the government.

There were also certain procedural differences. The quorum clause of these commissions was less exclusive than usual, merely requiring that any three or more commissioners should act both in ordinary and extraordinary acts;[4] there also seem to have been special rules relating to the examination of witnesses and the admission of interrogatories.[5]

[1] There is one recorded instance of recourse to extra-judicial proceedings in 1655 when the Council of State directed that the Lords Commissioners of the Great Seal should endeavour to 'compose the differences' between one John Buck and his wife; this early experiment in marriage guidance was not a success and does not seem to have been repeated (see *C.S.P.D.*, 1655–6, pp. 115 and 375–6).

[2] (1652), DEL 8/71/pt. 1/57.

[3] *Davenport* v. *Lucy and others* (1652), DEL 8/71/pt. 1/59.

[4] The quorum clause of a mixed commission would normally require the presence of at least one member of each group of judges (other than the civilians) to be 'present and consenting' to judgment.

[5] For these, see pp. 114–55 *post*.

APPEALS FROM THE DELEGATES TO THE HOUSE OF LORDS

Long before the abolition of the Court of Delegates, the House of Lords was recognized as a tribunal of last resort for all litigation in the secular courts. Its jurisdiction over appeals in common law matters was established in medieval times, while its appellate jurisdiction in equity was finally confirmed after the Restoration.[1]

Its relationship with the ecclesiastical courts, however, was rather more obscure. Until the Reformation, the Upper House seems to have asserted no claim, as the rights of the Pope to the ultimate appeal in religious litigation were apparently unchallenged. After the creation of the ecclesiastical Delegates the true interpretation of 25 Hen. VIII, c. 19 was, as will be seen, a matter for debate and the right of an unsuccessful party before the Delegates to make a further appeal was the subject of much litigation.[2] The power of the Crown to grant a commission of review as an act of grace cannot be said to have been settled until the third decade of the seventeenth century, but so limited was the relief which this provided that disputants in the ecclesiastical courts had begun to explore a new possibility—appeals from the Delegates to the House of Lords.

The earliest application for such an appeal which has been found in the course of this enquiry was made in 1628 in *Vaughan's Case*.[3] Vaughan petitioned the House of Lords for relief against a sentence of the Delegates in a testamentary cause, but the Lords, after debate, rejected his petition, contenting themselves with the significant suggestion that the correct course was to apply for a commission of review. There seem to have been no other applications of this nature for the next fifty years, and it may well be that this rebuff was sufficiently decisive to inhibit further petitions. So infrequently, however, were commissions of review granted to unsuccessful litigants before the Delegates that any other means of questioning a decision of that court must have seemed worth investigation and exactly half a century after *Vaughan's Case* another attempt was made to invoke the jurisdiction of the Lords.

On 10 June 1678, a Mr Cottington presented a petition to the

[1] See T. Beven. 'The Appellate Jurisdiction of the House of Lords', *Law Quarterly Review*, xvii (1901), pp. 155–70.

[2] See pp. 62–6 *post*.

[3] Unreported: referred to in Yale (ed.), *Lord Nottingham's Chancery Cases*, vol. 2, p. 663.

Upper House, praying relief from a decision of the Court of Delegates that he had been lawfully married at Turin to Signora Gallini 'a very lewd woman'.[1] Lord Nottingham was chancellor at the time and, as Mr Yale has demonstrated, he viewed extensions of the appellate jurisdiction of the Lords with considerable reserve.[2] This petition must have seemed to him a convenient opportunity for demonstrating beyond doubt that the precedent of *Vaughan's Case* still stood, and he set about the task with great ingenuity. After a forceful speech from Nottingham, directed mainly to the point that appeals to the Lords in ecclesiastical matters would infringe the royal prerogative, the petition was referred to the Committee of Privileges for further consideration and precedents were cited.[3] In a closely reasoned speech, the chancellor gave a rationale of his opposition to such appeals, taking his stand partly upon law and partly upon expediency. The statute, he explained, did not prevent commissions of review, but these were to be allowed only by way of grace and the Lords could not be concerned with them 'for the Lords sit here only to dispense right, not to dispense matters of grace, which the King reserves to himself'. The arguments *ab inconvenienti* were equally persuasive, for to allow appeals to the Lords from the Delegates either in matrimonial or testamentary matters would be productive of all sorts of inconveniences; there was no limit of time for bringing appeals to the Upper House and the distribution of estates and the legitimacy of children would never be secure if such appeals were possible.

With these arguments the Committee of Privileges was convinced and when the decision was reported to the House it was, after further debate, accepted. The ruling was emphatic and well supported by precedent, and Nottingham seemed justified in ending his report of the proceedings with language which suggested that no more would be heard of the matter.[4] Only a few days after

[1] *Ibid.*, p. 661. This account by Nottingham of the proceedings upon the petition was first printed as a note to the report of *Kennedy* v. *the Earl of Cassillis* (1818), 2 Swans. 313 at 326.

[2] Yale, (ed.) *Lord Nottingham's Chancery Cases*, vol. 1, p. cix.

[3] There seem to have been few relevant authorities available, as Nottingham says of the material put forward on Cottington's behalf that none of it 'did any way come near the point in question' (*ibid.*, vol. 2, p. 662).

[4] 'the House agreed with the committee; and now it is settled that no appeals from the Delegates can come before the Lords' (*ibid.*, vol. 2, p. 664). Nottingham repeated the point in the course of a judgment he gave in 1679; see p. 72 *post*.

the resolution in *Cottington's Case*, the Lords rebuffed two other attempts to appeal to them from the Delegates in testamentary matters,[1] and in fact no appeal was ever successfully brought before them from that tribunal. However, the belief that such appeals were possible was curiously persistent; as late as 1746 a work of practice could state that access to the Lords was available from the Delegates,[2] and the same view could be held by laymen at the very end of the court's life.[3]

For this erroneous opinion there seem two possible explanations. Nottingham's account of the proceedings upon Cottington's petition did not find its way into print until 1818,[4] and no other report seems to have been published before that date; it follows that in the absence of printed evidence of what the Lords had themselves decided there was no great difficulty in believing that their appellate jurisdiction, which by 1700 was agreed to extend over the whole field of common law and equity, was in fact universal.

A more compelling reason for this belief was the existence of two reports which, when read together, might appear to uphold it. In *Saul* v. *Wilson*[5] the headnote begins: 'No appeal lies to the House of Lords, from a sentence by the delegates.' This is an unexceptionable statement of the law but it is *obiter* only (the cause turned upon the interpretation of the Statute of Charitable Uses) and based upon doubtful reasoning. In *Warner* v. *North*[6] the decision in *Saul* v. *Wilson* was reversed, and this led Shower to add a *Quaere* to his report implying that an appeal might in fact lie from the Delegates to the Upper House. This may well have added to the confusion.

[1] *Ibid.*, vol. 2, p. 664.

[2] P. Floyer, *The Proctor's Practice in the Ecclesiastical Courts* (London, 1746), p. 21.

[3] Charles Dickens, *David Copperfield*, ch. 26.

[4] See note 1 on p. 52 *ante*.

[5] (1689), 2 Vern. 118.

[6] (n.d.), Shower, 110.

CHAPTER III

COMMISSIONS OF DELEGACY

Before considering the procedure of the court, the study of which forms the central portion of this book, it seems desirable to discuss the substantive law relating to commissions of delegacy, i.e. the rules which determined whether a petition for an appeal should be granted or refused.

The right to decide this issue was given by 25 Hen. VIII, c. 19 to the Lord Chancellor,[1] whose judgment was apparently final.[2] In the great majority of causes, commissions were granted without question, but if an application was contested, the chancellor's function was narrowly confined to a consideration of the law applicable to the granting of commissions and he had no business with the merits of the cause.[3]

A review of this law may well begin by considering the nature of the right to appeal. It was commonly said that this right was *ex debito justitiae*,[4] and a contrast is made with commissions of review where there was no 'right' to a commission and the petitioner could do no more than ask for grace.[5] But it must not be

[1] This Act, with its requirement that petitions should be directed to the chancellor, applied in terms only to the ecclesiastical courts. It seems that appeals from the other civilian courts were initiated by whatever means had become customary; thus petitions of appeal from the Court of Chivalry were always directed to the Crown, by whom they were normally referred to the chancellor (*H.C.C.*, p. 222) or on rare occasions, to other persons (e.g. *Copley* v. *the Earl of Kingston* (1637), *C.S.P.D.*, 1636–7, p. 495, where the petition was considered by the Earls of Northumberland and Dorset and two other persons (cited in *H.C.C.*, p. 222).

Petitions for commissions of review, however, were always addressed to the king in Council; the exercise of the royal discretion in respect of them was entrusted to the chancellor or (rarely) to others; see p. 76 *post*.

[2] The Act makes no provision for an appeal from the chancellor's decision and no evidence has been found of any attempt to question it.

[3] 'An objection was taken in the arguing of this case, that the *Lord Chancellor* upon a petition for an appeal, is not to try the merits of the cause; this is undoubtedly true, but then the *Lord Chancellor* must determine, whether an appeal will lie or not, though he will not enter into the merits' (Lord Hardwicke in *Sir Henry Blount's Case* (1737), 1 Atk. 295 at 298).

[4] e.g. the statement of Lord Nottingham (Yale (ed.), *Lord Nottingham's Chancery Cases*, vol. 1, p. 358).

[5] *Ibid.*, vol. 1, p. 358. Reviews were granted to hear appeals from decisions of the Court of Delegates; they are discussed at pp. 62–79 *post*.

imagined that the phrase *ex debito justitiae* implied that there was an automatic right to a commission and indeed the use of the phrase in other contexts shows that a 'right' properly described as *ex debito justitiae* might be refused upon the exercise of sound discretion. In *Goodwin* v. *Giesler*,[1] for example, a party was summoned before the Irish Court of Delegates at only four days' notice and his advocates' request for a short adjournment to prepare his cause was peremptorily refused. Upon application for a commission of review, the Lord Chancellor declared that the party was entitled to this adjournment *ex debito justitiae*, but he admitted that it could have been refused upon a due exercise of the court's discretion.

But perhaps a better way of looking at the matter was that suggested by Lord Nottingham on one occasion; there may be circumstances where the granting of a commission may not be *ex debito justitiae* and in such cases there was, in fact, a duty to refuse it. In particular, this situation would arise whenever, in the chancellor's opinion, the party against whom a commission was sought would have a reasonable prospect of terminating proceedings before the Delegates by obtaining a prohibition. The rule was laid down by Nottingham in *Hugh Revell's Case*.[2] Revell, a bastard of Sir William Willoughby, died intestate and left a substantial personal estate. At the king's direction, the ordinary granted administration to Henry Killigrew, but Mary Dixey (Revell's aunt) demanded a commission of appeal. Nottingham held that a commission should not be granted because on the facts Killigrew could obtain a prohibition from the courts of common law and 'Where the courts of Common Law may justly award a prohibition to the Delegates, there ''tis not *ex debito justitiae* to grant a commission of appeal, but it [is] rather a duty to deny it'.[3]

Subject to what has been said above, the Act imposed no limitation upon an appeal from a decision of a lower court on the merits.[4] An appeal from a *gravamen*,[5] however, was limited by a principle

[1] (1794), Ridg. Ir. T. 371.

[2] Yale (ed.), *Lord Nottingham's Chancery Cases*, vol. 1, p. 258.

[3] *Ibid.*, vol. 1, p. 259.

[4] Restriction of the right to appeal based upon act of the parties (i.e. agreement not to appeal) is discussed at pp. 59–60 *post*. For various attempts to limit appeals in causes of correction, see Gibson, *Codex Juris Ecclesiastici Anglicani*, vol. 2, p. 1080, and the references there cited.

[5] A *gravamen* or 'grievance' was a decision on some interlocutory matter (e.g. rejection of witnesses) by which a party was injured (*O.J.*, CCLXXVII/1–2).

which derived from a difference between the rules of the civil and the canon law; an appeal governed by the latter code could be made from any *gravamen*, whereas an appeal under the civil law could be made from a *gravamen* only if it was *irreparabile*.[1] This rule, a commonplace of the older authorities, was well enough established by the Reformation, but the question which remained to be resolved was the precise nature of a *gravamen irreparabile*. The most lucid account of the matter was the judgment of Lord Hardwicke in *Sir Henry Blount's Case*,[2] where the petition for an appeal turned on precisely this point. An action was begun in the Court of Chivalry against Sir Henry Blount for the improper assumption of arms. In the course of the trial Blount alleged that all pedigrees entered in the books of the College of Arms ought to be signed by the parties who requested the entries to be made, and then objected that certain entries used against him had not been so signed and ought therefore to be rejected. When this allegation was itself rejected by the judge of the Court of Chivalry, Blount petitioned the Chancellor for a commission of Delegates to try the matter, while a cross-petition was put in by the other side declaring that no appeal lay in such a case.

Hardwicke rightly saw that the cause turned on the nature of the *gravamen* and in his discussion of the authorities cited before him there is implicit the rule by which a *gravamen irreparabile* could be distinguished from one which is not. Is the decision of the *judex a quo* such as to destroy the complainant's cause completely? If it is, the *gravamen* is *irreparabile* and the appeal to the Court of Delegates will properly lie; if, on the other hand, the judge's ruling merely weakens the complainant's case, but does not destroy it, he cannot appeal at this stage but must wait until the definitive sentence is given on the merits. If that goes against him, he may then appeal and the point involved in the *gravamen* may then be argued before the appellate court.[3]

[1] 'By the Canon law, you are admitted to appeal from all grievances in general, but in the Civil law only where *gravamen est irreparabile*' (Lord Hardwicke in *Sir Henry Blount's Case* (1737), 1 Atk. 295 at 296).

[2] (1737), 1 Atk. 295.

[3] The reason for refusing appeals from *gravamina* which were not irreparable was neatly put by Bentham, who approved of the civil law rule and incorporated it into his proposed appellate system: 'From an interdiction of this sort, no prejudice to justice can arise. If, notwithstanding the interlocutory order complained of, the definitive decree is such as the complainant would have wished, the appeal would have been of no use; if otherwise, it is then time enough to appeal

The enhanced precision in the definition of *gravamina irreparabilia* which Hardwicke's judgment provided was no doubt welcome to those who practised before the civilian courts, but it must have made all the more painful the contrast between the rules of the civil law, which held appeals within reasonable bounds,[1] and those of the canon law, which knew of no such limitation. By the time of the Reformation, the burdensome nature of the wide canonical rule had become apparent and a petition presented to Parliament during Cranmer's archiepiscopate expressed what was apparently a widely held view.[2]

Which remedy, [the appellate system] like as it was at the first most holsomely provided for the avoyding of thiniquity of partiall Juges; so it is nowe moost wickedly abused for the maintenance of yll doers in their wrongful causes and avoyding of due execution of justice, by reason that they be infinite; specially, after the Canon lawe. For by Civile, there is but appellacion permitted; and that not without penaltie on him that shal than appeal without cause: and that is more reasonable.

At the back of this statement there seems to lie at least a hint that the adoption by the canonists of the civil law rule would be the best solution of the problem. This was in fact proposed as early as 1533,[3] and the *Reformatio Legum Ecclesiasticarum*, which placed stringent limits upon appeals before definitive sentence,

and one appeal at that ultimate stage answers every purpose of 20 appeals at so many intermediate stages. Well or ill-grounded appeals from interlocutory orders are therefore equally useless' (*Collected Works* (Edinburgh, 1843), vol. 4, p. 343).

[1] This consideration weighed with Lord Hardwicke, who was anxious that the decision which he gave in *Blount's Case* should not be an indirect means of extending appeals in the Court of Admiralty. 'It has been said there can no great mischief ensue, if such a commission should issue out of the court; but what weighs with me is the making of a precedent for future applications to Chancery of this kind; for it would be of mischievous consequences to allow of such dilatory appeals, because as the court of admiralty proceeds by the same law, it would be an authority for such sort of appeals from the interlocutory orders of that court, and would create great expence and delay, and the suitors there are too necessitous for the most part to allow of any affected delays.' (1737), 1 Atk. 295 at 298.

[2] Strype, *Memorials of Thomas Cranmer*, vol. 2, pp. 723–4.

[3] *L. & P. Hen. VIII*, 1533, p. 53 (Suggestions concerning the regulating of appeals in ecclesiastical causes). The document begins: 'By the law of civil, no man can appeal afore sentence.' It advised that no appeals should be allowed for any grief before judgment except in cases allowed by the civil law. The experiment of limiting such appeals had already been attempted but without success; see Gibson, *Codex Juris Ecclesiastici Anglicani*, vol. 2, pp. 1079–80, and authorities there cited.

excepted those made from *gravamina irreparabilia*.[1] But this code never passed into law, and the divergence between the rules of the civil and canon law governed the Court of Delegates until its end.[2]

The right to appeal to the Court of Delegates was statutory and Lord Nottingham, in one of his later judgments, showed that limitations of this right were to be decided by a due interpretation of the Act which gave it and by nothing else. The possibility of intruding other considerations had arisen in the case of Hurst, a Canterbury attorney, against whom proceedings had been taken in the secular courts for not receiving the sacrament in his parish church.[3] Similar proceedings were taken against him in the Archdeacon's Court, but the plea of prosecution in a temporal court which he advanced there was overruled. He then appealed to the Delegates, but being apparently unfamiliar with the niceties of ecclesiastical procedure, he seems to have imagined that the onus of prosecuting the suit lay on the other side and no action was taken for three years. It was then held that the appeal had lapsed and the case was remitted to the Archdeacon's Court, where Hurst repeated his original plea, which was again overruled. Hurst again appealed and his opponents sought to prevent the granting of a commission by pointing out that he now appeared to be a factious appellant and that under Canon 98 no such person was to be admitted to an appeal.

After disposing of the technical point that Hurst had not yet been found to be a factious appellant by legal process, and thus was not within the terms of the canon, Nottingham passed to the substance of the case. Whether Hurst was within the canon or not was irrelevant because the canon was itself irrelevant. 'The canon in this point is void, for the statute of 25 H. 8, having given the subject the benefit of appeal, so as to be prosecuted within 15 days, it is not in the power of the Convocation by any canons they can make

[1] Cardwell (ed.), *Reformatio Legum Ecclesiasticarum*, p. 302.

[2] The matter was still being canvassed as late as 1832. In that year the Royal Commission set up in 1830 to inquire into the proceedings and jurisdiction of the ecclesiastical courts suggested that the number of appeals could be reduced if 'by regulations which might be found expedient, checks could be given to appeals from grievances in intermediate steps in the cause' (*Eccl. Courts Rep* (1831–2), p. 8). This recommendation was given statutory authority by 3 & 4 Vict. c. 86, s. 13, which limited such appeals to those approved of by the judge whose decision it was sought to question.

[3] Yale (ed.), *Lord Nottingham's Chancery Cases*, vol. 2, p. 934.

to lessen or weaken this remedy or to obstruct it by superintroducing any new conditions or qualifications upon it which the Act of Parliament doth not require: and therefore the canon which bars all such appeals until conformity is void.'[1]

A problem which occasionally fell to be considered was the effect of renunciation of the right of appeal; could the party who had renounced when proceedings were going on in a lower court later change his mind and apply for a commission? Here also, it was Nottingham who provided the most lucid answer. Applications of this kind came before him on several occasions and when considering them, he was quick to seize on the distinction, very relevant in this connection, between commissions of delegacy and commissions of review. His view of the matter is best understood by contrasting two causes, *Ellis* v. *Layton*[2] and *Cole* v. *Mordant*.[3] The first was a testamentary cause, where a decision was given in the court of first instance against two pretended wills. Both the parties claiming under the wills acquiesced in the judgment and agreed not to appeal, but one of them later applied for a commission of delegacy. Nottingham granted it, apparently on the ground that, since the appeal was *ex debito justitiae*, it was not the business of the chancellor to judge the merits of a possible bar to it, the validity of which was uncertain.[4] The commission should be issued and the matter then raised before the Delegates.[5]

Nottingham's decision in *Cole* v. *Mordant* shows that he thought the position very different when what was renounced was the 'right' to a commission of review. This cause also turned upon a pretended nuncupative will; there had been proceedings before the Delegates and then a feigned trial at law which had been agreed to by the other side only when Mrs Cole had consented to be bound by any

[1] *Ibid.* vol. 2, p. 925.

[2] *Ibid.* vol. 1, p. 358.

[3] *Ibid.*, p. 356.

[4] See Lord Nottingham's comment on this decision in *Cole* v. *Mordant*: 'I admitted the appeal and granted the commission of Delegates notwithstanding [the agreement not to appeal], because the appeal was due *ex debito justitiae*, and if the consent barred it, it was pleadable before the Delegates who knew how to judge of it.'

[5] The same problem had come before Sir Leoline Jenkins some years before and he had given his opinion on it in a letter to the Earl of Clarendon (the then Lord Chancellor), who had consulted him. He reached the same conclusion as Nottingham; a commission should be issued and the first duty of the commissioners would be to consider the validity of the pact not to appeal (Wynne, *Life of Sir Leoline Jenkins*, vol. 2, pp. 722–3).

decision the Delegates might give upon the verdict at law. When judgment went against her, she petitioned for a commission of review. Since reviews were a matter of grace and not of right, the chancellor had a discretion here which he could not exercise when a commission of delegacy was in issue and there was no reason (as there had been in the other cause) to leave to the commissioners of review the decision as to the validity of the agreement not to appeal. Nottingham's refusal of the application was peremptory; a commission of review was a mere matter of favour and 'he that departs from his own consent is not entitled to any favour'.[1] Mrs Cole's position was exactly the same, he declared, as that of a man who had agreed before the chancellor not to bring a writ of error, but who later brought one. Such a man would lose both his injunction and his trial 'because all favour is forfeited'.[2]

When an appeal to the Delegates involved chattels, an appeal might properly lie against a decision by a lower court on possession, although that decision did not involve any question of title. In *Legatus Hispaniae* v. *Plage*[3] the king of Spain, through his legate, sued Plage for goods which the king claimed to be forfeit to himself. The judge of the Admiralty found that the king was entitled to possession, but he did not determine the question of title. Plage then applied to the Lord Chancellor for a commission of delegacy, and it was argued that an appeal would not lie because the sentence did not concern right or interest, but merely possession. On this point the chancellor heard argument 'Et en fine le Seignior Chancellor ala en son closet, & dilonques il amesnust un livre del Civil Ley, en que il trove un text precise que appeal gist cy bien lou le sentence est del possession come lou sur le interest & droit. Et sur ceo il grant un appeal.'

The right to be heard by the Court of Delegates was not confined to parties to the suit in the court below; anyone with a legitimate interest in it could appeal. This rule, which may be found in the older authorities,[4] was confirmed in its application to the Delegates in *Jones* v. *Bougett*.[5] Mr Bougett began a suit in the ecclesiastical courts against Mrs Jubert upon a contract of marriage. Before

[1] Yale (ed.), *Lord Nottingham's Chancery Cases*, vol. 1, p. 358.

[2] *Ibid.*, p. 358.

[3] (1610–11), Moo. K.B. 814.

[4] See *D.* 49. 1. 4. 2; Ayliffe, *Parergon Juris Canonici Anglicani*, p. 73, and the anonymous cause there cited.

[5] (1739), 1 Atk. 298.

sentence was given, Mrs Jubert married Jones and a child was born of that union; Mrs Jubert later died. The court found for Mr Bougett, and Mr Jones, who with the child was interested in the sentence, although not a party to the original suit, petitioned the Lord Chancellor for a commission of delegacy. The chancellor held that the older authorities applied to appeals to that court and the petition was granted.

CHAPTER IV

COMMISSIONS OF REVIEW

The litigant who was unsuccessful before the Delegates might wish to take his cause further and in this chapter his right to do so will be considered.

By the end of the court's life, the position (for both ecclesiastical and secular business) was clear enough. The party against whom the Delegates decided was not entitled to a further appeal *ex debito justitiae*, but he might present a petition to the king in Council asking for a further consideration of the cause by judges appointed under an instrument known as a commission of review.[1] This petition was usually referred to the Lord Chancellor,[2] who would hear counsel on both sides and then advise the Crown.[3]

This position was not reached without a struggle, however, and the development of the law governing reviews requires examination under several heads. As the legality of reviews in secular and spiritual causes depended upon different arguments and lines of decision, these must be separately considered, as must the criteria by which it was decided (once the lawfulness of reviews had been established) to grant or refuse an application. Other matters requiring investigation are the procedure to be followed when applying for a commission of review and the law which governed the execution of such commissions.

The first aspect of reviews which attracted attention in the courts was their legality, and for ecclesiastical causes a convenient starting point for an enquiry into this problem is the Act 25 Hen. VIII, c. 19; this stated that the sentence of the ecclesiastical Delegates was to be 'definitive' and that there was to be no further appeal from it.[4] This might well be understood as setting an end to further litigation, and much learning was expended in elucidating the true meaning of the words. The earliest and most

[1] *Eccl. Courts Rep.* (1831–2), p. 20.

[2] See pp. 75–6 *post*, where the procedure is described in greater detail.

[3] It would not, as a rule, be successful. Applications of this kind were considered in a rigorous light 'as it is only some important misconstruction of Law, or error of Fact, in the sentence of the Court of Delegates, which is considered sufficient to warrant the exercise of this interposition of the Royal Prerogative' (*Eccl. Courts Rep.*, (1831–2) p. 20). [4] 25 Hen. VIII, c. 19, s. 4.

important of the reported causes on this matter is *Halliwell* v. *Jervoise*.[1] A parson sued for tithes before the bishop of his diocese and then appealed to the Court of Audience, where the first sentence was confirmed. There was then a further appeal to the Court of Delegates which reversed both the earlier decisions. The unsuccessful litigant then obtained a commission under the Great Seal to certain commissioners 'ad revidendum les sentences', whereupon his opponent caused a prohibition to issue.

The matter was recognized as an important one and the cause was adjourned into the Exchequer Chamber for Debate. Here two opposing arguments were advanced. Popham argued that the common law could not interfere with commissions of review by way of prohibition because such reviews had formerly been allowed by the Pope from sentences given by his legates and this prerogative had been transferred to the Crown by the Statute 25 Henry VIII, c. 19. A more radical view was advanced by Fenner; the authority of the Pope had been extinguished here, he declared, and since no appeal beyond the Delegates is given by statute, none can lie. Popham's view, however, proved decisive, and after a further conference the court agreed to grant a consultation.[2]

As this account makes clear, the reported argument turned mainly on the question whether or not the powers formerly exercised by the Pope over the Church in England could be said to reside in the Crown and it is not without significance that it was this wider question, touching the royal prerogative, which exercised the mind of the court whenever the problem of interpreting the statute arose. Coke, in his discussion of the cause, stated the problem in the same light: 'the said Acts of 24 and 25 H. 8 do upon certain appeals make the sentence definitive as to any appeal,

[1] (1596–7). Reported in Moo. K.B. 462 and Cro. Eliz. 571. (*sub nomine Gervis* v. *Hallewel*) and noted in 4 Inst. 341 (*sub nomine Hollingworth's Case*); Moore's report is the most complete.

Several earlier decisions, apparently unreported, are referred to by Coke in his discussion of commissions of review in 4 Inst. 341. They are *Michelot's Case* (1586–7), *Goodman's Case* (1586–7) and *Huet's Case* (1586–7). *Halliwell* v. *Jervoise* may well have gone to the Exchequer Chamber for Debate because these earlier decisions were conflicting or obscure.

[2] This was the writ by which the judges of the common law could order the return to the ecclesiastical courts of some cause which had been removed from those courts by prohibition. It derived its name from the 'consultation' or deliberation of the king's judges, by whom it was decided that the prohibition did not properly lie. (T. Cunningham, *A New and Complete Law Dictionary* (London, 1764), vol. 1, *s.v.* 'Consultation').

for the words be (shall be definitive) and that no further appeal should be had'. But, he went on, commissions of review are possible, and the words of the Act which might appear to prohibit them are to be understood in the light of two facts: (i) the Acts of Henry and Elizabeth had transferred the Pope's powers as Supreme Head of the Church in England to the Crown and these powers included the granting of reviews; (ii) there is nothing in the Act which directly forbids such reviews.

This gave the considerable weight of Coke's authority to the proposition that the definitive nature of a sentence by the ecclesiastical Delegates did not prevent subsequent review, and for the next four decades no further litigation on this point seems to have appeared in the reports. Early in Charles I's reign, one final attempt was made to establish the invalidity of such reviews in the cause of *Haver* v. *Thorol.*[1] This was a matrimonial dispute where a review was sought and the matter came before the Common Bench when a prohibition was moved for. The argument, as reported in Littleton, was long and complex. Counsel for the petitioners directed their minds to the precise words of the Act and raised a fresh point of interpretation; reviews and appeals were distinct things and the sole intention of the statute was to regulate the latter.[2] Thus the words which interdicted 'further appeals' merely prohibited further commissions of delegacy and had nothing to do with reviews. Reliance was also placed upon the number of reviews which had already been granted.[3] The other side declared that the distinction between commissions of review and commissions of delegacy was unreal,[4] and that the Act was meant to set a definite limit to any re-examination of the Delegates' decisions. The significance in this connection of the royal prerogative was realised, and both sides, in further argument, debated for and against the proposition that the prerogative could be bound by statute.

[1] (1628–9), Lit. 228.

[2] This point is implicit in Coke's account of *Halliwell* v. *Jervoise* (4 Inst. 341), *sub nomine Hollingworth's Case*) but it does not seem to have been raised in argument before, if one may judge from the reports.

The reference in Littleton's report of the discussion to 35 Hen. VIII, c. 19 is a misprint for 25 Hen. VIII, c. 19.

[3] 'Le melieur exposicion des leies est le use; & in temps Eliz. & apres tiels Commissions ount este grant' (at 229).

[4] '& coment que diversity est mise inter Appeal & Review uncore ceo est forsque in parols & nemy in reason & meaning del ley' (at 230).

But the invitation to express himself on so weighty a matter was one which Richardson J. was disinclined to accept, and his cautious judgment was largely confined to a reiteration of the linguistic niceties surrounding the precise words of the Act. The substance of his judgment contains two propositions. First, there is a valid distinction between appeals and reviews, so that the words of the Act 'and no further Appeals to be had'[1] cannot apply to the latter. Second, the true meaning of the word 'definitive' is to be sought by contrasting it with the word 'final'. The statute 24 Hen. VIII, c. 12[2] required that matters which came before the archbishop should be 'finally determined' and that decisions of Convocation (which was given jurisdiction in matters touching the king, his heirs and successors) 'should be taken for a final decree, sentence, judgment, definition and determination'. In respect of these 'final' decisions, then, there could be no review, but the later Act[3] merely made judgments of the ecclesiastical Delegates 'definitive' and thus there was nothing in it to bind the Crown.

To make a clear distinction between the words 'definitive' and 'final' is a tempting way of solving the problem, but the logic of Richardson's judgment did not have a universal appeal. If a review is to be allowed from a sentence which is 'definitive' merely and not 'final' it follows that when a sentence is 'final' there can be no review. There are lines of cases, however, in which this distinction is obliterated; thus the statute 28 Hen. VIII, c. 6 (which established a Court of Ecclesiastical Delegates in Ireland) provided that the sentences of that court should constitute 'the final determination of all causes and griefs contained in the provocation or appeal', yet commissions of review were granted in respect of decisions of that court which would have been impossible if the word 'final' had borne the meaning attributed to it by Richarson.[4] Again, the statute 8 Eliz. I, c. 5, which purported to regulate appeals in civil and marine causes, stated that decisions of the Delegates appointed to hear such causes should be 'final', but here also reviews were granted.[5]

The truth seems to be that in a litigious age the demand for

[1] 25 Hen. VIII, c. 19, s. 4.

[2] The Act in Restraint of Appeals, further discussed at pp. 6–10 *ante*.

[3] i.e. 25 Hen. VIII, c. 19.

[4] The significance of these decisions is commented on in Brodrick and Fremantle, *A Collection of the Judgments of the Privy Council*, p. xlii.

[5] See pp. 67–9 *post*.

reviews was too strong to be denied. Moreover, to deny the possibility of review meant to deny the royal prerogative to grant it.[1]

The line of decisions referred to above clearly established that reviews were possible in ecclesiastical causes. These decisions, however, had no direct relevance to secular litigation, as they were all intended to interpret the Acts of Appeals,[2] and those statutes were meant to define the course of appeal in ecclesiastical causes alone. Secular civil law appeals were governed by different statutory enactments and (to some extent) by different considerations of policy; thus it follows that the law governing review in such causes requires separate consideration. This consideration must in practice be confined to Admiralty and prize business, as no evidence survives for the other secular courts.[3]

The idea that some limit should be set to appeals is to be found running through the whole administration of marine law in England from a relatively early period. In a judicial sphere where litigants were so often transient seamen or merchants domiciled abroad, it must have seemed especially desirable that justice should be speedy and that causes should be brought to a quick determination without those opportunities for delay which appeals so readily afforded. At one time, it is true, there seems to have been no limit to the number of appeals by which an ordinary marine cause could be protracted,[4] and the lengthening of suits which resulted was the subject of a petition as early as Richard II's reign.[5] This petition may have had no immediate result, but it is clear that by the sixteenth century the need for limitation, at least in certain fields of maritime jurisdiction, was recognized. Thus, treaties between England and France in the early years of Henry VIII's reign, which established special courts for the trial

[1] It is significant that Coke, who appeared in *Halliwell* v. *Jervoise*, stated that his function in that case was 'to maintain the Queens power' (4 Inst. 341, *sub nomine Hollingworth's Case*.)

[2] 24 Hen. VIII, c. 12 and 25 Hen. VIII, c. 19.

[3] i.e. the Court of Chivalry and the Courts of Oxford University. No reference to a review in any cause emanating from these courts has been found in the Delegates' archive, nor is there any material relating to unsuccessful applications for reviews. Since, however, the secular civil law courts were in general governed by the same law (see the comment of Lord Hardwicke in *Blount's Case* (1737), 1 Atk. 295 at 298), it is likely that the rules evolved for Admiralty causes were considered to apply (*mutatis mutandis*) to the others.

[4] Thus the litigation upon appeal in *Gernesey* v. *Henton* seems to have extended from 1389 to 1404 (Marsden (ed.), *Select Pleas in the Court of Admiralty*, vol. 1, pp. 17–26).

[5] *Ibid.*, vol. 1, p. lxxix.

of piracy, gave only a limited right of appeal to the King's Council, and later in that century the special commission granted to Dr Lewes (*c.* 1575) for the trial of certain maritime causes specified that there was to be no appeal from his judgments.[1] But of more immediate importance is the Act 8 Elizabeth I, c. 5 which, by stating that decisions of the Delegates in marine causes should be 'final, and no further Appeal to be had or made from the said Judgment or Sentence definitive' seemed on its face to prohibit any further investigation of any matter coming up from the Court of Admiralty.[2]

This enactment was the subject of varying interpretations. The earliest comment available is contained in a letter of Dr Lewes (the then judge of the Court of Admiralty) in 1566, which is referred to by Sir Leoline Jenkins in a legal opinion which he wrote for Lord Keeper Bridgman in 1668:

> I have seen a Letter from one of my Predecessors, Dr. Lewis, to Secretary Cecil, wherein he desires his Favour to promote a Bill in Parliament, (which no doubt was this very Statute, 8 Eliz., c. 5, for his Letter bears Date Nov. 5 1566.) which he says he had brought into the Lower House, for reducing Admiralty Causes, in point of Appeal, to the same Standard the Ecclesiastical Causes were, by the statute 25 H. VIII. And in Answer to some Question that Secretary had put to him, he adds these Words: 'My Lord Keeper cannot grant any Commission upon Appeal, but in communi forma, without he have a special Warrant from the Queen's Majesty, wherein also I have some doubt'. Meaning, I suppose, (as the Civil Law led him to believe) that no Man could be precluded (at leastwise before this Statute was made) from making his Complaint to the Prince.[3]

The natural meaning of these words is that the statute was intended to prevent a 'Complaint to the Prince', by way of petition for a review, and it seems likely at the least that such was the intention of its author; the words of the Act appear unambiguous and Squibb, in his comment on it, interprets it in this way.[4] Coke, on the other hand, clearly implies in the Institutes that he

[1] *Ibid.*, vol. 2, p. xiii.

[2] It seems that the Act was drafted in response to complaints by foreigners of excessive dilatoriness in the conduct of maritime litigation in this country. Dr Lewes, who was responsible for the measure, wrote in the letter to Cecil, referred to below, that he had caused the Bill to be introduced into Parliament 'upon occasion of complaynte of straungers for longe sutes in cyvill and marittime causes, by reason of dyvese appeles permytted in those causes' (S.P. Eliz. I, vol. 41, no. 11).

[3] Wynne, *Life of Sir Leoline Jenkins*, vol. 2, p. 721.

[4] *H.C.C.*, p. 222.

did not regard the legislation as excluding reviews in marine causes, but he provided no authority for this proposition other than his own *ipse dixit*.[1] Jenkins, writing in 1668 and with some experience of the workings of the Court of Delegates behind him,[2] was more cautious,[3] and the matter was still apparently in dispute in 1677 when the question was considered by Lord Nottingham.

By this time, there had been decisions in favour of reviews,[4] but the propriety of granting them was still, apparently in doubt.[5] In a careful judgment, Nottingham confirmed the legitimacy of his predecessors' actions. After referring to the unanimity of practice in this field and invoking the authority of Coke, he went on to consider the consequences of the view that there could be no commission of review in marine causes. These, he thought, would be deplorable, for it would be 'absurd' and 'would tend to a failure of justice' to deprive the king of his right to grant reviews. It would also involve a logical absurdity, for the king, who was the sole fount of justice, would be deprived of the right to remedy decisions of judges who derived their authority from him alone: 'What is this but to exhaust the fountain of justice and have him without power who gives power to others, as a fountain does waters cumulative not privative'.[6]

Nottingham had still to explain away the very emphatic negative words of the Act, and this he did neatly. Their function, he declared, was to make it clear that commissions of review were only matters of grace and thus prevent them from becoming as common as appeals, which would result in their abuse.[7]

This judgment is not, perhaps, entirely convincing (in particular, Nottingham ignored the distinction between 'definitive' and 'final' and between appeals and reviews, made in *Haver* v. *Thorol*).[8] But the decision seems to have been accepted as decisive, and no later

[1] 4 Inst. 341.

[2] He first sat as a judge delegate in *Norwood and Mayer* v. *Norwood* (1665), DEL 8/71/pt. 2/22.

[3] 'I have not known any [review] in that little Time wherein I have had the Honour to serve in the Admiralty' (Wynne, *Life of Sir Leoline Jenkins*, vol. 2, p. 721).

[4] Two have been identified in the records: *Lightfoot* v. *Zerbi and others* (1664), DEL 8/71/pt. 2/18; *Clinkard* v. *Jolly and others* (1668), DEL 8/71/pt. 2/36.

[5] 'the civilians made some doubt whether any review at all did lie in Admiral causes by reason of the words of the statute of 8 Eliz. cap. 5' (*The Ralph and Mary and The Constant Thomas* (1677), 2 Nott. Chan. Cas. 573).

[6] The sentiment is Coke's (4 Inst., p. 341).

[7] *The Ralph and Mary and the Constant Thomas*, *supra*, at 574.

[8] (1628–9), Lit. 228.

cause has been found in which the matter was re-opened. Commissions of review in marine causes were not encouraged by the judgment, however, as only one later example has been identified.[1]

The possibility of granting commissions of review in prize causes is a problem which requires separate examination, for with these it could be claimed that different considerations applied and the arguments against review may have appeared more convincing. The point seems to have attracted very little attention from the reporters, but counsel opposing a review in *Matthews* v. *Warner*,[2] a testamentary appeal, lighted upon a judgment of Lord Camden in *The Hoogscarpel*,[3] a prize cause where the decision, in the opinion of counsel, could be made to admit of a wider application. Camden, like Coke and Nottingham before him, had grasped the significant relationship between reviews and the royal prerogative, but his view of what this relationship ought to be was very different from theirs: 'this Prerogative is not to be countenanced; being the growth of base and despotic times; founded on the usurpation of the powers assumed by the Emperors or the Church of *Rome*, and introducing expedience into the administration of Justice'.

But by a general application of this argument Lord Loughborough was not impressed and he placed it firmly in the context of prize law: here, he was prepared to admit, it had great cogency:

> I cannot but suppose...all, that fell from Lord *Camden*, was pointed and applied to the case of frequent trials upon questions of Prize; upon which undoubtedly very strong arguments occur against going beyond the usual limits, which the course of the Admiralty and the observance of foreign treaties prescribe; that from the sentence of the Vice-Admiralty there may be, and there must be, an appeal to the King in Council. It is to be decided there only upon appeal. The decision is very solemn. The mode is sanctioned by public engagements; and the most obvious inconvenience arises from keeping in suspense the question, whether a dividend is to be made among the captors, or the capture is to be restored.[4]

The problem had already been considered by Sir Leoline Jenkins,[5] but he had reached a very different conclusion. The opinion which he gave at the request of Lord Keeper Bridgman in

[1] *Brathwaite and others* v. *Gallopp and others* (1682), DEL 8/72/pt. 1/60.

[2] (1798), 4 Ves. J. 186 at 202.

[3] Apparently unreported. The substance of the judgment is given in vol. 2 of A. Browne, *A Compendious View of the Civil Law, and of the Law of the Admiralty* (London, 1802), App. 5 and (in a rather more cursory form) in 4 Ves. J. 202.

[4] 4 Ves. J. at 205–6.

[5] Wynne, *Life of Sir Leoline Jenkins*, vol. 2, pp. 721–2.

1668 related to the possibility of a prize cause being the subject of a review. Much of the argument, it is true, turned upon factors peculiar to the cause,[1] but even setting these aside, Jenkins was clearly of opinion that by international law a foreign subject could not be refused the right to apply for a review in a prize cause. The passage in which this view is expressed is emphatic and precise:

> But that, My Lord, which inclines me very strongly to believe there lies a Review in this Case is, that the petitioner, for it is a Stranger, [*sic*] and a Subject to one of his Majesty's Allies, and consequently has, as well by the Law of Nations, as by several Treaties with Spain, a Right to implore his Majesty's Justice, and to be instant for it by all Ways and Means, not only ordinary in our courts of Justice, but extra-ordinary also, before his Majesty by his special Delegates.

Almost forty years later, this view of the matter was confirmed by Richard Crawley, the then Admiralty registrar. Writing to Richard Warre,[2] he answered the question whether a particular prize cause could be reviewed:

> her Majesty may, *praerogativa regia et plenitudine potestatis*, grant a review if she thinks fit, on a petition from Groen, by an order to the Lord Keeper. But before such a commission be granted it will be proper to consider very well of it; for there was but one all the last war, and the difficulties which attended it were so great that no other was ever attempted.[3]

The evidence, as has been shown, reveals a clear division of opinion. On the one hand, reviews in prize causes are declared to be politically undesirable and this opinion is re-inforced by arguments *ab inconvenienti*, while on the other hand the rules of international law and the practice of the courts are produced in defence of the prerogative to grant reviews. The statements of Jenkins and Crawley are strongly in support of the view that the right to apply for a review existed[4] (at least in the case of foreigners), and it should be noted that both Camden and Loughborough inveigh against the undesirability of reviews in prize causes, not against their illegality. Despite this limitation, their arguments were

[1] e.g. the effect upon it of the Act 17 Car. I and of a Proclamation of September 1660.

[2] H.M.C. Portland MSS. vol. 8, pp. 148–9; letter dated 12 September 1704.

[3] This is probably a reference to *Brathwaite and others* v. *Gallop and others* (1682), DEL 8/72/pt. 1/60; see p. 71 *post*.

[4] There was never any suggestion that there was a right to a review itself, as it was always *ex gratia*.

eminently cogent and they probably reflect the attitude of those who were charged with deciding, in particular cases, whether or not to grant a review.[1]

This reluctance is reflected in the records, which make it clear that, at least for a substantial part of its life, the Court of Delegates was rarely called upon to consider a prize cause by way of review. Entries in the Repertory Books,[2] which run from 1619 to 1789, always state the name of the court from which the cause came up to the Delegates on appeal, and if the cause is a review of a previous decision, the entry makes this clear.[3] Only one review of a cause coming from the Lords Commissioners of Prize Appeal is recorded,[4] and this confirms the validity of the arguments advanced above; such reviews were legal but were granted with exceptional rarity.

It is clear from all this evidence that the possibility of reviewing decisions handed down by the Delegates (whether in ecclesiastical or secular causes) was eventually established beyond dispute, and it now remains to consider upon what principles reviews were granted. The decision fell very largely to the chancellors;[5] they had a discretion in the matter, but one which the crystallization of practice and the authority derived from reported cases came increasingly to direct. A review of the authorities may conveniently begin with the accession to office of Lord Nottingham,[6] which resulted in a number of decisions in which careful thought and subtle reasoning were applied to this branch of the royal prerogative. Although inclining to the view that appeals should be carefully regulated,[7] he could not be said resolutely to set his face against commissions of review. Purely frivolous objections he would sweep aside, and in *Gravenor* v. *Cartwright* (*et e contra*)[8]

[1] It will be seen that chancellors were always reluctant to recommend reviews, except upon very strong grounds; see pp. 71–5 *post.*

[2] See p. 228 *post* for the form and purpose of these books.

[3] e.g. *Bainbrigg* v. *Benskyn* (1647), DEL 8/71/pt. 1/33; the entry reads 'Judices Delegati in causa appellationis'.

[4] *Brathwaite and others* v. *Gallop and others* (1682), DEL 8/72/pt. 1/60. The cause is described as an appeal from 'Judices delegati in omnibus causis appellationum et querelarum quoad naves et bona jure belli capta et seizita'. The facts are briefly rehearsed in *C.S.P.D.*, 1684–5, p. 137 in which a second commission of review was (unsuccessfully) sought.

[5] Occasionally to other persons; see p. 76 *post.*

[6] No examples have been found earlier than 1673, the year when Lord Nottingham accepted the Great Seal.

[7] Yale, *Lord Nottingham's Chancery Cases*, vol. 1, p. cix.

[8] (1679), 2 Nott. Chan. Cas. 733.

he brusquely dismissed the argument that an application for a review should be rejected because, after the original hearing, there were not enough common law judges left to make up a commission.[1] Again, he was not slow to grasp the implications of his hard-won victory in *Cottington's Case*,[2] and he made it clear that the decision of the House of Lords not to hear appeals from the Court of Delegates must have an affect upon the exercise of the chancellor's discretion.[3]

But Nottingham's instinct was against prolonging litigation by way of appeal when this could be avoided. In *Gravenor* v. *Cartwright* (*et e contra*),[4] where the parties were involved in litigation in Chancery as well as before the Delegates and a commission of review was applied for, he recommended instead acceleration of the suit in equity and finally refused to grant a review on the ground that the supplicant's remedy in equity was adequate.

By Lord Hardwicke's time, it is clear that the rules which governed the chancellor's discretion in this field were already acquiring a certain rigour. In an interesting decision in *Savile* v. *Savile*[5] he lays down three rules which are widely enough expressed to be of general application:

First the weight of evidence was against the sentence: Secondly, the question had only been once heard and examined; for the Appeal to the Delegates was brought upon one preliminary point; and the course of that Court in such a case is to take possession of the whole cause:[6] Thirdly, the sentence tended to establish a proposition of great importance in future cases; and which had not been before established by any decision in this country; *viz.* that forgiveness of adultery may be collected from facts and circumstances, so as to bar the husband from the right of divorce.

[1] 'I take it to be no objection that there have been six judges of the Common Law at the Delegates, for that may happen in most cases and then there should be never any review at all' (*Gravenor* v. *Cartwright* (*et e contra*), *supra*, at 734.

[2] (1678), 2 Nott. Chan. Cas. 661. An account of the case is also given in 2 Swanston 326 based on Nottingham's (then unpublished) papers. Its effect in settling the relationship between the Court of Delegates and the House of Lords is discussed on pp. 51–3 *ante*.

[3] 'though a commission of review be only *ex gratia*, yet now there ought to be a greater propensity to it than ever because there can be no resort to Parliament by way of appeal for any injustice done in the spiritual courts' (*Gravenor* v. *Cartwright* (*et e contra*), *supra*, at 734–5.

[4] (1679), 2 Nott. Chan. Cas. 733.

[5] Apparently unreported, but referred to in *Matthews* v. *Warner* (1798), 4 Ves. J. 186 at 202.

[6] This was not always so; see pp. 43–5 *ante*.

Although no less than twenty-four commissions of review were granted from 1666 to 1741,[1] and no doubt many more unsuccessful applications were made, the subject still does not seem to have attracted the reporters.[2] But details of practice were accumulating and by the end of the eighteenth century, the chancellor's discretion to grant commissions of review was found to be governed by rules as precise as those which controlled his discretion in many other fields.

The subject gave rise to two detailed judgments in 1798 and 1803. The first of these, *Matthews* v. *Warner*,[3] was an application for a review of a decision of the Court of Delegates in a testamentary cause, and Lord Loughborough's judgment is a useful statement of the law governing such applications as it had by then developed. He made it clear that, although applications should be granted only 'upon grounds of sound discretion', he was not in principle unsympathetic to them. The law of England was determined that the rights of litigants should not be established by 'quick conclusions', as he showed by analogies drawn from practice in error and retrial at common law. But he went on to concede that more than his private opinion that the judgment of the Delegates was wrong would be needed to justify the granting of a commission of review. In effect he accepted (and amplified) the rules governing discretion adumbrated by Hardwicke. The point to be argued here was a material one, the evidence affecting it was complex and conflicting and, he implied, the decisions hitherto given in the case ran counter to it: 'with this evidence... I should have no difficulty, sitting, as I have sat, in a Court of Law, to put it so to the jury, that I should expect a verdict, that he had not devised.'[4] In the light of these facts the Lord Chancellor certified that a review should be granted.

The last of the modern cases, in which the mode of exercising the royal discretion is touched upon, is *Eagleton* v. *Kingston*,[5] also

[1] See the list in *Matthews* v. *Warner* (1798), 4 Ves. J. 186 at 194–5.

[2] There is some evidence to suggest that it was not usually the practice of the chancellors to state in open court the reasons for the advice tendered to the Crown; see Lord Eldon's comment in *Eagleton* v. *Kingston* (1803), 8 Ves. J. 438 at 464, where he seems to regard the giving of reasons as undesirable. A statement of reasons must have been given sometimes, however, as some have found their way into the reports (e.g. *Franklin's Case* (1725), 2 P. Wms. 299 at 300; *ex parte Fearon* (1800), 5 Ves. J. 633 at 644–6). The substance of the chancellor's certificate to the Crown is given in *Eagleton* v. *Kingston*, *supra*, at 480–1.

[3] *supra*. [4] (1798), 4 Ves. J. 186 at 209. [5] *supra*.

a testamentary cause, in which the petition for review came before Lord Eldon. His judgment is somewhat diffuse, slipping imperceptibly from the question of review to the merits of the cause, but the passage in which he sums up his conclusions provides so admirable an example of his judicial manner, and is so neat a statement of the law, that it deserves quotation *in extenso*:

> the case, as established on the part of the memorialists, does not furnish any such doubts respecting the sentence pronounced by the Court of Delegates, considered either with reference to the facts, which it can be understood to have decided upon, or with regard to important points of law, which it may be supposed to establish, as makes it expedient, that his Majesty should grant such Commission of Review as hath been prayed. This Commission is prayed of the grace and benignity of the Crown. Its sound discretion, by which its grace and benignity are guided, has upon obvious grounds of public expediency usually induced it to withold Commissions of Review, unless there are very cogent reasons for believing, that the sentence sought to be reviewed is founded upon error in fact or in law; or, unless the doctrines of law, upon which the sentence is supposed to be founded, are so questionable or important, as to make it clearly fit, that they should be considered in the most solemn manner.[1]

It is clear from the foregoing that the chancellor, in exercising his discretion, usually considered particular defects in the conduct of a cause, and of these a mistaken finding of fact or a mistaken application of law seem to have been the most common. On occasions, however, the petition for a review might be based upon a more general ground, e.g. the complete insufficiency of the hearing; if the Delegates, in their ordering of the cause, had been grossly partial or incompetent, a commission of review would be granted. A striking example (and the only one which seems to have found its way into the reports) is *Goodwin* v. *Giesler*.[2] This was a testamentary cause, turning upon a will the validity of whose execution was doubted. After some of the witnesses for the will had been examined *viva voce* in the court of first instance in Ireland, their evidence was found to be conflicting, but despite this the judge found for the will. The other side at once appealed to the Irish Court of Delegates and the usual inhibition was granted. The court met after only four days' notice and for the first time the seals of the transmiss were broken.[3] The judges at once

[1] *Eagleton* v. *Kingston* (1803), 8 Ves. J. 438 at 480–1.

[2] (1794), Ridg. Ir. T. 371 (which refers to a decision of the Irish Court of Delegates).

[3] This document is usually referred to as the process; see pp. 216–17 *post*.

called on the appellant to support his appeal and his advocates (not previously having been able to examine the transmiss to ensure that it was an accurate record of proceedings in the court below) asked for time to prepare the cause and also to make ready printed cases for the judges delegate. This request was peremptorily refused. One of his advocates then undertook to be ready on the following morning, if the court would adjourn. This was also refused, whereupon the appellant's advocates and proctor withdrew. The judges then called for the depositions of the subscribing witnesses to the will which were at once read and, without any further examination of the cause they affirmed the sentence of the court below.

Upon an application for a commission of review, the Lord Chancellor's comments were scathing:

> It is a very painful duty to me to be obliged to make any comment upon the proceedings of the Court of Delegates. But I cannot avoid stating my decided opinion, that the judges-delegate, who ought to have heard this appeal, could not in any manner be warranted in this most precipitate judgment... If they were determined to dispose of the appeal, without hearing the appellant in support of it, surely it was their bounden duty, minutely to have examined the whole transmiss, to weigh the evidence which it contained...In making this report, I have to lament deeply, that I must detail a proceeding which will not reflect credit upon the jurisprudence of this country.[1]

No procedure by which a commission of review might be applied for was provided by statute, and persons seeking a review made use of the usual means whereby an exercise of the royal prerogative was sought—a petition to the king in Council.[2]

This document was presented by the petitioner's proctor, who usually signed it.[3] It generally contained a statement of the facts of the cause and the decision of the Court of Delegates and of the court or courts from which the appeal had come, while the claim to a review might be strengthened by an allegation of some specific

[1] *Goodwin* v. *Giesler* (1794), Ridg. Ir. T. 371 at 383–4.

[2] They were not addressed to the chancellor and were not handled by his secretary for Commissions of Appeal (*Eccl. Courts Rep.* (1831–2), p. 209). Twelve have been identified among the State Papers Domestic falling between the years 1671 and 1704.

[3] The application for a review was referred to in the records of the court as a *supplicacio* (e.g. *Waltham and others* v. *Rawley and others* (1603), DEL 4/2/188); the party apppealing by way of review was known, not as *pars appellans*, but as *pars supplicans* (*Rawley and others* v. *Waltham and others* (1602), DEL 4/2/123).

act of omission by the Delegates which the petitioner found objectionable.[1] The petition was then referred to the Lord Chancellor (or on occasions some other person)[2] and a day fixed for the hearing of argument.

The investigation of the petitioner's claim was usually thorough. The process and original papers might be brought in for investigation,[3] and members of both the civilian and common law bars might be heard.[4] Legal argument seems to have been based partly on the general expediency of granting a review and partly on the merits of the cause.[5] If the Lord Chancellor thought fit, the parties or one of them might be required to appear.[6]

The chancellor's decision was embodied in a certificate of advice to the Crown which would on occasions contain reasons for the decision arrived at.[7] When this had been considered by the king in Council, a formal order in Council was made in accordance with its terms.[8]

A commission of review was in substance an appeal, and may well have been regarded by most litigants as no more than a second

[1] Thus Dacres Barrett complained that, although the court which heard his cause had ten members, the allegation which contained the substance of his claim was considered by only two of them, who rejected it (*C.S.P.D.*, 1697, p. 509). In another cause, which had come from the Prerogative Court of York, the petitioner alleged that the evidence of two witnesses, favourable to him, had been suppressed by the Delegates 'contrary to the practice of York and the known laws of the nation' (*C.S.P.D.*, 1696, p. 27).

[2] The task was usually delegated to the holder of the Great Seal; the Lord Chancellor (e.g. *C.S.P.D.*, 1697, p. 509), the Lord Keeper (e.g. *C.S.P.D.*, 1684–5, p. 259) or the Lords Commissioners of the Great Seal (e.g. *C.S.P.D.*, 1689–90, p. 399). Other persons might act on occasions; thus one petition was referred to 'the Attorney or Solicitor General' (*C.S.P.D.*, 1689–90, p. 39).

[3] See the entry in the Account Book kept 'in Mr Rushworth's Time' for *Gernon* v. *Gernon* (1753), DEL 8/52.

[4] e.g. *Eagleton* v. *Kingston* (1803), 8 Ves. J. 438, where each side was represented before the Lord Chancellor by two civilians and two others.

[5] e.g. the arguments in *Matthews* v. *Warner* (1798), 4 Ves. J. 186.

[6] e.g. *C.S.P.D.*, 1671, p. 90. Petition of Robert Prujean in a cause involving his grandmother, now the wife of Serjeant Maynard. The petition was referred to Sir Orlando Bridgman, who made an order requiring Maynard and his wife to attend him.

[7] e.g. the report of the chancellor on a petition of Lord Decies in 1677; to allow a review would be undesirable, as it might result in a finding against two judgments already given for a consummated marriage (and thus bastardize the issue of that marriage) and might call in question a resolution of all the judges of England in Queen Elizabeth's time on an important point of matrimonial law (*C.S.P.D.*, 1677–8, p. 291).

[8] e.g. the order in respect of Lord Decies' petition (*C.S.P.D.*, 1677–8, p. 291).

commission of delegacy.[1] However, the law which governed the execution of reviews differed in some important respects from the law by which commissions of delegacy were regulated and these differences must now be considered.

It was a well-established rule that, when a cause was heard by way of review, new evidence could be pleaded only if the commission of review permitted it,[2] such permission being contained in a so-called 'clause of new matter'. The granting of such a clause was within the chancellor's discretion, and the principles which underlay its exercise were set out with some precision by Lord Eldon in *Eagleton* v. *Kingston*.[3] Such applications, he declared, should be regarded with great reserve and the most cogent justifications for them must be provided. The petitions for a commission of review must expressly request such a clause of new matter and must state the grounds upon which such a request may be justified, while counsel who appeared before him must direct their arguments to the point. Such a clause should not be granted for the admission of evidence which could have been admitted below, unless the petitioner could satisfy the court that with reasonable diligence he could not have discovered those facts beforehand or brought them to the attention of the court; it was not enough that he did know them but was misled by bad advice into suppressing them.

One effect of the rule that the granting of a commission of review was a matter for discretion, was that there was no time limit to applications for such reviews.[4] The propriety of granting an application after a long lapse of time was considered by Lord Chancellor King in *Hill* v. *White and White* (*et e contra*),[5] where

[1] 'Now tho' a Commission of Review is not properly an Appeal, yet 'tis a remedial Course of Proceeding, and 'tis not material by what Name an injured Person hath remedy, so as he is relieved' (*arguendo* in *Philips* v. *Bury* (1692), 4 Mod. 106 at 117).

[2] The rule was succinctly expressed in *Popping: on Rhodes's Will* (1725), Sel. Cas. Chan. 48. 'On Appeal may bring new Matter, but in Review must proceed *ex eisdem* Acts.' The rule must have ceased to be the subject of dispute at an early stage of the court's life; the earliest reported case discovered in which it was referred to is the one cited at the beginning of this note, and here it is merely given in the course of the Lord Chancellor's judgment and is not the subject of argument by counsel. It had clearly been accepted in the practice of reviews much earlier; the first example of the express admission of new matter discovered in the course of this investigation is *Staper and Leake* v. *Tite and Pate* (1613), DEL 4/6/66.

[3] (1803), 8 Ves. J. 438 at 464–9.

[4] It was otherwise with commissions of delegacy; see p. 10 *ante*.

[5] (1728), Mos. 29.

the space of six years had elapsed between the passing of sentence and the application for a review.[1]

Counsel opposing the petition drew attention to the fact that limitations were normally placed upon the time within which the decisions of a spiritual court could be appealed (fifteen days being allowed by statute)[2] and to the strictness with which these limits were observed.[3] He also stressed the hardship which would result, in a testamentary cause such as the present one, from upsetting the disposition of the estate by the executor.

The soundness of these arguments was accepted by the Lord Chancellor, although he held that they were susceptible of qualification. As a general rule, he declared, he would not advise the Crown to grant a commission of review after so long a time 'for that would render property unsettled and precarious', but a different conclusion might properly be reached if a clause of new matter were applied for or if there were other special circumstances.

An applicant for a review could not be required to pay the costs of proceedings before the Delegates.[4]

The grant of a commission of review did not, in strict law, operate to stay execution of the sentence given by the Court of Delegates, but suspension of execution usually resulted in fact.[5]

The legality of granting more than one commission of review for any cause remained long in doubt. By its very nature, the problem could not have arisen very often; only the wealthiest and most determined litigant could face the prospect of a fifth or sixth judicial conflict and the chancellor's reluctance to allow even one commission of review was likely to extend with even greater force to a second. In fact, the matter seems never to have been finally decided. In *Halliwell* v. *Jervoise*[6] it seems to have been agreed by the court that one review should be final, but Richardson J. in *Haver* v. *Thorol*[7] suggested that more than one review was possible (he accepted the argument that the king's power to grant repeated reviews was the same as that formerly exercised by the

[1] The petition sought a review of a decision by the English Court of Delegates; there was also a cross-petition in respect of a sentence by the Irish Court of Delegates.

[2] 24 Hen. VIII, c. 12, s.7.

[3] 'I have known an Appeal disallowed that was brought on the sixteenth Day' (*Hill* v. *White and White* (*et e contra*), *supra*, at 30).

[4] *Popping: on Rhodes's Will* (1725), Sel. Cas. Chan. 48; *Eccl. Courts Rep.* (1831–2), p. 21.

[5] *Ibid.*, p. 21.

[6] (1596–7), Moo. K.B. 462 at 463.

[7] (1628–9), Lit. 228 at 232.

Pope). He went on to admit that 'est doubtfull inter Civilians ou Commission de Review poet estre grant apres Commission de Review' but the better opinion, to his mind, was that they could be.[1]

The Crown continued to grant commissions of review from time to time, but the indefinite extension of litigation which reviews made possible was widely held to be undesirable and the Royal Commission on the Ecclesiastical Courts suggested in its special report of 1831 that, if the jurisdiction of the Court of Delegates were transferred to the Privy Council, reviews could be abolished.[2] This advice was followed, and the Act which resulted from the Commission's recommendations provided that the decisions of the Privy Council should not be subject to review.[3]

NOTE ON PRIZE APPEALS

The precise relationship between the Prize Appeal Court and the Court of Delegates is not easy to grasp on the basis of evidence now in print.[4] The problem is one which it is not the function of this book to solve, but some comments may properly be made here, based on information which came to light when the records of the Delegates were examined.

These records make it clear that for a long period the relationship between the two tribunals was an intimate one (and indeed there may have been no formal distinction until 1628 when a permanent bench was set up for the hearing of prize appeals).[5] The Report of the Royal Commission which inquired into certain of these courts, issued in 1824,[6] emphasized the closeness of the

[1] The only example of repeated reviews found in the course of this investigation is *Waldrond* v. *Pollard* (1567–8), Dy. 273. This litigation resulted from the various changes in the religious settlement in the mid sixteenth century, and the considerations affecting it were so peculiar that it does not seem to have been regarded as a precedent; it was not cited in either *Halliwell* v. *Jervoise*, *supra*, or in *Haver* v. *Thorol*, *supra*.

[2] *Eccl. Courts Rep.* (1831–2), p. 7.

[3] 2 & 3 Will. IV, c. 92, s. 3.

[4] e.g. the rather confused account of the matter given in ch. 6 of E. S. Roscoe, *A History of the English Prize Court* (London, 1924).

[5] Rymer, *Foedera*, vol. 19, p. 7, cited in Roscoe, *op. cit.*, p. 87. The Delegates were given a jurisdiction in prize appeal during the Interregnum (Firth and Rait, *Acts and Ordinances*, vol. 2, p. 74) and this may have been a reversion to an older practice.

[6] *Admir. etc. Courts Rep.* (1824).

connection between them, and this is borne out by the records. By this time they apparently employed the same officials and used the same seal[1] and prize appeal documents of various periods are to be found today among the Delegates' records.[2]

[1] *Ibid.*, p. 91. This point is illustrated by several prize appeal records, which are now filed among the Delegates' papers. The inhibition, citation and monition in *The Priscilla* (1795), DEL 2/7, was signed by Lord Arden, who was registrar of both courts. The same mandate in *The Bedford* (1814), DEL 2/7, is described as issuing 'under Seal of our High Court of Delegates', while in *The Maria Theresa* (1758), DEL 8/79, the document still has a complete seal attached and it is identical in form with that used by the Court of Delegates.

[2] e.g. the sentence in the prize cause *Birde and others* v. *Hopkins and others* (1595) is filed in DEL 5/2; see also note 1 above.

CHAPTER V

PROCEDURE—CAUSES *INTER PARTES*—THE PRELIMINARIES

The procedure of the Court of Delegates does not seem to have attracted the attention of text-book writers during any part of its life and in the course of this investigation no treatise has been found devoted solely to this subject. Nor is this surprising, for both Clerke and Oughton touched on appeals in their works on procedure,[1] and the latter in particular has given a tolerably full account of civilian appellate procedure in its broad outline in his celebrated book, the *Ordo Judiciorum*.

It may be argued, then, that there is no room for a further discussion of this subject as it affected the Court of Delegates, or at least for no detailed discussion. Such an argument is not without cogency, but there is nevertheless reason to believe that a full statement of the procedure followed by a typical appellate tribunal within the civilian system will be of some value. Little is known about this subject, or indeed about civilian procedure in general; the only modern account is to be found in Squibb's investigation of the Court of Chivalry and the chapter devoted to procedure,[2] while it provides a clear general picture, is necessarily limited in scope by the fact that so few of the records of that court have survived,[3] as well as by its specialized jurisdiction. The older writers, such as Clerke, Oughton and Law, are somewhat inaccessible and suffer from a certain dryness which is the inevitable result of describing procedure *in vacuo* and without reference to illustrative material drawn from the archives of particular tribunals. The importance of procedural studies has only recently been stressed,[4] and the need for such a study in the present case, if this account of the Court of Delegates is to be complete, is clear

[1] Oughton, who was deputy registrar of the Court from *c.* 1668 to 1720, and had attended upon its proceedings 'ex Ephebis' (*O.J.*, *Praefatio*), seems to have drawn fairly heavily upon this experience in his account.

[2] *H.C.C.*, ch. 13.

[3] On this see *H.C.C.*, App. 1.

[4] A. S. Diamond, 'Some New Thoughts on Legal Procedure', *The Journal of the Society of Public Teachers of Law*, (N.S.), v (1959–60), pp. 192–204.

enough. A final incentive lies in the fact that the records of the court are peculiarly rich in procedural material.

The following account is derived very largely from these records.[1] It relates to procedure in causes *inter partes*, while the procedure in causes of office (which is not substantially different) is touched on briefly in a later section.[2] The subject is considered under the three heads into which it naturally falls—the preliminaries of a cause, proof, sentence and execution.

A convenient starting point is the application for a commission of delegacy by a prospective appellant.[3] Originally, it seems, his proctor[4] would tender to a Master in Chancery (especially appointed for this purpose) a draft of the commission of appeal which was sought, together with the instrument of appeal (if the appeal had been made extra-judicially before a notary public) or a true copy of the relevant acts of the court appealed from (if the appeal was *apud acta*, i.e. made before the *judex a quo* himself).[5] By the time Oughton wrote, however, the procedure had changed.[6] The appellant's proctor would first draw up a petition, addressed to the Lord Chancellor (or the Lord Keeper or the Lords Commissioners of the Great Seal);[7] this contained the names of the parties to the litigation in the lower court, the nature of the appellant's case,

[1] It will be observed that most of the material illustrating procedure has been drawn from the Act Books of the early seventeenth century (as a part of the investigation of the records made for the purpose of this study, the whole of the Acts for the period 1601–21 have been read). It was found best to pay particular attention to these books as they are far more informative than those produced later, while the limited time available made it impossible to examine everything with equal care. However, a certain number of the later Act Books and Assignation Books have also been examined in part (at least one for every fifteen years after 1621) and the more important procedural changes that occurred after that latter date have been noted.

[2] See pp. 175–7 *post*.

[3] The steps previously taken before the *judex a quo* (the formal protest at the sentence from which it is sought to appeal, the application for apostles and the rest) belong rather to procedure before the lower court and are therefore omitted here. A full account may be found in *O.J.*, CCLXXXIX–CCXCVI.

[4] Towards the end of the Court's life, at least, solicitors may occasionally have handled petitions (*Eccl. Courts Rep.* (1831–2), p. 208).

[5] *O.J.*, CCCII/1–3.

[6] His book was apparently written between the years 1712 and 1715 (J. T. Law, *Forms of Ecclesiastical Law* (London, 1831), tit. III/1/6).

[7] These petitions were dealt with by an official in the Chancellor's office. Oughton gives him the rather cumbrous title of 'A Libellis Supplicum Secretarius (in Causis Appellationum Delegandis)' (*O.J.*, CCCII/2/e/ii) and he is later referred to as the Secretary of Commissions of Appeal to the Lord Chancellor (*Eccl. Courts Rep.* (1831–2), p. 207). For an example of a petition, see App. 1.

the decree of the judge below and a formal statement of appeal from that decision to the king in Chancery, together with a request for a commission of delegacy with judges chosen at the chancellor's discretion,[1] and the usual clauses regulating the structure of the commission.[2] Certain other details might also be included when they were necessary,[3] and by the end of the court's life it had become customary to add the names of counsel in the cause in a memorandum at the foot of the petition.[4] If the petition were accepted, the names of the judges chosen to determine the appeal were endorsed on it and the document was signed by the chancellor.

It was then, apparently, returned to the appellant's proctor. He would prepare a draft of the commission of appeal,[5] which was deposited together with the petition with the Clerk of the Hanaper;[6]

[1] The phrase used by Oughton ('Judices...Delegati, Arbitrio suo nominandi' (*O.J.*, CCCII/1/e/i)) must not be taken to imply that the chancellor was always personally responsible for the choice of judges; in fact he seems rarely to have been concerned with it. The matter is further discussed at pp. 185–8 *post*.

[2] There were two of these; the first laid down the minimum number of judges whose presence was necessary at various stages of the hearing and the second (the 'quorum clause') specified the various categories of judges which had to be represented at these stages. It was probably to these clauses that Oughton referred when he spoke of the commission containing 'clausuli...usitati' (*O.J.*, CCCII/2/e/i).

Quorum clauses were often contained in commissions issued by the Crown (Usher, *The Rise and Fall of the High Commission*, p. 45).

[3] Thus an applicant who could satisfy the regulations governing admission *in forma pauperis* might add to his petition a request to be admitted in this form, so that he might be relieved of the charges of applying for a commission; if the necessary conditions were satisfied, the chancellor, in his endorsement of the petition, would direct that the petitioner be so admitted (e.g. the petition of Francis Crumpe (1660), DEL 9/1/134). For the law relating to admissions *in forma pauperis*, see *F.E.L.*, XXIII/XXV and pp. 92–4 *post*.

[4] *Eccl. Courts Rep.* (1831–2), p. 207.

[5] These commissions must be distinguished from commissions of adjuncts; the latter were issued whenever it was found necessary to join new judges with those appointed under the original commission. Oughton gives among the commonest reasons for their issue the absence, death or refusal to act of some of the original judges (*O.J.*, CCCII/2/e/iv). For an example of a commission of adjuncts, see App. III.

[6] Several copies of these petitions have been found among the Delegates' archives; see *Higgins* v. *the Archbishop of Dublin* (1719), DEL 2/40, *The Parochial School-Masters of Scotland* v. *Frazer and others* (1829), DEL 7/8/391, and the petitions of Francis Crumpe and John Dunne (DEL 9/1/134–5). The style of these petitions, which were presented at various dates from 1660 to 1829, conforms to Oughton's description (*O.J* CCCII/2/e, which has been used as the basis of this account) and it seems likely that petitions were of the same general character throughout most of the period when they were in use. Petitions were apparently the same in substance whether the cause were ecclesiastical or secular,

under the authority of the latter the petition would pass the Great Seal.[1]

If the application were not contested, the commission could be issued without any formalities other than those already described.[2] If, however, the adverse party objected, he could put in a counter petition praying to be heard by counsel against the allowing of the appeal.[3] The Lord Chancellor, having heard counsel on both sides, would make an order giving his reasons for granting or refusing the original petitioner's request and giving such other directions as might seem proper.[4] The refusal of a commission might be absolute, or it might allow the applicant to put in an amended petition and the order might direct that pleadings in the appeal, if allowed, be limited to some specified matter.[5]

The Second Act of Appeals laid down that petitions for appeals in ecclesiastical causes should be made to the king in Chancery and this requirement seems always to have been adhered to. The Act, however, did not pretend to regulate the method of applying for appeals in secular causes which had long been dealt with by commissions of delegacy, and applications from the Court of Chivalry continued to go to the king in Council after jurisdiction over such appeals had been absorbed by a single Court of Delegates.[6] It was the usual practice for such petitions to be delegated

as the petition of Henry Howel in an appeal from the Court of Chivalry (printed in *H.C.C.*, App. xxv) follows the same general pattern as those cited above, all of which related to ecclesiastical causes.

[1] It is not certain that the Great Seal was used for every appeal. For a discussion of the problem, see the note at the end of this chapter.

[2] Viner refers to what was apparently a widely held belief that no commission of delegacy could be issued without a warrant under the Royal Sign Manual (*A General Abridgment of Law and Equity*, vol. 17, p. 250). He correctly observes that 25 Hen. VIII, c. 19 contains no such provision and suggests that the rule applies only to ecclesiastical causes which are outside the statute. He refers in this connection to suits 'upon a Commission general of the king' and he states that these causes could not come before the court without a royal warrant. He is probably speaking here of certain causes where the Delegates had original jurisdiction (for this, see pp. 45–6 *ante*).

[3] An alternative procedure was to enter a caveat against the granting of the petition; e.g. *Jameson and Co.* v. *Merry and others* (1773), DEL 2/46.

[4] See the order in *Higgins* v. *the Archbishop of Dublin*, (1719), DEL 2/40. It should be noted that the chancellor was never required to consider the merits of the appellant's cause (*Sir Henry Blount's Case* (1737), 1 Atk. 295 at 298).

[5] e.g. *Higgins* v. *the Archbishop of Dublin*, *supra*.

[6] e.g. the petition of Henry Howel presented in 1688 (*H.C.C.*, App. xxv). Petitions of appeal in marine causes, however, had always been directed to the king in Chancery (Marsden (ed.) *Select Pleas in the Court of Admiralty*, vol. 1,

to the Lord Chancellor,[1] by whom no doubt they were dealt with in the same way as petitions relating to ecclesiastical causes.

Once the commission had passed the Great Seal, the cause could proceed. The first stage in the hearing before the court involved the presentation of the commission to certain of the judges, their acceptance of it and the decreeing of an inhibition and citation against the *judex a quo*[2] and the respondent.[3]

The commission, which was engrossed on parchment, issued in the name of the Crown and was addressed to the judges who were to try the cause. It recited the names of the parties, the judgment given in the court below and the appeal to the king in Chancery or in Council, and concluded with a formal committal of authority to the judges, the details of the quorum clause[4] and the instruction that procedure was to be summary.[5] It was presented by the appellant's proctor (or, occasionally, by the appellant himself),[6] and at least two judges-delegate had to accept it before the cause could proceed further.[7] As the whole of the hearing prior to informations[8] and sentence was normally conducted by the civilians alone,[9] they were usually the only judges to whom a formal presentation was made, but this ceremony was not confined to civilians by any rule of the court and if other members of the commission chose to take part in the earlier stages of a hearing

p. lxxix). There is no evidence available which relates to the practice of the Oxford university courts.

[1] See p. 54 *ante*.

[2] i.e. 'judex a quo est appellatum' (*O.J.*, XIX/1).

[3] As long as the records of the court were kept in Latin, the parties to an appeal were known as *pars appellans* and *pars appellata*. It seems preferable to refer to the latter as 'the respondent' rather than 'the party appellate', especially as the term 'respondent' is invariably used in the records by the end of the eighteenth century.

[4] See p. 83 *ante*.

[5] See p. 100 *post*. For an example of a commission, see App. II.

[6] e.g. *Churche* v. *Clerk* (1602), DEL 4/2/73.

[7] *O.J.*, CCCII/4/f.

[8] For this term, see *F.E.L.*, CXLIX and p. 161 *post*.

[9] The civilian members of a commission were usually referred to as the 'Condelegates' to distinguish them from their colleagues, and the two categories into which judges-delegate usually fell (i.e. civilians and others) are often distinguished in this way; thus a form of proxy might speak of proctors appearing 'before the said Right Honorable Judges Delegates or their Condelegates' (*Watson* v. *Thorpe* (1809), DEL 2/90). On rare occasions, the term is applied to other members of the commission (e.g. to the common law judges, as in *Clarke* v. *Reed* (1733), DEL 6/39/23, where the civilians assigned the cause for Serjeants' Inn 'whensoever the Judges Condelegates shall appoint').

it might be presented to them also.[1] In causes of importance, when proceedings at the opening session were conducted with somewhat greater solemnity than usual, the commission might be read aloud.[2]

Presentation would usually take place at Doctors' Commons, where the civilians had their chambers,[3] but if at least two of the judges were not to be found there, they would have to be sought for elsewhere, and in such a case the task of presenting a commission cannot have been unattended with practical inconvenience for the appellant's proctor and the registrar or his deputy (who had to transcribe the formal act). Thus in *Waltham and others* v. *Reynolds and others*,[4] they had first to attend upon Sir Daniel Dun at his house in Aldersgate Street, then upon Sir Christopher Parkyns, who lived at Cannon Row, Westminster and finally upon Dr Henry Kirkham, whom they found in the house of a relative in the parish of St. Dunstan's in the West. It was even necessary on occasions to go out of London, if the requisite number of judges could not be found within it; the presentation in *Kemis* v. *Rosser*,[5] for example, involved a journey to Rochester to receive the acceptance of Dr Masters.

The number of judges present at the opening session varied from cause to cause, being governed by no other rule than that requirement of the quorum clause which usually specified that at least two must be present for 'ordinary acts'. By the eighteenth century the presence of persons other than civilians at this stage was rare, and it was never common, but in the earlier period they did on occasions attend, and in causes involving parties of importance there might be a glittering array of persons prominent in Church and State; the opening session of *the Earl of Hertford* v. *Lord Mounteagle*.[6] for example, was attended by the Archbishop

[1] It is clear that acceptance by any two commissioners was enough to initiate a cause and these two need not be civilians. Oughton merely states that the commission was to be presented 'aliquibus eorum duobus, vel pluribus' (*O.J.*, CCCII/4/f) and this rule is confirmed by the records. Thus in *Aldebroughe* v. *Brakenburye and Graye* (1605), DEL 4/3/65 the opening session of the cause was held in the chambers of Sir David Williams, J.K.B., and the presentation was made to him and to Sir George Snigge B. and Dr John Hone. The usual orders appropriate to a first hearing were decreed and it was not until the next hearing that a second civilian (Dr Amye) also accepted the commission.

[2] e.g. *the Earl of Hertford* v. *Lord Mounteagle* (1605), DEL 4/3/65, where the opening session took place 'in conclavi...prope Cameram Stellatam', in the presence of the Archbishop of Canterbury, the Bishop of London and other notables.

[3] e.g. *Berbloke* v. *Morley* (1602), DEL 4/2/136.

[4] (1614), DEL 4/6/148.

[5] (1607), DEL 4/4/140.

[6] *supra*.

of Canterbury, the Earl of Northampton, the Bishop of London, Sir John Fortescue, Chancellor of the Duchy of Lancaster, Sir John Harbert, the second secretary of the king, the Chief Baron of the Exchequer, a judge of the King's Bench and the deans of Westminster Abbey and St Paul's Cathedral.

As soon as the commission was presented and accepted, the judges present would proceed to decree an inhibition and citation, the purpose of which was to prevent execution of the judgment given below and to ensure that the respondent entered an appearance.[1] The document was engrossed on parchment and issued in the name of the Crown.[2] It was addressed to all and singular clerks and literate persons whomsoever (except when absolution was included, as such absolution could be given only by clerks).[3] After reciting in full the commission of delegacy, it further recited acceptance by at least two judges and the application to them by the appellant for an inhibition and citation. It finally instructed those judges to inhibit or cause to be inhibited the *judex a quo* or his deputy and his registrar, together with the respondent, so that the appellant should not be hindered in his prosecution of the appeal; it also required that the respondent should be cited to appear on a fixed day and at a fixed place to answer the appellant.[4]

The inhibitions of courts belonging to the Archbishop of Canterbury were required by Canon 96 to be signed by an advocate practising in the court (unless there was no advocate exercent there, in which case the signature of a proctor would suffice).[5] The Court of Delegates, not being a tribunal belonging to the archbishop, was

[1] After this decree had been executed, any attempt to continue proceedings in the lower court, or to take advantage of a judgment given there, was known as an 'attentat', and upon complaint by the party aggrieved to the Delegates it would be revoked. See e.g. *Stone and Stone* v. *Linter* (*in the grievance*) (1617), DEL 4/7/25 & 29, a testamentary cause where letters of administration were granted by way of attentat to Linter by the judge of the Prerogative Court of Canterbury. Upon complaint by the appellants' proctor, the Delegates revoked the grant and ordered Linter to deliver up the letters. It appears from the records that grants of probate or of letters of administration were the attentats most commonly complained of. [2] For an example, see App. VI. [3] *O.J.*, CCCIII/7.

[4] Like other decrees of the Delegates, the inhibition and citation was not allowed to exceed the authority given to the judges by the commission under which they acted. In *Dawkes* v. *Francklyn* (1646), DEL 4/18/110 & 114, the respondent's proctor successfully petitioned for the relaxation of a 'clausula quaedam inconsueta' which had been included in the inhibition and citation served upon his party; the Delegates revoked the offending clause 'quatenus non comprehenditur in auctoritate Comissionis Regie eis et eorum condelegatis concessa'. [5] *O.J.*, CCCI/1/a/ii.

not bound by this rule and most of the earlier examples of this decree which have been discovered among the records are unsigned;[1] by the latter part of the eighteenth century, however, it had become the usual practice for the appellant's advocate to sign inhibitions.[2]

The inhibition and citation, when it had passed the seal of the court, would be served upon the persons against whom it was directed;[3] they might be required to specify an address for service, if there was any uncertainty about the matter.[4]

Service in London was usually effected by an officer of the court, permanently employed for that and other purposes, but any of the 'clerks and literate persons whomseover' to whom it was directed might act,[5] and examples have been found where the decree was served by a schoolmaster,[6] a yeoman[7] and a clerk.[8] When service had to be effected in provincial dioceses, the process server of the local consistory court would sometimes act.[9]

The decree would be served upon the persons named in it, and, if it were directed against more than one respondent, each would be served separately.[10] Service was effected by showing the sealed decree to the person concerned[11] and leaving with him a note of

[1] None of them is earlier than 1700.

[2] Advocates signed documents at the bottom *left*-hand side (*H.C.C.*, p. 193), although examples may sometimes be found where they signed on the right; e.g. the libel in *Hayton and others* v. *Braine and Hurst* (1735), DEL 2/38, signed by Henchman, Strahan and Audley. Proctors usually signed at the bottom *right*-hand side.

[3] The method of serving mandates of the court is discussed in some detail at this point, as the inhibition and citation was usually the first mandate decreed by the judges-delegate; the same procedure was employed, *mutatis mutandis*, for the service of all other decrees, and some of the illustrations which follow are drawn from these decrees.

[4] e.g. *Bainton* v. *Mountague* (1608), DEL 4/4/219, where the appellant's proctor declared that the respondent 'non habere aliquem certum domicilii locum ubi possit citari' and the court required that a place for service should be designated within three days. The problem was especially acute if the respondent were abroad. In *Gobine* v. *Le Mayre* (1618), DEL 4/7/180 & 202, it was complained that Le Mayre resided 'in partibus ultramarinis' and his proctor then nominated a public building in Shrewsbury ('pretorium in villa Salopie') as an address for service.

[5] 'Omnis Literatus possit citare et inhibere' (*O.J.*, CCCIII/8).

[6] e.g. *Ricraft* v. *Cox* (1757), DEL 2/68.

[7] e.g. *Robertson* v. *Hutchinson and Hutchinson* (1775), DEL 2/68.

[8] e.g. *Revell* v. *Turton and Groome* (1827), DEL 2/71.

[9] e.g. *Hopper* v. *Davis and others* (1753), DEL 2/108/1.

[10] e.g. *Plowden* v. *Paxton and others* (1740), DEL 2/65, where there were nine respondents.

[11] The servant or wife of such a person would apparently suffice, if he were not available; see the certificate of service in *Campbell* v. *Moore and others* (1727), DEL 2/19.

the contents (which before 1733, when the decree itself would be in Latin, was known as the 'English Note').

On the back of the mandate would be a certificate, signed by the mandatary, giving details of the precise day and place at which service was effected,[1] and it seems that service was not valid unless these details were included.[2] The purpose of the rule was to ensure that, if service were disputed, the person against whom the decree was directed should have a chance to prove that he was elsewhere at the time when service was alleged.[3] The point arose in a characteristic form in *Seymor* v. *Seymor*,[4] where the argument turned on the service of a mandate for payment of alimony. The appellant claimed that on the day when service was alleged to have taken place (apparently in London) he was at his house at Frampton Cotterell in Gloucestershire; the attack on the certificate failed, however, as a witness was produced who swore that he had seen Seymor on that day in a house in Foster Lane in London.[5]

The certificate of service was often re-inforced by a further document, an affidavit of service which was attached to the inhibition and citation,[6] and which declared that the mandatary had been sworn to the truth of the certificate of service before some

[1] This was usually in English, but occasionally in Latin (e.g. the certificate (on a monition for process) in *Bleasby* v. *Lupton and Alcock* (1712), DEL 2/11). A brief note of these details might also be written on the back of the (papered) seal; e.g. *Blew* v. *Barnard* (1743), DEL 2/11.

[2] e.g. *Owen* v. *Owen* (1614), DEL 4/6/200, where the point was taken that service was bad because the certificate did not state in what parish or in what place the respondent was cited.

[3] *F.E.L.*, XLII/4/2/i. The rule also enabled such a person to prove that, although the mandate had been duly executed, he had not been given sufficient time to act in accordance with its directions, a matter which often arose in connection with the transmission of process from the lower court; e.g. *Baxter* v. *Egmore* (1613), DEL 4/6/126, where the *judex a quo* was accused of contumacy in failing to transmit the process on time, but the respondent's proctor was able to point out that, according to the certificate of service, the mandate had been executed only one week before.

[4] (1614), DEL 4/6/252.

[5] The certificate might be attacked by the evidence of witnesses (as here) or by an affidavit of the party objecting to it; e.g. *Pomeroye* v. *Close* (1608), DEL 4/4/161, where Pomeroye swore 'That he was not monished or cited in the parishe of Ilsington in the Countye of Devon or in any other place by John Jewell supposed mandatary...or on any other daye before or since'.

[6] Occasionally the affidavit was instead entered in the Act Book; e.g. *James* v. *Farthing* (1670), DEL 4/21/352, where it was signed by the process server and two judges.

competent person.[1] These affidavits were sometimes sealed with an official seal.[2]

Process serving was a notoriously dangerous calling,[3] and the mandataries of the Court of Delegates had their full share of risk. This might involve assault or the threat of it, as in *Alven* v. *Babb and Richards*,[4] where Anthony Henborough attempted to serve an inhibition and citation of the court upon Babb, the principal respondent. No sooner had he approached Babb than the latter threatened to assault him, snatched the document from his hands, tore off the seal and threw it away. When Henborough expostulated with him, reminding him that the decree was issued under the authority of the Crown and of a royal court, Babb spoke contemptuously of the process server and the king and added 'verba scandalosa & contemptuosa' of the ecclesiastical courts in general and of the Court of Delegates and its officials in particular. Babb's contempt was later dealt with in the usual way, by the initiation against him of a cause of office.

If he were lucky, however, the mandatary might escape with nothing but hard words, as was the case in *Holte* v. *Savage* (*in the principal cause*),[5] where the appellant's wife, after unsuccessfully attempting to tear up a mandate which had been served upon him, swept a copy (which the process server had left) into the gutter with her broom and then 'did call the sayd mandatary raskall and knave and badd him gett him goenge and sayd if he would not be goene she would sett him further or the like in effect'.

The method of service described above was applicable when the inhibition and citation was private, i.e. susceptible of execution upon the respondent personally. If for some reason personal service proved impossible, the appellant might apply to the court for permission to cite the respondent *viis et modis*, i.e., with a public

[1] Usually two judges-delegate if the certificate was sworn in London, or a Master Extraordinary in Chancery if it was sworn elsewhere. Other persons might sometimes act; e.g. *Hopper* v. *Davis and others* (1753), DEL 2/108/1, where an affidavit relating to service of a monition for process was sworn before a Commissioner for the Court of Common Pleas.

[2] e.g. *Huleat* v. *Higgins* (1735), DEL 2/37; the affidavit was sworn before the vicar-general of the diocese of Dublin and the seal of the consistory court of that diocese was affixed.

[3] For examples, see *H.C.C.*, p. 197; G W. Sanders, *Orders of the High Court of Chancery* (London, 1845), vol. 1, p. xi.

[4] (1614), DEL 4/6/160.

[5] (1614), DEL 4/6/275.

citation.[1] If the court made the necessary decree, service would be effected by fixing the mandate, complete with its seal, to the outer door of the dwelling house occupied by the person to be served,[2] or of the dwelling house where he was thought to have last lodged. It might also be affixed to the outer door of the parish church during the time of divine worship.[3] If the party to be served were in prison, the mandate could be attached to the outer door of the prison and a copy left there.[4]

For service upon foreign merchants, sailors and the like the Royal Exchange was used.[5] The method of service here involved the affixing of the original decree to one of the pillars of the Royal Exchange 'Dureing the time of the usual Resort of Merchants there'[6] and leaving it for several hours; it would then be taken down and replaced by a copy.[7]

A particular form of public citation was that addressed to all persons in general who might be presumed to have an interest in the cause. They were especially used in testamentary matters (such as the granting of letters of administration)[8] and were served in the same way as an ordinary citation *viis et modis*. A typical example of this form of citation was decreed in *Egerton* v. *Egerton*;[9] it was addressed to 'all persons whomsoever in generall having or pretending to have any right, title or interest in the letters of administration, or last will and testament or goods chattells and debts of Sir Rowland Egerton deceased', and was served by affixing the original citation to the market cross at Brackly in

[1] For the distinction between public and private citations, see *F.E.L.*, XXXI/4.

[2] e.g. *Holte v. Savage* (*in the principal cause*) (1614), DEL 4/6/275. The mandate had to be attached to the outer surface of the door, for to enter the house without the owner's consent would amount to trespass; see *F.E.L.*, XLI/4/1 and authorities there cited. A window shutter would serve as well as a door; e.g. *Soux* v. *Soux* (1702), DEL 2/81.

[3] e.g. *Lady Osborn* v. *Williams* (1718), DEL 2/59.

[4] e.g. *Reddaway* v. *Taylor* (1712), DEL 2/72, where a decree for answers was served upon Taylor in the Fleet Prison.

[5] e.g. *Dumble* v. *Towns* (1604), DEL 4/2/303.

[6] *Plowden* v. *Paxton and others* (1740), DEL 2/65.

[7] There were some causes in which this procedure could cause the parties embarrassment. In *Burnett* v. *Webb and others* (1652), DEL 6/3/15, a matrimonial cause, the court found it necessary to decree that no further citations in the cause be served in this way 'to prevent any scandall that may be imposed on ye persons litigant' from so public a display of the mandates.

[8] *F.E.L.*, XXXVII/1/4/vii.

[9] (1651), DEL 6/4/43–4.

market time and leaving a copy after the original had been displayed for a brief period.[1]

The presentation of the commission of delegacy and the decreeing of the inhibition and citation was the most important (and often the only) business done at the opening session. There were, however, other matters which might receive attention then and, in particular, claims to proceed *in forma pauperis* were usually raised at this stage.[2] The party seeking to be admitted in this form (and either appellant or respondent might apply)[3] was required to swear that he was not worth five pounds;[4] his personal appearance was apparently necessary for this purpose.[5] When the oath had been administered, the party might then be admitted.[6] If the party applying was a married woman, her husband would be required to take the oath,[7] and it was a valid objection to the admission of a female party that, although she was married at the time of admission, she alone, and not her husband, had been sworn.[8] If a party who was below age could satisfy the requirements of the oath, his *curator ad litem* might be admitted to act on his behalf *in forma pauperis*, once he had sworn an affidavit as to the minor's means.[9]

[1] These were the regular methods of citation *viis et modis* which are referred to in the records of the court. No trace has been found there of the more picturesque modes of citation to which Law refers; i.e. citation *per tubam* (by sounding a trumpet), *per campanam* (by tolling a bell) and *per vexilli erectionem* (by erecting a banner) (*F.E.L.* XLI/4/2).

[2] But not necessarily then. See e.g. *Kendel and Nelham* v. *Shorditche* (1614), DEL 4/6/201, where one of the parties applied at the ninth hearing, on the ground that he had then been brought to a state of poverty by reason of the numerous law suits he had been compelled to pursue.

[3] e.g. *Pope* v. *Fry* (1613), DEL 4/6/93 (appellant); *Henrick* v. *Derrick* (1613), DEL 4/6/86 (respondent); *F.E.L.*, XXIII/1.

[4] In the early seventeenth century, at least, appeals from certain ecclesiastical courts in London were affected by the rule mentioned by Oughton that persons seeking admission *in forma pauperis* in these courts must not be worth more than forty shillings (*O.J.*, VIII/7); e.g. *Fleetwood* v. *Harrison* (1613), DEL 4/6/79, where both the parties belonged to the diocese of London and the appellant swore herself to be worth not more than that sum. By the time that Oughton wrote, however, the sum universally accepted was five pounds.

[5] Oughton thought it probable that personal appearance was always necessary for this purpose (*O.J.*, VIII/2/d); no example has been found in the records of the Delegates in which the oath of a pauper was taken by his proctor.

[6] Admission was entirely at the court's discretion and it might be refused even though the party was prepared to take the oath; e.g. *Algar and Algar* v. *Coote* (1634), DEL 4/14/245.

[7] e.g. *Cooke* v. *Bowcher* (1617), DEL 4/7/135.

[8] e.g. *Meridithe* v. *Baron* (1605), DEL 4/3/64.

[9] e.g. *Burrowes* v. *Blenerhasset* (1647), DEL 4/19/16 & 19.

Admission might be opposed by the adverse party on the ground that the petitioner was worth more than five pounds, and the court might then require proof of his means. He might be admitted conditionally 'ad effectum probacionis paupertatis sue tantum' and the matter would be gone into in the usual way by allegation, personal answers and the evidence of witnesses and documents.[1] A petitioner might anticipate opposition and support his application by whatever means he thought would be acceptable,[2] while the judges themselves, if they entertained any doubts as to the bona fides of an applicant, might question him closely in open court.[3] The reasons for a petitioner's poverty as well as its extent might also be adverted to in the application.[4]

Once a petitioner had been admitted *in forma pauperis*, the court would assign advocates and proctors to act on his behalf.[5] They were required to act 'without any hope of fee or reward'.[6]

After admission, a pauper was usually relieved of future charges arising from the conduct of the cause.[7] However, the court retained the right to revoke his admission if due cause were

[1] e.g. *Stevenson* v. *Watson* (1606), DEL 4/3/244 *et seq.*

[2] e.g. *Shrimpton* v. *Randall* (*Goodine intervening*) (1606), DEL 4/3/192; Randall produced a certificate attesting his poverty signed by several of his neighbours. In *Ward* v. *Sherman* (1621), DEL 4/8/248 the application of the respondent was supported by the affidavit of one John Rowland who swore that the respondent's husband was not worth the sum of five pounds 'nor indeede the some of five groats'.

[3] e.g. *Davyes* v. *Grace* (*second cause*) (1607), DEL 4/4/44. Davyes, a clerk in Holy Orders, applied for admission *in forma pauperis*, but Grace objected on the ground that Davyes had a benefice worth at least thirty pounds per annum. The court then questioned Davyes as to the value of his benefice, the number of his cures and the precise extent of his debts.

[4] e.g. *Kennedy* v. *Sparrow* (1722), DEL 2/48. Mary Sparrow, having taken the usual oath, went on to declare that she was 'reduced to this Low Condition by ye said Thomas Kennedy who has much of her money in his hands, and by ye great expenses she has been at for some years in ye Courts of Leighlin, Dublin and Doctors' Commons in constraining the said Kennedy to do her right'.

[5] e.g. *Wandeford* v. *Wandeford* (1604), DEL 4/2/310. The appellant was allowed three advocates and three proctors. This was the usual number assigned in such causes, but the court at its discretion might always make a different allotment; e.g. *Wetherall* v. *Hayton* (1617), DEL 4/7/22, where the respondent was allowed two advocates and six proctors.

[6] *F.E.L.*, XIII/1.

[7] But not of those already incurred (*F.E.L.*, XXIII/5). A letter written by Sir Leoline Jenkins to Samuel Pepys in 1677 suggests that the registrar of the Court of Admiralty found it necessary to waive his right to those fees which were payable to him by paupers (Wynne, *Life of Sir Leoline Jenkins*, vol. 2, pp. 709–10); the same may well have been true of the other civilian courts.

shown,[1] and the court might also insist that a party, even when allowed to sue as a pauper, should undertake to pay costs if he were able to later.[2] Moreover, a pauper might renounce this status.[3]

Admission as a pauper (when this was necessary) usually completed the business to be done at the opening session, and the Delegates would then adjourn the cause to the next court day.[4] On this day, the next main stage in the procedure of the Court of Delegates would occur: the appearance of the respondent. His proctor would appear on his behalf, and exhibit his proxy; after a formal protest against the jurisdiction of the court,[5] he would demand that a libel should be tendered by the appellant or the cause remitted to the judge from whom it came and the respondent dismissed with costs. The court would then assign a day *ad libellandum*.[6]

The only other business generally dealt with at this (second)

[1] e.g. *Carter* v. *Pope and Spencer* (*Hussey intervening*) (1619), DEL 4/8/63; the court revoked Carter's admission after the respondents had tendered a petition, previously presented to the Lord Chancellor and endorsed by him, protesting against it. This revocation was known as 'dispaupering'; e.g. *Turner* v. *Smith* (1712), DEL 6/33/77.

[2] e.g. *Newport* v. *Huggenson and others* (1605), DEL 4/3/45; two of the respondents were admitted *in forma pauperis* upon condition that they should pay costs 'cum ad pingiorem [*sic*] fortunam pervenerint'.

[3] e.g. *Stedman* v. *Edwards* (*in the grievance*) (1614), DEL 4/6/219. If a party renouncing were engaged in more than one cause, a separate renunciation was required for each; e.g. *Stedman* v. *Edwards* (*in the principal cause*) (1614), DEL 4/6/219.

[4] The Court of Delegates, like other civilian courts, followed a year divided into four terms, the court days within each term being fixed with reference to certain saints' days. The Delegates sat on the third day after the appropriate festival (following the Court of Arches and the Prerogative Court, which sat on the first and second days respectively); they followed the usual civilian practice by having four court days in each term, to which was usually added one extra day (known as the *dies extraordinarius* or bye day) towards the end of the Hilary, Trinity and Michaelmas terms, the precise date being fixed by the judges themselves in the course of the term. For the civilian court days, see *O.J.*, II, which should be read in conjunction with *F.E.L.* (Apps. 4 to 8).

[5] These formal protests by a proctor against every act of the adverse party or of the court are a characteristic feature of civilian procedure. Their general significance is nowhere explained in the procedural treatises, but they seem to be based upon the principle that a party was taken to accept and to be bound by every one of those acts whose validity he did not expressly contest. This explanation is suggested both by a study of the records of the Delegates and by Law's account of particular protests; e.g. F.E.L. cv/5/5 (if a party did not protest against witnesses of the adverse side when they were produced, he would be taken to approve of their persons (and therefore, presumably, could not later attack them on the ground of character)).

[6] e.g. *Baker* v. *Holland* (1603), DEL 4/2/222.

hearing of the cause was the giving of security.[1] The older authorities agreed that both sides ought to give security,[2] but the practice of the civilian courts in this country appears to have differed. In the Court of Chivalry, security was always required from both parties,[3] but in the Court of Delegates, maritime appeals were the only sort of cause in which security seems always to have been demanded.[4] The sureties of the appellant undertook that their principal would prosecute the suit, abide by the judgment of the court and pay costs if awarded against him, while the respondent's sureties gave a similar guarantee.[5] The sureties appeared in open court and gave their undertakings verbally;[6] these were then usually embodied in bonds.[7] At the time of their appearance, the party on whose behalf they bound themselves might verbally indemnify them,[8] but such indemnifications were unusual.

Two sureties were usually required from each party,[9] but there might be more than two and a greater number would tend to be offered if the sum were large.[10] The same sureties might be tendered for a party in more than one action,[11] and this rule held even when

[1] Roman law knew several sorts of surety; the sponsor, the fidepromissor and the fideiussor (Buckland, *A Text Book of Roman Law*, p. 445). Only the last is to be found in the practice of the Court of Delegates.

[2] *F.E.L.*, LXXXI/3 and the authorities there cited.

[3] *H.C.C.*, p. 198.

[4] The parties, however, might dispense with it by agreement; e.g. *Matthewson* v. *Adrianson* (1603), DEL 4/2/225.

[5] Sureties might also be required in some causes appealed from the ecclesiastical courts, in particular from the administrators of deceaseds' estates (e.g. *Birde* v. *Hassall* (1603), DEL 4/2/200) and from the persons into whose hands the profits of a living were to be paid if the benefice were sequestrated (e.g. *Jones* v. *Pusy and Shury* (1707), DEL 2/46). If parties before the Delegates agreed to go to arbitration, they might be required to furnish sureties 'de stando et acquiescendo laudo arbitrio et finali determinacioni dictorum venerabilium virorum [arbitrorum]' (*Aldebroughe* v. *Brakenburye and Graye* (1605), DEL 4/3/80), while persons appointed by the court as guardians over minors might have to give security 'de bene & honeste educando' the minors in question (*Stone and Stone* v. *Linter* (*Walwyn and Walwyn intervening*) (1618), DEL 4/7/160).

[6] e.g. *Dumble* v. *Townes* (1604), DEL 4/2/291.

[7] Examples have also been found of what may have been an alternative procedure; the conditions upon which the sureties bound themselves were set out *in extenso* in the Assignation Book and were signed by them (e.g. *Wilmer* v. *Pix* (1680), DEL 6/20/27).

[8] e.g. *Bowlinge* v. *Longe* (1618), DEL 4/7/154.

[9] e.g. *Dumble* v. *Townes* (1604), DEL 4/2/291.

[10] e.g. *De Geere and De Geere* v. *Gribble and Greenfield and Co.* (1658), DEL 6/8/24, where four sureties were required to bind themselves in the sum of £2000.

[11] e.g. *Marriott and partners* v. *Freeman*, *Marriott* v. *Man*, *Marriott* v. *Jenny* (1634), DEL 4/14/189; the appellant produced the same two sureties in all three actions.

the sums involved were considerable,[1] provided that the sureties themselves were of sufficient substance.

Sureties were not confined to a particular class (as commissioners *ad partes* largely were) and all that seems to have been required of them was that they should be good security for the sum in question and live within the jurisdiction. Among those who are to be found in the Delegates' records were 'generosi',[2] seamen,[3] innkeepers[4] and tradesmen of all sorts.[5] Foreign merchants were acceptable,[6] but it seems that they had to be domiciled within the jurisdiction.[7]

The sureties tendered in connection with the administration of deceased's estates, who were often required to bind themselves in considerable sums, tended to be men of greater substance than those involved in marine causes; they were usually landowners, considerable merchants and the like. A typical example occurs in *Fitton* v. *Broughton* (*in the principal cause*),[8] where the respondent's proctor petitioned that administration of the estate in dispute should be entrusted to his party *pendente lite*, and he offered as sureties Sir William Hamner, Sir Richard Grovener (both landowners) and Sir Thomas Marberry of London. The court chose Grovener, who was required to bind himself, together with Broughton, in the sum of £2000. Similarly, in *Layer*. v *Rugge* (*in the principal cause*),[9] a testamentary cause where Rugge had been granted administration of an estate *pendente lite* by the *judex a quo* and the sureties he had then provided were later attacked by the appellant, Rugge insisted that they were adequate, as one was a knight and a good security for a greater sum than that at issue, while the other was a gentleman with a landed estate of £100 per annum. The court, however, was not impressed and threatened to revoke probate unless more substantial sureties were provided.

[1] e.g. *Russell and others* v. *Lenthall and partners*; *Russell and others* v. *Marston and partners* (1642), DEL 4/18/32; the same two sureties for the appellants were accepted in the sums of £4100 in the first action and £640 in the second.

[2] e.g. *Nurse* v. *Nurse* (1605), DEL 4/3/3.

[3] e.g. *Reekes* v. *Mempas* (1605), DEL 4/3/2.

[4] *Ibid.*

[5] e.g. *Rickman* v. *Fitche* (1605), DEL 4/3/18 (haberdasher); *Betts* v. *Goodwin* (1643), DEL 4/18/35 (tailor and 'Sattin Cutter'); *Reekes* v. *Mempas*, *supra*, at f. 9 (ironmonger).

[6] e.g. *Cowper* v. *Halley and others* (1605), DEL 4/3/4.

[7] In all the examples noted in the Act Books, such merchants were always stated to be domiciled within an English parish. In *Von Thienen* v. *Von Thienen* (1731), DEL 2/89, the court insisted that the sureties offered should reside in England.

[8] (1608), DEL 4/4/192.

[9] (1617), DEL 4/7/50 & 58.

The amount in which the sureties bound themselves was not normally disputed in open court, and no doubt proceedings at an earlier stage of the cause would often enable the parties to decide upon a sum acceptable to both sides. This was not always so, however, and sometimes the amount would be left to the court to fix, either at its entire discretion[1] or by way of compromise between the conflicting claims of the litigants.[2] The court might also insist that the sum originally agreed on should be altered if this seemed reasonable.[3] The sums in which sureties were bound were not usually large in Admiralty causes but in testamentary appeals they could be considerable.[4]

It was clearly essential that sureties should be good security for the sum in which they were bound, and neither the adverse party nor the court could be expected to accept them without some investigation into their standing. It seems that the enquiry was usually made by the court itself and the task was often delegated to the process-server.[5] Sometimes the court thought it proper that the adverse party should be given a chance to make an investigation himself,[6] while it was open to any interested third party who was dissatisfied with the security offered to make his own enquiries.[7]

[1] e.g. *Brooke* v. *Luys* (1607), DEL 4/4/130; the appellant's proctor offered to provide sureties 'obligandos in competentem sumam per dominos assignandam'.

[2] e.g. *Wright* v. *Marston and Chapman* (1643), DEL 4/18/42. The appellants offered sureties in the sum of £1050, the respondents insisted that the sum should be £2000 and the Court then fixed it at £1500.

[3] e.g. *Juris* v. *Chelston* (1651), DEL 6/4/4. The court directed that the amount in which sureties were bound should be increased if an appraisement of certain of the goods at issue showed them to be more valuable than had been thought.

[4] e.g. *Von Thienen* v. *Von Thienen* (1731), DEL 2/89 (£50,000); *Hutcheson* v. *Naylor* (1730), DEL 2/108/1. (£40,000).

[5] e.g. *Lutwidge* v. *James and others* (1739), DEL 2/51. A report as to the means of the sureties tendered by both sides was drawn up and signed by Peter Powell, who was then the Delegates' mandatary. Such a report might also be made to the judges in open court (*Andrewes and Draper* v. *Pile* (1656), DEL 6/6/118). What may have been an alternative procedure is to be found in *De Farier* v. *Da Silva* (1790), DEL 2/108/1, where the sureties were required to swear as to the adequacy of their means.

[6] e.g. *Barners* v. *Tailboies* (1612), DEL 4/5/227; the Delegates insisted that the appellant should nominate sureties before a certain time 'ut pars [adversa] eorum nomina habere possit ad effectum inquirendi ad eorum sufficienciam'.

[7] e.g. *Chelston* v. *The Great Christopher* (1654), DEL 2/117, where a protest was entered against certain sureties by the commissary of the Queen of Sweden (apparently the cause was one in which Swedish subjects were involved). His investigations had left him with grave doubts as to their standing, as two of them were already engaged for considerable sums and were 'persons of noe certaine or visible estates, but wholly depend upon trade and casualty', while the third had been a prisoner of the Upper Bench for several years.

As a result of such investigations, the adverse party might find occasion to object to the sureties tendered by the other side, financial insufficiency being naturally the most frequent ground of complaint; if the court held that the complaint was well-founded, it would order the tender of more substantial security.[1] The basis of the objection to a surety was either general (as, for example, that he was '[nec] sufficiens nec idoneus')[2] or particular (a frequent objection to a surety was that he was not taxed in the subsidy book,[3] or that the sum offered was insufficient).[4] Objections of the latter sort generally related to the financial standing of the sureties, but they might touch upon other matters also.[5] If the insufficiency of sureties was established at a later stage of proceedings, the party on whose behalf they had bound themselves might be required to furnish additional sureties.[6]

Attacks upon a surety might be rebutted by such evidence as the party on whose behalf they had bound themselves could produce as to their sufficiency. In *Matthewson* v. *Admanson*,[7] for example, when the respondent's proctor objected to one of the sureties put forward by the appellant, the latter was able to reply that the

[1] e.g. *Bannister and partners* v. *Turner and partners* (1679), DEL 6/19/71. Two sureties, a sailor and an ironmonger, appeared for the appellants and bound themselves on the usual terms in the sum of £150. Five days later, one Charles Martin appeared in court and declared that he had enquired after the 'worth and credite' of these two, and had been told by their neighbours 'that neither of them would be trusted for five pounds'. The court then required the appellants to provide better sureties.

[2] e.g. *Matthewson* v. *Admanson* (1605), DEL 4/3/2.

[3] In the seventeenth century, the subsidy seems to have been much relied on as an indication of financial standing. A typical example of the use the court made of it is *Waltham and Geare* v. *Mingart* (1604), DEL 4/2/323, where one proposed surety for the appellants, when questioned by the court, admitted that 'he is not taxed in the subsidie book'. When the appellants' other surety made a similar admission the court accepted them, but only on the condition that their principals should provide a further surety who was so taxed.

[4] e.g. *Reekes* v. *Mempas* (1605), DEL 4/3/2; the appellant offered two sureties in the sum of £200, while the respondent petitioned that the sum should be at least £350.

[5] e.g. *Dumble* v. *Townes* (1604), DEL 4/2/303; the point was taken that the sureties did not in fact live at the places where they had been said to live.

[6] e.g. *Manny* v. *Grolier* (1633), DEL 4/14/95. Manny provided two sureties at an early hearing of the cause who were accepted by the court; it was later discovered that one of them was in the Fleet prison while the other had left London. Manny was then required to produce 'uberiores fideiussores'. The production of such additional sureties was known as 'corroboration' of the original security (*Bannister and partners* v. *Turner and partners*, *supra*, at f. 72.

[7] *supra*.

surety in question owned fee simple lands and tenements to an annual value of £186 or more and that he had been assessed in the last Royal subsidy at £5 and had paid the assessment. It was also in favour of a surety that he had been admitted below.[1]

Once sureties had been accepted by the court, they could be joined in any order for costs decreed against their party,[2] and their property could be seized.[3] Sureties might also be attached for non-payment of costs.[4]

It is clear that the giving of sureties was regulated by the court's discretion. The Delegates could, as has been shown, insist on the production of additional sureties or of sureties who were *uberiores* than those already produced, and they might also, on rare occasions, dispense with sureties altogether in a cause where they would otherwise have been necessary. This discretion might in particular be exercised where one party was so circumstanced that he could not reasonably be expected to provide them. The situation arose in *Baker* v. *Foster*,[5] where the appellant produced one surety and later, at the court's insistence, another. When his proctor insisted on sureties from the respondent, Foster himself appeared in court and pleaded that he was 'extraneum et a domicilio suo longe remotum atque in hiis partibus penitus ignotum ita quod non possit fideiussores introducere'. This plea was apparently regarded as reasonable, for the case continued without any surety being tendered by Foster.[6]

Even in causes where the court insisted on sureties, its discretion might extend to a reasonable latitude in the time allowed to find them if there was some valid difficulty. Such a difficulty was most likely to arise if the sum involved were a large one and the problem occurred in a characteristic form in *Shirley* v. *Bassilier and others*,[7] where the appellant was required to give sureties in

[1] e.g. *Baker* v. *Foster* (1606), DEL 4/3/213.

[2] e.g. *Shirley* v. *Bassilier and others* (1608), DEL 4/4/226 (costs of suit); *Lord Baltimore* v. *Jones* (1634), DEL 4/14/247 (costs of transmission of process).

[3] e.g. *Hooper* v. *Johns* (1645), DEL 4/18/95, where the successful respondent proceeded against the sureties of the appellant and possessed himself of an eighth share which they owned in a ship.

[4] e.g. *Carnabie* v. *Nottingham* (1611), DEL 4/5/148. One of Carnabie's sureties was attached and later released when the costs were paid.

[5] *supra*, at f. 212.

[6] Sureties might also be remitted for other valid reasons: e.g. *Trigg and Trigg* v. *Jones and Vassall* (1604), DEL 4/2/332; the appellants were not required to provide sureties as they were 'paupertati [*sic*] gravati ita quod non possint fideijubere'.

[7] *supra*, at ff. 92 *et seq.*

£1000.[1] On the day assigned for the furnishing of sureties by Shirley, his proctor was constrained to admit that he had been unable 'racione magnitudinis sume' to find a sufficient number of suitable persons in or around London; he had therefore been compelled to have recourse to his tenants on his estates in Sussex and to friends living there, and he expected them to arrive in London shortly. At his request, the court adjourned the cause to the next term, so that the sureties might have ample time to reach town.

At the next hearing, the most important business was the tender by the appellant of his libel; this would be admitted by the Delegates who would assign a term to prove it,[2] and at the same time decree that the cause should proceed *summarie et de plano*.[3]

The libel in the Court of Delegates differed from libels in a court of first instance in that the information it contained was largely formal. The detailed pleading which was the basis of the appellant's claim (whether as plaintiff or defendant below) would be included in the process which was shortly to come before the judges-delegate,[4] and nothing would have been gained by repeating it, while any new pleading which the appellant wished to rely on could be put forward in a separate allegation.[5] As a result, the

[1] *supra*, at f. 173.

[2] e.g. *Baggott and Baggott* v. *Broughton* (1602), DEL 4/2/158.

[3] In the civil law, procedure upon appeal was usually the same as that which had been followed in the court below; thus causes which were summary at first instance were heard summarily upon appeal and the like rule was followed for plenary causes (for the distinction between plenary and summary causes, see *F.E.L.*, XXI). But all causes before the Court of delegates were heard summarily, even if they had been plenary at first instance, a practice which was held to result from a clause always inserted in commissions of delegacy which required that the judges-delegate should proceed in a summary manner (*O.J.*, CCCXII/8).

[4] For the process, see pp. 216–17 *post*.

[5] The precise relationship between the libel and any allegation which the appellant might choose to tender is difficult to establish on the basis of evidence now available, for the earlier seventeenth century at least (the problem is made particularly acute by the fact that no cause papers survive from this period). It is clear from the Act Books, however, that in that period the libel could be very much longer than the usual seven paragraphs of the eighteenth-century libel, and it is likely that in such cases it contained fresh pleading as well as formal matter.

The description of the libel which follows has had, of necessity, to be taken from eighteenth century examples. The precise form of those libels in the earlier period which contained pleadings cannot now be established with certainty, but where no fresh pleading was tendered by the appellant, it seems not unlikely that the form was substantially the same as that of the later libels.

libel was usually confined to formal details concerning the appeal, of which the most important was the *praesertim* which set out the substance of the decision appealed from.

The libel was in writing[1] and on paper;[2] it was signed by the appellant's advocate.[3] One advocate might sign for another,[4] and a party unrepresented by counsel might sign for himself.[5] It was addressed to the judges-delegate and began by reciting their styles and titles and the names of the parties. The rest of the document recited briefly proceedings in the court below and the judgment from which an appeal was made, the application to the king in Chancery for a commission of appeal, the issue of that commission and its acceptance by at least two judges and the fact that the respondent was subject to the jurisdiction of the Delegates.[6] There was a formal closing paragraph.[7]

By the first decade of the eighteenth century, the drafting of the libel conformed to a rigid precedent and the matter it contained was normally fitted into seven paragraphs. However, slight variations from this pattern occur from time to time without involving

[1] As the procedure in the Court of Delegates was always summary (see p. 100 *ante*), libels might well have been given orally and entered in the court minutes, as the rules for summary procedure permitted (*F.E.L.*, LXXIV/1/2). The practice of the Delegates, however, seems always to have required a written libel, as the relevant entries in the Act Books which have been examined always specified that the libel was 'in scriptu conceptus'. However, pleading contained in a later allegation might always be parol; e.g. *Ticheborne* v. *Swale and others* (1620), DEL 4/8/148. In such cases, the substance of the pleading was entered in the Act Book and the allegation was said to be 'apud Acta facta'.

[2] cf. the practice of the Court of Chivalry, where libels were on parchment (*H.C.C.*, p. 199).

[3] It might be signed by more than one. Parties appearing before the Delegates frequently took the precaution of being adequately represented; it was common for a party to have two advocates and by no means rare to have three or four. It appears from the sentence porrected for the appellant in *Powys* v. *Andrews* (1722), DEL 5/32/unfoliated, that he was represented by five advocates. This practice must have grown to extravagant lengths, as by an order dated 6 July 1812 the court directed that for the future no more than four counsel (of whom no more than two were to be advocates) were to be heard on either side (DEL 6/54/facing 1).

[4] e.g. *Isherwood and others* v. *Rich* (1824), DEL 2/43; the libel is signed 'John Lee for Dr J. Addams'.

[5] e.g. *Keith* v. *Trebeck* (1742), DEL 2/48, where the libel is signed only by Keith.

[6] For a typical libel, see App. VII.

[7] This was usually confined to the formal 'Item quod premissa sunt vera etc.', but it was sometimes expanded to include a statement of the relief required by the appellant (e.g. *Filewood* v. *Talbot* (1789, DEL 2/27).

any alteration in the substance of the document,[1] and there are occasional examples which contain pleading on the merits of the cause as well as the usual formal material; these may represent a reversion, for some reason which cannot now be established, to the older type of libel which, if the argument advanced earlier is correct,[2] did on occasions contain such pleading.[3]

The respondent was entitled to a copy of the libel,[4] and the court might make its reception of the libel conditional on the tender of a copy to him or his proctor within a specified period.[5] If there was more than one appellant, each might tender a separate libel.[6]

The appellant was under an obligation to tender a libel, and failure to do so on the appointed day was likely to be punished by remission of the cause to the *judex a quo* and the condemnation of the appellant in costs.[7] Here as elsewhere, however, a reasonable excuse for failure to libel on time would be accepted.[8]

The civil law allowed a party to obtain personal answers to his pleading from his opponent,[9] the latter being required to admit or deny each item in the pleading.[10] In the Court of Delegates, the respondent might be required to give such answers to the libel (if it contained pleading)[11] or to the pleading contained in a separate allegation.[12] Moreover, if the principal cause were retained, the Delegates would continue to hear it from the point to which the

[1] e.g. *Bowes* v. *Lady Strathmore* (1787), DEL 2/12 (five paragraphs); *Franks* v. *Cockburn and others* (1798), DEL 2/27 (eight paragraphs).

[2] See p. 100 *ante*.

[3] e.g. *Phipps* v. *Stewart* (1737), DEL 2/62; the matter is contained in fourteen paragraphs.

[4] *F.E.L.*, LXX/2/3/iii.

[5] e.g. *Harrison* v. *Elwes* (1612), DEL 4/5/178.

[6] e.g. *Hyde and Mason* v. *Limbery* (1733), DEL 2/38.

[7] e.g. *Stokes* v. *Stokes* (1603), DEL 4/2/196.

[8] e.g. *Chatfeeld* v. *Hull* (1613), DEL 4/6/126; the appellant's proctor had been obliged to write to his client in Sussex to arrange for the appointment of counsel and had also to obtain copies of certain documents necessary for framing the libel. He was allowed until the next court day.

[9] For an elaborate classification of such answers, see *F.E.L.*, LXXXV; for an example of a decree for answers, see App. VIII.

[10] The purpose of this rule was to save time and expense by relieving a party from the obligation of proving such parts of his case as his adversary was prepared to admit (*F.E.L.*, LXXXVI/I). Thus in *Lord Berkeley* v. *Hussey* (*Lady Dillon intervening*) (n.d.), DEL 2/10, Lady Dillon declared that she 'hoped and expected to have been so fully releived by his Lordship's Answers to her said former Allegation as not to have had any Occasion of examining any Witnesses thereto'.

[11] e.g. *Hall* v. *Repes* (1603), DEL 4/2/226.

[12] e.g. *Speke and others* v. *Pitt* (1740), DEL 6/40/177.

judex a quo had taken it, and if the defendant below had not yet given answers to the plaintiff's libel, such answers could be decreed by the judges-delegate.[1]

Personal answers were written on paper.[2] They were set out in numbered paragraphs, corresponding to the paragraphs of the libel or allegation which contained the pleading being answered, and each paragraph in the pleading was wholly denied, wholly admitted or admitted in part.[3]

Like the depositions, answers were usually given before an examiner, if the party giving them were in London,[4] or before commissioners, if he were in the country and the answers were taken by commission *in partibus*.[5] On rare occasions, they might be given before the judges-delegate in open court.[6] Answers also resembled depositions in that they were repeated and acknowledged by the party giving them, before judges or commissioners. They were then signed by the party, counter-signed by the judges or commissioners and also by the notary public who attended (in London, often the deputy registrar, but in the country a local notary appointed *ad hoc*).

[1] e.g. *Prichard* v. *Prichard* (*in the principal cause*) (1621), DEL 4/8/241.

[2] They were occasionally given verbally and entered in the Act Book; e.g. *Pike* v. *Yeardlie and Tracher* (*Ayre intervening*) (1608), DEL 4/4/216.

[3] In the last case, the extent of the admission was as a rule precisely stated. The value of personal answers to the party demanding them, even when the admission was only partial, is well-illustrated by *Dodshon* v. *Dodshon* (1671), DEL 2/111/1. The appellant pleaded, *inter alia*, that the deceased had at least £40 in gold and certain other articles of value during his last illness in a trunk or some other place in the house where he died and that the respondent, or some person acting under her orders, had hidden them, so that the executors could not find them when they searched the house. In her personal answers the respondent admitted that there were articles of value in the house, but no gold, at the time pleaded, but denied the rest of the article. As a result, the appellant was relieved of the obligation to prove the existence in the house of the valuables, but he would have to prove that the gold was there and that the respondent was responsible for removing both gold and valuables.

[4] In which case, he would be produced personally in court by the appellant's proctor, sworn by the judges and monished to give his answers before the next court day; e.g. *Gunston* v. *Hubberd* (1608), DEL 4/4/180.

[5] e.g. *Hewetson* v. *Peirson* (1707), DEL 2/40. For such commissions for the purpose of taking answers, see pp. 104–5 *post*.

[6] e.g. *Speke and others* v. *Pitt* (1740), DEL 6/40/177. The respondent was required to appear in court 'in order to be examined as a party principal upon the Articles of the Allegation admitted in this Cause on the behalf of [the appellants]'. It appears from the account in the Assignation Book that Pitt's examination took over eighteen hours and it may be that the length and complication of his answers was the reason why the judges performed the task.

Answers were usually given by the party himself, but the answers of a minor would be given by his *curator ad litem*.[1] If there was more than one party, they might give joint answers,[2] or each might give his answers separately;[3] even if a decree for answers had been obtained against all the respondents, the appellant might, if he pleased, renounce the answers of one or more of them.[4] If the appellant tendered more than one set of pleadings, the respondent might be required to give personal answers to each set.[5] Answers could be required, not only from the original parties to a cause, but also from anyone intervening *pro interesse suo*.[6]

If the appellant was dissatisfied with the answers given in by the respondent, he could petition the court that fuller answers be given, and demands for fuller answers, like the administration of interrogatories,[7] could apparently continue until the party demanding them was satisfied that they were complete.[8] Usually a petition for *pleniora et planoria responsa* would be allowed without further enquiry, but if there was some real doubt as to the insufficiency of the original answers, the court might require formal written exceptions against them from the party petitioning for fuller answers.[9] Fuller answers, like original answers, were usually given in writing and without direct intervention by the petitioner, but exceptionally the court might allow the petitioner to obtain them from his opponent by a method akin to cross-examination.[10]

If the respondent lived reasonably close to London, he was

[1] e.g. *Herbert* v. *Cotton* (1690), DEL 3/21/unfoliated.

[2] e.g. *Waller and others* v. *Joyce* (1685), DEL 3/21/unfoliated; joint answers were given by five of the appellants.

[3] e.g. *Martin* v. *Pine and Ude* (1688), DEL 2/53.

[4] e.g. *Goodall* v. *Biggar and Gossard* (1605), DEL 4/3/85; Goodall obtained a decree for answers against both respondents but later renounced Biggar's answers.

[5] e.g. *Rea and Mason* v. *Mansell and Collins* (1692), DEL 3/22/unfoliated; a respondent was required to give answers to three separate allegations.

[6] e.g. *Aldebroughe* v. *Brackenburye and Graye* (*Tunstall intervening*) (1606), DEL 4/3/240; personal answers were demanded from Tunstall.

[7] For these, see pp. 130–6 *post*.

[8] e.g. *Hyde and Mason* v. *Calamy and Limbery* (1731), DEL 2/38; the respondents were required to give 'secunda pleniora' and later 'tertia pleniora'.

[9] e.g. *Davenport* v. *Lucy and others* (1652), DEL 6/5/17.

[10] e.g. *ibid.*, at f. 24. Lucy had required fuller answers from Davenport, but these, when they were given, were also claimed to be insufficient. The judges then directed that both the principal parties should appear before them in private and Lucy was permitted to elucidate Davenport's answers, for which purpose he was directed 'to remind her of former passages and to aske her what questions he should think fitt'.

expected to appear personally to give his answers, the length of time he was given for appearance depending upon his distance from the capital.[1] As has been seen, however, answers might be taken before commissioners *ad partes* if the party from whom they were required was living in the country.[2] The procedure employed in such a case was (*mutatis mutandis*) identical with that used to take evidence by commission; letters commissory were issued under the seal of the Delegates (to which were attached the pleadings to which answers were required) and presented to commissioners living locally, who would accept them. The party appeared and was sworn, his answers were taken down by the registrar assumed and the whole sent back to the court with a certificate attesting due execution of the commission.[3] The same device could be employed if the party lived abroad,[4] unless, of course, he was inaccessible to any jurisdiction.[5]

A decree for personal answers lay entirely within the court's discretion, and although it was usually granted without question it might be refused if it seemed to the court that no good purpose would be gained by conceding it; thus the court's discretion might be exercised against a petitioner if it seemed unlikely that his opponent could add to admissions already made on his behalf by his proctor.[6] Moreover, the petitioner was expected to take advantage of any offer by his opponent to give personal answers *sua sponte*, and if the offer were refused, the court might absolve the person

[1] e.g. *Alcock* v. *Digges* (1601), DEL 4/2/34; the respondent was given three days if he lived 'in Civitate London aut Suburbiis' and otherwise seven days.

[2] See p. 103 *ante*.

[3] For a typical commission, see the relevant documents in *Lord Berkeley* v. *Hussey* (*Lady Dillon intervening*) (1734), DEL 2/10. For a detailed account of commissions *ad partes* for the examination of witnesses, see pp. 115–41 *post*.

[4] e.g. *Blackett* v. *Rollo* (1788), DEL 2/12; answers were taken from the respondent, who lived at Nancy in Lorraine, by virtue of a commission directed to the magistrates of that city. For such commissions *ob mutuae vicissitudinis obtentu*, see *F.E.L.*, cxx/1/4 and pp. 141–6 *post*.

[5] e.g. *Forrest* v. *Harris and others* (1707), DEL 2/27; answers were demanded of the respondents and sworn evidence was given by an attorney that they 'are as he has heard and beleives at Sea aboard Severall Ships severall Voyages [*sic*] by reason of which it is impossible for either of the said parties to give their personnall answers as requested to an allegacion given in ...on the part and behalf of the said Edmund Forrest'.

[6] e.g. *Williams* v. *Williams and Williams* (1611), DEL 4/5/164. The respondents' proctor tendered an allegation and sought a decree for answers from the appellant in the usual way. The appellant's proctor, 'animo excusandi dominam suam a personali comparicione', then made an admission, which the court apparently considered adequate, as the petition for answers was refused.

making it from the obligation to give answers at any later stage of the cause.[1] The benefit of answers given by the respondent might be denied to the appellant if the latter failed to pay the costs incurred in giving them.[2]

Personal answers were usually required of a principal party rather than of his proctor, on the ground that the former, through his personal knowledge of all the facts, was better able to relieve his opponent than any proctor could.[3] Occasionally, however, the position was reversed and answers were insisted on from the adverse party's proctor in cases where he was better informed.[4]

The next stage in procedure was the presentation to the Delegates of the process, a document containing a full account of the proceedings in the cause before it was appealed.[5] The court's decree for transmission was usually made immediately after tender of the libel.[6] It was addressed to 'all and singular clerks and literate persons'.[7] It recited the names of the parties, the nature of the cause and the fact that the court had decreed transmission of process; it went on to require that the *judex a quo*, his surrogate, registrar or actuary or any other person in whose custody the relevant documents might be,[8] should cause them (or copies of them)[9] to be transmitted. This decree was served in the usual manner;[10] it was customary for the mandatary to leave with the

[1] e.g. *Goodall* v. *Biggar and Gossard* (1605), DEL 4/3/69.

[2] e.g. *Maye* v. *Stapeley and Pelham* (1608), DEL 4/4/235.

[3] The decree for answers would normally contain a recital to this effect.

[4] e.g. *Wollaston* v. *Geares* (1611), DEL 4/5/145; personal answers were required from the appellant's proctor to an allegation concerning fees charged by the Court of Audience, in which court that proctor was exercent.

[5] For a fuller discussion of the process, see pp. 216–17 *post*.

[6] For an example of a decree for transmission of process, see App. ix.

[7] Some of the later examples were addressed to the process server alone, e.g. *Fletcher* v. *LeBreton* (1829), DEL 2/28, where the decree was addressed merely to 'Henry Rutter, Officer of our High Court of Delegates'.

[8] Almost always, of course, they were in the registry of the lower court. Occasionally, however, they might be in the hands of a private person and in such a case, a monition for process would be directed to him; e.g. *the Earl of Hertford* v. *Lord Mounteagle* (1605), DEL 4/3/96, where a monition was addressed to Sir Edward Coke, the attorney-general. In the event, he proved uncooperative and it was only after he had been declared contumacious several times that he consented to part with the documents.

[9] In practice, the originals of court records were very rarely tendered, but a request might be made for them in special circumstances; e.g. *Earle* v. *Murves and Mowsehurst* (1601), DEL 4/2/4, where the appellant's proctor demanded transmission of the originals because of a defect in the copy which had been sent up.

[10] For service of mandates, see pp. 88–92 *ante*.

official upon whom it was served a sum to cover the cost of transmission.[1] If the cause had passed through more than one court below, the order for transmission would embrace all the processes.[2]

On the appointed day, the process would be presented to the judges-delegate; the task was usually performed by a proctor acting on behalf of the *judex a quo* or his registrar,[3] although anyone might act.[4] There seems usually to have been only one copy of the process provided, but occasionally other copies were made available.[5] Although, as has been seen, the process sent up was usually a copy of records kept in the archives of the lower court, the nature of a cause might also require the production of original documents of one sort or another. This need most frequently arose in testamentary causes, where the original will would be required,[6] but other documents might also be needed.[7] This need was met by the decreeing of a monition for originals which was, *mutatis mutandis*, the same as a monition for process.[8]

As soon as the process was tendered, the costs which were owed in respect of it to the registrar (or his deputy) of the *judex a quo* were taxed by the Delegates and a monition for payment decreed.[9] No separate bill appears to have been tendered,[10] and no doubt an allowance was made by the court at the current rate per folio for law copying. It follows that the sum allowed varied with the size of the process and the cost of a long process could be heavy.[11]

[1] This varied from 13*s*. 4*d*. to one guinea.

[2] e.g. *Tyme* v. *Wilson* (1604), DEL 4/2/312.

[3] e.g. *Berebloke* v. *Morley* (1602), DEL 4/2/149.

[4] e.g. a servant of the registrar (*Trigges and Trigges* v. *Vassall and Jones* (1605), DEL 4/3/45) or the deputy registrar in person (*Pick* v. *Pick* (1614), DEL 4/6/252).

[5] e.g. *the Earl of Hertford* v. *Lord Mounteagle* (1605), DEL 4/3/121; at the request of the appellant's proctors, the court decreed copies of the process for the parties, if they desired it.

[6] e.g. *Barnes* v. *Robson* (1752), DEL 2/9.

[7] e.g. ships' wages books (*Kester and others* v. *Farrant and others* (1726), DEL 2/49). The precise nature of the document might be unspecified, as in *Cowper* v. *Halley and others* (1607), DEL 4/4/23, where the process was accompanied by 'librum quendam et sacculum...cum scriptis in eodem inclusis et repositis'.

[8] e.g. *Barnes* v. *Robson*, *supra*.

[9] e.g. *Hill* v. *Haselwood and Hill* (1604), DEL 4/2/291. Failure to pay these costs was met by excommunication; e.g. *Marwood* v. *Baylie and others* (1605), DEL 4/3/58.

[10] A formal note of taxation, signed by the judges present at that hearing, is usually to be found on the back of the process.

[11] e.g. *Cavendishe* v. *Cavendishe* (1612), DEL 4/5/184; the Delegates taxed the cost of a process in three volumes at £32, while in *Astill* v. *Bickles* (1601), DEL 4/2/19, they allowed £53 for a process of unspecified length.

The taxed charges were payable by the appellant;[1] if there were several, the court's order for payment would normally be made against all of them, but one might be required to pay the whole sum in certain cases (e.g. if it could be shown that he had undertaken the appeal without the consent of the others or had made himself solely responsible for payment).[2] The appellant could, as a rule, insist upon tender of the process before these charges were met,[3] but in some cases the court would require the previous payment of at least part of the sum due when this precaution seemed reasonable.[4]

If a clerical error was alleged in the process, the court could require the registrar of the *judex a quo* to exhibit the original; this would then be compared with the process and if the mistake was found to exist, the Delegates would order reformation of the process.[5] Alternatively, an official of the court might be sent to inspect the original, with power to make any alteration in the process which this inspection might show to be necessary.[6]

Such was the procedure when the process was transmitted on the due date. Very often, however, transmission was delayed,[7] and this could be a serious hindrance in the conduct of proceedings.[8] The reasons advanced by way of excuse were almost infinite; the vagaries of the climate,[9] the pressure of other business upon the

[1] *O.J.*, CCCXV/7. But the respondent might make himself liable by his misuse of the process; e.g. *Rock* v. *Heydon* (1613), DEL 4/6/44 (the respondent's proctor borrowed the process and then refused to return it; he was required to pay for the cost of a copy).

[2] e.g. *Gilbert and others* v. *Edinge and others* (1604), DEL 4/2/306.

[3] e.g. *Blades* v. *Warde* (1605), DEL 4/3/9. The appellant's proctor complained that the deputy registrar of the *judex a quo* was present in court and had the process with him but refused to tender it; the latter declared his willingness to exhibit the process but only if the costs were paid immediately. Otherwise, he insisted, he was under no obligation to exhibit. But the court rejected the argument, and insisted upon immediate exhibition.

[4] e.g. *Goare* v. *Goare* (1612), DEL 4/5/184; the appellant had been out of the country for at least six months when the process was due to be tendered and the court directed that fifty shillings should be paid to the registrar of the *judex a quo* before transmission.

[5] e.g. *Salisburie* v. *Griffith* (1613), DEL 4/6/128 & 135.

[6] e.g. *Lambert and Phillippes* v. *Merland* (1611), DEL 4/5/68.

[7] Or even, it seems, entirely omitted, a circumstance attended with great hardship to the appellant, who might thereby lose his cause (*O.J.*, CCCXXXII/1).

[8] See *O.J.*, CCCXV/1–4, for the difficulties caused by non-transmission.

[9] e.g. *Wood* v. *Smithe* (1634), DEL 4/14/244; delay was said to have occurred 'racione nivis et per aeris intemperiem'.

officials of the lower court,[1] and natural disasters such as the plague.[2] The allowing by the Delegates of too short a time to transmit a long process might also be pleaded,[3] as might obstruction by the *judex a quo*,[4] or by the adverse party.[5]

An excuse very often advanced (and no doubt with justification) was the practical difficulty involved in the safe despatch of such documents from the more distant provinces. In 1722 Thomas Sale, the registrar of an Irish ecclesiastical court, wrote indignantly to a London correspondent, in answer to a recent letter from the latter complaining about delays in the despatch of the process in a cause before the Delegates. Nothing but the refusal of a reliable messenger to wait for its completion, Sale declared, had prevented its transmission long before and even now such people were not easy to find: 'I am now under the greatest difficulty in procureing a safe hand to deliver it at Doctors Commons, tis very large being 590 folios and you may depend upon it, by the first that goes for London, & at ye same time I will signifie to you by whom it goes'.[6]

Perhaps the commonest cause of delay, however, and the one which lies behind most of the instances where no particular reason was assigned, was mere dilatoriness on the part of the officials of the *judex a quo*. A characteristic example is to be found in an affidavit sworn (apparently on behalf of the appellant) in *Carty* v. *McClintock and others*.[7] John Hallwood, a scrivener of Dublin, attested that by the appellant's order he had called 'above twenty several times' at the registrar's office of the Consistory Court of Dublin and had requested preparation of the

[1] e.g. *LeFeve* v. *Stearwell and others* (1619), DEL 4/8/16; the registrar complained that he had 'permultos processus ad transmittendum ante proximum'.

[2] e.g. *Maye and others* v. *Stapeley and others* (1606), DEL 4/3/221; a decree for process was renewed 'racione pestis'.

[3] e.g. *Allen* v. *Lake* (1611), DEL 4/5/140; only three weeks were allowed, although the process would take at least ten weeks to transcribe.

[4] e.g. *Wright* v. *Nelson and others* (1618), DEL 4/7/226; the process was ready for transmission but the judge refused to seal it.

[5] e.g. *Miles* v. *Woodroffe* (1614), DEL 4/6/245; an injunction was served upon the registrar of the lower court, which prevented him from preparing the process.

[6] *Bryan* v. *Bryan* (1720), DEL 2/6. In *Duchemin* v. *Lewin* (1678), DEL 2/116/2, also an Irish appeal, the officials of the Consistory Court of Dublin could find no speedier way of transmitting the process to London than to entrust it to a merchant who was then despatching goods to a kinsman in Chester, in the hope that the latter would forward it safely to Doctors' Commons.

[7] (1729), DEL 2/18.

transmiss. He had been told it would be ready by the beginning of the next term, but when he later called for it the registrar told him 'that the same was a prepareing and would be got ready in a fortnight or three weeks time at the furthest, or words to that purpose'.

The Court of Delegates evolved its own procedure to meet a failure to transmit. If no representative of the *judex a quo* or his registrar appeared with the process on the appointed day, the appellant's proctor would petition that they be declared contumacious and in pain thereof excommunicated.[1] The court would usually declare them contumacious but reserve penalty until the next court day (thus providing a further opportunity to present the process, so that contumacy would be purged).[2] This petition and decree might be repeated several times from one court day to the next until the process was presented.[3] The court might indicate that further delays *ex gratia* would not be allowed by making a final adjournment 'sine spe ulterioris dilacionis',[4] and when the court's patience was finally exhausted, excommunication or attachment would be decreed.[5] Absolution or release would not be granted until the process had been handed in.[6]

Only one other preliminary in the procedure of the Court of Delegates remains to be noticed—the exhibition of the instrument of appeal.[7] This document was the formal record of the fact that the appeal had been made. It was usually on paper,[8] and issued in the name of the notary public representing the appellant, declaring

[1] If the appeal came from one of the secular courts, where excommunication was not employed, attachment would be sought; e.g. *Dumble* v. *Townes* (1604), DEL 4/2/312.

[2] e.g. *Wroughton* v. *Wroughton* (1602), DEL 4/2/153.

[3] Two or three court days were usually allowed and on occasions the court would be very lenient. In *Matthewson* v. *Admanson and others* (1605), DEL 4/3/98, for example, the *judex a quo* and his registrar were declared contumacious on 26 April 1604, and did not purge their contumacy until 23 November of that year.

[4] e.g. *Marwood* v. *Baylie and others* (1603), DEL 4/2/227. In this case the registrar produced the process promptly at the next session.

[5] e.g. *De Swinega* v. *Offield and Dike* (1611), DEL 4/5/152; an appeal from the Court of Admiralty, where Harward the registrar was attached by order of the Delegates and placed in the custody of the Admiralty Marshal.

[6] e.g. *Tyme* v. *Wilson* (1605), DEL 4/3/4.

[7] For an example, see Appendix x.

[8] Under the Commonwealth, it was not uncommon for these instruments to be on parchment (e.g. *Wiche* v. *Antrobus and Wyche* (1650), DEL 8/74). Later examples are almost always on paper, but see *Helyar* v. *Helyar* (1756), DEL 2/104, and *Taylor and Paget* v. *Young* (1733), DEL 2/87, where parchment was used.

the intention to appeal from proceedings 'hereinafter mentioned'. It recited the name of the *judex a quo*, the nature of the cause and the decision from which it is sought to appeal; it then declared that the notary public 'does by these presents rightly and duly appeal' to the king in Chancery and specified that the due formalities had been observed (i.e. the demand for apostles[1] and the interposition of the appeal within fifteen days after sentence).[2] The body of the document concluded with a reservation of the right to reform the appeal; below was an authenticating certificate signed and sealed by the notary public who had drawn up the instrument.[3]

The instrument had to be exhibited in the presence of the respondent or his proctor; it was not sufficient merely to deposit it in the registry.[4] Exhibition might occur at any time before the conclusion of the cause,[5] but it usually occurred at a fairly early stage of proceedings, and the court might order exhibition on a particular day before conclusion.[6]

An abbreviated version of the instrument of appeal, known as the protocol of appeal, might be exhibited when the inhibition and citation was sought. This contained the first few lines of the text of the formal instrument and the substance of the last two paragraphs; it apparently served as an earnest of the appellant's intention to tender a complete and valid instrument at a later stage.[7]

[1] These were letters dimissory from the *judex a quo* to the *judex ad quem*. By the time that Oughton wrote (1712–15) the practice of sending apostles had fallen into desuetude, as the information they contained was all to be found in the process. However, the practice of demanding them continued; see *O.J.*, CCLXXXIX/2/a and CCXCI/CCXCIII.

[2] The older civil and canon law had allowed only ten days (Gibson, *Codex*, vol. 2, p. 1081); the period was lengthened to fifteen days by 24 Hen. VIII, c. 12, ss. 6–7. The usual form of the instrument of appeal suggests that the time began to run against the appellant from the time that he first knew of the sentence (and not from the time that it was actually pronounced); e.g. *Brown* v. *Brown* (1791), DEL 2/11, where the relevant section of the instrument reads 'And I do protest there are not Ten or at most Fifteen Days fully elapsed since the Grievances aforementioned were done to my Party the said Susannah Brown or at least since they came to her Knowledge.'

[3] Occasionally it might also contain the substance of the appellant's pleading, but this was unusual (e.g. *Collins and others* v. *Hoyland and Beilby* (1715), DEL 2/19).

[4] *O.J.*, CCCXVI. In *Carye* v. *Halsey and Feeld* (1605), DEL 4/3/120, the appellant's proctor described the instrument as 'alias penes registrum remanens'.

[5] *O.J.*, CCCXVII/1.

[6] e.g. *Marwood* v. *Baylie and others* (1602), DEL 4/2/163.

[7] *O.J.*, CCCIV/1/a/i. The instrument and its protocol are sometimes to be found filed together (e.g. *Brown* v. *Brown, supra*.

NOTE ON THE USE OF THE GREAT SEAL FOR COMMISSIONS OF DELEGACY

Some confusion has arisen from the conflicting statutory requirements which related to the sealing of commissions. The Act which provided for ecclesiastical Delegates (25 Henry VIII, c. 19) directed that the Great Seal should be used (s. 4), but a later statute (8 Eliz. I, c. 5), which was intended to regulate appeals in civil and marine causes, stated that judges-delegate should be appointed for such causes 'by Commission under the Half Seal, as it hath been heretofore used in such Cases'.[1] If the two statutes are read together, an intelligible rule may be deduced from them; the Great Seal was to be used in ecclesiastical causes and the Half Seal in secular causes. The insuperable difficulty in the way of this interpretation, however, is that by the end of the court's life (and for a very long time before it) the Great Seal was used in every cause, ecclesiastical and secular alike.

Little assistance can be had from examining the seals themselves; no commissions survive earlier than 1660, and in almost every case the seal has either been removed from the documents *in toto* or has been so broken and defaced that its form is unrecognizable. The few examples (all very late) in which the seal has survived in an identifiable condition are all of the Great Seal. Moreover, the entries in the Act Books or Assignation Books which refer to the presentation of commissions invariably speak of them issuing 'sub Magno Sigillo Anglie' from a date as early as *c.* 1700. In the seventeenth century, this formula is not always employed but it often is, and it may be found applied to appeals in marine causes in the decade preceding the Interregnum.[2] The negative evidence is also significant; in the course of this investigation not a single instance has been found of a commission described as issued under the Half Seal, and this was also Rothery's experience.[3]

It is difficult to avoid the conclusion that from a very early date appeals in marine causes to the Court of Delegates issued under the Great Seal. The true explanation of the conflict between this fact and the requirements of the Elizabethan statute cannot be

[1] For the Half Seal, see H. C. Maxwell-Lyte, *Historical Notes on the Use of the Great Seal of England* (London, 1926), pp. 304–9.

[2] e.g. *Chamberlaine* v. *Wood and others* (1642), DEL 4/18/30.

[3] *R.R.*, p. xix.

certainly given on the basis of evidence now available, but an hypothesis may be tentatively proposed. The Act purported to regulate marine appeals at a time when this business had not yet been attracted to the single Court of Delegates which, if the argument advanced earlier is correct,[1] had come into being by the early seventeenth century. Until that time, these appeals were dealt with by *ad hoc* commissions which had no permanent administrative or judicial machinery behind them and which, to judge from the wording of the Elizabethan Act, had always been appointed under the Half Seal; when, however, this business was combined with other civil law appeals, it may well have been felt that appeals in all causes which came before the Court of Delegates should be subject to a uniform practice. Since commissions in ecclesiastical causes were always far more numerous than those from the Court of Admiralty, it must have seemed appropriate to follow the usage established for the former by 25 Henry VIII, c. 19. The fact that Admiralty appeals were now being heard in circumstances very different from those prevailing when 8 Elizabeth I, c. 5 was passed, may have been held to justify neglect of that Act.

[1] See pp. 17–19 *ante*.

CHAPTER VI

PROCEDURE—CAUSES *INTER PARTES*—PROOF BY WITNESSES

The preliminaries of the cause completed, the hearing could proceed to proof; this could be offered in two ways, by witnesses or by documents.

New evidence was often produced before the Delegates, and its admission was governed by liberal rules. In an appeal from a definitive sentence, it was possible for both parties to plead matter not previously pleaded and to offer new proofs.[1] Moreover, the Delegates had a fairly extensive original jurisdiction,[2] and when they heard a cause at first instance evidence was, of course, freely admissible.

The evidence of witnesses was the proof most frequently offered, and in accordance with the usual practice of the civil law it was for the most part taken privately and in writing and not given orally in open court.[3] This system, however slow and expensive it may have seemed to common lawyers, was vigorously defended by practitioners in the civilian courts;[4] it was held to prevent collusion between witnesses or intimidation of a witness by the party producing him,[5] while the informality of this method of taking evidence was deemed to make it less formidable to a witness than oral examination and cross-examination amid the panoply of an open court.[6] Witnesses before the Court of Delegates were

[1] *O.J.*, CCCXVIII/1. It should be noticed, however, that this liberality did not extend to appeals *a gravamine*, where the parties were confined to pleadings and proofs admitted below (*O.J.*, CCCXVIII/2).

[2] For this, see pp. 42–50 *ante*.

[3] This procedure seems to have been universal among the civilian courts in this country. For the ecclesiastical courts, see *F.E.L.*, CX/2; for the Court of Admiralty, see G. H. Main Thompson, *Admiralty Registrars, Some Historical Notes* (London, 1958), p. 26; for the Court of Chivalry, see *H.C.C.*, p. 200. For exceptions, see pp. 153–5 *post*, and *H.C.C.*, p. 206.

[4] *Eccl. Courts Rep.* (1831–2), pp. 144–5 (evidence of Dr Addams) and pp. 155–6 (evidence of Dr Phillimore).

[5] This is implied in *F.E.L.*, CX/1, where these objections to the customary method of examination at common law are stressed.

[6] e.g. *Brisco* v. *Brisco* (1815), DEL 7/11/199. One of the parties, in a letter to a lady whose evidence he desired to make use of, remarked: 'You need not be

examined in this way until the end of its life,[1] and it follows that this technique of examination requires careful study if this account of the court's procedure is to be complete.

If a witness lived outside London and he could not reasonably be expected to come to town to give evidence, the party seeking to produce him would petition the Delegates for the appointment of commissioners;[2] before these representatives of the court, his depositions could be taken locally.[3] On occasions the court would decree a commission without any cause for it being put forward by the petitioner,[4] but it was usual to assign some reason and these, for the most part, turned upon the impossibility or the grave difficulty involved in bringing the witness to London.[5] Ill-health was, of course, a valid reason,[6] as was the 'molestia et incomoditas' of the roads,[7] the inclemency of the weather[8] or the fact that the person whose presence was required in London was engaged 'in

at all afraid, for you will not have to appear personally in Court, but your Evidence will all be taken down in Writing in a private room, as all the other Witnesses' Evidence was.'

[1] Written examination continued to be used by the ecclesiastical courts until 17 & 18 Vict., c. 47 allowed them to employ oral examination if they preferred. Similar permission was given to the Court of Admiralty by 3 & 4 Vict., c. 65, s. 7 and to the Courts of Oxford University by 17 & 18 Vict., c. 81, s. 45.

[2] They were known as commissioners *ad partes* (*F.E.L.*, CXI/2). See App. XII for an example of such a commission.

[3] It may seem more reasonable to begin by discussing the examination of witnesses in London, as this was far commoner. It has seemed better, however, to deal first with depositions taken by commission, as most of the material used in this discussion has been extracted from documents (of which a prolific number survive among the cause papers) relating to this method of examination. Thus the discussion of examination in London has been largely confined to matters not already touched upon when commissions *ad partes* were considered, and the two sections taken together provide a comprehensive account of the civil law procedure for taking evidence.

It should also be noticed that commissions *ad partes* could be used for other purposes (e.g. taking personal answers), and a number of the illustrations which follow are drawn from commissions of this character.

[4] e.g. *Savile and others* v. *Shepard* (1611), DEL 4/5/49.

[5] But other factors, such as social standing, were also considered; e.g. *Button* v. *Longe* (1610), DEL 4/5/4 (the appellant was granted a commission (for taking his personal answers) solely on the ground that, as a knight, he was an 'egregia persona' and as such entitled to this consideration).

[6] e.g. *Stevenson* v. *Watson* (1605), DEL 4/3/31; the court granted a commission (for the taking of the appellant's personal answers) as it was alleged that she was 'valetudinariam et comode non posse ad hanc Civitatem accedere sine periculo salutis sue'.

[7] e.g. *Maye and others* v. *Stapeley and others* (1607), DEL 4/4/10.

[8] e.g. *Browne* v. *Cheny* (1618), DEL 4/7/254; the impossibility of coming to London 'presertim hoc brumale tempore' was advanced.

negociis Regiis'.[1] Even the home counties were thought sufficiently remote in the early seventeenth century to justify the issue of a commission, so that witnesses living in Sussex might be so examined.[2] These reasons might be supported by appropriate evidence,[3] but the court was usually satisfied without it.

Commissions were for the most part granted by the Delegates without demur, but on occasions they would insist on the personal appearance of the individual concerned in London,[4] or they would grant a commission only 'sub certis condicionibus'; thus the petitioning party might be required to give the judges the names of those witnesses whom it was proposed to examine, and if the execution of the commission was likely to involve the adverse party in great expense in representation (if, for example, it was to be executed abroad) the Delegates might insist that a sum be paid into court for the use of that party before the commission was extracted.[5] Moreover, any attempt by a litigant at whose application a commission had been granted to abuse the privilege (for example, by using it as a means of putting his opponent to unnecessary expense) would be checked by the award of costs.[6]

As soon as the decision to decree a commission had been taken,

[1] e.g. *Porter* v. *Towerson* (1613), DEL 4/6/3.

[2] e.g. *Gilberd* v. *Beylie and others* (*in the principal cause*) (1614), DEL 4/6/250.

[3] e.g. *Hill* v. *Newporte* (1617), DEL 4/7/84; the respondent's proctor applied for a commission on the ground of illness and this statement was supported by an affidavit sworn by one Edward Kirkes. In *Dighton* v. *Bennett* (1634), DEL 4/14/164, where the appellant wished to have witnesses in Ireland examined by commission, the court first required him to take an oath that the witnesses existed and were necessary to prove his case.

[4] e.g. *Owen* v. *Owen* (1614), DEL 4/6/159; the court decreed for the personal appearance of the respondent (to give his answers) 'sine spe Commissionis obtinendae pro eius responsis'.

[5] e.g. *Nevell* v. *Nevell* (1611), DEL 4/5/153. A commission was to be executed for the appellant in several different towns or cities on the continent. He was required, before extraction, to inform one of the judges, in the presence of the registrar, of the witnesses' names and to deposit £10 for the expenses of the respondent.

[6] e.g. *Baker* v. *Browne and Bacon* (1602), DEL 4/2/156. The appellant had been granted a commission, which was to be executed at the parish church of Bury St Edmunds. The proctor of one of the respondents later complained to the court that his party had been represented at the church on at least three of the days assigned for execution, had caused his commissioners to be present and had prepared written interrogatories to be put to the appellant's witnesses; as a result, he had incurred heavy expenses and this, he claimed, was the sole reason why the commission had been applied for: 'scienter et ex proposito concedi obtinuisse ut hoc modo pars dicti Browne imanibus sumptibus et laboribus fatigetur'. The court awarded costs of retarded process against the appellant.

the court would appoint commissioners to act on its behalf. The Delegates, however, were not usually responsible for choosing the commissioners, as the parties were allowed this privilege;[1] those who were to act on behalf of the party petitioning for the commission were usually named and appointed in open court when the commission was decreed, and at the same time it was customary for the judges to give their approval to any commissioners whom the adverse party chose to nominate within a certain period (three or four days was the usual time allowed).[2] It seems that these latter nominations were not normally brought to the attention of the Delegates when they were made, but sometimes the court would insist that a judge be informed of them.[3]

It was usual for each side to nominate three or four commissioners, although the full number appointed would rarely act; this was a necessary rule, as there could be no certainty when the commission was decreed how many would be able or willing to speed it. The propriety of appointing more than four commissioners was canvassed in *Harrison* v. *Lord Reay*,[4] where the appellant's proctor nominated no less than nine and the point was taken for the respondent that the 'consuetudo curie' did not allow of more than four. The court made the true position clear by appointing all the appellant's nominees, but adding a proviso that no more than four of them were to join in expediting the commission.

The number of commissioners nominated by each side was, as a rule, equal (or almost so), as neither party would wish to be at a disadvantage, but occasionally there was a discrepancy; thus in *Arscott* v. *Hender and Moldesworth*[5] the appellant nominated three commissioners but the respondent only one.[6]

If a commission *ad partes* was decreed by any ecclesiastical tribunal other than the Court of Delegates, it would allow the

[1] At one time it was the practice in the ecclesiastical courts for the judge himself to nominate commissioners (*F.E.L.* CXI/7), but it is clear from the Delegates' Act Books that by the early seventeenth century nomination by the parties was the rule.

[2] e.g. *Hinde* v. *Chetwyn* (1632), DEL 4/14/23.

[3] e.g. *Harrison* v. *Lord Reay* (1632), DEL 4/14/14. There may have been some uncertainty whether the persons likely to be chosen would be suitable.

[4] *supra*.

[5] (1605), DEL 4/3/143.

[6] Such cases may be explained by the difficulty of finding persons willing to act, in the short time allowed by the court to the adverse party to nominate; in this case, for example, the respondent was allowed only three days to find commissioners to sit in Cornwall.

commissioners to proceed *conjunctim et divisim*, so that proceedings could be validly conducted by only one commissioner.[1] Proceedings before the Delegates themselves, however, always required at least two judges,[2] and it followed that the presence of at least two commissioners was necessary for the valid execution of any commission decreed by that court,[3] unless both the parties consented to only one, in which case he could act alone.[4]

Although the usual form of commission did not require it, it seems that at least one commissioner from each side had to be present before the commission could be properly sped.[5] However, there was no need for all the commissioners appointed to act and it frequently happened that some of those named took no part at all in the proceedings.[6]

The provenance of the commissioners was dictated by convenience and they were usually drawn from the country surrounding the place where the commission was to sit.[7] There was, however, no firm rule in the matter and they might come from further afield.[8]

The type of commissioner chosen depended upon the nature of

[1] *F.E.L.*, CXI/3/1/i (at p. 230).

[2] A rule which derived from the usual wording of the quorum clause. See *F.E.L.*, CXI/3/1/i–ii (at p. 230).

[3] e.g. *Forrest* v. *Wilson and Reid* (1768), DEL 6/45/215; a commission was granted anew because it had been mistakenly sped by only one commissioner 'whereas the Tenor of the Commissions in the Delegates requires two'.

[4] *F.E.L.*, CXI/3/1/ii (at p. 230). This rule may explain the not infrequent issue of commissions by the Delegates *conjunctim et divisim* in the earlier seventeenth century, although consent by the parties is never referred to in the Act Books.

[5] The rule was the same in the Court of Chivalry, as was no doubt the reason for it; the commissioners were not required to be unbiassed, so that it would be dangerous to allow proceedings to be conducted by the representatives of one side alone (*H.C.C.*, p. 201). Thus in *Mathew* v. *Earnely* (*in the principal cause*) (1642), DEL 4/18/18, an affidavit was sworn on the respondent's behalf that two commissioners named by him had attended at the parish church of St Thomas in Monmouth to expedite a commission granted to the appellant, but 'noe Commissioners named by the sayd Mathew did come into the sayd Church upon any of the sayd dayes to speed the sayd Commission, by meanes whereof the sayd Comission was not exequted'.

[6] e.g. *Jones* v. *Cox* (1679), DEL 2/116/2; the parties nominated six commissioners of whom three did not act.

[7] e.g. *Stoddard* v. *Carmarthen* (1605), DEL 4/3/108; a commission *ad partes* was decreed for execution at Greenwich and the appellant's proctor nominated commissioners living at Greenwich, Lee and Deptford.

[8] e.g. *the Archbishop of York* v. *Hutton and Hutton* (1607), DEL 4/4/121–2. The commissioners included cathedral dignitaries from Ripon, York and Southwell and the vicar of Sherborn; they sat at Cawood.

the cause, and seems to have followed the practice of the court from which the appeal came. If the cause was ecclesiastical, the persons appointed were almost always clerks in Holy Orders.[1] They were usually parochial clergy if the commission was to sit in a parish church (as was the usual custom), but if proceedings took place in a cathedral or university town, some of the dignitaries there would often act.[2] The bias in favour of clergymen is no doubt to be explained by the fact that in many rural communities they were the only persons of the necessary standing who were sufficiently well-educated to undertake the task.[3] There was, however, no rule of the court which made the employment of clerks obligatory in ecclesiastical causes and 'mixed' commissions of clerks and laymen do occasionally occur.[4]

If the appeal came from a secular court, the Delegates would appoint laymen as commissioners rather than clerks; a typical example is *Harrys and others* v. *Wogan*,[5] a marine cause, where the commissioners included the mayor of Barnstaple, a knight, a bachelor of Laws and various gentlemen.

Whatever the nature of the cause, it was uncommon for persons with legal experience or qualifications to act; on occasions, however, commissioners were appointed who were officers of ecclesiastical courts[6] or who held degrees in law,[7] and use might also be

[1] During the Interregnum, however, laymen seem invariably to have been employed. A commission typical of that period was the one issued in *Maynwaring* v. *Maynwaring* (1659), DEL 6/8/84; it was directed to eight persons, all of whom are described as 'Esquires' or 'generosi'.

[2] e.g. *Arthur* v. *Law and Dunkin* (1666), DEL 4/21/36. The commission sat in St. Patrick's Cathedral, Dublin, and the commissioners included the Dean of St. Patrick's, the Dean of Christ Church and the Archdeacon of Dublin. In *Lewes* v. *Daye* (*the Archbishop of Canterbury intervening*) (1618), DEL 4/7/270, a commission for the scrutiny of records sat in the chapel of Oriel College, Oxford, and all the commissioners were fellows.

[3] It must be borne in mind that many of the documents used in the course of their proceedings were wholly or partly in Latin until 1733.

[4] In *Harrison* v. *Lord Reay* (1632), DEL 4/14/14, the appellant's nominations were of this character and the court overruled an objection to them on this ground by the respondent's proctor. In *Aldebroughe* v. *Brakenburye and Graye* (*Tunstall intervening*) (1606), DEL 4/3/292, the court appointed three knights after the respondents' proctor had asked for a commission directed 'discretis et illustribus viris'.

[5] (1611), DEL 4/5/129.

[6] e.g. *Gunston* v. *Guibbon* (1608), DEL 4/4/188; one of the commissioners was William Thurrowgood, commissary of the Bishop of Norwich.

[7] e.g. *Hunwick* v. *Barnes* (*Hunwick intervening*) (1606), DEL 4/3/208; the commission included three doctors and two bachelors of Laws. Such appointments were not uncommon in university or cathedral towns.

made of advocates who were exercent before the Court of Delegates itself.[1]

Although the parties (or their proctors) were usually allowed to nominate the commissioners of their choice, it is clear that the court retained a general control over appointments; it might refuse to accept particular persons as commissioners,[2] and sometimes even persons who had been nominated and accepted by the Delegates were struck off before the commission began to sit.[3]

The reason most often given for rejecting a nomination (when the court saw fit to assign one)[4] was that the nominee was likely to act in a manner prejudicial to the interests of the adverse party.[5] The point was usually taken by that party's proctor who would 'except' against particular nominations of the other side. Anything which was likely to make a nominee unsuitable could be referred to, but the most frequent ground of objection was some 'dependence' upon one of the parties. Thus in *the Bishop of Durham* v. *the Archbishop of York*[6] the Delegates refused to sanction the appointment of one John Craddock, nominated by the respondent's proctor, after the appellant's proctor had pointed out that Craddock was the archbishop's chaplain, while in *Scarlett* v. *Chatterton*[7] the appellant's proctor made an exception against a nominee of the respondent because he was a 'consanguineus' of that party and an 'inimicus' of the appellant. However, an obvious connection

[1] e.g. *Baker* v. *Foster* (1607), DEL 4/4/99; Dr Marten, described as 'Advocatus huius Curie', was appointed to act alone in the execution of a commission at Henley-on-Thames.

[2] e.g. *Frampton* v. *Frampton* (*in review*) (1602), DEL 4/2/97; the respondent's proctor was allowed to nominate anyone 'exceptis Hanson et Bastard'.

[3] e.g. *Baker* v. *Browne and Bacon* (1602), DEL 4/2/134; one of the respondent's proctors nominated five persons who were accepted, but a marginal note in the Act Book states that two of them were later removed.

[4] Reasons were not always assigned; e.g. *Astill* v. *Bickles* (*in the principal cause*) (1601), DEL 4/2/31.

[5] The fact that nominations were usually made by the parties' proctors rather than by the court, naturally made this a frequent risk. The sort of behaviour expected of commissioners was discussed in *Owen* v. *Lloyd* (1639), Cur. Mil. Boxes 6/141 (a decision of the Court of Chivalry which also used the system of commissions *ad partes*, cited in *H.C.C.*, p. 201); they were not expected to be unbiased but they had to treat both parties fairly. As Law put it, they were required to be 'open, kind, just, and honest, towards both parties alike, without partiality, or prejudice for or against one more than another' (*F.E.L.*, CXI/3/2/iv (at p. 230)). For a fuller discussion of the dangers of nominations by proctors, see *F.E.L.*, CXI/3/2/iii–iv (at p. 230); CXI/6–8.

[6] (1610), DEL 4/5/28.

[7] (1619), DEL 4/8/17.

between a party and persons nominated as commissioners on his behalf was never an inevitable cause of their rejection, and provided that they were likely to behave in an impartial manner they might be accepted.[1]

The suitability of prospective commissioners was usually gone into when the commission was decreed. Sometimes, however, partial commissioners did not show themselves in their true colours until proceedings under the commission began, and in such cases it would not be possible for the court to take action until the commissioners' process was returned. If it appeared from the process that any of the commissioners had been guilty of such conduct as would ground a successful 'exception' against him, the entire proceedings might be suppressed and a new commission decreed from which the offending commissioners were removed.[2]

The need to make new nominations might arise, not only from the rejection of original nominees by the court, but also from the refusal of nominees to act; the reasons most frequently advanced were ill-health[3] and the pressure of other business.[4] In such cases, a fresh application might be made to the court and the vacant places filled.[5]

As well as choosing commissioners, the court had to select a suitable person to act as the registrar or actuary of the commission. It was customary to appoint the registrar of the Delegates himself or his deputy, but they were given the right to delegate the task to some person 'partibus indifferens' whom they chose to nominate; on rare occasions, the deputy registrar performed the office

[1] e.g. *the Bishop of Bristol* v. *the Bishop of Worcester* (1618), DEL 4/7/283; the court accepted all the nominees of the appellant, although they were prebendaries of his cathedral.

[2] e.g. *Chatterton and Chatterton* v. *Cavendishe* (*Bruce intervening*) (1612), DEL 4/5/239 & 278. The appellants' proctor complained that the proceedings in the commission granted to the respondents had been irregular, as the commissioners nominated by his parties had been prevented by the appointees of the other side from taking part in its execution. Upon investigation, the Delegates found the accusation proved, suppressed the proceedings and decreed a new commission.

[3] e.g. *Montagu* v. *the Bishop of Winchester* (*in the principal cause*) (1619), DEL 4/8/29; several persons chosen were unable to take part 'ratione invalitudinis et infirmitatis eorum corporum'.

[4] e.g. *Meynell* v. *Thornley* (1667), DEL 2/107.

[5] e.g. *Montagu* v. *the Bishop of Winchester* (*in the principal cause*), *supra*, at f. 30. Such a step was essential only when so many of the original commissioners refused to act that proceedings could not be validly conducted by those who remained.

in person,[1] but as a rule the right to delegate was exercised and a substitute chosen,[2] a note of the fact being endorsed at the foot of the commission.[3] It might also happen that the court would nominate particular persons to act for the commissioners, other than the registrar of the Delegates or his deputy.[4]

The registrar assumed was usually a man who lived in the locality where the commission was to be executed; the requirement of 'indifference' seems to have ensured that he was not nominated by the parties.[5] Only one was chosen as a rule, but occasionally a second might be assumed to act *conjunctim et divisim* with the first, if the original appointee had occasion to absent himself from sittings of the commission.[6] The form of appointment usually employed specified that the registrar assumed should be a notary public,[7] but if no such person was available in the locality where the commission was executed,[8] other persons of sufficient standing might serve instead.[9]

[1] e.g. *Sharp and Smith* v. *Ward and Leech* (1728), DEL 2/75; James Pinfold acted as registrar for a commission executed at York.

[2] Once chosen in this way, the actuary had to be accepted by the commissioners (if he was willing to act) or reimbursed for any loss of time. In *Scarlett* v. *Chatterton* (1619), DEL 4/8/99, one Cresfeld was appointed as registrar for a commission decreed on behalf of Chatterton; he presented himself at the time and place appointed but the commissioners, at Chatterton's suggestion, then appointed another man. Chatterton was later required by the Delegates to pay Cresfeld's expenses.

[3] e.g. *Banks and others* v. *Finch and others* (1712), DEL 2/9; the commission bears at its foot a note by Thomas Oughton, the then deputy registrar, stating that he was 'variis negotiis impeditus' and therefore constituted one Richard Rider, notary public, 'pro Expedicione huiusmodi Comissionis vice et loco meis'.

[4] e.g. *Ingham and Fisher* v. *Russell and Stubbes* (1603), DEL 4/2/215; the court nominated three persons successively, the registrar having the power to appoint a substitute only if all of them were unable to act.

[5] There were occasional exceptions to this rule; e.g. *Masters* v. *Masters* (1741), DEL 2/54 (one of the parties was able to achieve the nomination of a registrar of his own choice).

[6] e.g. *Keene* v. *Madden and others* (1726), DEL 2/48.

[7] *F.E.L.*, CXI/3; it was otherwise, on occasions, if the commission was to be executed outside the jurisdiction. For such commissions, see pp. 141–6 *post*.

[8] Such a shortage was sometimes the result of a deliberate act by one of the parties: e.g. *Dicklegge* v. *Halton* (1614), DEL 4/6/198; the respondent's proctor complained that it had proved impossible to execute the commission as all the persons suitably qualified in the locality had refused to act 'idque...sollicitacione et persuacione' of the appellant.

[9] e.g. *Chatterton* v. *Nicholls* (1828), DEL 2/17; a commission for answers was executed in Chichester and attested by two householders of that city 'There being no Notary Public at this time within Chichester...or within ten miles thereof'. See also *Egerton* v. *Egerton* (1653), DEL 2/41, where two 'literate persons' were chosen by the commissioners for the same reason.

No doubt care was taken to choose an impartial and efficient registrar assumed but this cannot always have been easy. Sometimes the court, when decreeing the commission, found it necessary to specify with some precision that particular persons should not be employed,[1] while any appointee could be 'excepted against' by one of the parties if doubts were felt about his suitability. The exceptions thus taken turned as a rule upon the partiality of the registrar assumed. In *Boothby* v. *Milborne*,[2] for example, the respondent objected that some of the witnesses had been approached by Mr John Fortune 'who is the Notary that takes the depositions in this cause' and told what they were to swear to, while in *Horne* v. *Lake and others*[3] an exceptive allegation in writing was directed against Thomas Holmes, the actuary who had been nominated by the deputy registrar of the Delegates, asserting that he had previously acted as a proctor in the cause and since the beginning of the appeal had 'expensed and managed the same'. To have any financial interest in the outcome of the cause was also enough to ground an exception, for in *Haughton* v. *Marfitt and Margrave*[4] objection was taken to William Campey, because he had made a wager with the local apothecary as to the result of the litigation.[5] These 'exceptions' were raised before the Delegates themselves,[6] or before the commissioners when they had begun to sit;[7] in the latter case, the commissioners might remit the point to London for the consideration of the court.[8]

In conclusion, the court had to appoint a place for the commissioners to sit and to fix a time for their sessions. If the cause was ecclesiastical, the Delegates would usually appoint as a meeting place a parish church convenient for the witnesses,[9] while if they

[1] e.g. *Fitton* v. *Broughton* (1608), DEL 4/4/224; the Delegates directed that certain persons may be assumed 'exceptis Magistro Colleyne ac omnibus aliis qui fuerint aut sint a consiliis dicti Fitton'.

[2] (1686), DEL 8/77.

[3] (1674), DEL 2/101/2.

[4] (1760), DEL 2/38.

[5] In the event, the commissioners confirmed Campey in his appointment, after written statements had been tendered, signed by him and by the apothecary, that the wager was to be deemed null and void.

[6] e.g. *Hickmott* v. *Munne* (*in the principal cause*) (1645), DEL 4/18/76.

[7] e.g. *Horne* v. *Lake and others* (1674), DEL 2/101/2.

[8] e.g. *Horne* v. *Lake and others, supra.*

[9] A typical example is *Bee* v. *Moore* (1667), DEL 2/111/1; the commissioners were directed to sit in the parish church at Ancaster in Lincolnshire for the purpose of examining witnesses who lived in Ancaster and Stowe Greene (a village nearby).

lived in or near a cathedral city the consistory court of the cathedral might be chosen.[1] The use of churches or consistories for causes of this nature was the invariable rule of the court throughout the whole of its life, except during the Interregnum, when the commissioners were usually instructed to sit in secular buildings.[2] There were also occasions when the court gave a choice of venue, but this was uncommon.[3] If the commissioners were required to perambulate (which might be necessary if the witnesses were too scattered to permit of their all attending at the one place), the Delegates would fix as many meeting places as were necessary.[4] The parties themselves had some say in the matter and objection could always be taken to the court's choice.[5]

The usual form of commission gave the commissioners the power to adjourn their proceedings from the locale fixed by the court to any other of their choice. This power was freely exercised, and it was customary to hold the formal opening session in the parish church and then adjourn to the local inn.[6] This arrangement was no doubt conducive to the ease and comfort of the participants, but it was not without the danger of abuse. In *Bovey* v. *South and others*,[7] for example, the most sinister construction was placed upon the adjournment of a commission (granted by the

[1] e.g. *Pollexfen* v. *Kingston* (1671), DEL 2/111/1; the commissioners sat in the 'locus consistorialis' of Exeter Cathedral. In *Layer* v. *Layer* (1617), DEL 4/7/110, where a commission was issued for taking the answers of the respondent (who apparently lived in or near Norwich), St Luke's chapel in the cathedral was used.

[2] e.g. *Newman* v. *Bennington* (1659), DEL 6/8/91 (an inn at Spalding); *Sandeford* v. *Shurt* (1659), DEL 6/8/92 (the town hall at Liverpool).

[3] e.g. *Hord and others* v. *Smith and Heylin* (1666), DEL 4/21/71; the commissioners were instructed to sit 'in ecclesia parochiali de Lechlade vel aliquo alio loco convenienti'.

[4] e.g. *Griffyn* v. *Jeffrye* (1606), DEL 4/3/182; the commissioners were to sit for two days at Cotstock and for two days at Hinton Marten.

[5] e.g. *Chatterton and Chatterton* v. *Cavendishe* (*Bruce intervening*) (1612), DEL 4/5/293 & 308. The respondent petitioned that a commission be decreed for execution at Derby. The appellants' proctor later objected to the choice of Derby on the ground that the respondent and his father were 'admodum graciosi in dicta villa de Darbie', and the appellants consequently feared that they would not be able to reach the town in safety if they wished to attend the execution of the commission.

[6] e.g. *Banks and others* v. *Finch and others* (1712), DEL 2/9; the first sitting of the commission was held in the parish church at Wigan and all later sittings in the house of Richard Toutell 'apud Signum Clavium Transfixarum, Vulgo vocatum The Cross Keys' in Wigan.

[7] (1649), DEL 8/87.

judex a quo) from the parish church at Ruscombe to the house of one Richard Aldworth, one of the respondents. It was alleged that Aldworth, having made elaborate preparations to entertain the witnesses, invited them to his house, and having plied them with 'very good meate and drinke...and liberall intertainement' attempted to discover what evidence they would give; he then arranged that their examination should take place in a room where anything that was said could be heard in the adjoining rooms. It was no doubt in order to guard against abuses of this sort that the power of adjournment was sometimes restricted.[1]

The use of ecclesiastical buildings for the conduct of commissions seems to have been confined to appeals from the Church courts. Commissions which were decreed in the course of marine appeals (which made up the bulk of the court's secular business) were usually conducted in town halls and similar buildings.[2]

The court was responsible for fixing the time as well as the place for the execution of commissions. Usually three or four days were allowed for the purpose,[3] the commissioners being permitted to decide for themselves at what hours they would sit during that period (although the court's directions were sometimes more explicit).[4] The judges would normall selecty particular days, but occasionally the choice was left to the commissioners themselves with the proviso that proceedings had to be completed within a certain period.[5] If the days were chosen by the court, they could be altered later if they were found to be unsuitable.[6] The court's directions as to the time of sitting had usually to be adhered to

[1] e.g. *Aldebroughe* v. *Brakenburye and Graye* (1605), DEL 4/3/144; the appellant had obtained a commission with the usual permissive clause, but later one of the respondents deposited in the registry of the court a certificate signed by five of the judges, which forbad the commissioners to sit anywhere except in the parish church of Doncaster, unless it was established on oath that it was impossible for the witnesses to attend there.

[2] e.g. *Fox* v. *White and others* (1618), DEL 4/7/235; the commissioners were directed to sit in a public building (*pretorium*) at Weymouth.

[3] e.g. *Colmer and others* v. *Marshe* (*Seaman intervening*) (1614), DEL 4/6/267; the commission was to sit on 27, 28 and 29 March 1614.

[4] e.g. *Garnett and Garnett* v. *Willmott and Willmott* (1606), DEL 4/3/206; the commissioners were to sit on 2 September 1606 between the hours of nine and three.

[5] e.g. *Pynce* v. *Groven* (1613), DEL 4/6/122; the commission could be sped at any time before Easter following.

[6] e.g. *Grundy and Boston* v. *Cannon* (1612), DEL 4/5/306; the court altered the days at the request of the appellants when they were found to clash with the sittings of the County Assize.

exactly, and evidence taken outside the appointed period was liable to be suppressed.[1]

All the foregoing details, when decided, were embodied in the commission (or letters commissory), the source from which the commissioners derived their authority.[2] This was engrossed on parchment and was addressed to the commissioners, whose names were set out in two groups (each comprising the nominees of one side) which were joined with the words 'nec non'.[3] It recited the granting of the commission and its purpose,[4] together with the details of the time and place of execution which the court had decreed; there was also a 'quorum clause' directing that proceedings could take place before all the commissioners or any two or more of them. They were directed to proceed against witnesses who refused to tell the truth 'per legitima juris remedia', and there was a formal committal to the commissioners of 'auctoritatem nostram...cum cuiuslibet legitima coercionis potestate'. The precise date by which the process of the commission was to be returned to the court was stated and the document usually ended with a note, signed by the deputy registrar of the Delegates, appointing a suitable notary public to act as registrar assumed of the commission.

When the letters commissory had passed the Delegates' seal, they were sent down to the place where the commission was to be executed, together with all the other documents which would be necessary for the speeding of the commission; the letters substitutional of the proctors in the cause,[5] the pleadings upon which the witnesses were to be produced and possibly the adverse party's interrogatories.[6] If necessary, the Delegates would order that any

[1] e.g. *Raye* v. *Forde* (1633), DEL 4/14/108 & 177. The Delegates assigned 8 January 1633 as the first day for executing a commission; certain witnesses were examined on 7 January, but their depositions were suppressed and a new commission decreed for their examination. [2] For an example, see App. XII.

[3] The same arrangement was used in the letters commissory decreed by the Court of Chivalry (*H.C.C.*, p. 201).

[4] Commissions were usually issued to examine witnesses, but they could be used for many other purposes; see p. 141 *post*.

[5] For these, see p. 127 *post*.

[6] The adverse party might, if he preferred, postpone the presentation of interrogatories until the commission had begun to sit (*F.E.L.*, CXI/4 & 10), while on at least one occasion, interrogatories were not presented until after the commission had terminated and the court decreed a second commission to administer them; *Hickmott* v. *Munne and others* (1645), DEL 4/18/79. For a full account of the purpose and function of interrogatories, see pp. 130–6 *post*.

documents in the hands of third parties which might be required for the due execution of the commission should also be despatched.[1] The responsibility of seeing that the documents were properly transmitted seems to have fallen upon the party in whose favour the commission was decreed.[2]

On the appointed day, the commissioners, the witnesses who were to be examined and the registrar assumed assembled in the church or other place assigned for their business. The parties naturally wished, in most cases, to be legally represented, but as it was usually inconvenient for proctors practising in London to attend at proceedings of this sort in the provinces,[3] they would appoint substitutes in their stead. Appointments of this sort were made by the original proctor by means of 'letters substitutional' under which two substitutes were usually appointed,[4] with power to act *conjunctim et divisim*;[5] only one, however, would normally appear.[6]

Proceedings began with the formal presentation of the letters commissory.[7] These were publicly read by the registrar assumed

[1] e.g. *Matthewes* v. *Spurlinge* (*in the principal cause*) (1620), DEL 4/8/159; the court decreed that a matrimonial contract which was in the possession of the *judex a quo* should be produced to the commissioners, so that the witnesses should be able to inspect it.

[2] Thus in *Reynolds* v. *Reynolds* (1618), DEL 4/7/165, the appellant is blamed by the respondent's proctor for not taking the necessary steps to send the documents down, so that the commission was delayed, while in *Dumbell* v. *Townes* (1605), DEL 4/3/118, the appellant excused himself on the ground of illness from seeing to this task. In practice the documents were usually presented to the commissioners by the rcpresentative of the party who had petitioned for the commission.

[3] By the end of the eighteenth century, however, it was not unknown for them to appear in person even when the commission was executed in a part of the country distant from London; e.g. *Walker and Walker* v. *Walker and Walker* (1803), DEL 2/90 (one side was represented by his original proctor at a commission executed at Bath). No doubt the improved state of the roads was largely responsible.

[4] It seems that whenever possible notaries public were employed as substitutes, but as persons with this qualification were not always available in the country, recourse might be had to anyone who was willing to act and who appeared suitable. A typical example is *Cartwright* v. *Fane* (1678), DEL 2/105/2; the appellant's proctor nominated two substitutes, of whom one was a bachelor of Laws and the other a master of Arts.

[5] e.g. *Banks and others* v. *Finch and others* (1712), DEL 2/9. If one side was represented by more than one proctor, they might issue joint letters substitutional; e.g. *Hewitson* v. *Peirson* (1707), DEL 2/116/2.

[6] More than one might act on occasions; e.g. *Harris* v. *Twittey* (1696), DEL 2/108/1, where two substitutes acted on behalf of Harris' proctor.

[7] e.g. *Banks and others* v. *Finch and others*, *supra*.

and the commissioners accepted the burden of their execution.[1] Letters substitutional were then exhibited by the legal representatives of each side,[2] and the business of examination could commence.

The witnesses were produced by the proctor's substitute of the party on whose behalf they were to give evidence;[3] they were then admitted and sworn by the commissioners and monished to remain in attendance until their evidence had been taken. Each witness was examined separately and in private, which was usually understood to mean, when evidence was taken by commission, that only the commissioners and their registrar should be present.[4]

[1] They might, of course, refuse to act. In *Meynell* v. *Thornley* (1667), DEL 2/107, a commission was decreed to take an inventory of a deceased's estate and to inspect the books of account. The commissioners met and the books were produced for their inspection; they immediately signed a certificate in which they declared: 'Wee finde the busines soe large and our owne affaires not permitting our whole tyme to be imploied therin wee wuld not proceed to any effect upon the said Comission nor can wee make any other returne of the State of that busines.'

[2] If he preferred, a party might always act for himself; e.g. *Arthur* v. *Lane and Dunkin* (1667), DEL 2/111/1 (a commission for the examination of Arthur's witnesses was presented by Arthur himself). Both sides were normally represented before the commissioners, but the adverse party's proctor was not bound to appear if he did not deem it necessary; thus, if interrogatories had already been prepared on behalf of the respondent and sent down with the commission, they could be administered to the appellant's witnesses without the intervention of the respondent's proctor; e.g. *Belfield* v. *Gustard* (1681), DEL 2/106/2.

[3] Sometimes the commissioners issued a warrant specifying the time and place for attendance of witnesses; e.g. *Egerton* v. *Egerton* (1653), DEL 2/41. The court itself, when the commission was decreed, might direct that certain witnesses should attend at a specified stage of the proceedings; e.g. *Watts* v. *Sacheverell* (1610), DEL 4/5/27 (four named witnesses were required to appear at a church in Leicester between two and four p.m. on the first day assigned for sittings of the commission).

[4] e.g. *Forrest* v. *Wilson* (*Reid intervening*) (1768), DEL 2/28; a protest was entered in the acts of the commission on behalf of one of the parties that 'the Method observed in all such Cases as this, is that no person shall be present at the Examination of Witnesses, but only the Commissioners and the Actuary'. This is confirmed by cases such as *Cunningham* v. *Lady Semple* (1699), DEL 6/29/5, where the court suppressed depositions taken by commission on the ground that the witnesses had been examined publicly and decreed a new commission 'expediendam secrete vemotis omnibus praeter Comissionarios Notarium & Testem examinatum'. The same rule was followed by the Court of Admiralty (see the instructions for executing a commission decreed by that court in *Sutherland* v. *Corbett* (n.d.), DEL 8/79) but not by the Court of Chivalry, which apparently permitted the presence of advocates or their substitutes for the purpose of examining witnesses or administering interrogatories (*H.C.C.*, pp. 203–4). On rare occasions (and for what reason does not appear) even the commissioners

The examination of witnesses was strictly confined to the pleading of the party producent;[1] this is clear from the fact that the depositions were always set out in an identical form, each paragraph beginning with a reference to the article of the pleading upon which it was based.[2] Moreover, no example has been discovered, among the very many examined, in which the evidence was founded upon any other material.[3] Either the commissioners or the registrar must have been responsible for conducting the examination,[4] and the latter seems in most cases to have taken down the answers.[5]

Each witness usually began his deposition with certain biographical details which were set out at its head; these might include his age, occupation, place of birth, parish and the approximate

were not allowed to be present during the examination; e.g. *Rea and Mason* v. *Mansell and Collins* (1693), DEL 2/100/2 (the commissioners certified that the registrar assumed 'in loco privato, in absentia nostra juxta potestatem Ei in dictis Litteris Comissionalibus datam, eosdem [testes] separatim Examinavit'. The witnesses later appeared before the commissioners to recognize and subscribe their depositions in the usual way).

[1] It might be further confined to part only of the pleading; e.g. *Hewetson* v. *Peirson* (1707), DEL 2/40 (a commission issued on behalf of Peirson was limited to the sixth and seventh articles of his allegation).

[2] The usual formula which opened each paragraph ran: 'Ad [primum] articulum allegationis respondit et dicit that...'

[3] The Court of Chivalry followed the same rule (*H.C.C.*, p. 203).

[4] Whether the witnesses attended in London or before commissioners, the court would issue exact instructions as to the method to be employed, if this seemed necessary. Thus in *Speke and others* v. *Pitt* (*in the grievance*) (1739), DEL 6/40/119, the Delegates directed that 'the Examiner be not permitted to read the Articles to the Witnesses as specifically laid but that he shall only frame general Questions to the Witnesses as to the Meaning and Intention of the Deceased by the Signs and Tokens specified in the several Articles wherein such Signs and Tokens are pleaded'. This could be taken to imply that the usual practice in the Court of Delegates was to read out each article of the pleading to the witness verbatim and then take down his comments on it: there is some evidence which suggests that by the nineteenth century (if not before) examiners in some ecclesiastical courts were able to use whatever method they pleased (*Eccl. Courts Rep.* (1831–2), p. 18).

[5] e.g. *Salisbury* v. *Bartlett* (1681), DEL 2/106/2; the certificate of the registrar states that the entire proceedings were 'manu mea propria totaliter conscriptum'. The task might, of course, be shared between the registrar and an assistant; thus in *Turvill* v. *Mullineux* (1668), DEL 2/106/2, the registrar certified that the depositions were written 'partim manu mea propria, partim manu aliena, me interim aliter impedito'. On occasions, a witness might be allowed to write his own answers; thus in *Haughton* v. *Marfitt and Margrave* (1758), DEL 2/108/2, the commissioners' acts declared that all the depositions were taken down by the registrar 'except only the Deposition of...John Clough which is in part drawn and altered or interlined by himself!'

time he had known one or both of the parties.[1] The evidence itself was taken down in English, but the common form parts of the depositions were usually in Latin until 1733.

When a witness's evidence on behalf of the party producing him was completed, the adverse party was then free to conduct his own examination. Like the party producent,[2] he was required to commit to writing the questions he wished to put to the witness, these questions being known as 'interrogatories'.

This system may seem somewhat analogous to cross-examination at common law, but the difference between interrogatories administered in the Court of Delegates (or any other civilian court)[3] and questions put by counsel cross-examining in a court of common law must be emphasized.[4] The latter can base his questions upon the evidence which he has heard the witness on the other side give; no such resource was available to the civilian advocate (since the depositions were taken in secret) but he would have a copy of the pleadings upon which the witness had been questioned, and his interrogatories could be based upon the answers which the witness was likely to have made in his original examination. In arriving at the sort of interrogatories which were most likely to assist his cause, the adverse party's legal adviser would be assisted by instructions from his principal and by his own judgment;[5] there were,

[1] Sometimes details of residence over a long period were given. Thus in *Littlehales* v. *Tayler* (1702), DEL 8/75, Jane Bright declared 'That shee lives at present in the parish of Bishopps Castle with her mother where shee has been about a month, & before that shee lived as a servant with one Mr Tomkins of Bromyard for some short time & before that with her mother at Bishopps Castle, before that at the Cock & Castle in Bridgworth, & before that at home with her mother, & before that in London in German Street for 4 years together, & before that for some years with one Mr Woolaston of Bishopps Castle'. As Squibb observes, such information may have biographical and genealogical value (*H.C.C.*, p. 203).

[2] The party on whose behalf a witness was examined was said to 'produce' the witness and was known as the party producent; the adverse party, by whose interrogatories his own examination of that witness was said to be conducted, was known as the party ministrant.

[3] They were also used in the Court of Chancery (*F.E.L.*, CIX/1/2).

[4] It should be noticed, however, that towards the end of the court's life, the administration of interrogatories was often (misleadingly) referred to as 'cross-examination'; e.g. *Spear* v. *Bone and Newsam* (1815), DEL 2/114/2.

[5] e.g. *Maye and Bulman* v. *Stapeley and others* (1607), DEL 4/4/39; the appellants' proctor explained that his principals had gone into the country at the time when the respondents' witnesses were produced, and in the absence of instructions from them he had been obliged to frame interrogatories 'ex coniecturis verisimilibus iuxta rei naturam et qualitatem negocii et ex intellectu suo proprio'.

moreover, many common form interrogatories which could be administered as a matter of course.[1]

The adverse party had usually more latitude in framing interrogatories than was allowed to the party producent in respect of his examination. Whereas the latter was required to confine himself to his pleadings (which had previously been scrutinized by the court and might have been reformed at its direction) no such limitation was placed upon the party ministrant; he was rarely required to submit his interrogatories beforehand for the court's approval,[2] while no case has been found where answers to interrogatories were suppressed on the ground that the questions were irrelevant or in some other respect improper (which suggests that considerable freedom was allowed in drafting them).[3]

Interrogatories were usually written on paper[4] and in English,[5] the questions being set out in numbered paragraphs. Drafting them was, it seems, a skilled task and one which was usually entrusted to advocates;[6] sometimes, at least, it was done by proctors or by a litigant,[7] and there is nothing in the works of practice to suggest that it could not be done by anyone. Interrogatories might be drawn up in London and sent down attached to the commission or drawn up on the spot after the commissioners had

[1] For these, see pp. 132–4 *post*.

[2] Occasionally, however, the court might insist upon this; e.g. *Robinson* v. *Evans* (1696), DEL 6/27/123 (the appellant was required to submit to the court for its approval questions which he proposed to use in the examination of two of the respondent's witnesses).

[3] There seems, however, to have been a closer supervision by the Delegates of interrogatories during the Interregnum (at least with causes of a certain class). Thus in *Davenport* v. *Lucy and others* (1652), DEL 6/4/144, one of the earliest causes tried under the Cromwellian Act relating to forced marriages (Firth and Rait, *Acts and Ordinances*, vol. 2, pp. 496–7), the court found it necessary to lay down procedural rules for the examination of witnesses 'according to the true meaning of ye Act of Parliament and ye Comission in this cause exhibited'; it was decreed that interrogatories which either party wished to administer should 'be viewed and admitted by ye Judges soe farre as they shall find them pertinent to ye case in Question'. The same rule may well have applied to all other causes tried under the Act.

[4] They were occasionally written on parchment; e.g. *Davies* v. *Chambers* (1684), DEL 2/38.

[5] The common form parts were often in Latin; e.g. *Hart* v. *Carey* (1669), DEL 8/83/1.

[6] This was the practice of the Court of Chivalry (*H.C.C.*, pp. 203–4).

[7] e.g. *Felton* v. *Devereux* (1645), DEL 4/18/99 (interrogatories drafted by a proctor); *Blackett and others* v. *Rollo* (1788), DEL 2/12 (interrogatories to be administered to the principal appellant's witnesses drafted by the respondent).

begun to sit.[1] In either case they were not to be made known to the witness until his examination on behalf of the party producent was completed.[2] Like depositions, interrogatories were administered to each witness privately and his answers taken down in writing;[3] it is possible that this method of administration was compulsory, even if the commission was executed in a country outside the jurisdiction of the court where a different system of cross-examination was employed.[4]

Interrogatories would often begin with certain instructions to the person conducting the examination.[5] Then could come certain common form questions which seem usually to have been intended to cast doubts upon the impartiality of witnesses or to impugn their character.[6] Thus a witness might be asked by whom he had

[1] The alternative was usually embodied in the court's decree, which would direct that the witnesses were to be examined 'super interrogatoriis Comissioni annectandis vel in partibus minis andis' (*Evans and others* v. *Rowe* (*Lloid intervening*) (1614), DEL 4/6/237). It seems that the latter course was usually followed, as witnesses who were examined *in partibus* were not produced before the Delegates in London; thus their identity was not known until the commission began to sit and not until then, in most cases, was it possible to frame 'apt and fitting interrogatories' (*F.E.L.*, CXVI/5/3/vi).

[2] e.g. *Savile* v. *Savile* (1739), DEL 2/78; the cover of the interrogatories administered to a witness produced on behalf of the appellant is endorsed 'not to be opened untill he shall have undergone his Examination on behalf of the said Dame Mary Savile by Vertue of the Commission annexed and to be certifyed accordingly.'

[3] e.g. *Banks and others* v. *Finch and others* (1712), DEL 2/9.

[4] e.g. *Forrest* v. *Wilson* (*Reid intervening*) (1768), DEL 2/28. A commission *ad partes* was decreed for the examination of witnesses in Scotland on behalf of the intervener. After the commissioners had begun to sit, the representative of the appellant declared that according to the universal practice in that kingdom, the party adverse to the party producent could be present when the witnesses were examined and had 'a right to cross interrogate the Witnesses for the discovery of Truth'. He proposed that this 'fair open and customary method of Examination' should be used, but after a protest from the other side that the procedure followed by the English civilian courts must be adhered to, the appellant's representative was refused the right to be present during the cross-examination and written interrogatories were administered in the usual way. (The significance of this example may be affected by the fact that the requisition was executed within the United Kingdom; it may have been difficult for the Court of Delegates to insist on the acceptance of its own rules of procedure if witnesses in causes before that tribunal were examined in a foreign country, where the method of taking evidence in civilian courts was different.)

[5] e.g. *Watkins* v. *Nendick* (1802), DEL 2/92; the witness was to be reminded of the oath he had taken and of the danger of perjury. He was to be required to answer fully, without reference to his depositions in chief or to answers given to other interrogatories.

[6] Some of the information as to character obtained in this way was somewhat imprecise; e.g. *Hill* v. *Webb* (1706), DEL 2/36 (Elizabeth Palmer, when asked

been requested to give evidence, what benefit (financial or otherwise) he expected to receive from giving it,[1] whether he had been instructed by the producent what he should say, where he had lived for a period of several years, what he was worth his debts paid and how long he had known the party producing him.[2] He might also be asked which side he wished to win.[3]

Questions which recurred somewhat less frequently related to religion and politics. Thus the conformity of a witness to the Established Church might be investigated, and he might be asked when he had last attended a service or received the Sacrament according to the rite prescribed in the Book of Common Prayer.[4] Interrogatories might also seek to establish that a witness was a Dissenter,[5] a Roman Catholic[6] or without religious belief of any sort.[7] His political views might be the subject of a similar scrutiny.[8]

what character was had by John Grant, another witness replied 'that she hath heard that he is reputed not to bee soe good as he should bee, but she does not charge him with any particular crime').

[1] The subornation of witnesses is a matter frequently touched upon in evidence. In *the Countess of Inchequin* v. *Lord Howard* (1699), DEL 8/78, Elizabeth Beckett quoted the statement of a fellow witness: 'There was mony enough to be gott on either side, for the Lawyers were so cunning, the Suit would never bee ended'. Beckett also claimed to have been told that the respondent had promised twenty pounds to one Francis Batty, if the latter would swear for him and find others to do the like.

[2] See the interrogatories in *Walker and Walker* v. *Walker and Walker* (n.d.), DEL 2/90, *Weedon* v. *Weedon* (n.d.), DEL 2/91, and *Yeoman* v. *Banbury* (1708), DEL 2/104, from which these examples of typical common form questions are taken.

[3] This question usually provoked the 'correct' response that the witness favoured both parties alike; e.g. the judicious answer of John Moland in *Marshe* v. *the Bishop of Dromore and others* (1715), DEL 2/55, that 'this respondent favours all the said parties alike, and were it in his power to decide or give the victory in this cause, he would after hearing what both parties have to say give the victory to such of them as should then appear to him this respondent to have the best right'.

[4] e.g. *Emerton* v. *Hyde* (1676), DEL 8/83/1. Questions of this sort could sometimes cause embarrassment; William Joyce, to whom this enquiry was put in *Hill* v. *Webb* (1706), DEL 2/36, caused the following rider to be added to his depositions: 'Hee adds that he goes constantly to Church, but never received the Sacrament which he speedily intends God willing to doe'.

[5] e.g. *Desborow* v. *Desborow* (1677), DEL 8/83/1; each witness was asked if he were an Anabaptist.

[6] e.g. *Harris* v. *Twittey* (1696), DEL 2/37.

[7] e.g. *Haswell* v. *Dodgshon* (1731), DEL 2/37; an objection was made to a witness that she had no 'due sense of Religion and a future State'.

[8] e.g. *Rhodes and others* v. *Rhodes and others* (1723), DEL 2/72; Ann Clayton was asked whether she acknowledged King George and whether she would take an oath to abjure the Pretender.

As well as questions which recurred often enough to be properly described as being in common form, the interrogatories might also, of course, contain detailed enquiries which related to the particular facts of the cause in which they occurred.[1]

In most cases, the party ministrant was content with one set of interrogatories, but if for some reason this was insufficient, others might be tendered, each set being distinguished from the rest by a numerical title as *primo loco*, *secundo loco* and so on.[2] The purpose of these repeated sets is not entirely clear. They can hardly have been intended to elicit further information from a witness when his original answers were felt to be incomplete, as the practice of examining witnesses in secret meant that their evidence was not known until publication;[3] moreover, it appears from *Evan* v. *Molesworthe* (*in the principal cause*)[4] that the insufficiency of the witnesses' answers to the original interrogatories could be mended by the decreeing of fuller answers, which were apparently analogous to the *pleniora et planiora responsa* demanded of a principal party.[5] The evidence of the Delegates' records suggests that in many cases the reason for administering interrogatories in this form was merely to divide them into manageable segments. The party ministrant might wish to address common form questions to all or most of the witnesses and in addition certain particular questions to some of them; in such a case, the interrogatories *primo loco* might be in common form, and administered to all, while those *secundo loco*, *tertio loco* and so on might each be addressed to a single witness.[6]

[1] *F.E.L.*, CIX/2.

[2] There seems to have been no limit to the number of sets which a party could administer; in *Baker* v. *Hand* (1702), DEL 2/110/1, one of the parties administered interrogatories 25° *loco*. See also *H.C.C.*, p. 205.

[3] Additional interrogatories in the Court of Chivalry have been explained in this way (*H.C.C.*, pp. 204–5), but the practice of that tribunal permitted the examination of witnesses by the legal representatives of the parties, so that the witnesses' answers were known as soon as they were given. The matter is nowhere discussed in *F.E.L.*

[4] (1611), DEL 4/5/62.

[5] For these, see p. 104 *ante*.

[6] The operation of the principle is neatly illustrated by interrogatories drafted for the respondent in *Purcell and Purcell* v. *Purcell* (1725), DEL 2/60. There were six sets in all, of which the first was apparently administered to all the witnesses produced by the appellants, while each of the remaining five was directed to an individual witness and was intended to obtain detailed information about certain matters mentioned in the first and third articles of the allegation upon which they had been produced.

An alternative procedure was to draw up a single set of interrogatories; when

The administration of interrogatories was a frequent occurrence, although the adverse party was, of course, under no obligation to tender them. The practice was, however, viewed with doubtful favour by text-book writers who drew attention, in general terms, to the dangers it involved;[1] several of these are illustrated by the records of the court and require discussion.

Interrogatories, as has been seen, often tended to impugn the reputation of witnesses, and if they were directed too pointedly against character, the party ministrant might find himself open to proceedings for defamation. Thus the cause of *Allen* v. *Steward*[2] was an appeal in an action of this nature brought by Anna Steward against Henry Allen because of 'nonnulla verba convitiosa opprobriosa vituperiosa scandalosa et diffamatoria' inserted in interrogatories for which Allen was responsible, which had been administered in a cause before the High Commission.[3]

There was also the risk that tactlessly drawn interrogatories would irritate the witness to whom they were addressed, especially when the draftsman failed to adjust them to the character of the witness and the nature of the information it was desired to elicit. The problem arose in *Dalrymple* v. *Dalrymple*,[4] where evidence was taken by requisition in Edinburgh concerning a point of Scots law and some interrogatories couched in rather peremptory language were addressed to several distinguished Scottish advocates. One of them, David Hume, concluded his answers by remarking that 'although he has answered the Additional, and further Additional Interrogatories, out of Deference for the Counsel whose Names appear at them, yet, still he cannot but consider them as being of an unusual, and an exceptionable Tenor and Style, and such as is fitter for the Detection of a Witness who is suspected of Perjury on a Matter of Fact, than of a Lawyer called to give a professional Opinion'. Another witness spoke of being

it was desired to administer a particular interrogatory to one witness only, his name would be incorporated in it; e.g. *Britland* v. *Carte* (1735), DEL 2/11.

[1] Thus Law speaks of the need for 'caution and skill' in drafting them, and adds a warning that 'for the most part interrogatories rather do good than injury to the party who produced the witnesses; and the contrary' (*F.E.L.*, CIX/6).

[2] (1641), DEL 5/12/67.

[3] This makes clear that in ecclesiastical courts the defence of privilege was not available in defamation actions brought for words used in judicial proceedings. The position in the Court of Chivalry was the same; see *H.C.C.*, p. 169 and causes there cited.

[4] (1809), DEL 7/4/341.

'teased and insulted' by the interrogatories and refused to make any answer to them.[1]

As well as harming the party ministrant, interrogatories might on occasions cause general inconvenience, especially when they were administered at great length. Thus in *Purcell and Purcell* v. *Purcell*[2] the appellants' witnesses were to be examined by commission at Stafford, but the proctor's substitute complained to the court that so much time was consumed by the interrogatories of the respondent that the period assigned for the commission had expired before all the depositions could be taken.

When the examination of a witness was completed,[3] his written depositions were read over to him and he would acknowledge them as correct,[4] after any necessary alterations had been made.[5] He would then sign the depositions, which were counter-signed by those of the commissioners who attended his examination and also by the registrar assumed.[6]

A witness may have refused to attend before the commissioners, in which case his appearance could be enforced by means of a compulsory, a decree analogous to the *subpoena* of the Court of Chancery. Such a decree could be issued by the commissioners themselves, by virtue of the authority delegated to them by the court,[7] but to ensure speedy execution it might be decreed by the Delegates themselves at the same time as the commission, against

[1] *Dalrymple* v. *Dalrymple* (1809), DEL 7/4/344. [2] (1725), DEL 2/60.

[3] This examination was confined to questions put on behalf of the party producent (based on his pleadings) and the interrogatories administered on behalf of the adverse party. The civil law did not allow re-examination of a witness by the party producent after the interrogatories had been answered (and since the entire proceedings were conducted in secret, re-examination as practised at common law would scarcely have been feasible). See *First Report of the Royal Commission on the Law of Divorce* (1853), Q. 91 (evidence of Dr Lushington) cited in *H.C.C.*, p. 205.

[4] Like the examination, this repetition was in private; e.g. *Bowes* v. *Lady Strathmore* (1790), DEL 2/12 (the commissioners' acts state that the repetition was made 'separately secretly and diligently' in the presence of the commissioners and the registrar assumed).

[5] e.g. *Barber* v. *Merriweather* (1668), DEL 2/106/2.

[6] Subscription by the witness might be omitted entirely in an appropriate case; e.g. *the Countess of Inchequin* v. *Lord Howard* (1699), DEL 8/78 (the commissioners appended to the depositions of Thomas Rugeley, a man aged over 80, a note that 'Antedictus Thomas Rugeley testis calamum contrectare et nomen et cognomen suum subscribere (uti dicit, et Nobis veresimile est) non potest').

[7] *F.E.L.*, CXIV/12/2/i. For an example, see *Stephens* v. *Ford* (1683), DEL 8/31/2; the decree issued in the name of the commissioners and was signed by their registrar assumed.

any witness who, it was thought, was likely to prove recalcitrant.[1] Alternatively, the commissioners might merely declare the witness contumacious, and reserve further proceedings against him for the court;[2] in such a case, he might later be required to attend for examination in London.[3]

The procedure for examining witnesses by commission which has been described above was followed when (as was usual) there was no disagreement between the commissioners about the conduct of proceedings.[4] If a dispute did arise, there seems to have been no settled method of dealing with it. Sometimes the decision of the majority was followed, as in *Duck* v. *Grey*,[5] where an objection was made to the admission of one witness on the ground that she had been excommunicated at an earlier stage of the cause (and thus had no *locus standi in judicio*). Two of the commissioners sitting at the time considered that proceedings should continue despite this impediment, while the third supported the protest; this was overruled, however, and the witness duly admitted.

On other occasions, however, the commissioners were divided by a protest into two hostile groups, and each group acted differently. Such a division occured in *Read* v. *Read*,[6] where a commission had been granted for the examination of witnesses produced by the appellant and an objection was lodged against one witness on the ground that she was the appellant's daughter. Four of the commissioners refused to admit her and suggested that the question of her admissibility should be referred to the court in London, while three were of opinion that she should be examined immediately but that her evidence should not be published until

[1] *F.E.L.*, CXIV/12/2/ii; e.g. *Heber and others* v. *Marlow and partners* (1708), DEL 2/36 (a compulsory was decreed against three named witnesses and attached to the commission). Compulsories might be issued both by the Delegates and by the commissioners; e.g. *Shaw* v. *Brathwaite and others* (1731), DEL 2/76.

[2] e.g. *Fitton* v. *Broughton* (1608), DEL 4/4/247 & 252; the reluctant witness was later excommunicated.

[3] e.g. *Silver* v. *Gaye and Ablett* (*Bachiler intervening*) (1618), DEL 4/7/220.

[4] The commissioners (as has been seen) were almost always persons without legal training or experience. It seems reasonable to assume that in their execution of a commission they were usually advised by their registrar or by the substitutes of the proctors in the cause. The substitutes were sometimes provided with guidance by the proctor appointing them; e.g. *Masters* v. *Masters* (1741), DEL 2/54 (one of the proctors in the cause sent a letter, containing a detailed account of the procedure to be followed, to the person representing him before the commissioners).

[5] (1681), DEL 2/106/2.

[6] (1667), DEL 2/111/1.

the court had heard legal argument on her standing as a witness. She was sworn and later examined by the members of the latter group while the others, after a formal protest, withdrew and (it seems) refused to sign the usual certificate.

In *Holdsworth* v. *Burwell*[1] a sensible compromise was reached; conditional admission of two witnesses was agreed to by the commissioners, but it was directed that their evidence should not be published 'nisi habita prius informatione'.

When all the witnesses had been examined, the documents which attested the due execution of the commission could be drawn up. For this purpose, it was necessary to draft the formal acts of the commission, containing a full account of proceedings. These were written on paper[2] and in Latin until 1733,[3] and contained a precise statement of each day's activities.[4] To this was added a certificate which served as a formal confirmation that all the documents were being transmitted to the court; this was signed by the commissioners who had taken part and was often sealed with an official seal.[5]

Following the certificate of the commissioners would come that of the registrar assumed and this was usually the last of the formal documents produced in the course of executing a commission.

[1] (1664), DEL 2/113/1.

[2] Occasionally parchment was employed; e.g. *Dodshon* v. *Dodshon* (1671), DEL 2/111/2.

[3] Until that date, Latin was always used if the cause were ecclesiastical. If, however, the commission was issued in connection with a marine appeal, the commissioners' acts might be in English; e.g. *Heber and others* v. *Marlow and partners* (1708), DEL 2/36. The use of English in such cases is no doubt to be explained by the fact that the commissioners were usually laymen with no knowledge of Latin.

[4] If the commission had not been executed, the certificate would state the precise reason; e.g. *Greenway* v. *Bever* (1769), DEL 2/30 (a commission *ad partes* had been decreed to examine the registry of the Archdeaconry of Berkshire, and the certificate stated that it could not be executed as the registrar had locked the registry and gone away).

[5] e.g. *Becket and others* v. *Risly* (1677), DEL 8/83/1; attached to the certificate is the seal of William Foster LL.D., Commissary and Official of the Archdeaconry of Bedfordshire. The use of seals of ecclesiastical officials to 'authenticate' documents was common (see *F.E.L.*, XLIII/2–3); commissioners' certificates and letters substitutional of proctors were often sealed in this way. The practice apparently gave a greater authority to the document than it would otherwise have had, and sometimes commissioners would explain that they had foreborne to use their own seals, as these were not sufficiently efficacious; e.g. *Bee* v. *Moor* (1667), DEL 2/111/1 (the seal of the Commissary of the Dean and Chapter of York was affixed to the certificate at the commissioners' request 'quia sigilla nostra non sunt authentica').

A typical registrar's certificate began by stating the diocese where he was born and went on to recite his appointment as a notary public, his attendance at the various stages of the commission's execution and the fact that he had committed the whole or a certain part of the proceedings to writing and had set his notarial sign to them 'in fidem ac testimonium eorundem'.[1] Below was his signature and his notarial sign.[2]

All that now remained to be done was to prepare the documents for return to London. The usual practice was to arrange the papers one on top of the other in book form and to cut a slit in the centre of the left hand margin; they were then folded vertically and the parchment commission (with a similar slit cut through the bottom of it) wrapped round them. A thin tongue of parchment was then threaded through these apertures and tied or sealed up, so that the documents and the commission were securely joined together.[3]

The bundle was sent off to London as it was, or enclosed in a paper or parchment wrapper.[4] It was usually brought into court by a proctor acting on behalf of the commissioners,[5] but sometimes their registrar was made responsible for its safe return and proceedings could be taken against him if the documents were not to hand by the due date.[6] If the commissioners themselves were to blame for delay in transmission, they might be summoned to answer articles of contempt.[7]

As soon as the process had been formally tendered, the Delegates would usually decree publication of the depositions;[8] they would

[1] e.g. *Pollexfen* v. *Kingston* (1671), DEL 2/111/1.

[2] For notarial signs, see *H.C.C.*, p. 205.

[3] The various documents which comprised the commissioners' process were often separated later, before they were filed in the archives of the court, but a certain number have survived intact; *Parsons* v. *Parsons* (1689), DEL 2/60 and *Wynn* v. *Webster* (1707), DEL 2/95 are typical examples. Sometimes the record of execution took a more idiosyncratic form; e.g. *Rea and Mason* v. *Munsell and Colls* (1693), DEL 2/116/1 (the entire proceedings were written on strips of parchment sewn together in the form of a roll).

[4] e.g. *Purcell and Purcell* v. *Purcell* (1724), DEL 2/60; *Plowden* v. *Paxton and others* (1743), DEL 2/65.

[5] e.g. *Harrison* v. *Lord Reay* (1635), DEL 4/15/65.

[6] e.g. *Harrys and others* v. *Wogan* (1611), DEL 4/5/159; the Delegates ordered the arrest of the registrar when the process was not tendered on the appointed day.

[7] e.g. *Astill* v. *Bickles* (*in the principal cause*) (1601), DEL 4/2/45. It was not usual, in such cases, to decree excommunication (*F.E.L.*, XLIX).

[8] They might, however, be later suppressed if there was found to be some irregularity in the manner of obtaining them; e.g. *Jefford* v. *Winter* (1633),

also order that copies be made for each of the parties;[1] if for some cause copies could not be provided within a reasonable time, the proctors might be given an opportunity to examine the originals.[2] If it was necessary to examine any part of the process before publication, an *apertura* might be ordered for this purpose.[3]

The costs of executing a commission were taxed by the court when the process was presented or at one of the later sessions. It seems to have been customary to follow a rule of apportionment, the party producent being required to pay for the costs of examining witnesses on his pleadings, while the adverse party was charged with the expenses of administering his interrogatories.[4] The execution of commissions could be expensive, especially if they were sped in a distant part of the country or involved the examination of many witnesses.[5] These costs, like others taxed by the court, could be paid by instalments if they were heavy.[6]

If the commission was not executed through the fault of the party on whose behalf it was decreed (if, for example, insufficient notice of the hours of expedition was given to the adverse party), the court might award costs of retarded process to the latter.[7]

DEL 4/14/74 & 78 (the Delegates rejected the first article of an allegation tendered by the appellant but later mistakenly authorized a commission to examine witnesses upon that article).

[1] e.g. *Metcalf* v. *Bishopp* (1601), DEL 4/2/44. It was only when these copies were available that the parties would know what evidence the witnesses had given.

[2] e.g. *Frampton* v. *Frampton* (*in review*) (1601), DEL 4/2/49.

[3] e.g. *Morden* v. *Nicholls* (1610), DEL 4/5/25. After return of the process, the respondent's proctor complained that a number of witnesses had failed to undergo examination before the commissioners, who had reserved punishment for the court. The Delegates then decreed an *apertura* in order to inspect the acts of the commission.

[4] e.g. *Baxter* v. *Egmore* (1614), DEL 4/6/208; the examination of witnesses was taxed at £3. 6*s*. 8*d*. and the administration of interrogatories at £2.

[5] There survives among the cause papers in *the Countess of Inchequin* v. *Lord Howard* (1700), DEL 2/105/1, a bill which was put in for costs incurred during the execution of a commission at Stafford in April 1699. The charges were claimed for travelling expenses and other costs when thirty witnesses were examined over a long period; the total of the bill was £40. 11*s*. 6*d*.

[6] e.g. *Walton* v. *Peard* (1606), DEL 4/3/228; the bill was taxed at £19 on 6 November 1606, and the court directed that half the sum was to be paid before the Feast of the Epiphany and the balance before the Feast of the Purification. For payment of costs by instalments, see also p. 166 *post*.

[7] e.g. *Warner* v. *Wentworth* (1637), DEL 4/15/181 & 207. A commission was decreed for the respondent but the appellant complained to the court that, although he had attended with two commissioners and a substitute proctor on all the three days appointed for its expedition at the church where the commis-

If it proved impossible to execute the commission, a renewal could be applied for;[1] this would be granted by the court if good cause were shown. The reasons usually advanced had to do with the physical difficulties involved in taking the necessary documents to the place where the commissioners were to sit,[2] or in executing the commission in the face of plague,[3] bad weather,[4] the obstructive tactics of the adverse party[5] or the like.

The usual reason for decreeing a commission *ad partes* was the examination of witnesses and it is in this context that the procedure employed to execute such commissions has been discussed. They were, however, a versatile device, and almost any judicial act which the court itself could perform might be entrusted to commissioners if the need arose. Examples are to be found in the records of the Delegates of commissions to administer an oath,[6] to take bonds,[7] to appraise property[8] and to view dilapidations.[9] The examination of documents by a commission *pro scrutinio* was also common.[10]

Most of the witnesses whose evidence was required before the Court of Delegates were within the jurisdiction of that tribunal, but causes were sometimes heard for which the evidence of persons

sion was to sit, the respondent had taken no steps to expedite it, nor had he informed the appellant and his party of his intention not to do so, although he must have been aware of their presence as his house adjoined the churchyard 'soe as it could not be butt notice was taken by him and his houshold of their such attendaunce'. The court later allowed the appellant £6. 13*s*. 4*d*. as costs of retarded process.

[1] *F.E.L.*, CXIX.

[2] e.g. *Snellinge* v. *Esmond and Pagett* (1634), DEL 4/14/146; the commission was to be executed in Ireland but the boat carrying the documents was delayed and did not arrive until after the date fixed for expedition.

[3] e.g. *Hill* v. *Haselwood and Hill* (1604), DEL 4/2/320.

[4] e.g. *Matthewe* v. *Spurlinge* (*Blundell intervening in the principal cause*) (1620), DEL 4/8/213.

[5] e.g. *Cooke* v. *Stokes* (1619), DEL 4/8/50; a commissioner nominated by the appellant had begun to act, but had later been prevailed upon by the other side to withdraw, so that the appellant was represented by fewer commissioners than he was entitled to.

[6] e.g. *Alder* v. *Alder* (1613), DEL 4/6/55.

[7] e.g. *Heseltine* v. *Waller* (1794), DEL 2/36.

[8] e.g. *Keene* v. *Madden and others* (1726), DEL 2/48.

[9] e.g. *the Bishop of Carlisle* v. *the Archbishop of York* (1671), DEL 2/111/2. Commissions of this sort, which needed expert knowledge for their execution, required the appointment of commissioners suitably qualified; e.g. *the Archbishop of York* v. *the Bishop of Durham and others* (1633), DEL 4/14/137 (a commission for the examination of Durham House in the Strand was issued to masons, bricklayers, carpenters and plumbers).

[10] For such commissions, see pp. 157–8 *post*.

living abroad was needed.[1] In such a case, the court would decree a commission *ob mutuae vicissitudinis obtentu*[2] addressed to persons exercising judicial authority in the foreign country concerned and requesting their assistance.[3] Commissions of this sort were not infrequently decreed by the Delegates for execution in distant parts of the world;[4] indeed, had not ready co-operation been offered by foreign jurisdictions in this way, the conduct of many causes would have been frustrated.[5] On rare occasions, one of the court's examiners would be sent abroad to assist in the execution of requisitions,[6] and it is possible that examiners sometimes acted as commissioners in foreign countries;[7] it is clear from the evidence given before the Ecclesiastical Commissioners in 1832 that examiners in some of the ecclesiastical courts could act alone overseas without the need for any requisition.[8]

The decree was in substance the same as those issued for execution within the jurisdiction, but with those differences which were made necessary by the fact of execution abroad. It was usually

[1] This was especially true of marine causes, although evidence in testamentary and matrimonial causes was sometimes taken abroad.

[2] Such commissions were often referred to by the rather less cumbrous title of 'requisition' (e.g. *Harrison* v. *Hartley* (1818), DEL 2/35; *F.E.L.*, CI/8/1) or *litterae requisitoriales* (e.g. *Lambell* v. *Lambell and Lambell* (1648), DEL 4/19/72). For an example, see App. XIV.

[3] Such decrees were based on the proposition that different jurisdictions should support each others' authority and provide such assistance as this for each other upon a reciprocal basis (*F.E.L.*, CXX/2).

[4] Among the examples noted in the records are commissions to Spain (*Baker* v. *Foster* (1606), DEL 4/3/212); South America (*Lopes da Rosa and others* v. *Lusitano de Pinna* (1737), DEL 2/69); Berlin (*Segond* v. *Bonnard du Marest and others* (1729), DEL 2/79; Madras (*Ennis* v. *Egan and Egan* (1743), DEL 6/41/101).

[5] The point may be illustrated by causes such as *the Earl of Exeter* v. *Lady Roos* (*in the principal cause*) (1619), DEL 4/8/69; commissions were issued to examine witnesses in Flanders, Italy and Spain, examinations which would otherwise scarcely have been possible at all, or possible only at great cost.

[6] e.g. *Brisco* v. *Brisco* (1815), DEL 7/11/185–98 & 248; a requisition was issued to the British Ambassador in Sweden and Charles Bowdler, an examiner of the Delegates, acted as actuary when the witness was examined at Stockholm.

[7] In *Blackett* v. *Rollo* (1787), DEL 8/73/pt. 3/57, when proceedings were taking place before a court in the province of York, a commission was decreed for execution at Nancy in Lorraine by foreign magistrates or by 'any other competent person or persons' and one of the proctors in the cause spoke of procuring 'a proper person from Doctors Commons London as Examiner to see the Execution of the Requisition already decreed'.

[8] *Eccl. Courts Rep.* (1831–2), p. 41. The use of all these expedients was probably confined to cases where there was some doubt about the competence of foreign magistrates or their willingness to act.

addressed specifically to persons exercising judicial office,[1] or to authorities who might be expected to exercise such office;[2] there was sometimes a restriction to judges with particular qualifications.[3] The use of laymen was unusual,[4] although commissions were sometimes directed to British diplomatists serving abroad.[5] Only those persons appointed were entitled to act, and if it became necessary to change the place originally assigned for execution, a new commission would have to be decreed to other judges.[6]

The commissioners were usually directed to sit in their accustomed place of judgment;[7] as was the case with commissions *ad partes*, the presence of at least two of them was required at each sitting.[8] A longer period was naturally allowed for execution than the three or four days usually assigned for the completion of commissions *ad partes*,[9] and the transmission of process from

[1] e.g. *Banks* v. *Holhead* (1703), DEL 2/9; the commission was directed to 'Jusdicentibus...Magistratibus Civitatis Amstelodami et Judicibus ad Causas Civiles et Criminales'. Cf. commissions *ad partes* which were usually addressed to laymen.

[2] e.g. *Gull and partners* v. *Western and partners* (1712), DEL 2/32; the commission was addressed to 'Proconsules et Senatores Civitatis Hamburgensis'.

[3] e.g. *Nevell* v. *Nevell* (*in the principal cause*) (1611), DEL 4/5/155; the execution of a commission at Brielle, Utrecht, the Hague and Flushing was entrusted to persons 'jurisdictionem ecclesiasticam in huiusmodi locis respective exercentibus', while in *Gobyne* v. *LeMayre* (1619), DEL 4/8/9, witnesses in a testamentary cause were to be examined in Italy by judges 'jusdicentes in negociis testamentariis'.

[4] The court might refuse to appoint laymen if judges were likely to be available; e.g. *Nevell* v. *Nevell* (1611), DEL 4/5/153 (the petitioning proctor asked for three named laymen to be appointed but the court did not consent).

[5] e.g. *Brisco* v. *Brisco* (1815), DEL 7/11/184–98; in the course of proceedings before the Court of Arches a witness was examined before the British Ambassador to the Swedish Court.

[6] e.g. *Wye* v. *Du Brevil and partners* (1716), DEL 2/111/3; a commission was decreed to the magistrates of Middleburg in Zeeland but when it was later found necessary to examine some of the witnesses in Amsterdam a new decree was applied for, addressed to the magistrates of the latter city.

[7] e.g. *Banks* v. *Holhead*, *supra*; hearings were to take place 'in loco Praetoriali Tribunali sive Judiciali dictae Civitatis Amstelodami'. Sometimes the venue might be more precisely specified; e.g. *the Earl of Exeter* v. *Lady Roos* (*in the principal cause*) (1619), DEL 4/8/75 (the witnesses in a testamentary cause were to be examined 'in loco Judiciali in dicta Civitate Neapolitana vocato La Vicaria').

[8] However, the consent of the parties would presumably validate proceedings before only one commissioner; see *F.E.L.*, CXI/3/1/i–ii (at p. 230) and causes such as *Harrison* v. *Hartley* (1818), DEL 2/35, where the commissioners were permitted to act 'jointly and severally'.

[9] e.g. *De Olavaga* v. *Philipps* (1655), DEL 6/6/48; the court decreed that an examination at St Sebastian in Spain was to take place at any time during the period of three whole months from the date of the decree.

foreign parts when the commission had been executed was subject to the same liberality.[1] The commissioners were instructed to choose their own registrar locally, the usual qualification being that he should be 'fidedignus' or 'partibus indifferenter favens'.[2] The commission would also contain such other mandatory or permissive clauses as were necessary.[3]

There was always a danger that such commissions might be entrusted for execution to persons with only an imperfect knowledge of English civilian procedure;[4] an attempt was sometimes made to overcome this difficulty by annexing to the commission a document explaining to those to whom it was addressed the precise way in which they should proceed, in order to satisfy the requirements of the civil law as administered in England.[5] An examination of the requisitions still surviving in the archives of the court suggests that they were for the most part executed with a due regard for these requirements.

The execution of these requisitions differed not at all (*mutatis mutandis*) from the execution of commissions *ad partes* within the court's jurisdiction. They were often attended, however, by difficulties which were peculiar to the conduct of proceedings abroad, and which resulted in many cases either from the jealousy with which foreign governments regarded such requisitions or from the ease with which they could be obstructed in places where the Delegates' authority could offer no protection. Thus the consent of the foreign government within whose jurisdiction the witnesses were to be examined might have to be obtained,[6] or various other

[1] e.g. *Lopes da Rosa and others* v. *Lusitano de Pinna and others* (1737), DEL 2/69; a commission which was to be executed in South America was issued on 4 March 1737 and was to be returned before the first session of the Trinity term 1739.

[2] e.g. *Banks* v. *Holhead* (1703), DEL 2/9.

[3] e.g. *Harford* v. *Morris* (1782), DEL 2/40 (power to appoint an interpreter); *Banks* v. *Holhead, supra* (notice of proceedings to be given to the adverse party).

[4] e.g. *Henrick* v. *Derrick* (*in the principal cause*) (1614), DEL 4/6/232; it was alleged that the witnesses examined by requisition had not been questioned in secret but in each others' presence and that the interrogatories annexed to the commission had not been administered at all.

[5] e.g. the instructions for the execution (at Rotterdam) of the requisition decreed by the Court of Admiralty in *Sutherland* v. *Corbett* (n.d.), DEL 8/79.

[6] e.g. *Blackett* v. *Rollo* (1788), DEL 2/12; the respondent who proposed to produce certain witnesses at Nancy in Lorraine found herself obliged to petition the Parliament at Nancy and obtain a decree of that Parliament permitting execution.

formal requirements satisfied before proceedings could begin.[1] The despatch of the necessary documents to a distant part of the world was not always easy,[2] and even the task of translating them into the local tongue might hinder proceedings.[3]

There might, in addition, be difficulties of a more sinister character. Those who were charged with the execution of a requisition could not be protected, as in England, by the direct imposition of the court's authority and the adverse party would sometimes have means of intereference to which he could not have had recourse if proceedings had taken place within the jurisdiction. A striking instance occurred in *Lady Grosvenor* v. *Fenwick*[4] where, in an earlier stage of the cause, the respondent attempted to secure the execution of two requisitions (one from Chancery and the other from the Dean and Chapter of Westminster) at Paris. An agent of the appellant caused Fenwick to be imprisoned and later, when some of the commissioners were sitting, had them haled before the Lieutenant Criminall at Paris, who forbad them to continue. When a companion of the respondent proposed to return to England in order to acquaint the authorities there with this state of affairs, the appellant's agent obtained an order from the French Court at Versailles to apprehend him, but he succeeded in escaping, and when the appellant's agent himself returned to London he was imprisoned at the order of the Lord Keeper.

A problem of the same order was the venality with which justice was administered in some foreign countries. Thus in *Wye* v. *Du Brevil and partners*[5] an agent of the appellant at Amsterdam

[1] e.g. *Lopes da Rosa and others* v. *Lusitano de Pinna and others* (1735), DEL 2/69; a requisition was decreed for execution in the Brazils, but under Portuguese law the commission itself and all the documents annexed to it had first to be translated into Portuguese, attested by a suitable authority and examined by the Court of India and the Mines before execution could begin.

[2] e.g. *Lopes da Rosa and others* v. *Lusitano de Pinna and others*, *supra*; the original requisition decreed by the court had first to pass through Lisbon, in order to catch the Bahia Fleet for Portuguese America, but as the ship in which it had been sent from London did not arrive at Lisbon in time, the requisition had to be returned to London and a new one decreed.

[3] e.g. *Stacie* v. *Rich and Gray* (1741), DEL 2/80. A requisition for the examination of witnesses at Brest was returned to London unexecuted, accompanied by a letter from the Parisian correspondent of the gentleman who had attempted to obtain its execution. It had proved necessary, as the letter explained, to abandon the task 'there being but two very bad translators in that country, who had ask't a months time to do it & ten Pistoles for their trouble'.

[4] (1703), DEL 2/31.

[5] (1716), DEL 2/111/3.

was given the task of obtaining from the clerks of the Admiralty there some papers which his principal needed for the examination of witnesses in that city; he soon found that he had occasion to write to another interested party of his fear that 'the Clerks of the Admiralty may be brib'd by the french People to keep up the papers till Doomsday'.

When proceedings were concluded, the commissioners' process was sent back to London and the depositions accepted and published in the usual way.[1] Sometimes the evidence had been taken down in Latin, but often it was in the vernacular tongue and in the latter case the court would arrange for translation into English.[2]

Almost the only use to which requisitions were put was the examination of witnesses about the facts of a cause, but like commissions *ad partes* they could sometimes serve other purposes; thus in a cause involving a foreign interest, questions of foreign law were sometimes in dispute and a requisition could be usefully employed to take expert evidence. A convenient illustration is to be found in *Harford* v. *Morris*,[3] where the respondent was alleged to have abducted the appellant (the illegitimate daughter of the Earl of Baltimore) from a boarding school in Chelsea and had gone through a ceremony of marriage with her at Ypres. One of the matters in dispute between the parties was the law by which the validity of the ceremony was to be judged, one side claiming that the marriage was governed by the laws of the Austrian Netherlands while the other insisted that the laws of Holland should apply. A commission was despatched to The Hague with a case stated and two advocates there gave their opinion.

The examination of witnesses in London involved substantially the same procedure as that required for the execution of commissions *ad partes*, but there were certain differences which need comment. The contrast between the two methods may conveniently be drawn by describing examination in London in broad outline.

[1] See pp. 139–40 *ante*.

[2] e.g. *Baker* v. *Foster* (1606), DEL 4/3/270; the process was written 'in lingua hispanica sive Lusitanica' and each side was allowed to nominate a suitably qualified person to act as translator. Sometimes the translation was made by the deputy registrar of the court; thus J. Pinfold translated a requisition in *Segond* v. *Bonnard Du Marest and others* (1730), DEL 2/79, while Ed. Rushworth performed the same task in *Stacie* v. *Rich and Gray* (1742), DEL 2/80.

[3] (1781), DEL 2/37.

If the depositions of a witness were to be taken at Doctors' Commons, he would be presented to the court by the proctor of the party proposing to rely upon his evidence.[1] When he had been formally received by the judges present,[2] they would administer the oath;[3] he would then be monished to undergo examination before the next court day. Witnesses were usually produced generally, that is, they were examined on all the pleading of the party producent, but they might be admitted *sub limitacione*, in which case their examination was limited in accordance with the court's direction.[4]

If a witness was challenged by the adverse party certain restrictions might be imposed upon the use of his evidence,[5] or he might be rejected *in toto* if the court was satisfied that his depositions would be inadmissible.[6] If they thought fit, the Delegates might limit the number of witnesses to be called.[7]

[1] e.g. *Murfett* v. *Tayler* (1604), DEL 4/2/232.

[2] As it was impossible for persons excommunicate to perform any legal act (*F.E.L.*, XXVI/1/3), the witness would be absolved by the court before being sworn, if he was unreconciled to the Church; e.g. *Wilson* v. *Piggott* (1618), DEL 4/7/157.

[3] The law relating to these oaths took on its modern form in the nineteenth century and before that time the only witnesses excused from taking the oath were Quakers, who were allowed instead to make a solemn affirmation (A. R. N. Cross, *Evidence* (London, 1963), p. 143). The precise date of this concession seems uncertain, but what is apparently one example of it has been found among the Delegates' records as early as 1736, for in *Blunt and others* v. *Walmsley* (1736), DEL 6/39/131, several witnesses were produced and they were all sworn in the usual way, except one Benjamin Godfrey 'who solemnly affirmed'.

[4] e.g. *Kippax* v. *Bradshawe* (1620), DEL 4/8/118; the court ordered that two witnesses were to be examined only in connection with a nuncupative will which was in dispute and only upon the second and eighth articles of the party producent's pleading.

[5] e.g. *Sunderland* v. *Conyers* (*in the principal cause*) (1620), DEL 4/8/220. The respondent's proctor produced a number of witnesses, among whom was a man to whom the appellant's proctor at once took objection on the ground that he had previously acted as a legal adviser of the respondent; the court received him on the condition that his depositions were not to be published 'nisi quatenus fuerint de jure recipiendae'.

[6] e.g. *Jervis* v. *Fuller* (*in the principal cause*) (1618), DEL 4/7/184; this was a testamentary cause in which the appellant's proctor produced two witnesses whom the court refused to admit, after the respondent's proctor had pointed out that one was the executor of the will in dispute and the other was the executor's mother.

[7] e.g. *Croker* v. *Yates and others* (1604), DEL 4/2/294; both sides were limited to four witnesses each. This cause suggests the existence of a discretion in the court, but this discretion seems very rarely to have been exercised against parties seeking to produce witnesses.

Witnesses were entitled to travelling expenses and other costs incurred in giving evidence.[1] These would either be agreed between the witnesses and the party on whose behalf they were to appear, or taxed by the court at the time of production;[2] in the latter case, witnesses might apply personally to the court for expenses or be represented by a proctor.[3] Unless a party had offered expenses to a witness, he could not obtain a compulsory against him.[4] It seems that expenses could be claimed only if the sole purpose of the journey to London was to give evidence.[5]

Within the time appointed by the Delegates, the witness would attend at Doctors' Commons to be examined.[6] His depositions were based upon the pleading of the party producent and the interrogatories of the adverse party, and the method of taking his evidence was the same as that employed before commissioners *ad partes*.[7] The examination was conducted by an examiner, an official of the court and the depositions were later repeated before any two or more of the judges who were sitting on the relevant commission.[8] The task of hearing repetitions was often shared among the judges on a commission,[9] and although it was normally

[1] These were known as *viatica* (*F.E.L.*, CIV/1/2).

[2] e.g. *Hill* v. *Haselwood and Hill* (1604), DEL 4/2/320; a witness applied to the court for expenses and was allowed 3*s*. 4*d*. which was to be paid to him at the time of his examination.

[3] e.g. *Watson* v. *Watson* (1614), DEL 4/6/263.

[4] *F.E.L.*, CV/3. The formula of application for a compulsory always stated that expenses had been tendered; e.g. *Haywood* v. *Light* (*in the principal cause*) (1617), DEL 4/7/96. See App. XI for an example.

[5] e.g. *Francis* v. *White* (1610), DEL 4/5/20; a witness claimed expenses but his application was contested on the ground that he had made the journey with the additional purpose of obtaining absolution from a sentence of excommunication previously decreed against him.

[6] Foreign witnesses might be provided with a sworn interpreter; e.g. *Lopes da Rosa and others* v. *Lusitano de Pinna and others* (1739), DEL 2/69 (the depositions of several Portuguese witnesses were taken down in English after being translated).

[7] See pp. 127–36 *ante*.

[8] The same rule which required that commissions *ad partes* should be executed by at least two persons (*F.E.L.*, CXI/3/1 (at p. 230)) made the presence of at least two judges necessary for the repetition of evidence taken in London. With the consent of both parties, however, one judge would suffice; e.g. *Cathcart* v. *Harvie and Steel* (1735), DEL 2/19 (an allegation upon which witnesses were examined was endorsed 'It is consented that the witnesses may be repeated before one Judge').

[9] e.g. *Took* v. *Beecher* (1702), DEL 2/85; of the three witnesses produced on the appellant's allegation, one was repeated before Oxenden and Herriot, one before Ayloffe and one before Harwood.

performed by civilians alone, others might on occasions take part.[1] The evidence would later be published in the usual way.[2] Witnesses who had refused to attend could be compelled to do so by means of a compulsory,[3] and the court had in addition a power to fine witnesses who, after being sworn, failed to undergo examination.[4]

The sole function of the examiner seems to have been to take down the witnesses' evidence in the form in which it was given; it was not his business, apparently, to elucidate obscurities in the depositions and if such obscurities were found upon publication, the witnesses might be recalled and examined afresh. Thus in *Willoughbie* v. *Willoughbie*[5] two witnesses were required to appear in open court to be examined by the judges after it had been objected that they were 'nimirum obscuros in eorum depositionibus', while in *Pope* v. *Rawe* (*Moore intervening from definitive sentence*),[6] a tithe cause where several witnesses had given ambiguous evidence 'quoad genera & qualitatem decimarum', re-examination took place not in open court but, so it seems, before the examiner.

The taking of depositions by an examiner was practicable when the witness lived in or close to London and was able to attend at Doctors' Commons for formal production and the subsequent examination. If, however, the witness, although present in London was unable to attend upon the court and the examiner, his evidence might be taken by means of a *descendendum*.[7] Upon application to the court by the proctor of the party producent, the Delegates would make the appropriate decree and one of the judges, accompanied by the deputy registrar of the court, would 'descend' upon the place where the witness was; there he would be sworn and monished to undergo examination.[8] The proctors on both sides would be present and interrogatories might be handed in on behalf of the adverse party for administration to the witness.[9]

[1] e.g. *King* v. *the Earl of Coventry* (1703), DEL 2/48; the evidence of one witness was repeated before Sir Thomas Trevor, Chief Justice of the Queen's Bench and Dr Raines.

[2] See pp. 139–40 *ante*.

[3] For these see pp. 136–7 *ante*.

[4] e.g. *Porter* v. *Towerson* (1613), DEL 4/6/126; witnesses were required to attend upon the examiner 'sub pena XL solidorum ab eorum singulis levanda'.

[5] (1617), DEL 4/7/120 & 161.

[6] (1618), DEL 4/7/205 & 223.

[7] *F.E.L.*, CXI/2/2/iv–vi.

[8] e.g. *Wheatly* v. *Hudson* (1605), DEL 4/3/25 & 29. The examination itself might be conducted then and there; e.g. *Montier and others* v. *Alesworthe* (1617), DEL 4/7/72.

[9] e.g. *Chatterton and Chatterton* v. *Cavendishe and Bruce* (1610), DEL 4/5/19.

Any valid reason which made the personal appearance of the witness impossible was a good ground for decreeing a *descendendum*. Incapacitating illness would serve,[1] as would imprisonment,[2] sequestration[3] or even the pressure of private business,[4] while persons engaged on the royal service were allowed the like concession,[5] as were expert witnesses, when the claims of their profession were too exigent to permit of their attendance in court.[6] The respect shown by the court to *egregie persone* was such that they might be accommodated by a *descendendum* even though there was no reason, other than their station, which prevented their appearance in the usual way.[7]

Witnesses in London usually gave evidence by one of the two methods which have just been described (i.e. before an examiner or by means of a *descendendum*). Occasionally, however, the court would direct that such witnesses should be examined by a commission, analogous to a commission *ad partes*. Sometimes, the reason may readily be guessed at; thus a commission might be decreed when the number of witnesses in a cause who were available for

[1] e.g. *Baker* v. *Greenewaye and Legier* (1614), DEL 4/6/257; it was said of a witness living in Westminster that 'morbo podagre laborare ut non possit ad hoc tribunal accedere'.

[2] e.g. *Wheatley* v. *Hudson* (1605), DEL 4/3/25; two witnesses were in the Comter Prison in Wood Street.

[3] i.e. the confinement of the female party during a matrimonial cause. If sequestration occurred in London, the party sequestrated could give her depositions, personal answers or the like by a *descendendum*; e.g. *Bridges* v. *Pledall* (1617), DEL 4/7/84.

[4] e.g. *Walthall and Robinson* v. *Walthall and Walthall* (1618), DEL 4/7/164; a *descendendum* was allowed to Maria Walthall on the ground that she was 'pluribus negociis adeo difficilibus & implicatis impedita quominus ad hoc judicium accedere potest'.

[5] e.g. *Finche* v. *the Countess of Southampton* (1602), DEL 4/2/159. The respondent wished to produce as witnesses the deputy Master of the Pipe Office, the Royal Auditor 'in officio vocato the Preste' and their clerks; a *descendendum* was decreed on the ground that the 'Regia negocia' in which they were engaged made their personal appearance impossible.

[6] e.g. *Clifford* v. *Clifford* (1607), DEL 4/4/95; several doctors who had been chosen to examine one of the parties complained that they had little time for the purpose. The Delegates decreed a *descendendum* for the administration of the oath 'pro fideli inspeccione facienda'.

[7] Usually only one judge was involved in a *descendendum* but if it was decreed to an *egregia persona* the court might show its respect by appointing a deputation; e.g. *the Earl of Hertford* v. *Lord Mounteagle* (1605), DEL 4/3/104 (a *descendendum* was decreed to examine the Countess of Sheffield, and the deputation (any two members to be a quorum) comprised a royal secretary, a Common Law judge, two senior civilians and the Dean of St Paul's).

examination in London was so great that the usual resources of the examiner would probably have been unable to cope with them.[1] The purpose of other commissions of this nature is more obscure; thus in *Greaves* v. *Babington*[2] the Delegates decreed, for no apparent reason, that witnesses should be examined by a commission of six gentlemen and clerks, who were to sit at the house of the Earl of Sussex in Covent Garden, while in *Muffet* v. *Fletcher*[3] depositions were taken by four Doctors of Divinity sitting as commissioners in the Consistory of St Paul's Cathedral. It is possible that the nature of the evidence or the convenience of the persons concerned dictated this departure from the usual procedure.

When necessary, the court could avail itself of expert evidence of one sort or another. A claim that documents were forged was sometimes raised, especially in testamentary causes; thus in *Franklyn and others* v. *Franklyn and others* (*in the principal cause*)[4] it was alleged that part of the will in dispute had been fabricated and the Delegates were asked to appoint 'aliquos in arte scribendi peritos' to look into the matter. The court appointed four proctors for the task, who were given an agreed example of the deceased's handwriting and asked to compare it with the will; they later rendered a written report on their findings.[5] Alternatively, the evidence of witnesses who were familiar with the handwriting of the deceased might be used.[6]

The opinion of merchants skilled in accounting might be called for when complicated questions of account rose. This point was taken by the appellants in *Staper and Leate* v. *Tite and Pate*[7] when

[1] e.g. *Staper and Leake* v. *Tite and Pate* (1613), DEL 4/6/66; a commission of four advocates was appointed to sit in London.

[2] (1647), DEL 4/18/137.

[3] (1607), DEL 4/4/2.

[4] (1602), DEL 4/2/130, 138 & 156.

[5] Expert advice of this sort was sanctioned by the civil law (*O.J.*, ccxxv/1–3 and 10–11) but its admissibility was disputed in the common law courts as late as the nineteenth century; see the conflicting judgments in *Doe d. Mudd* v. *Suckermore* (1837), 5 Ad. & El. 703. Such evidence is now admissible in those courts (Cross, *Evidence*, p. 503) and its reception may well have been influenced by the civilian practice.

[6] e.g. *Plowden* v. *Paxton and others* (1743), DEL 2/65; four witnesses, who claimed to have seen many examples of the deceased's handwriting, deposed that a will was genuine. Such evidence was accepted at common law at a time when the evidence of expert witnesses was still a subject for debate; see *Doe d. Mudd* v. *Suckermore*, *supra*, at 719–20.

[7] *supra*, at f. 76

they proposed that merchants should be appointed to examine books of account which had been tendered as evidence; this was necessary, it was declared, as the exhibits 'non facile...intelligi potest per dominos judicantes huius Curie in hac causa delegatos sine inspeccione, industria, scrutamine calculo et relacione mercatorum...peritorum'.

Marine appeals would on occasions raise technical points in which the Delegates required guidance. In accordance with the well-established practice in the Court of Admiralty, the matter might be submitted to some of the Elder Brethren of the Trinity House for their opinion.[1] Thus in *Hutton* v. *Stoker*,[2] where the litigation arose out of a collision, the complicated facts of the dispute were put to several of the Brethren, who advised that the decision of the lower court be reversed and the losses equally apportioned, as both crews were equally blameworthy; they also set a value upon one of the ships and its cargo. Experts in maritime matters other than the Elder Brethren might be consulted, as in *Gull and partners* v. *Western and partners*,[3] where the court directed that '4 skillfull Comanders of Ships be named on each Side out of four to be appointed by ye Court to attend Informations here to inform ye Court in Such Questions as may be put concerning Sailing none of those to be of ye Trinity House'. If the nature of the cause made it necessary, the qualifications of the experts might be narrowly defined; thus in *Dove and partners* v. *Masters and partners and Pute*[4] the Delegates required the assistance of two masters 'skilled in the Newcastle Trade'.

Medical evidence was sometimes required in matrimonial causes, when an examination of one or both of the parties was called for. The usual practice is well illustrated by *Muffet* v. *Fletcher*;[5] the court directed that the husband should be examined by nine persons (six to be a quorum), all of whom were doctors of medicine, and the wife by any four out of six 'honestae matronae' whose qualifications were not then more precisely stated.[6] The propriety of employing doctors for this purpose does not seem to have been called into question, but complaints were sometimes made about the 'honest matrons' and doubts might be cast both

[1] See E. Edwards, *A Treatise on the Jurisdiction of the High Court of Admiralty* (London, 1847), p. 183 and the authority there cited.

[2] (1789), DEL 8/81.

[3] (1710), DEL 6/33/18.

[4] (1698), DEL 6/28/74.

[5] (1607), DEL 4/4/1.

[6] Four of them are later described (at f. 23) as 'obstetrices'.

upon their competence and their capacity to withstand subornation. Thus in *Clifford* v. *Clifford*[1] the appellant's proctor complained that the inspection of the female party (which had been ordered by the lower court) had been made 'per personas imperitas valde partiales et affectionatas dicte Clifford mulieri et valde inimicas dicto Clifford viro'.

Some causes required the elucidation of foreign law and here it was necessary to apply to an expert in the appropriate jurisprudence. A typical example may be drawn from *Harford* v. *Morris*,[2] where one of the matters at issue was the validity of an alleged marriage which the parties had contracted within the dominions of the king of Denmark. An application was made to an advocate at Gluckstadt for his opinion, and his evidence on Danish law was taken by requisition.

As has been seen, the civil law required that witnesses should be examined privately.[3] This was a fundamental principle of civilian procedure and was regarded as an essential means of preventing certain abuses which public examination made possible. The authorities nowhere state that exceptions to this rule existed, but it is clear that there were occasions when witnesses whose evidence was required in civilian causes were examined in open court. This departure from the accustomed practice was not confined to any one tribunal, and those investigations which have recently been made into the civilian courts suggest that the right to sanction public examination was general. Thus some few examples have been found in the records of the Court of Chivalry,[4] and it has been suggested that the Court of Admiralty was always able to allow production of witnesses in this way,[5] although here again it was unusual.[6]

The records of the Court of Delegates reveal the like position; private examination was the rule but examination by the judges in open court a permissible deviation from it. Sometimes the reasons for open examination may be deduced with some certainty

[1] (1607), DEL 4/4/19.
[2] (1774), DEL 2/40.
[3] See pp. 114–15 *ante*.
[4] *H.C.C.*, p. 206.
[5] Main Thompson, *Admiralty Registrars*, p. 26.
[6] Private examination remained the rule in civilian tribunals until after the abolition of the Court of Delegates. In 1840, the Admiralty Court Act (3 & 4 Vict., c. 65, s. 7) gave that court a discretionary right to permit open examination and a similar discretion was extended to the ecclesiastical courts by the Ecclesiastical Courts Act of 1854 (17 & 18 Vict., c. 47).

from the facts of the cause. In *Milward* v. *Howe and others*,[1] for example, it was apparently permitted for convenience and to save time. The appellant had brought in certain evidence late, and the court, although unwilling to rescind conclusion because of the pressure of business, was prepared to hear as much as was necessary 'ad informandas conscientias suas'; the witnesses were at once brought in and sworn and three of the judges, sitting in two divisions, examined them.[2] Moreover, there were, it seems, certain sorts of evidence which might be regularly taken in open court; a Digest of Causes preserved among the Delegates' records refers to one such category when it cites authority for the proposition that 'witnesses may be examined Viva Voce, in regard to alimoney'.[3]

The procedural reforms of the Interregnum offer another possible example, although one of limited application. In *Davenport* v. *Lucy and others*,[4] one of the earliest causes to be heard under the Act relating to forced marriages,[5] the court was required to lay down rules for the examination of witnesses 'according to the true meaning of ye Act of Parliament and ye Comission in this cause exhibited'. The Delegates decreed, *inter alia*, that the witnesses produced on either side should be examined by any three or more of the judges.

There are, however, other examples of open examination to which no certain explanation can be assigned. One of the most striking occurred during a hearing of *Shrimpton* v. *Randall*

[1] (1602), DEL 4/2/169.

[2] It may be objected that this illustration is not necessarily an example of public examination, as the court may have been cleared for the purpose. There are two arguments available by way of rebuttal: (i) the relevant act does not state that the court was cleared; (ii) there is no reference to the publication of evidence taken in this way. If the depositions were taken in private and there was no subsequent publication, the adverse party would be in an intolerable position as he would have no means of knowing what evidence had been given against him; this must surely have resulted in a protest from his proctor, but no such protest is recorded. The only reasonable explanation of the absence of publication is that publication was not necessary because the evidence was given in open court, where anyone who wished might hear it.

[3] *Digest of Causes before the Ecclesiastical Courts 1750–58* (DEL 8/74); this is apparently one of the private case books kept by advocates exercent in the civilian courts (for these see E. S. Roscoe, *Lord Stowell* (London, 1916), p. 34). The decision cited in support of the proposition is *Whitmore* v. *Whitmore* (at f. 2; the name of the court giving the decision is not stated).

[4] (1652), DEL 6/4/144.

[5] Firth and Rait, *Acts and Ordinances*, vol. 2, pp. 496–7.

(*Goodine intervening*).[1] This cause was originally brought against Shrimpton for maladministration of a deceased's estate and in the course of the appeal Goodine tendered certain pleadings which involved charges of incompetence against the appellant. Goodine was then offered a choice by the Delegates of producing his witnesses in or out of court,[2] and at the next hearing he chose the former course, bringing in several witnesses 'interrogandos et examinandos per dominos judicandes'; their examination by the judges is recorded in a lively passage in the Act Book.[3]

In those situations where a witness might be examined in open court, he might be available for production in London, or he might live in the country; in the latter case, the court could decree a commission *ad partes* which would permit of such open examination.[4]

[1] (1606), DEL 4/3/277.

[2] The phrase used in the Act Book is 'in judicio vel extra'.

[3] *Shrimpton* v. *Randall* (*Goodine intervening*), *supra*, at f. 268.

[4] e.g. *Sydall* v. *the Bishop of Lichfield and Coventry* (1738), DEL 6/40/69; the Delegates indicated their willingness to grant 'a Commission for Examination of Witnesses Openly'.

CHAPTER VII

PROCEDURE—CAUSES *INTER PARTES*—PROOF BY DOCUMENTS

The production of witnesses was perhaps the commonest method by which a party chose to prove his pleadings, but in the Court of Delegates, as in other civilian tribunals, frequent use was made of documentary evidence.[1]

The documents tendered were of the most varied kinds. They were often the records of civilian courts,[2] but documents from the archives of other tribunals might be put in,[3] as might purely private writings, such as letters of institution and induction,[4] books of account,[5] indentures[6] and the like. The number of instruments tendered could be formidable in a complicated cause, and in *Staper and Leate* v. *Tite and Pate*[7] the appellants offered, as well as records of the Court of Admiralty and books of account 'centum et quinquaginta literas instrumenta et scripta hanc causam concernentia'. Documents in a foreign language were supplied with a translation duly certified by a notary public.[8]

The 'discovery' of documents was a principle recognized by the Delegates and either party could apply for documents in the hands of the other. Thus in *Porter* v. *Towerson*[9] the appellant's proctor

[1] Instruments were known as proof *mortua voce* while the depositions of witnesses were proof *viva voce* (*F.E.L.*, CXXIX/1). For an elaborate classification of instruments, see *F.E.L.*, CXXIX/3–5.

[2] e.g. *Piper and others* v. *Phillippes and Phillippes* (1601), DEL 4/2/13 (depositions of witnesses in the Prerogative Court of Canterbury); *Kempe* v. *Pratt* (*from definitive sentence*) (1601), DEL 4/2/93 (copies of acts of the London Consistory Court); *Robinson* v. *Robinson* (1602), DEL 4/2/116 (a definitive sentence given in the Court of Delegates in another cause and the relevant act).

[3] e.g. *Franklyn and others* v. *Franklyn and others* (1602), DEL 4/2/93; copies of depositions and interrogatories in the Court of Chancery.

[4] e.g. *Fisher* v. *Pilton* (1602), DEL 4/2/160.

[5] e.g. *Staper and Leate* v. *Tite and Pate* (1613), DEL 4/6/76.

[6] e.g. *Cobbe and Cobbe* v. *Stilman* (1606), DEL 4/3/244.

[7] *supra.*

[8] e.g. *Gage* v. *the Earl of Stafford* (1750), DEL 2/31; part of the appellant's proof was a copy of a decree extracted from the registry of the Court of the Parliament of Paris, to which was annexed a version in English certified as 'Faithfully Translated out of French' by one Benjamin Bonnet, a notary public.

[9] (1613), DEL 4/6/130.

claimed that a reckoning (*computum*) had been made between the respondent and a third party and he petitioned that Towerson should be monished to exhibit it, while in *Tanner and Moore* v. *Butler and others*[1] an application was made for the respondents that the appellants should be compelled to produce a legal opinion given by certain advocates, which they were believed to have in their possession.

The customary practice was that the documents in question should be tendered by the proctor of the party relying upon them 'in subsidium probacionis' of the pleadings. They would then be admitted by the Delegates, kept with the other papers in the cause in the archives of the court and returned to their owner when the cause was over.[2] If the instrument was such that its retention by the court for a long period might inconvenience the owner, the court might decree that a copy should be made, collated with the original and retained among the court records, while the original was returned to the party tendering it.[3] Copies seem usually to have been entered in books kept for that purpose, known as 'Muniment Books',[4] but sometimes documents were copied into the Act Books.[5]

The method of production described above was appropriate when the documents were brought into court, or could be brought in, in the court's opinion.[6] If, however, their production was impossible (which might be the case if they were the records of another tribunal and kept in the registry of some distant provincial diocese) the Delegates might decree a commission *pro scrutinio* to certain persons who were charged with the task of making copies.[7]

[1] (1706), DEL 2/85.

[2] A receipt would often be written in the margin of the relevant act; e.g. *Hall* v. *Repes* (1604), DEL 4/2/244.

[3] e.g. *Wells* v. *Agas* (1606), DEL 4/3/269. This procedure was no guarantee that the original would be returned quickly; in the cause just cited, letters of institution and induction were tendered on 28 January 1606 and copies were decreed on that day but the letters were not returned until 17 November 1609.

[4] For an account of these, see pp. 228–9 *post*.

[5] e.g. *Reynolds and others* v. *Waltham and others* (1606), DEL 4/3/241; a certificate tendered by one of the appellants, and signed by four of the judges in the cause, is transcribed as a part of the relevant act.

[6] The court might choose to insist upon production of the originals if this seemed at all feasible. In *Rusheton* v. *Tighe* (1608), DEL 4/4/243 & 248, the appellant's proctor produced in evidence copies of certain rolls which he declared to be in the possession of Sir Edward Paston, but the Delegates rejected the copies and required that the rolls themselves be produced.

[7] For an example of such a commission, see App. XIII.

Such a commission was clearly analogous to a commission *ad partes* for the examining of witnesses and operated (*mutatis mutandis*) in the same manner. A typical example is provided by *Boughton* v. *the Dean and Chapter of York*,[1] a cause in which the respondents wished to make use of certain 'Libri, munimenta, actus capitulares, statuta et alia instrumenta' which were housed in the registry of the dean and chapter. The commissioners, who were the nominees of the parties,[2] sat in the registry of York Minster, a local notary acting as their registrar and both sides being represented before them by proctors' substitutes. The relevant documents were produced and read out by the registrar 'alta et inteligibili [*sic*] voce' and the commissioners then directed that copies of them should be made within the next three days and duly collated with the originals. These copies, which were examined and certified by the commissioners, were then returned to the court together with letters substitutional, the commissioners' acts and the original commission itself.[3]

As an alternative to a commission, the Delegates might allow the production of copies taken privately, accompanied by sworn evidence that the copies agreed with the original.[4]

As well as documents, other exhibits might be tendered by way of proof in appropriate cases. Thus in *Diggens* v. *Leighe*[5] an attempt was made to prove the existence of a marriage by tendering a gold ring, set with a diamond and a ruby, around which were written the words: 'Quos deus coniunxit homo non separet' and 'Amor omnia vincit'. Diggens, it was alleged, had given the ring to Leighe, with these words: 'Take this ringe in token of my constant love and affection towards yowe in the waye of matrimonye and in case yowe consent thereunto keepe the same and think of the

[1] (1716), DEL 2/10.

[2] Commissioners were usually of the same type as those chosen to execute commissions *ad partes*, but if a scrutiny was decreed in London, members of Doctors' Commons might be chosen; e.g. *Stoddeid* v. *Carmarthen* (1605), DEL 4/3/108, where the Delegates decreed a scrutiny of documents in the registry of the Court of Arches and appointed three advocates as commissioners.

[3] There might also be a separate monition directed to those persons in whose keeping the documents were, requiring production before the commissioners at the time and place specified for execution of the commission; e.g. *Warham and Parsons* v. *Legge* (1617), DEL 4/7/107.

[4] e.g. *Milwarde and Howe* v. *Flaskett* (1604), DEL 4/2/282; one of the respondents produced copies of certain depositions taken before the Star Chamber and one Robert Browne then swore that he had collated them with the original records of that tribunal.

[5] (1607), DEL 4/4/73.

writings therein conteyned.'[1] Exhibits were also tendered by way of proof in *Watson* v. *Watson*,[2] although the significance of the curious collection of articles put forward in that cause can only be guessed at.[3]

[1] The cause presumably turned on the distinction between *verba de praesenti* (the exchange of which was enough to make a marriage immediately binding) and *verba de futuro* (which required subsequent consummation to give them effect); see P. M. Bromley, *Family Law* (London, 1962) p. 35.

[2] (1614), DEL 4/6/243.

[3] They comprised 'duos anulos, viz. one small gould ringe and thother a little blewe ringe' together with 'duas loras Anglice twoe stringes viz. thone of black and yellowe silke with letters or words wrought in it and the other of haire', and an 'effigiem seu specium clavis Anglice the print of a key or of part of a key in past'.

CHAPTER VIII

PROCEDURE—CAUSES *INTER PARTES*—SENTENCE AND EXECUTION

When the various stages of procedure previously described had been completed, the cause could pass to informations and sentence.

For this purpose it was necessary to require the attendance of the legal advisers of the parties, who were summoned by a formal warrant.[1] This document, which was on paper, bore the names of the parties and their proctors, fixed the precise time and place for hearing and required proctors on both sides to attend with their counsel; on the back was a complete list of the judges belonging to that commission divided, in the case of a full commission, into the four categories which comprised it (*judices e foro seculari*, *doctores*, *proceres* and *episcopi*). The warrant was signed by a number of the judges, presumably those to whom it was tendered and who intended to sit at the hearing to which it related. Upon the back was a certificate that it had been personally served upon one or both of the parties' proctors; it does not seem to have been the practice to serve it upon counsel. Warrants were usually drafted in common form, but if the provisions of a particular warrant were at all unusual, it might be expanded.[2]

The warrant seems always to have been signed by enough members of each group on the commission to form a quorum; thus in *Boughton* v. *the Dean and Chapter of York*[3] the commission comprised five peers, five bishops, three common law judges and seven civilians and at least one member of each group signed. One of the functions of the warrant may have been to obtain sufficient signatures to ensure that a quorum was likely to attend.

If more than one hearing was needed for informations and sentence a separate warrant would usually be issued for each,[4] but

[1] For an example, see Appendix XV.

[2] e.g. *Marks* v. *Hutchinson and Mayer* (1782), DEL 2/56. The warrant was issued in February but the date fixed for the hearing was towards the end of April; the reason for the delay (the respondents' absence abroad) is set out in the body of the warrant.

[3] (1716), DEL 2/10.

[4] e.g. *Blackwood* v. *Jansen* (1782), DEL 2/13; three warrants survive, the second and third specifically fixing a time 'to hear further informations'.

if the judges agreed to sit *de die in diem* until the cause was completed, one warrant alone would suffice.[1] If the time fixed for hearing by the original warrant was altered, it would be countermanded by the issue of a new one.[2]

It seems that warrants were not issued for the earlier stages of a cause, when only ordinary acts were sped. Their use, however, was not confined to informations and sentence, as they might be issued on certain other occasions (apparently those when a full quorum was required).[3]

On the day appointed by the warrant for hearing and determining the cause, the judges assembled and business began with 'informations'. In the procedure of the Delegates, as has been seen, much business which would have been done in the judges' presence in a trial at common law, was committed to paper out of court; before sentence could be given, therefore, everything which was relevant to the decision (the pleadings of the parties, their personal answers, the depositions of their witnesses and the like) had to be communicated to the judges, who had also to hear and consider counsel's arguments. The purpose of informations was to permit all this to be done.[4]

The records of the court tell us very little about the method by which this stage of a cause was carried out before the Delegates, but it seems likely that they followed the procedure of the other ecclesiastical courts as that is described by Oughton.[5] The pleadings, personal answers and depositions tendered by each side in the course of the appeal were read out and also, presumably, the process.[6]

[1] *Jenner and others* v. *Tyrrell* (1830), DEL 2/45; the warrant is endorsed in these terms.

[2] e.g *Seaforth and Spencer* v. *Cock* (1808), DEL 2/77.

[3] e.g. *Procurator General* v. *Burrows* (1795), DEL 2/36 (hearing of petition by proctors; *Hughes* v. *Sloper and others* (1737), DEL 2/36 (consideration of admissibility of allegation).

[4] The term 'informations' is properly confined to the recitation of proofs and legal argument on the merits of the whole cause. At an earlier stage of the hearing, the court might require a similar recitation of proofs and legal argument on some emergent matter (e.g. the admission of a witness) but in the latter case, by way of distinction, the records speak of 'hearing the pleasure of the judges'; the Latin formulae are *ad informandum* and *ad audiendum voluntatem* respectively. This distinction in nomenclature is clearly stated by Oughton (CXXII/a/i–ii) but it is not always adhered to with scrupulous precision in the records; in particular, 'informations' is sometimes used when 'hearing pleasure' would be more appropriate; e.g. *Pope* v. *Fry* (1612), DEL 4/5/302.

[5] *O.J.*, CXXII.

[6] The practice of reading the depositions aloud is referred to in *Hervey* v. *Hervey* (1773), DEL 6/46/169.

When this was done, the court would hear legal argument by advocates. Informations would continue until the Delegates were satisfied that every fact or argument which they ought to hear had been brought before them;[1] in a 'heavy' cause, there might be repeated adjournments.[2]

When the court was fully informed it could proceed to sentence, but with the Delegates, as with other civilian tribunals, this involved a procedure very different from that of the courts of common law. The drafting of the sentence was the responsibility not of the judges but of the parties,[3] each side drawing up, within the broad limits of the standard formula, the judgment which was most favourable to his cause.[4] These drafts,[5] which were on parchment, were then 'porrected' or handed to the judges and the one tendered for the party in whose favour the court found was then read out.[6]

A blank space was always left in the sentences at the appropriate point and the word *justitiam* inserted in the one accepted by the court, in order to distinguish it from the other.[7] There were also blank spaces in which were entered in due course the amount of taxed costs and the due date of payment.

The successful sentence was signed, on the bottom right-hand

[1] e.g. *Pexall* v. *Brocas* (1605), DEL 4/3/43; the court refused one party's request to give sentence, as informations were not sufficiently full.

[2] e.g. *the Bishop of St David's* v. *Lucy* (1698), DEL 6/28/107 *et seq.*; there were fifteen separate sittings for this purpose, most lasting several hours.

[3] On rare occasions, the court might draft its own sentence; e.g. *Somervile* v. *Smithe* (*in the principal cause*) (1605), DEL 4/3/20 (both sides porrected sentences in the usual way, but the judges proceeded to deliver 'Sententiam per seipsos conceptam'). See also *Robow* v. *Thompson and others* (1682), DEL 6/21/69, where the court ordered a sentence to be drafted in terms dictated by itself.

[4] In some civilian courts the sentence was drafted by an official of the court on the basis of instructions given to him by the parties' legal advisers (*F.E.L.*, CLV/3/2/i).

[5] As a rule, each side would porrect only one sentence, but if there were, say, several respondents and the appellant sought a different remedy from each, he might porrect several sentences; e.g. *Cardinall* v. *Martyn and others* (1617), DEL 4/7/49 (two sentences were porrected for the appellant, directed against the various respondents).

[6] In most of the civilian courts, where only one judge sat, the sentence was read out by him, but this task was usually performed for the Delegates by the registrar (or, presumably, his deputy) in Oughton's time (*O.J.*, CXXVII/3/b/v). Occasionally, however, one of the Delegates would read the sentence: e.g. *Paston* v. *Thwaytes* (1602), DEL 4/2/132; *Allen and Aldworth* v. *Tilston* (1596), DEL 5/2/76.

[7] On this, see Note I at the end of the chapter.

corner,[1] by those judges who accepted it,[2] while from *c.* 1600 it was customary for the advocates of the party on whose behalf a sentence was porrected to sign on the bottom left-hand corner;[3] at the bottom of the instrument or on the back, a certificate of promulgation was endorsed by the official of the court in whose presence the sentence had been delivered. This certificate usually set out the precise time and place at which sentence was pronounced and the name of the official responsible for the endorsement;[4] the names of the witnesses to the formal promulgation are to be found not in the certificate but in the Act Books.[5]

In appropriate cases, other documents might be annexed to the sentence; thus in testamentary causes, it might be accompanied by a copy of the disputed will,[6] while in a disciplinary or defamation cause, where the unsuccessful party was required to do penance, a schedule of penance might be fastened to the sentence, setting out the formula he was required to repeat.[7]

If the judges were divided in their opinions, sentence was given for the party in whose favour the majority found,[8] the names of the dissenting judges being entered in the Act Book.[9] On occasions, however, a dissenting minority might go further in signifying

[1] Occasionally at the bottom left-hand corner; e.g. *Besey* v. *Elam* (1586), DEL 5/1/27.

[2] A judge might signify acceptance of a sentence (without attending the sitting at which the sentence was promulgated) by signing it beforehand; e.g. *Hill* v. *Archbold and others* (1619), DEL 4/8/102 (sentence was delivered for the appellant in the absence of the bishops of Durham and Rochester, but with their consent which was indicated 'per subscripciones suas dicte Sententie factas').

[3] See DEL 5/2/*passim* (sentences for the period 1594–1601).

[4] These certificates are not referred to in Oughton's treatise, but they occurred on some sentences promulgated by the Court of Chivalry (*H.C.C.*, App. XXII; there is, however, no certificate on the other sentence reproduced in this book, in App. XXI). Sentences surviving among the records of the Court of Admiralty (except for a few of the earliest examples) all bear these endorsements (Marsden (ed.), *Select Pleas in the Court of Admiralty*, vol. 1, p. lxiv). They seem to have been invariable in the practice of the Court of Delegates until *c.* 1740.

[5] e.g. *Fitche* v. *Oxford* (1614), DEL 4/6/178.

[6] e.g. *Clenche* v. *Smithe* (1585), DEL 5/1/13.

[7] e.g. *Withers* v. *the Bishop of Exeter and others* (1611), DEL 5/4/no. illegible. More rarely, other documents are found; e.g. *Salmon and Salmon* v. *Tunstall* (1673), DEL 5/22/13 (the suppletory oath and deposition of the respondent).

[8] The majority would have to be so constituted as to satisfy the terms of the quorum clause. Thus if the commission was made up of common lawyers and civilians (and the quorum clause was drafted in the usual form for such a commission) a valid majority would have to include at least one common lawyer.

[9] e.g. *Layer* v. *Rugge* (1617), DEL 4/7/129; the court found in favour of the respondent by five to one, Dr Ridley dissenting.

its disapproval of the decision. Thus in *Davenport* v. *Lucy and others*[1] there was a long and acrimonious debate at the end of which the majority found for the defendants;[2] the sentence porrected on their behalf was then signed by those of the judges who assented to it, but a minority of the Delegates emphasized their dislike of this decision by signing the plaintiff's sentence and insisting that it should be filed among the records of the court (a procedure which the others referred to as 'null, illegall and voyd').

The judges of the Court of Delegates never gave reasons for their decisions.[3] It was the only civilian court to retain this rule into the nineteenth century; some at least of these tribunals had abandoned it as early as *c.* 1750.[4] This reticence is for several reasons to be regretted, especially as it makes any study of doctrinal development in the court very difficult.

As soon as the court had delivered sentence, it would usually direct its attention to the taxation of costs.[5] Each party's costs were engrossed on strips of parchment;[6] these were several inches wide and sometimes of considerable length.[7] The various items which comprised the bill were shown individually, but the total was for the most part taxed at a round sum until the latter half of the

[1] (1653), DEL 6/5/78.

[2] The cause was heard by the Delegates at first instance in the exercise of their original jurisdiction.

[3] For a statement of the rule and its practical effects, see Note II at the end of this chapter.

[4] The matter is touched on in *H.C.C.*, pp. 162–3; the earliest extant reports of reasoned judgments in the Court of Arches are those of Sir John Lee, beginning in 1752 (but not published until 1833), while in the Court of Admiralty reasoned judgments were reported as early as 1766 by Sir William Burrell. There is, it is true, no indication that such judgments were given in the Court of Chivalry until the recent decision in *Manchester Corporation* v. *Manchester Palace of Varieties Ltd*, [1955] P. 133 but that court held no sittings from 1737 until this century, and had it continued to be active it would in all likelihood have conformed to the practice of the other civilian tribunals.

[5] The civilian courts and the Court of Chancery had always (with certain reservations) allowed the successful party costs, following the rule of Roman law 'in expensarum causa victus victori condemnandus est' (*H.E.L.*, vol. 4, p. 536, adopting *C.* 3. 1. 13. 6); cf. the practice of the common law courts where the awarding of costs only gradually replaced the amercement of the unsuccessful party (*H.E.L.*, vol. 4, pp. 536–8).

[6] Occasionally strips of paper might be used; e.g. *Lady Osborn* v. *Williams* (1718), DEL 8/83/2, where the taxed bill is written on several sheets stitched together in book form. The document, whatever its form, was known as a *billa* or *schedula*.

[7] e.g. *Hussey* v. *Viscountess Dillon and the Earl of Berkeley* (1736), DEL 8/56; the bill porrected for the Earl of Berkeley was over 18 feet long.

eighteenth century; thereafter the taxed figure was usually precise. The bill would sometimes embrace costs incurred in the lower courts as well as before the Delegates,[1] and the expenses of proceedings in the grievance and in the principal cause might also be combined.[2] Each party's bill was usually signed by his advocates and the judges would sign the bill of the successful party below their formal endorsement of the sum allowed.

The successful party would porrect his bill as soon as sentence was given in his favour.[3] The Delegates would usually tax it immediately, but causes of difficulty might be adjourned so that the court could have the benefit of counsel's argument.[4] When the court had allowed a sum by way of costs, the proctor of the party in whose favour it found would take the usual oath,[5] and a monition for payment would be decreed; execution might be stayed, however, if an application was made for a commission of review, until the Lord Chancellor's decision was signified to the king in Council.[6] If there were several unsuccessful parties, costs would be divided between them.[7]

In certain circumstances, both sides might be awarded costs by the Delegates; if, for example, the court gave judgment both in the grievance and the principal cause, it might find for one party in the former case and for the adverse party in the latter. When this happened, the court might simplify payment by ordering a

[1] e.g. *Cottington* v. *Cottington* (1678), DEL 8/53/1. This reservation of taxation until the end of proceedings was sometimes decreed by court order (e.g. *Higgens* v. *Elye* (*in the grievance*) (1604), DEL 4/2/307); it might also, presumably, have resulted from agreement between the parties that costs should be allowed to accumulate so that a single taxation might be made when the cause had reached the ultimate tribunal.

[2] Here too the decision might rest with the court, which could reserve the taxing of costs in the grievance when it retained the principal cause, so that both might be taxed together; e.g. *Salisburie* v. *Griffith* (1614), DEL 4/6/177.

[3] e.g. *Pocock* v. *Longe* (1620), DEL 4/8/185. If there were several successful parties, more than one bill might be porrected on their behalf; e.g. *Lynold* v. *Maylard and others* (1618), DEL 4/7/234 (the court found against the appellant on a charge of contumacy and one bill was porrected for seven of the respondents with a separate bill for the eighth).

[4] e.g. *Barnardiston* v. *Barnardiston and Barnardiston* (*in the grievance*) (1604), DEL 4/2/326.

[5] i.e. that the expenses had been incurred; e.g. *Vaughan and others* v. *Powell* (*in the grievance*) (1601), DEL 4/2/19.

[6] e.g. *Hervey* v. *Hervey* (1773), DEL 6/46/180.

[7] e.g. *Aldebroughe* v. *Brakenburye and Graye* (*Tunstall intervening*) (1606), DEL 4/3/291; each respondent was required to pay half the appellant's taxed costs.

compensatio or set-off so that only the balance was due.[1] The precise limits of *compensatio* are uncertain and some attempts to make use of it were disallowed.[2]

The sum originally decreed by the court was not necessarily final; if good cause was shown, the decree might be rescinded and costs taxed anew. Thus in *Heale* v. *Upton* (*in the grievance*),[3] the successful respondent was originally allowed only £16, although his proctor declared himself ready to swear that more than £50 had been spent; later, however, further evidence on costs seems to have been offered, and the court revoked its first decree, increasing the sum allowed to Upton to £20. There were other ways, as well, in which the court might vary an award of costs; sometimes, for example, the Delegates would make only a partial taxation of costs, reserving their right to make a further taxation at a later stage 'si eis visum fuerit'. The principles underlying this practice are obscure but it may have been used as a disciplinary device.[4]

The monition for payment would usually require the whole sum taxed to be discharged by a certain day, but if the amount was heavy, the Court might allow payment by instalments; thus in *Stoddard* v. *Carmarthen*[5] the respondent's costs were taxed at £40 and the appellant was ordered to pay half this sum before the Feast of St Bartholomew and the balance by All Souls' Day.[6]

The Court of Delegates had a complete discretion as to costs. Where the litigants could not agree about costs,[7] the court was

[1] e.g. *Hersey* v. *Barker* (1611), DEL 4/5/103; the court found for the respondent in the principal cause, taxing his costs at £20 and for the appellant in the grievance with costs at £8. Costs were discharged by the payment of £12 by the appellant to the respondent.

[2] e.g. *Staper and Leate* v. *Pate* (1612), DEL 4/5/280; costs were awarded to the respondent and the appellants alleged that her husband was indebted to them 'per billam obligatoriam' and that the amount owed on the bill should be set off against costs; this the court refused to sanction. The only examples of *compensatio* discovered in the course of this investigation relate to the set-off of costs incurred in the grievance and the principal cause.

[3] (1608), DEL 4/4/206 & 213.

[4] e.g. *Mather* v. *Godbould* (1611), DEL 4/5/128; Mather's costs were taxed at 20 marks and Godbould was told that he would be relieved from further taxation if he paid in time and took an oath *de bene gerendo*.

[5] (1608), DEL 4/4/180.

[6] The practice of the Court of Chivalry also allowed for payment of costs and damages by instalments (*H.C.C.*, p. 215).

[7] The litigants might themselves agree that no costs should be awarded; e.g. *Lardner* v. *Westwood and others* (1642), DEL 4/18/21 (the parties came to a compromise which involved remission of the cause to the lower court 'sine expensis').

under no obligation to allow them to a successful party and the refusal of costs was by no means uncommon.[1] In this the Delegates followed the general rule (so it seems) of the ecclesiastical courts which viewed the practice of awarding costs with some reserve.[2] Often no reason at all was assigned for denying them and reasons, when they were given, were varied in character. Sometimes the exercise of discretion against the successful party was a punitive measure;[3] it might also amount to a recognition that costs were, in the circumstances of the case, practically irrecoverable.[4] There were occasions, moreover, when the court used its discretion as a means of furthering policy; thus, commissions of review, which were always looked on with disfavour,[5] might be discouraged by a judicious order as to costs.[6]

Not only might the court refuse the successful party costs, it might also (although more rarely), require him to pay the costs of his opponent.[7] The circumstances in which such an order might be made are a little obscure. In the examples which have been noted, the Delegates often gave no reason;[8] when an explanation is vouchsafed, the record may state merely that the order was made 'ex causis justis et racionalibus' or the like.[9] Presumably this action was taken when the successful party's cause was entirely devoid of merit.

If the judges who delivered sentence did not tax the costs

[1] In such a case, the clause relating to costs would be struck out of the successful party's sentence; e.g. *Sheffeild* v. *Cassan* (*in the principal cause*) (1731), DEL 5/32/unfoliated.

[2] Oughton states that the unsuccessful party should not be condemned in costs 'si justam...litigandi causam...habuerat' (*O.J.*, CXXXIV/a/9).

[3] e.g. *Clifford* v. *Clifford* (1608), DEL 4/4/182; the respondent was denied her costs because the bill was not left for taxation by the day assigned by the court.

[4] e.g. *Tate* v. *Mildmay* (1739), DEL 6/40/100; the court found for Mildmay but refused to allow costs 'by reason of the poverty of Mrs. Tate, and not from the Merits of her Case'.

[5] For this, see pp. 71–5 *ante*.

[6] e.g. *Greenhill* v. *Thomas* (1680), DEL 6/20/33; the court found for the respondent and taxed his costs at £20 but further directed that 'if Greenhill renounce a Review before Midsomer the Costs not to be recovered of him'. An order to the same effect was made in *Hallum and Smith* v. *Lee and Jones* (1680), DEL 6/20/85.

[7] The discretion of the other ecclesiastical courts might also be exercised in this way (*O.J.*, CXXXIV/a/9).

[8] e.g. *Pincomb* v. *Norton* (1633), DEL 4/14/56; the successful appellant was required to pay the substantial sum of £300 by way of costs to the respondent.

[9] e.g. *Brickwood* v. *Brickwood* (1607), DEL 4/4/94.

themselves, their discretion would be exercised by those to whom the task of taxation was delegated.[1] In these cases the court might give some indication of the severity with which costs were to be taxed by an endorsement on the sentence itself, such as 'moderate taxentur'.[2] If a taxation made out of court in this way was disputed, the person responsible for it might attach to the taxed bill a certificate containing his justification of the taxation.[3]

A survey of the bills of costs preserved in the archives of the court suggests that the expenses incurred by litigants were not unduly high as a general rule, if regard be had to the fact that the proceedings were conducted before the highest appellate tribunal and that it was a common practice for each party to employ several counsel.[4] Costs, however, could be extremely heavy in the longer or more complex causes; thus in *Zuizan* v. *Shelly*[5] costs were taxed at £400, a considerable sum in the seventeenth century, while in *Lopez and partners* v. *Le Clarke and partners*,[6] of about the same date, they amounted to the enormous figure of £1,500. Certain aspects of civilian procedure, such as the taking of evidence abroad, could be particularly expensive and costs in causes such as *Harford* v. *Morris*,[7] where many witnesses were examined by requisition, were much inflated by this means.[8] The court seems to have followed no settled policy of leniency or

[1] i.e. the civilian condelegates, or the person discharging the office of registrar. The employment of the latter for this purpose does not seem to have been common until the second half of the eighteenth century, by which period taxation of costs in the Court of Admiralty was often delegated to the registrar or his deputy (Main Thompson, *Admiralty Registrars*, p. 27). Officials of the Delegates were on occasions allowed to tax costs somewhat earlier; e.g. *Smith* v. *Smith* (1716), DEL 6/34/pt. A/2, where the Court made an order for taxation by the registrar and *Purcell and Purcell* v. *Purcell* (1725), DEL 2/60, where a letter from one of the appellants to James Pinfold the deputy registrar speaks of a bill of costs 'taxt by you'.

[2] e.g. *Buckenham and Crouch* v. *Gunter* (1682), DEL 5/26/3. Such endorsements did not always go undisputed; thus in *Stratton and others* v. *Heron and Tenche* (*in the principal cause*) (1634), DEL 4/14/227, two of the judges subscribed the sentence with the words 'Taxentur admodum parce' but their three colleagues dissented.

[3] e.g. *Girdler* v. *Lamb* (1813), DEL 2/32.

[4] Out of 26 bills of costs chosen at random from seventeenth-century examples, only three claim amounts in excess of £100 and with only one of these did the court allow more than £100.

[5] (1634), DEL 4/14/172.

[6] (1634), DEL 4/14/189.

[7] (1785), DEL 8/58.

[8] The appellant claimed £2,117. 13*s*. 8*d*. of which she was allowed rather more than half.

severity in taxing, but to have approached each bill on its merits; it could on occasions be severe.[1]

Expensae litis (i.e. the usual costs arising from the conduct of a cause) were the commonest sort and they were never taxed until after sentence. Other costs might also be incurred, however, the most frequent being costs of contumacy in connection with excommunication,[2] and costs of retarded process, which arose from a deliberate attempt to delay the suit.[3] Such costs might be taxed at any stage of a cause, whenever the court decreed that contumacy or retardation had occurred.

As bills of costs were always arranged on a terminal basis, they are a convenient means of discovering the length of time taken by a cause before the Delegates and if costs below were included, the length of the entire cause.[4] It is clear that litigation before the ecclesiastical courts was rarely expeditious. Proceedings before the Delegates themselves seem usually to have lasted at least one year,[5] and causes with only one earlier instance were sometimes dependent before the courts for very much longer.[6]

Bills of costs may also be consulted to see how the various stages of an appeal to the Delegates were spread over the terms taken to hear and determine it. A typical example is *Somersett and others* v. *Dingley*[7] where proceedings took place over six terms. In the Easter term of 1666 and the vacation preceding, the commission of delegacy was presented, the inhibition and citation decreed and executed, the monition for process decreed and the libel tendered. In the Trinity term, the process was transmitted, but in the Michaelmas

[1] e.g. *Powell* v. *Beresford* (1707), DEL 8/54; a bill for £89. 3*s*. 6*d*. was taxed at £5.

[2] *F.E.L.*, CLXII (footnote 1).

[3] Among the commonest examples of retardation which occur in the records of the Delegates were the failure of a party to expedite a commission *ad partes*, which had been decreed on his behalf (e.g. *Cooke* v. *Stokes* (1619), DEL 4/8/57) or failure to appear with counsel when required to do so (e.g. *Marston* v. *Van Segling* (1652), DEL 6/4/90). For an example of such a bill, see App. XIX.

[4] Squibb drew attention to this use of bills of costs in *H.C.C.*, p. 218.

[5] On occasions, of course, causes could be disposed of more quickly; e.g. *Smith and Haddon* v. *Lee and others* (180), DEL 8/53/2 (the hearing of the entire cause, from the introduction of the commission of delegacy to sentence, was confined to the Trinity term, 1680, and the vacation preceding).

[6] e.g. *Jackson* v. *Mug* (1674), DEL 8/53/1. This cause was before the Court of Arches from the Trinity term 1666 to the Trinity term 1669; it was introduced into the Court of Delegates in the Michaelmas term 1669 and sentence was not given there until the Trinity term 1674.

[7] (1666), DEL 8/53/2.

and Hilary terms no steps were taken to forward the cause. In the Easter term of the following year, witnesses were produced and examined and in the Trinity term their depositions were published and sentence promulgated.

When sentence had been given and costs taxed in a cause, the Delegates had largely finished with it. There might, however, be certain matters relating to the execution of the sentence which required the attention of the judges, and in matrimonial or testamentary appeals, for example, they might take further action to complete the judgment; thus the litigants might be required to go through a ceremony of marriage or a grant of probate might be made.[1]

Deserving more detailed attention (because less fully discussed in the printed authorities) is the imposition of penance,[2] for whenever it was appropriate the sentence of the Delegates might include an order for the performance of penance.[3] Little documentary evidence on the subject has survived in the records of the court, but this suggests that these penances resembled, both in their form and their method of enforcement, the submissions which the Court of Chivalry imposed in defamation causes.[4]

The formula of penance imposed in a defamation cause (where they were most commonly employed, to judge by the surviving examples), and the procedure involved in its performance, is well illustrated by the order of penance imposed on one Samuel Weyman, the appellant in *Weyman* v. *Byle*[5] who had been found guilty of defaming the respondent.[6] In defamation causes, the penance usually consisted of a formal apology to the person defamed, made in a manner as public as the utterance of the defa-

[1] e.g. *Berebloke* v. *Morley* (1603), DEL 4/2/199 (parties required to solemnize marriage); *Hugason* v. *Hugason and Hugason* (1634), DEL 4/14/235 (probate granted).

[2] The matter is briefly touched on in *O.J.*, CCLXVIII/5–9 and CXXXVII/1/a/5.

[3] The only examples given by Law relate to contempt of court and wilful refusal to seek discharge from sentence of excommunication (*F.E.L.*, LII/2 and LIX/2). It is clear from the records of the Court of Delegates, however, that that tribunal, at least, could also impose penance for defamation and misconduct.

[4] For these, see *H.C.C.*, pp. 212–14.

[5] (1697), DEL 2/115/2.

[6] In several causes, these schedules are to be found attached to the sentence porrected by the party defamed; e.g. *Garrard* v. *Humble* (1677), DEL 5/23/23 (an 'Order of pennance' is fastened to Garrard's sentence and is signed by the judges who signed the sentence).

matory words,[1] and Weyman was required to attend at the vestry of St Olave's church in Southwark (which was the parish church of the respondent) and there, in the presence of the minister and churchwardens, the respondent herself and three or four of her friends (if they chose to be present)[2] he was required to repeat the following formula 'with an audible voice' as it was dictated to him by the minister:

WHEREAS I Samuel Weyman have utter'd & spoken certain scandalous and opprobrious Words of and against Lydia Byle Widow to the great offence of Almighty God, the scandal of my Christian Religion, & the injury & reproach of my Neighbour's credit and reputation, by calling her the said Lydia Byle a Whore and by saying She lay with a Quaker in the Cellar I do therefore before God and you humbly confess and acknowledge such my offence, and am heartily sorry for the same, & do ask her forgiveness, & do promise never hereafter to offend her in the like, God Assisting Me.

When the penance was completed, a note of its proper performance was endorsed at the foot of the schedule which was returned to the registry of the Delegates;[3] it could then be produced in court if there was any dispute as to its due performance.[4] Refusal by the party upon whom the penance had been imposed to perform it in the manner decreed would also be certified to the judges, and they might them make a fresh order.[5]

In the Court of Delegates, penances seem most often to have been imposed upon persons found guilty of defamation, but there

[1] The way in which this principle was applied is set out in *O.J.*, CCLXVIII/6–7; if the words had been spoken in public, the parish church of the injured party was usually chosen for the performance of the penance, but if they were spoken in a private place, penance would usually be done in the house of the person defamed. Even in the latter case, however, the court's order might ensure that performance was sufficiently public; e.g. *Crant* v. *Raven* (*in the principal cause*) (1633), DEL 4/14/37 (penance was decreed to be done in the house belonging to the curate of Armagh, with the proviso that if the door of the house was shut at the time appointed for the penance, it was to be performed in the porch outside).

[2] It was a characteristic both of penances and submissions that the party defamed and his friends had the right to 'attend and gloat over his defeated adversary' (*H.C.C.*, p. 214). The court would usually regulate the number of persons who were entitled to be present in the entourage of the injured party and might also specify their character; thus in *Crant* v. *Raven* (*in the principal cause*) *supra*, the respondent was allowed to bring eight friends with her, provided they were not Presbyterians or Papists.

[3] e.g. the certified schedule in *Weyman* v. *Byle* (1697), DEL 2/115/2.

[4] e.g. *Mallard* v. *Clerk* (1618), DEL 6/7/213.

[5] e.g. *Crant* v. *Raven* (*in the principal cause*), *supra*, at f. 17.

were certain other offences for which this decree was deemed appropriate. Thus in *Withers* v. *the Bishop of Exeter and others*,[1] a cause which arose out of Withers' dismissal from his post of vicar choral in Exeter Cathedral, the Delegates restored him on the condition that he performed a penance by way of apology for his 'intemperate and undutyfull cariage and behaviour' towards the bishop and certain of the canons,[2] while in *Salsbury* v. *Bartlett and others*,[3] the appellant, who was apparently a clerk in Holy Orders found guilty of misbehaviour, was required both to recite a penance and also 'to make a recantacion Sermon of the debauchery libellate'. Curiously, no example has been found of a penance inflicted in a cause of office, but the fact that so few of these causes were prosecuted to conclusion may be the reason for this.[4]

NOTE I (INSERTIONS IN THE SENTENCE)

The insertion of the word *justitiam* in the sentence porrected by the successful party, in order to distinguish it from that of his rival, is described by Law as the usual procedure in the ecclesiastical courts,[5] but the records of the Delegates suggest that, although customary, it was by no means the invariable practice of that tribunal. Sometimes a word other than *justitiam* was inserted; *sententiam* was often used and by the beginning of the eighteenth century it was commoner,[6] while later in that century the single word was often expanded to the formula 'sentence to be given for justice'.[7] Moreover, the insertion of one of these words does not seem always to have been certain proof that the sentence concerned was accepted by the court, despite Law's account of the matter. Until *c.* 1740 certificates of promulgation were endorsed on sentences delivered by the Delegates,[8] and as long as sentences were porrected it was customary for the judges to sign those which they

[1] (1611), DEL 5/4/no. illegible.

[2] The schedule of penance is printed in full in *R.R.*, p. 6.

[3] (1681), DEL 6/20/138.

[4] In *Office of the Judges* v. *Babbington* (1611), DEL 4/5/52, a cause of office promoted against a witness who had prevented a sentence of excommunication being delivered against him, the court abstained from inflicting penance because he had acted 'non ex malicia sed ex errore'.

[5] *F.E.L.*, CLV/7.

[6] See DEL 5/30/*passim.*

[7] e.g. *Wise and Brown* v. *Johnson* (1755), DEL 5/33/unfoliated.

[8] For these, see p. 163 *ante.*

consented to; nevertheless, there are preserved among the records a number of sentences which bear the words *justitiam* or *sententiam* but which have no certificate of promulgation and which are not signed by the judges.[1] It seems possible that these were unsuccessful sentences, and that the insertions were mistaken or made for some reason which cannot now be discovered.

The practice of the Court of Chivalry seems also to have diverged from Law's account; the word *justitiam* occurred in the usual formula of sentence porrected in that court, but apparently it was not inserted in the way described by Law.[2]

NOTE II (REASONED JUDGMENTS IN THE COURT OF DELEGATES)

Throughout the whole of its life, the judges of the Court of Delegates never set out the reasons upon which their decisions were based, either at the time when sentence was delivered, or later. The rule they followed is accurately stated in a fragment of conversation between Sir Julius Caesar and Sir Daniel Dun, recorded in the account of *the Countess of Essex* v. *the Earl of Essex* given in the State Trials:[3] '"I know the king expecteth we should say no more, than I do like this sentence, or, I do not like it. And that you know, Sir Daniel Dun, is the manner of the delegates, and not to go farther." "It is so," said Sir Daniel.' This practice was still adhered to in the closing days of the tribunal,[4] and reports of the Delegates' judgments had to be cast in a form which took account of it.[5]

To penetrate below the surface of the records (which usually contain no more than a bare finding for one side or the other),

[1] e.g. *Villiers* v. *Lady Osborne* (1729), DEL 5/32/unfoliated.

[2] *H.C.C.*, p. 211 and App. XXI.

[3] (1613), 2 St. Tr. 786 at 828.

[4] *Eccl. Courts Rep.* (1831–2), p. 62.

[5] 'The decisions of the "Court of Delegates" being only conveyed to the public in the terms of their "*decrees*", it is *necessary*, in reporting the proceedings of *that* court, to accompany the "*case*", with the "*argument and decree*", instead of the "*judgment*", which follows the "*case*", (and, generally speaking, *at once*) in *other* instances. This is stated, to explain what might seem *anomolous*, in the conduct of these Reports, to the reader, unacquainted with the practice of the "Court of Delegates" in this particular.' (J. Addams, *Reports of Cases...at Doctors' Commons, and in the High Court of Delegates* (London, 1823), vol. 1, Advertisement.)

although difficult, is not always impossible. The basis of the court's judgment may sometimes be arrived at by deduction, although this expedient is not often available.[1] Occasionally, there is more direct evidence, when a brief note exists, giving the reasons for judgments in the records themselves; thus on the final leaf of the Assignation Book 1671–3 there is a memorandum setting out the opinions of the various judges in *the Bishop of Carlisle* v. *the Archbishop of York*, while some of the notes on f. 157 of the Assignation Book 1654–6 appear to be of the same character.

For a vehement and closely reasoned statement of objections to the Delegates' practice, see Archbishop Abbot's protest in *the Countess of Essex* v. *the Earl of Essex*;[2] he had prepared a reasoned judgment, but was not allowed to deliver it.

[1] For examples, see the comments of counsel *arguendo* in *ex parte Fearon* (1800), 5 Ves. J. 633 at 644 and of W. M. Pulley in his evidence before the Ecclesiastical Commissioners (*Eccl. Courts Rep.* (1831–2), pp. 62–3).

[2] (1613), 2 St. Tr. 786 at 828.

CHAPTER IX

PROCEDURE—CAUSES OF OFFICE

The greater part of the business which came before the Court of Delegates consisted of causes *inter partes*, but a complete account of procedure must contain some reference to causes of office. These were disciplinary actions which were promoted 'either on account of some crime committed; or, on suspicion of some crime'.[1] They fell into two categories; causes instituted by the mere office of the judge (i.e. begun by the judge in his own name) and those instituted by the office of the judge promoted, which were begun by some other person; they are commonly referred to as necessary and voluntary causes respectively.[2]

Causes of office might be promoted in a lower court and come to the Delegates on appeal,[3] but not infrequently they were begun before that tribunal itself and arose out of some litigation already depending before it. Any 'crime', it seems, which came within the cognizance of ecclesiastical courts might be the basis of such an action, but the commonest ground for promoting them was apparently contempt of court.[4] Most of the causes promoted before the Delegates arose from specific acts of contempt,[5] but they might also arise from omissions,[6] and contempt of commissioners *ad partes* appointed by the court was as valid a reason

[1] *F.E.L.*, App. 2 (11).

[2] The practical distinction between the two classes of action seems to have resided in the nature of the act complained of. If it was something which fell within the immediate cognizance of the court (e.g. contempt committed in the face of the court) the judge would himself take steps to punish it and the cause of office would be necessary. If, however, the act complained of could not by its nature be known to the court until it was brought to the court's attention by judicial action (e.g. uncanonical behaviour by a clerk in Holy Orders) some private person would have to initiate proceedings and the cause would be voluntary.

[3] e.g. *Sunderland* v. *Conyers* (*in contempt*) (1620), DEL 4/8/132.

[4] The only examples given by Law are of this character (*F.E.L.*, XLVII–LIII), as are also all the causes of office noted in the course of this investigation.

[5] e.g. *Office of the Judges* v. *Fuller* (1619), DEL 4/8/60 (insulting words directed against the court); *Office of the Judges* v. *Wrothe* (1620), DEL 4/8/180 (solemnization of a marriage in defiance of the court's order); *Office of the Judges* v. *Andrewes* (1618), DEL 4/7/244 (commission of an attentat).

[6] e.g. *Office of the Judges* v. *Bridges* (1611), DEL 4/5/78 (refusal of a clerk to read a decree of excommunication).

for beginning a cause of office as contempt of the judges themselves.[1]

The procedure employed in hearing these causes was substantially the same as the procedure for causes *inter partes*. No new commission was required, as the Delegates had, no doubt, an inherent jurisdiction to punish any contempt of their authority. The action began with the reading by an advocate of a schedule setting out in some detail the acts or omissions complained of;[2] if it saw fit, the court would then decree that the person responsible be cited to answer articles of contempt (these articles constituting the pleadings in the action and taking the place of the libel or allegation in a cause of instance). The articles were then admitted, personal answers to them were demanded and the cause proceeded to proof and sentence in the usual way.

There were, however, two aspects of procedure which distinguished the cause of office from the cause of instance and which deserve brief attention. Voluntary causes were conducted by the persons promoting them, but if the cause were necessary (i.e. initiated by the judges themselves) they would have to appoint promoters of their office to act on their behalf. This appointment was made at an early stage of proceedings and the person chosen was often a proctor;[3] alternatively, someone interested in an action already before the court might act, if the cause of office arose in some way out of that action.[4] It was also a characteristic of the cause of office that the person against whom it was promoted could not be represented by a proctor until he had given in his answers to the articles of contempt pleaded against him, which he would thus have to do personally.[5] This general rule is laid down in

[1] e.g. *Silver* v. *Gaye and Ablett* (*Bachiler intervening*) (1618), DEL 4/7/220.

[2] e.g. *Watson* v. *Watson* (1614), DEL 4/6/238. A proctor would serve if no advocate was available; e.g. *Office of the Judges* v. *Ingram and others* (1611), DEL 4/5/89.

[3] e.g. *Office of the Judges* v. *Kensbeare* (1608), DEL 4/4/180; the court appointed three proctors.

[4] Thus if an appellant flouted the Delegates' authority in some way the court would institute a necessary cause of office against him and might appoint the respondent or an interested third party as the promotor of it. Thus *Office of the Judges* v. *Ludovic Watson* (1614), DEL 4/6/263 was promoted against the appellant in *Watson* v. *Watson*, *supra*, at f. 237, after he had assaulted a process server, and Thomas Watson (the respondent's father) was made the promotor.

[5] See *F.E.L.*, LI/5 and *Office of the Judges* v. *Ingram and others*, *supra*, at f. 104, for an elaborate statement of the rule.

works of practice without modification,[1] but it is clear from the records of the Delegates that its rigour (in that tribunal at least) was on occasions relaxed if some good reason could be shown.[2]

Causes of office promoted before the Delegates themselves were not pursued with any great vigour; thus thirteen such causes were initiated between 1605 and 1615, but only one proceeded to sentence.[3] This reluctance to punish contempt of judicial authority is a little surprising, but a probable explanation is to be found in the structure of the court. The continually changing groups of advocates who comprised this tribunal may have felt little incentive to pursue affronts to their authority once the appeals out of which these affronts arose were determined, and it is likely that only the most flagrant examples of contempt were heard to the end.

[1] See the formulation of it in *F.E.L.*, *loc. cit.*

[2] e.g. *Office of the Judges* v. *Ingram and others*, *supra*, at f. 109; a cause was promoted against two judges of an ecclesiastical court and the Delegates allowed them to be represented by proctors before their answers had been given 'ex eo quod. . . sunt judices in partibus et in alia provincia degentes et ex eo quod est tempus hyemale ita quod ipsi non possunt sine magnis impensis comparere'.

[3] *Office of the Judges* v. *Babbington* (1611), DEL 4/5/52.

CHAPTER X

THE PERSONNEL OF THE COURT

JUDGES

The Court of Delegates had no permanent judges; a separate commission was issued for each cause appointing judges to hear it, and their authority terminated when the cause was concluded. The Act providing for ecclesiastical Delegates imposed no particular qualifications,[1] but it was inevitable that advocates, with their professional training in the civil law, should usually be chosen as commissioners. Often, however, they were afforced by others and in particular common law judges, bishops and peers;[2] each of these groups will be considered separately.[3]

Almost without exception, advocates formed the basis of commissions.[4] Throughout the whole period for which evidence survives there were usually five appointed for each cause,[5] and there were rarely fewer than three.[6] The number naturally rose in commissions of adjuncts (which were often issued for the purpose

[1] 25 Hen. VIII, c. 19, s. 4 merely required that judges-delegate should be 'such Persons as shall be named by the King's Highness'. The corresponding Irish statute laid down that judges of the Irish Court of Delegates should be 'discreet and well-learned persons' (28 Hen. VIII, c. 6).

[2] A somewhat similar variety is to be found in the early appellate practice of the secular civil law; in the middle ages, appeals from the Court of Chivalry were sometimes heard by knights and peers as well as by civilians, and the arrangements for marine appeals were much the same (*H.C.C.*, p. 221; *C.P.R.* 1405, p. 95; *C.P.R.* 1413–16, p. 398).

[3] The errors propagated by the printed authorities about the composition of the court (in particular, the suggestion that bishops and peers were often appointed as commissioners) make such consideration essential. For a typical statement of the mistaken view frequently held on the subject, see Sir M. Foster, *An Examination of the Scheme of Church Power* (London, 1840), p. 36; Blackstone, *Commentaries*, vol. 3, p. 66.

[4] The only two causes discovered in which no advocates sat are *Aisgill* v. *the Archbishop of Canterbury and Bargrave* (1627), DEL 8/70/pt. 1/33 and *Leslie* v. *Aunger* (1628), DEL 8/70/pt. 1/39; all the judges in these causes were bishops.

[5] Commissions including four or six civilians were not uncommon in the early seventeenth century.

[6] This ceased to be the case during the Civil War, when the number of civilians available was greatly reduced by the disturbances; see the appellant's comments in *Hayward* v. *Tufton* (1644), DEL 4/18/70.

of increasing the number of judges)[1] and fell in commissions of review; the decline in the latter case is probably to be explained by the fact that so many advocates had already been concerned in a review cause as counsel or judges that few practising members of the civilian bar were available who were unconnected with it.

In mixed commissions (i.e. those not composed solely of civilians) advocates rarely formed part of the quorum;[2] thus in the form of commission which had become usual by the beginning of the eighteenth century (containing three common law judges and five civilians) no binding sentence could be given unless at least one of the common lawyers consented to it. This had been a source of complaint long before commissions of this nature were common and as early as 1640 Sir John Lambe had included it among the list of matters which Archbishop Laud was asked to remedy.[3] In fact, the position of the civilians was rather stronger than their absence from the quorum might suggest, as they usually had a numerical majority which prevented the judges of Westminster Hall from out-voting them. In a full commission, however, in which bishops and peers were also included, the advocates lost their majority and it was a valid complaint that a decision could be given in such causes which was not acceptable to the only members of the bench who were professionally qualified in the civil law.

Although the civilians formed the majority on most commissions, the judges of the common law were allowed a share, which became increasingly important, in the workings of the Court of Delegates. Their names occur by *c.* 1600[4] (if not before), although the surviving records make it impossible to tell how frequently they were appointed until the third decade of the seventeenth century.[5]

[1] e.g. *Newman and Kingesley* v. *Mockemes* (1623), DEL 8/70/pt. 1/15 and *Lake* v. *Lake* (1643), DEL 8/71/pt. 1/20; each commission had eleven civilian members. For commissions of adjuncts, see p. 83 *ante*.

[2] For the quorum clause, see p. 83 *ante*.

[3] In his letter to Laud he wrote: 'We meddle not in common law causes and they have little or no skill in ours, yet they have been not only our judges, but always of the quorum and never any of us. So that we could do nothing without them but they what they pleased without us' (*C.S.P.D.*, 1639–40, p. 350).

[4] See DEL 4/2, *passim*.

[5] Any study of the court's composition must be based upon the commissions of delegacy or the Repertory Books, which are the only important documents containing full lists of the commissioners who were appointed for particular causes. As no commissions survive earlier than the Restoration, the material for this chapter has been largely derived from the Repertory Books which extend from 1619 to 1789.

Throughout the remainder of that century practice gradually hardened. The presence of common lawyers was at first quite infrequent, and until the Civil War they sat on one cause in every seven, or thereabouts. From August 1652 until the end of the Interregnum they were present on every commission,[1] and this reform (like several others in that period) was anticipatory of later practice. In the reaction which followed the Restoration, commissions from which common lawyers were completely excluded were again issued, but their number steadily dwindled and none is to be found later than the first decade of the eighteenth century.[2] That common lawyers were by now regarded as an essential part of each commission may be confirmed from other sources; in 1701 a petitioner seeking a review gave it as a principal ground of his application that the Court of Delegates which found against him was composed of five civilians only,[3] while in 1728 counsel in *Hill* v. *White and White* (*et e contra*)[4] declared that common lawyers had become 'necessary in the Commissions' in recent years.

The practice regulating the number and standing of the common law judges on a commission underwent a similar change in the course of the seventeenth century. In the earlier part of this period, it was not uncommon for only one or two to sit,[5] although on occasions there might be many more;[6] the available evidence suggests that at this time they were usually excluded from ordinary causes (for which the usual commission consisted of five civilians, sitting alone) and were employed largely on commissions of review or of adjuncts and in causes where persons of importance were involved. They might be drawn from all the common law benches

[1] DEL 8/71/pt. 1/60–89. In this period common lawyers were introduced into other civilian courts; three of the judges of the Court of Admiralty were from Westminster Hall during the Interregnum, while the Solicitor-General and the Recorder of London were among the commissioners named to exercise jurisdiction over heraldic matters (Main Thompson, *Admiralty Registrars*, p. 9; Firth and Rait, *Acts and Ordinances*, vol. 1, pp. 838–9).

[2] The last two causes of this nature were *Moulding* v. *Mytton* (1703), DEL 8/73/pt. 1/6 (seven civilians); *Deye* v. *Deye* (1703), DEL 8/73/pt. 1/7 (eight civilians).

[3] *C.S.P.D.*, 1700–02, pp. 395–6.

[4] (1728), Mos. 29 at 32.

[5] e.g. *Alford and Collyns* v. *Bower* (1620), DEL 8/70/pt. 1/5 (two common law judges); *Selby* v. *Faldoe* (1621), DEL 8/70/pt. 1/6 (one common law judge).

[6] e.g. *Harries* v. *Leake* (1625), DEL 8/70/pt. 1/19; nine common law judges were appointed to this commission (a substantial part of the common law benches).

or from only one.[1] By the end of the century when the position of the common lawyers was established, and they sat in every cause, it was customary for each commission to include three judges; usually they were puisnes (from *c.* 1730 one from each of the common law benches) but one or more of the Chief Justices might be included in certain circumstances.[2]

Attendance by the judges at sittings of the court was largely confined to informations and sentence and they took little part in the earlier sessions of a cause. Even their attendance at the final hearings, however, was a cause of increasing irritation to their civilian colleagues. In the early seventeenth century, there are some signs that Westminster Hall was prepared on occasions to cooperate with the College of Advocates and the common lawyers sometimes sat at Doctors' Commons.[3] This was not common, however, and seems never to have occurred after the Restoration; from that time onwards it was always the civilians who had, at some inconvenience, to go down to one of the Serjeants' Inns for sentence. The fixing of a time for this purpose seems also to have been the prerogative of the common lawyers and the conventional assignation for informations and sentence in the eighteenth century records is 'whensoever the Common Law Judges shall appoint'.[4]

In the face of this self-assertion by the common lawyers, the civilians involved in the work of the Court of Delegates found themselves powerless. That they resented the position there can be no doubt; attendance at the Serjeants' Inns was, it seems, especially burdensome and Sir John Lambe, in his letter to Laud already quoted,[5] spoke indignantly of the expense and inconvenience occasioned by it.[6] His protest, however, had no effect and another attempt, made some twenty years after the Restoration, to exchange the Serjeants' Inns for a meeting place more congenial

[1] e.g. *the Bishop of Winchester* v. *the Bishop of Durham* (1630), DEL 8/70/pt 2/3; the three common law judges who served on this commission were all from the King's Bench.

[2] e.g. *Johnson* v. *Glascock and others* (1687), DEL 8/72/pt. 2/19 (the Chief Justice of the Common Pleas and the Chief Baron of the Exchequer); *Hyland* v. *Hyland* (1694), DEL 8/72/pt. 2/50 (the Chief Justice of the King's Bench).

[3] e.g. pp. 204–5 *post.*

[4] e.g. *Butler* v. *Butler* (1757), DEL 6/44/58.

[5] See p. 179 *ante.*

[6] 'To attend at Sergeant's Inn was to the great trouble and extreme charge of the subject, in carrying down the proctors, advocates, registrars, and judges thither' (*C.S.P.D.*, 1639–40, p. 350).

to the civilians, was frustrated by the common lawyers themselves.[1] It seems that the matter was never raised again and for the rest of the court's life the arrangements for informations and sentence were dictated by the judges' convenience.

The extent to which the common lawyers were able to insinuate their own doctrines into the decisions of the Delegates is a matter of some uncertainty. Reasoned judgments, properly reported, might have made the matter clear, but these are not available and such evidence as is to hand yields uncertain conclusions. Sir John Lambe, it is true, had no doubts; his complaint to Archbishop Laud in 1640 is mainly concerned with the ill effects of allowing common lawyers to share in the judgments of the court and the chief evil, as he saw it, was the inevitable infection of the civil law by the tenets of the rival system. This, he declared, 'by little and little will ruin our profession, and deduce and turn all ecclesiastical judicature into the common law, and consequently all ecclesiastical jurisdiction, for no proceeding can be by any ordinary, but the subject may appeal, and it must terminate there if the wilful party please'.[2]

It is difficult to avoid the conclusion that the case is overstated (deliberately, no doubt, as Lambe had an interest in making the situation appear as black as possible). At the time when he wrote, commissions of delegacy containing common lawyers were of no very frequent occurrence and were destined not to become so for over half a century. By 1700, the argument may seem to have a greater cogency but even then the civilians had a protection which Lambe had either forgotten or deliberately ignored. Although they were never on the quorum they were almost always able to outvote the common lawyers, and thus to reject any heresy which Westminster Hall might require them to embrace. It seems likely, then, that common law doctrines made little mark upon the Court of Delegates.

Precise evidence which would serve to explain how the common lawyers were able to intrude themselves so successfully into the court is also lacking, but an explanation may perhaps be conjectured, as there were several circumstances which must have helped them. There was no statutory limitation upon the classes of judges whom the Crown might choose for civil law appeals and

[1] See pp. 205–6 *post*.

[2] *C.S.P.D.*, 1639–40, pp. 350–1.

medieval practice, as has been shown, allowed for some variety.[1] It has been plausibly suggested that the Act providing for ecclesiastical delegates permitted the inclusion of laymen (including common law judges) as the loyalty of bishops and civilians to the reformed Church was suspect;[2] this motive must have lost its cogency by the beginning of the seventeenth century, but by then the precedents for employing common lawyers may well have been of respectable antiquity and in the unified Court of Delegates the practice continued, although, as has been seen, they were included in only a small minority of commissions at that time. The opportunity to consolidate their position came during the Interregnum when some reason (probably the uncertain allegiance of the civilians to the Commonwealth)[3] led to the inclusion of the judges of Westminster Hall in all commissions. After the Restoration, the inevitable reaction to the older practice was of surprisingly short duration and by the end of the century the common lawyers were again present in every commission. This final success we must surely attribute to the general triumph of the common law over its old rival in the last four decades of the seventeenth century. The trickle of prohibitions had turned into a flood, the jurisdiction of the Court of Admiralty had been inexorably reduced and the ecclesiastical courts found themselves in the same plight.[4] The constitution of the Court of Delegates made it peculiarly vulnerable to penetration by the common lawyers and here, as elsewhere, they pressed their advantage home and won their victory.

The judges of the common law, although imperfectly acquainted with the civilian system, had at least received legal training and had a proper respect for forensic mysteries; the same could hardly be said for bishops and peers, who made up the two other categories from which Delegates were usually chosen. Little use was made of them, however, and the evidence for their activities is meagre. Their appearance on commissions was far less frequent than that of the judges. Even in the seventeenth century, bishops sat on only a small proportion of the causes and peers were even less frequently employed; commissions including them became steadily more uncommon in the century following and from 1750

[1] See p. 178 *ante*.

[2] Gibson, *Codex Juris Ecclesiastici Anglicani*, vol. 1, p. xxi.

[3] *H.E.L.*, vol. 5, p. 18.

[4] See pp. 26–7 *ante*.

until 1789 (when the series of Repertory Books came to an end) only six have been found.[1]

The circumstances in which it was thought proper to add bishops and peers to commissions are obscure.[2] The composition of a commission fell within the discretion of the Lord Chancellor and the principles involved were presumably considered by him from time to time, but the only reported decision on the matter which has come to light in the course of this enquiry is *ex parte Hellier*.[3] In this cause, an important point of testamentary law was at issue and one party petitioned for a full commission, which was answered by a cross-petition from the other side seeking the appointment of civilians and common lawyers alone. Hardwicke's judgment suggests that, in his view, full commissions were to be confined to purely ecclesiastical appeals (i.e. those involving the canon law, the jurisdiction of bishops and the like) as these were causes in which the presence of lords spiritual and temporal was desirable to achieve balanced judgments. No other reason (not even the importance of the cause) could justify such commissions.

In the absence of other decisions on the same point, it is impossible to trace the development of the rules which governed the chancellor's discretion in the course of the court's life. It is well enough established, however, that by about 1750 the exercise of that discretion in purely equitable matters was hardening,[4] and the appointment of judges to the Court of Delegates can hardly

[1] This is perhaps a convenient point to correct the curious error of Bishop Gibson concerning the composition of the court before the Civil War. In his *Codex* he declares: 'there are no footsteps of any of the Nobility or Common-Law-Judges, in Commission, till the year 1604, (i.e. for 70 years after the Erecting of the Court;) nor from 1604 are they found in above one Commission in forty, till the year 1639; from whence (i.e. from the downfall of Bishops, and their Jurisdiction, which ensued) we may date the present Rule of Mixtures in that Court' (pp. xxi–xxii). The records, however, tell a very different story. The first Repertory Book gives a complete list of commissions issued from 1619 to 1639 while from the earlier Act Books it is possible to extract the names of all the judges who attended sittings of the court from 1601 to 1619 (for the ecclesiastical Delegates, the same information is available for the period 1538–44). This evidence makes it abundantly clear that noblemen and common lawyers did sit before 1604 and that from that date until 1639 they sat far more often than Gibson suggests. For a detailed discussion of the matter, see Brodrick and Fremantle, *A Collection of the Judgments of the Privy Council*, pp. xlvii–lviii.

[2] The question of their sitting alone, without civilians or judges of the common law, hardly arose; only two causes have been found in which bishops sitting alone formed the entire commission, and none in which peers, or peers and bishops, sat alone (see p. 178 *ante*).

[3] (1754), 3 Atk. 798.

[4] See *H.E.L.*, vol. 12, p. 262.

have escaped this tendency; it is at least likely, then, that in the sixteenth and seventeenth centuries full commissions were granted upon rather more liberal principles. The virtual absence of such commissions from 1750 to 1789 (and possibly beyond) suggests either that there were no causes of the limited kind to which Hardwicke's judgment refers, or that the rule which he enunciated was later abandoned and that bishops and peers were allowed no further share in the workings of the court.

Civilians, common law judges, bishops and peers made up the great majority of commissions, but there was no obligation to choose Delegates from these alone and in the earlier part of the court's life others were included from time to time. This latter group has no fixed character and it is probable that in most cases its members were chosen as an alternative to bishops or common lawyers; thus deans and doctors of divinity recur[1] as do serjeants and (more rarely) the law officers of the Crown. Persons in the immediate employment of the Crown as secretaries and the like were sometimes put into commissions;[2] their employment was perhaps confined to those causes in which royal interests were intimately concerned.

Appointments of this nature were not infrequent until the Restoration.[3] They occur from time to time in the following four decades,[4] and are not to be found thereafter.

The choice of Delegates for a particular commission was a matter for the authorities. Before the Reformation, litigants who had appealed to Rome might themselves choose some of the judges,[5] but no such concession was made by the Act which provided for ecclesiastical Delegates and it is clear that the practice subsequently evolved made no provision for it. The most that an

[1] e.g. John Donne, who as Dean of St Paul's was appointed to fifteen commissions from 1619 to 1629.

[2] The names of Suckling, Cook, Vane, Windebanke and Nicholas are all to be found in the first Repertory Book.

[3] During the Interregnum the composition of the group naturally altered; clerks were excluded and a variety of persons well disposed to the government brought in, army officers and city aldermen being especially common. The matter is further discussed on p. 24 *ante*.

[4] Twelve examples have been found over this period.

[5] F. W. Maitland, *Roman Canon Law in the Church of England* (London, 1898), pp. 114–15; some striking examples are given in R. Brentano, *York Metropolitan Jurisdiction and Papal Judges Delegate (1279–1296)* (Berkeley, Cal., 1959), pp. 153–5. It has been suggested, however, that this was not the usual practice (A. Morey, *Bartholomew of Exeter* (Cambridge, 1937), p. 48).

appellant could do was to suggest, in general terms, the type of commission which he would prefer;[1] the respondent, if his own preference was different, could then advance it in a cross-petition.[2]

From *c.* 1690 to the end of the court's life the usual commission was made up of civilians and common law judges alone and most of the surviving evidence which relates to the choice of Delegates has to do with commissions of this type. It is apparent from the Report of the Ecclesiastical Commissioners in 1832 that by this time the selection of Delegates was largely mechanical. A rota was kept in the Lord Chancellor's office containing the names of all the puisne judges and all the doctors of the civil law (the latter being entered on the roll in the order of their admission to that degree); for each cause of appeal, the names of three common law judges and six civilians (three senior and three junior) were chosen in order.[3] The rota is known to have been kept at least from the chancellorship of Lord Eldon,[4] and there is little doubt that this system of choosing civilians (or one very like it) was in use long before. A survey of commissions issued in the seventeenth and eighteenth centuries shows that both senior and junior advocates were represented in most causes.[5] No pattern occurs in the names of common law judges appointed to commissions and some sat far more frequently than others. As the total number of common law judges was so small and their other judicial work so pressing, it may well have been the custom to approach them individually whenever a commission was to be issued.[6]

[1] Thus Henry Howell, petitioning in 1688 for an appeal from the Court of Chivalry, requested a commission 'directed to such Noblemen of this Kingdom and learned Judges of the Common Law and Civilians as hath been used in the like Cases' (*H.C.C.*, App. XXV). Similarly, in 1696, when it was still possible for commissions to be issued to civilians alone, a petitioner seeking a review requested a commission 'directed to the judges of the common law' (*C.S.P.D.*, 1696, p. 27).

[2] Thus in *ex parte Hellier* (1754), 3 Atk. 798, one party petitioned for a full commission, while the other in his cross-petition asked that only common law judges and civilians be appointed.

[3] *Eccl. Courts Rep.* (1831–2), pp. 207–8.

[4] *Ibid.*, p. 208.

[5] It should be noticed, however, that most of those who attended sittings of the court were of junior standing; see p. 29 *ante*.

[6] It is significant that although entries such as 'recusavit' appear not infrequently against the names of civilian Delegates in the Repertory Books, the names of common law judges are never so endorsed. This suggests that the latter were always consulted before their names were placed on commissions, while the civilians were not.

No surviving evidence, even of the most meagre sort, relates to the choice of bishops and peers. The matter was not touched on in the evidence given before the Royal Commission of 1832, as it had ceased to be at all usual to appoint spiritual and temporal lords as judges-delegate about eighty years earlier. The keeping of a permanent rota would hardly have been practicable, and it is likely that a list of those who would be suitable and who might be prevailed upon to act was drawn up whenever such a commission was to be issued.[1]

Causes of the more considerable sort (important either for their legal significance or from the standing of the litigants involved in them) were subject to special considerations and Delegates to judge them were selected with some care. The importance of a judicious choice was formally recognized during the chancellorship of Lord Bacon who made an order in 1619 that no commission of delegacy should be issued 'in any case of weight' without reference to the chancellor 'who will name the commissioners himselfe; to the end, that they may be persons of convenient quality, having regard to the weight of the cause, and the dignity of the Court from whom the appeale is'.[2] This order may have done no more than confirm previous practice, as there is evidence from an earlier period that the scrupulous choice required by Bacon in such causes was already being exercised. In 1605, for example, the litigation between the Earl of Hertford and Lord Mounteagle came before a Court of Delegates whose members had been carefully selected, as a document in the Hatfield House archives reveals.[3] The paper is headed 'Persons considerable for delegates in the commission of appeal of the Earl of Hartforde'; twenty names are included, among them those of the Archbishop of Canterbury and the Bishop of London, the Lord Chancellor, the Lord Treasurer, the Lord Chamberlain, three common law judges and six of the most prominent civilians. Below are set out objections to certain other persons (who had apparently been considered and rejected); two had been employed as counsel for the appellant, one had been 'privately used' at an earlier stage in the proceedings, while another

[1] There is some evidence that this procedure was followed when it was necessary to choose Delegates for important causes; the matter is discussed in the paragraphs which follow.

[2] Sanders, *Orders of the High Court of Chancery*, vol. 1, p. 122 (Order 97).

[3] H.M.C. Salisbury MSS., part xvi, p. 440. Two similar lists are to be found in H.M.C. Salisbury MSS., part xvii, pp. 182–3.

was 'privy to the close carriage of the appeal and...near in blood to the Earl of Hertford'. A similar method of scrutiny was presumably employed in other causes of a like nature.

In every cause, the ultimate responsibility for the choice of judges-delegate lay no doubt with the Lord Chancellor, but the day to day workings of the system were entrusted to others. Towards the end of the court's life, the rota of civilians and common law judges was controlled by an official of the chancellor's office,[1] and this had clearly been the practice for at least several decades. Earlier, however, the responsibility (for the choice of civilians at least) lay with the king's advocate. Immediately after the Restoration, a petition of appeal was put in by one John Dunne, and in the course of it he requested the chancellor to nominate civilians as commissioners 'or otherwise to authorize the Kings Majesties Advocate to appoint the said Judges Delegates as alwaies heretofore (untill the late troubles) was and hath beene accustomed'[2]. The practice was confirmed by Lord Clarendon in his endorsement of another petition of the same date, in which he required the king's advocate to name the judges for that appeal 'as alsoe for other Appeales for the future'.[3]

Despite this delegation of authority, it is clear that the chancellor retained the right to intervene on occasions. Bacon's order of 1619 had required this intervention for causes of importance,[4] and later in the century Chancellor Hyde, while confirming the right of the king's advocate to act for him in the appointment of Delegates, was careful to add the proviso 'except I be specially moved to name them myselfe'.[5] It is probable that this stipulation was most often invoked when the parties differed as to the composition of a commission; such disputes came before the chancellor personally, who after hearing argument gave a formal judgment.[6]

The Court of Delegates, as has been seen, had no permanent judiciary, a separate commission being issued for each cause. This arrangement, however novel it may appear today, was sanctioned by respectable precedents; thus before the Reformation, appeals to Rome from the English provinces were usually decided by judges

[1] The Secretary of Commissions of Appeal to the Lord Chancellor (*Eccl. Courts Rep.* (1831–2), p. 207). [2] DEL 9/1/134–5.

[3] DEL 9/1/134 (petition of Francis Crumpe).

[4] See note 2 on p. 187 *ante*.

[5] DEL 9/1/134 (petition of Francis Crumpe).

[6] e.g. *ex parte Hellier* (1754), 3 Atk. 798.

who were appointed *pro hac vice* by the Roman Curia and who lived in the province concerned,[1] while appeals in marine and chivalry causes were entrusted to commissions appointed by the Crown on an identical basis.[2] Such makeshift arrangements were not without grave inconveniences, however, and they were gradually replaced by those involving a greater permanency. The innovating zeal of the Council of Trent was directed to the system of Papal judges-delegate, which was drastically reformed,[3] while in England a tardy step was taken in the same direction in 1628 when a standing commission was established to hear appeals in prize causes.[4] This arrangement must have been successful enough, as it was continued for the rest of that tribunal's life,[5] but it had no immediate effect upon the constitution of the Court of Delegates, and it was not until some sixty years later that a determined attempt was made to reform that tribunal in like manner. From a letter bearing date 13 May 1685, signed by twelve of the most prominent advocates and representing, it seems, the general wishes of the profession, it appears that a petition, asking for 'stated Judges in the Court of Delegates' had been presented to Sir Leoline Jenkins, then judge of the Court of Admiralty and the Prerogative Court, who was no doubt thought to be the most influential civilian. Jenkins promptly advised that it should be presented to the king by the Archbishop of Canterbury; the petitioners fell in with this proposal, but requested that Jenkins himself and Sir Richard Lloyd, another prominent civilian, should be present to add their support when the petition was handed in, or should perform the task themselves, if the Archbishop refused to do so.[6]

Jenkins is known to have approved of the proposal and may be presumed to have given it his full support;[7] despite this, however, the constitution of the court continued as before and the attempt

[1] Appeals from all other provinces of the Church were decided in the same way; Morey, *Bartholomew of Exeter*, p. 46.

[2] Marsden (ed.), *Select Pleas in the Court of Admiralty*, vol. 1, p. lxxix; *H.C.C.*, p. 221.

[3] Van Espen, *Ius Ecclesiasticum Universum*, bk. 3, pt. 5, tit. 2, chs. 23–7.

[4] Roscoe, *A History of the English Prize Court*, p. 87.

[5] There was a temporary reversion to the older practice of appointing special commissions during the Interregnum; *ibid.*, p. 87.

[6] Wynne, *Life of Sir Leoline Jenkins*, vol. 2, p. 695.

[7] Wynne states that Jenkins was anxious to avoid the 'many inconveniences' resulting from separate commissions and that he drew up a draft set of rules to govern the standing commission which he hoped would be conceded by the king (*ibid.*, vol. 1, p. lii).

at reform must be considered, for whatever reason, a failure.[1] Whether the project was acceptable to the Crown in principle and languished merely for want of later encouragement,[2] or whether the plan for a permanent bench was liable to serious objection, we shall never know. The latter explanation is at least likely, as the scheme is known to have contained an aspect which can hardly have recommended it to a Stuart monarch. Hitherto, those who had acted as judges in a cause before the Delegates had received, by way of recompense for their services, a small sum of money from the successful party.[3] Such casual payments could not provide the fixed stipends which a permanent judiciary would expect, and Jenkins warned his colleagues, when they first presented the petition to him, that they 'should think of a Fund, out of which the Salaries should issue'. The implication of the warning is clear enough; a favourable answer could hardly be expected if one effect of the proposed reform was to charge the judges' salaries upon the straitened resources of the Crown. The plaintive answer of the petitioners suggests that this difficulty was likely to meet with no immediate solution: 'at present we have only this to say, that in case his Majesty shall be pleased to favour our Petition, we do not despair of finding out such a Fund, as shall not be any great Detriment to his Majesty's Revenue'.[4] This, in all likelihood, is the rock upon which the scheme foundered.

REGISTRAR

The principal official of the Court of Delegates (as of other civilian courts) was the registrar.[5] The position was an important one and

[1] There is no evidence that the petition was ever, in fact, presented; neither the document itself, nor a copy of it, is to be found among the State Papers Domestic.

[2] Jenkins, who could have given this, died shortly after, and Wynne is of opinion that this was a likely reason for the failure of the scheme (Wynne, *Life of Sir Leoline Jenkins*, vol. 1, p. lii).

[3] By the end of the court's life, Delegates were paid at the rate of one guinea for each day's attendance at informations and sentence (*Admiralty etc. Courts Rep.* (1824), p. 74). Earlier practice was rather erratic, but the evidence of the bills of costs makes it clear that, from the early seventeenth century at least, the judges received some payment for their work.

[4] Wynne, *Life of Sir Leoline Jenkins*, vol. 2, p. 695.

[5] His Latin title was *registrarius*, but in English documents of the seventeenth and early eighteenth century he is usually called the 'register'. Later this is converted into the modern form 'registrar', although the older title is occasionally found as late as the end of the eighteenth century and beyond; thus in *Wattell* v. *Wattell* (1788), DEL 2/95, the certificate of service on the monition

the records of the court contain information about his qualifications, functions and mode of appointment which may serve as a supplement to the general account of this office which is contained in the printed authorities.[1]

No formal qualifications for the position of Delegates' registrar are specifically referred to in the records of the court, although it is very likely that he had always to be a notary public (at least, if he acted in person); he is often referred to in documents by this title and the authorities suggest (although with some hesitation) that it was necessary.[2] It seems that he had also to be a person capable of taking the oaths of supremacy and allegiance, as they were tendered to him upon appointment.[3] When the office was to be discharged in person and not by deputy,[4] regard was no doubt had to the personal qualities which work of this nature required.[5]

The functions of the Delegates' registrar were those which the nature of the office would suggest; the more important of them are embraced in the three-fold division of duties attributed by Ayliffe to any registrar of a civilian court.[6] A detailed analysis of the office in the Court of Delegates was made in 1824,[7] and it added to Ayliffe's list certain other requirements; in particular the registrar was obliged to attend when parties or witnesses were sworn, to make out

for process in the cause refers to the 'register' of the Court of the Dean and Chapter of St Peter's Westminster, while in the report on certain civilian courts issued in 1824 the older spelling is also used (*Admiralty etc. Courts Rep.* (1824), p. 74).

The full style of the Delegates' registrar is given in Letters Patent of Queen Anne's reign as 'Principalis Registrarius et Clericus ac Processuum Negotiorum Prothocollorum Instrumentorum et Actorum Quorumcumque Scriba' (DEL 9/5/53).

[1] See in particular *F.E.L.*, IX which is largely derived from Ayliffe, *Parergon Juris Canonici Anglicani*, pp. 382–6.

[2] Law declares that 'it seems to be a necessary qualification to his office' and cites Ayliffe and Burn as authority (*F.E.L.*, IX/1/iii). In *the Earl of Hertford* v. *Lord Mounteagle* (1606), DEL 4/3/203, it was stated that the registrar of the Court of Arches had always to be a notary public.

[3] e.g. DEL 4/14/264 (appointment of Sir John Oldbury in 1635).

[4] In fact, deputies were often employed; see pp. 302–4 *post*.

[5] The position was recognized as a responsible one; a return of 1734 said of the office that it 'requires great experience and ability, and is a place of great trust and consequence' (*Admiralty etc. Courts Rep.* (1824), p. 75).

[6] These were (i) to enrol all the acts of the court, (ii) to give the parties copies of court proceedings if they were asked for, (iii) to preserve all the original records of the court (*Parergon Juris Canonici Anglicani*, p. 383). The recitation of the registrar's duties in the instrument appointing James Pinfold as deputy in 1720 covers substantially the same ground (DEL 9/6/11–12).

[7] *Admiralty etc. Courts Rep.* (1824), pp. 74–5.

probate of wills or letters of administration granted by the court, to draw, engross and sign all the decrees issued by the judges and to have the custody of moneys paid into court and of the official seal. At one time the registrar was required to help in examining witnesses; references to this are quite common in the early seventeenth century,[1] and it was still apparently the rule as late as 1734.[2] Later, however, the task was always performed by an examiner approved by the registrar.[3] In the same way, the entering of personal answers, which at one time was also, it seems, an obligation of the registrar, later became a function of the proctors.[4]

The entry of the registrar upon his office was usually referred to in the appropriate Act Book or Assignation Book and was attended with some formality. A typical example was the accession of Sir John Oldbury who succeeded Sir George Paule, upon the latter's death or retirement. The ceremony took place at the beginning of the first session of the Easter term 1635, when Oldbury appeared in court in the presence of the advocate general and ten doctors of law; he presented his Letters Patent under the Great Seal and took the oaths of supremacy and allegiance.[5]

From the latter part of the seventeenth century the office of the Delegates' registrar seems always to have been granted in reversion and this may have been the practice very much earlier.[6] The oldest patent of which a copy survives among the court records was issued in the ninth year of Queen Anne's reign,[7] and it is, to judge from

[1] e.g. *Blades* v. *Warde* (1605), DEL 4/3/55; *Heylyn and others* v. *Wicherley* (1608), DEL 4/4/216. The registrars of other civilian courts also acted as examiners on occasions; e.g. *Hickmott* v. *Munne and others* (*in the principal cause*) (1645), DEL 4/18/96 (Court of the Commissary of Canterbury).

[2] *Admiralty etc. Courts Rep.* (1824), p. 74.

[3] *Ibid.*, pp. 74–5.

[4] *Ibid.*, pp. 74–5.

[5] DEL 4/14/264. The same form was used very much later; see DEL 6/44/79, which records the appearance in court of Godfrey Lee Farrant upon his appointment as registrar in 1758. These entries suggest that registrars of the Delegates were always appointed by such Letters Patent. Several are set out *in extenso* in the Muniment Books (see DEL 9/5/53–8 and DEL 9/8/115–22).

[6] There is evidence for this in a letter written by Sir William Trumbull to William Blathwayt (2 August 1695) relating to a reversionary grant of the office to the nephew of Sir Charles Hedges: 'If the King scruples because of the name of a reversion, you should inform him that the grants of this office have always passed for two lives' (H.M.C. Downshire MSS., vol. 1, pt. 2, p. 527). The propriety of certain reversionary grants had earlier been doubted, however, as a petition presented in 1660 for the grant of the office in reversion was endorsed: 'The King will grant no such reversion' (*C.S.P.D.*, 1660–61, p. 446).

[7] DEL 9/5/53–8.

later examples, a typical one; the appointment was granted to Richard Hill when the interest of Richard Crawley (the then registrar) had determined and to Sir Charles Hedges upon the determination of Crawley's and Hill's interests. In the earlier part of the court's life the office was sometimes exercised by two persons jointly,[1] although this practice does not seem to have survived the Civil War; later, however, two or even three persons acted jointly as deputy registrars.[2]

In the period when a substantial amount of business was passing through the ecclesiastical courts, the office of Delegates' registrar must have been a source of respectable profit to the holder. Some indication of its value in the period immediately following the Restoration is contained in an offer made by an unnamed person who had apparently applied for the registrarship (in reversion) of the Court of Delegates and of the High Commission;[3] for the two offices together he was prepared to give £400 or £500 immediately and to make further payments of £300 or £400 per annum when the reversion fell in.[4]

The discharge of such offices by deputy, the principal registrar receiving most of the profits and paying his appointee with the balance, seems always to have been common and from the beginning of the seventeenth century, if not before, the functions of the Delegates' registrar were usually performed in this way; it has proved possible to compile an unbroken list of such deputies from *c.* 1600 to the end of the court's life.[5] The older practice of the court may well have required the registrar to discharge most of his duties in person and such evidence as is available suggests this; thus entries on many sentences dating from the last two decades of the

[1] Thus the registrarships of John Plomer and Sir George Paule overlapped and they occasionally appeared together; e.g. *the Earl of Hertford* v. *Lord Mounteagle* (1605), DEL 4/3/77.

[2] See the list on pp. 302–4 *post*.

[3] He may well have been the John Brydall who had made an unsuccessful application for the reversion of the registrarships of these two courts five years before (*C.S.P.D.*, 1660–61, p. 446). It was not uncommon for two or more civilian courts to share the same registrar; earlier in the seventeenth century, one man had discharged this office both for the Delegates and the High Commission (see the entries relating to Plomer, Oldbury and Paule in the list of Delegates' registrars at pp. 297–9 *post*) and from the end of that century the same registrar always acted for the Court of Delegates and the Court of Admiralty.

[4] *C.S.P.D.*, 1665–6, p. 176.

[5] For this, see pp. 302–4 *post*.

sixteenth century make it clear that the then registrar (Edward Barker) often acted himself.[1] In the following decades, however, such appearances are far less frequent and after the Civil War, there seem to have been only two registrars who ever acted in person.[2] Nevertheless the widespread use of deputies to discharge offices of this sort was not universally approved and Sir Leoline Jenkins, for example, advanced several cogent reasons against their employment in the Court of Admiralty, some of which were equally applicable to the Court of Delegates.[3]

Although the appointment of a principal registrar was a matter for the Crown, it seems that the principal could appoint and dismiss his deputy at his pleasure;[4] the right to act by deputy was sometimes specifically conferred by the Letters Patent appointing the principal.[5] A single deputy filled the post throughout most of the court's life, although in the early seventeenth century some appointments overlapped,[6] and by the end of the century following it was customary for two or three deputies to act concurrently.[7]

OTHER OFFICERS

The registrar or his deputy had under his control a number of persons who helped with the clerical work of the court and performed certain other functions. In 1824, the officers employed consisted of a cryer, a sealer, examiners and clerks and this, it seems, was a typical civilian establishment.[8]

The most important function of the cryer (who is often referred

[1] See DEL 5/1/*passim*.

[2] Richard Crawley (registrar 1695 to 1712) seems to have largely dispensed with a deputy, but Lord Arden (registrar 1790 to 1832), although he did part of the work himself, employed several deputies.

[3] Wynne, *Life of Sir Leoline Jenkins*, vol. 2, pp. 709–10.

[4] When Godfrey Lee Farrant became registrar in 1758 he appointed George Bellas as his deputy (DEL 6/44/79); in the following year Farrant exhibited to the court an instrument revoking Bellas' appointment and another instrument appointing Nathaniel Bishop (DEL 6/44/117). Both these instruments were admitted by the court without question.

[5] Thus the Letters Patent, granting the office of principal registrar for two lives after the determination of the interest of Richard Crawley, allowed the appointees to act 'per Se vel per Sufficientem Deputatum Suum Sive Deputatos Suos Sufficientes' (DEL 9/5/58).

[6] Thus William Barker and Nicholas Webbe were both acting as deputies in 1633.

[7] See the list on pp. 302–4 *post*.

[8] The officers of the Court of Chivalry were substantially the same (*H.C.C.*, p. 137) as were those of the Court of Admiralty (*Admiralty etc. Courts Rep.* (1824), pp. 50–73) and of the Court of Arches (*Archbp. of Canterbury's Courts Rep.* (1823), pp. 18–20).

to as the mandatary) was to serve decrees of the court. In practice, the discharge of his duties was confined to London and if process was to be served out of the capital, someone living in the neighbourhood was usually employed (sometimes a servant of the proctor on whose behalf the decree was issued).[1] The cryer was also used to make enquiries as to the sufficiency of sureties and to certify his findings to the court,[2] while other investigations which the court required might fall to him.[3] He had also to attend the sittings of the court for the purpose of keeping order and making proclamations.[4]

The duty of the sealer was to keep the seal and to use it for sealing all the mandates which were issued under the authority of the court. As early as 1734 (and possibly for long before that) the office was discharged by the registrar, who had the custody of the seal and received the fees for its use.[5]

[1] e.g. *Edwardes* v. *Morgan* (1617), DEL 4/7/117. It seems that the Delegates' cryer had an exclusive right of service within a certain area, although its precise extent was disputed. In the Presentment of 1734 it was said to be confined 'to the bills of mortality' but the cryer employed in 1824 claimed that his rights were subject to no such limitations; the commissioners suggested that his privilege should be confined to an area within ten miles of Doctors' Commons, and that beyond that limit he should be employed to serve process only if the parties so desired (*Admiralty etc. Courts Rep.* (1824), p. 88).

[2] *Admiralty etc. Courts Rep.* (1824), p. 88. Many of these certificates survive among the cause papers; e.g. *Shemeld* v. *Stokes* (1745), DEL 2/78 (Peter Powell, the then mandatary, certified: 'I have made enquiry after James Cooke Esq.... and....I find him to be a Sufficient Security to be bound in a Bond of the penalty of Eight hundred pounds for Alice Shemeld...for her due administration of the said deceased's Goods, Chattells and Credits').

[3] e.g. *Soux* v. *Soux* (1705), DEL 6/31/77; the cryer was sent to make enquiries about the appellant's health, after she had claimed to be unable to appear in court because of illness.

[4] *Admiralty etc. Courts Rep.* (1824), p. 88.

[5] *Ibid.*, p. 88. This is perhaps a convenient place to describe briefly the seal of the court. An order of 3 April 1703 to Henry Harris, Chief Engraver of the Seals, describes the usual pattern; he was to prepare a seal 'with the Royal Arms and Crown, a lion and unicorn for supporters, with this inscription round the same: "Sigillum Annae, D.G. Mag. Brit. Fra. et Hib. Reginae, fidei defensoris &c., ad causas ecclesiasticas et maritimas" a ship under our arms, with this motto: "Ab Edgare Vendico"' (*C.S.P.D.*, 1703–4, pp. 450–1). A fairly complete example has survived attached to a compulsory issued in *Arabin* v. *Arabin* (1788), DEL 2/3; this is a large papered seal (the protective paper covering measures 5 in. by 5½ in.) displaying the arms and supporters referred to in Harris' warrant; the ship is a three-masted vessel, of later design than the one to be found on the seal of the Court of Admiralty reproduced in Marsden's book. It is clear from documents surviving among the cause papers that it was common to impress only part of the seal on the wax (usually the upper segment showing the Crown); this practice may well have been dictated by

The examiners were required to take down the depositions of all the witnesses produced in causes before the Delegates (except those who gave evidence by commission) and to certify exhibits tendered by witnesses. By 1824 (and no doubt for some time before) the same officers discharged this duty both for the Court of Delegates and the Court of Admiralty. They were notaries public appointed by the registrar or his deputies without the formal approval of the court being obtained.[1]

There was an establishment of clerks, the number of whom no doubt varied according to the amount of business passing through the court. Some of them were notaries public who might on occasions perform the functions of the deputy registrar during his absence.[2]

PROCTORS

A proctor is defined by Law as one 'who has the management of another man's business committed to him by the warrant and authority of his client or principal, which warrant is in English called a proxy'.[3] In the Court of Delegates (as in other civilian courts) his functions approximated to those of an attorney or solicitor in the courts of law and equity; his principal duty on behalf of a litigant was to guide the cause through the various stages which lay between the presentation of a commission and sentence, appearing before the judges to tender pleadings and personal answers, to produce witnesses, to make protests and the like. It seems that all proctors exercent in the Court of Arches had the right to practice before the Delegates,[4] although not all the practitioners before the Arches may have done so.

By the nineteenth century, the regulations governing entry to the

considerations of economy, as it seems unlikely to have been modelled on the use of the Half Seal (for which see Maxwell-Lyte, *Historical Notes on the Use of the Great Seal of England*, pp. 304–9).

[1] *Admiralty etc. Courts Rep.* (1824), p. 50.

[2] Thus Nicholas Bristowe, who is described in *Verny* v. *Andrewes* (*in the principal cause*) (1618), DEL 4/7/268, as 'unus clericorum huius Curie', attended the presentation of commissions in several causes in July, August and September 1618 (DEL 4/7/199–200). He later became a deputy registrar.

[3] *F.E.L.*, XI/2.

[4] e.g. *Salmons* v. *Squire* (1793), DEL 2/82; James Farquhar, who acted as a proctor in the cause, is described in the proxy as 'one of the Procurators General of the Arches Court of Canterbury and as such one of the Proctors exercent in his Majesty's High Court of Delegates'. In many proxies, the proctor is described merely as exercent in the Court of Arches. The rule in the Court of Chivalry seems to have been the same (*H.C.C.*, pp. 135–6).

profession were precise.[1] Persons proposing to practise in the Court of Arches were required to serve under articles for seven years with one of the thirty-four senior proctors, none of whom was allowed (as a general rule) to engage a second articled clerk until the first had served for at least five years. Before articles were entered into, a clerk was required to show that he was reasonably proficient in classical learning and some proctors, at least, had degrees in law.[2] There is some evidence that the system of articles was in force in the eighteenth century,[3] and it may have a much earlier origin.

Proctors usually acted under the terms of a written proxy, which they were required to exhibit whenever they appeared for a client,[4] the appointment in such a case being known as extra-judicial.[5] A litigant might, however, appoint a proctor judicially by making a nomination before the registrar.[6] The proctor was given full authority to conduct the litigation on his principal's behalf and a power of substitution was usually included.[7] Proxies could, if necessary, be executed abroad.[8]

Proctors exercent in the Court of Delegates were apparently subject to the disciplinary control of the judges. Abuses for which proctors were or might be responsible were corrected by *Monitiones Generales*. These were orders decreed by all the judges of causes in dependence at the time when the monition was issued and were directed to all the proctors exercent in the court at that time; they

[1] *Eccl. Courts Rep.* (1831–2), p. 14.

[2] Thus Alexander Serle, who appeared as procurator general in *Serle* v. *Nottingham* (1610), DEL 4/5/5, is described as an LL.B.

[3] The Orders and Injunctions made by the Judges and Advocates in Commons Assembled on 12 November 1742 (DEL 9/7/84–5) refer to practitioners who had 'served a regular Clarkship' and provides that each proctor of the Arches might have two 'Entred Clerks or Writers'.

[4] *F.E.L.*, XI/5. Proxies were usually written in longhand but occasionally printed forms were used; e.g. *Carty* v. *Mc.Clintock and Henderson* (1729), DEL 2/18. For examples of general and special proxies, see Apps. IV and V.

[5] *F.E.L.*, XII/4.

[6] *F.E.L.*, XII/3. Such appointments were rare in the Court of Delegates, but an example occurred in 1608 when Thomas Ayre 'iam ad partes ultramarinas profecturus' appeared before William Barker, the deputy registrar and appointed Milbury as his proctor in any litigation in which he might be concerned before the court (DEL 4/4/140).

[7] e.g. *Rutton* v. *Rutton* (1796), DEL 2/65; a form of proxy surviving in this cause gives the proctor named in it 'full Power and Authority to nominate and appoint one or more Substitute or Substitutes as need shall be or occasion require'.

[8] e.g. *Pancier* v. *Tourton* (1737), DEL 2/62; an intervener executed a proxy in Paris, appointing a proctor to represent him before the Delegates.

were required to conform to the terms of the order upon pain of suspension.[1] Proctors guilty of individual acts of misconduct were punished in the same way.[2]

ADVOCATES

In the civilian courts, advocates performed substantially the same functions as those which in the courts of law and equity fell to barristers.[3] They obtained the right to practise by admission to the Court of Arches, whereupon they became entitled to appear in the Court of Delegates and all other ecclesiastical tribunals.[4] Certain qualifications were required for practice; these did not remain constant but they were eventually three in number: possession of a doctorate in civil law, membership of Doctors' Commons and the 'year of silence'.[5]

Barristers had no right of audience in the civilian courts but from the beginning of the seventeenth century, if not before, they

[1] Several of these orders are entered in the Act Books of the early seventeenth century; most of them were intended to facilitate the conduct of business in the court. A typical example is the monition decreed on 18 February 1610; in order to avoid 'tumultuosum strepitum et confusam vociferacionem', it was directed that no proctor was to arrange for a cause to be heard in any other civilian court at a time set down for the transaction of judicial business by the Delegates (DEL 4/5/30).

[2] On 27 June 1605 the Act Book records that all the judges of the court suspended Mr Willett, a proctor, on the ground that he had addressed Dr Amys, who was then sitting as a judge, 'iniuriose et contumeliose contra bonos mores et obsequium per eum debitum'; the suspension was to continue until Willett was reconciled to Dr Amys (DEL 4/3/58). There is a further note that on 9 October of that year, in the presence of six judges and the deputy registrar, Willett tendered a formal apology, declaring 'That he is sorry that he hadd offended Dr. Amys' whereupon, with the latter's consent, the suspension was lifted.

It seems that the Dean of the Arches exercised some disciplinary control over proctors exercent in the Court of Arches (as were all those practising before the Delegates); see *Lee's Case* (1690), Carth. 169.

[3] *Eccl. Courts Rep.* (1831–2), p. 142.

[4] Advocates wishing to practise in the Court of Admiralty had in addition to be admitted by the judge of that court (*Eccl. Courts Rep.* (1831–2), p. 65). See *H.C.C.*, p. 133 and the authority there cited for the method of obtaining admission. The Court of Delegates, like the Court of Chivalry, seems to have had no special ceremony for the admission of advocates.

[5] A degree in law was not always required, as at one time other evidence that a candidate was learned in the civil law would suffice (*F.E.L.*, x/3). Membership of Doctors' Commons was not essential until the latter part of the seventeenth century (if not later) and examples may be found in the records of several persons who acted as advocates before the Delegates and who did not belong to the Commons. (I am indebted to G. D. Squibb, Q.C. for the suggestion that the Delegates' archives might reveal this.)

attempted to obtain it.[1] Early in the reign of James I it was proposed in the House of Commons by members of the common law bar that they should have a general right to practise in the ecclesiastical courts.[2] This attempt to encroach on the civilians' monopoly in their own tribunals was unsuccessful, but about twenty years later the common lawyers returned to the attack, and when the Court of Chivalry was revived in 1623 they argued that 'the Professors of the Common Lawes of England' should be entitled to practise there.[3] This suggestion also met with scant success.[4]

The position of the Court of Delegates was rather different, however, and barristers were able to gain an audience before it with some frequency. References to their appearance are to be found in the records in the last two decades of the seventeenth century,[5] and early in the century following the judges found it necessary to emphasize that their permission had to be obtained before common lawyers could plead in that court.[6] Barristers became well established in the course of that century,[7] and towards the end of the court's life it had become the almost invariable rule for each

[1] According to Law, they were to be heard in those tribunals only when questions arose 'concerning the supposed interposition of the municipal law', in which case they might appear with the licence of the judge (*F.E.L.*, p. xvii).

[2] It was apparently this suggestion which led to the creation of the university seats. In a petition to the king the civilians asked for some means of protecting their interests in Parliament and royal charters were then granted to Oxford and Cambridge, allowing each university to return two members who were to be 'skilful in the Imperial laws' (Halsbury, *Laws of England*, vol. 11, p. 503; notice, however, that Halsbury cites as his authority for this proposition Phillimore, *International Law*, vol. 1, preface, which gives a different explanation).

[3] *H.C.C.*, p. 133.

[4] There seems to have been only one recorded instance when a barrister pleaded for a client before that tribunal (*H.C.C.*, p. 134).

[5] e.g. *Greenhill* v. *Thomas* (1680), DEL 2/118/1; in an affidavit annexed to the warrant in this cause, the appellant explained that his reason for wishing to have the time for hearing and determining altered was that Serjeant Pemberton and Serjeant Baldwyn, who were to represent him before the Delegates, were engaged for trials at the King's Bench on the day originally assigned for the Delegates' hearing.

[6] Thus a Standing Order was unanimously decreed on 24 April 1703 'that no Common Lawyer be admitted to plead as Council in this Court unless leave given by ye Judges on ye Court day before' (DEL 6/30/52). Attempts were apparently made to evade this order as it was repeated, in rather more rigorous terms, in 1706 (DEL 6/31/105).

[7] e.g. sentences were recorded in thirty-two causes in the Assignation Book for the years 1720–4 and common law counsel were heard in twenty-four of them; in the years 1737–40, twenty-four sentences are recorded in the relevant Assignation Book and common lawyers appeared in fifteen of them.

litigant to employ at least one counsel learned in the common law.[1]

It is tempting to associate the appearance of barristers before the Court of Delegates with the inclusion of common law judges on commissions. References to the former begin to recur with some frequency about 1690 and it is about that time that the rules which governed the composition of the court (and which required that some common law judges should be included in every commission) finally hardened. The Court of Delegates was the only civilian tribunal in which the judges of Westminster Hall ever gained a permanent foot-hold and once they had done so, it would clearly be easier for barristers to obtain permission to plead there.

As well as pleading for a client before the Court of Delegates barristers might perform other functions for litigants there; thus they might draft documents and give legal opinions.[2]

[1] An analysis has been made of the causes entered in Appeal Case Books 5–7 (1816 to 1828). In all (except four) of the causes in these books, in which the litigants' legal representatives can be identified, each party retained at least one common lawyer.

[2] e.g. *Gardner* v. *Gardner* (1606), DEL 4/3/161 (certain schedules annexed to the respondent's allegation were said to have been drafted 'judicio consilio directione ac opinione' of Serjeant Harrys and Mr Hitchcock, a barrister; *Eman* v. *Molesworthe* (*in the principal cause*) (1611), DEL 4/5/166 (the appellant's proctor made use of a legal opinion given by Sir Henry Hobart, the Attorney General and Serjeant Montague as to the effect of a recently passed statute upon his client's interests).

CHAPTER XI

THE LOCALE OF THE COURT

The ecclesiastical courts of England have for the most part chosen to conduct their business in places deemed appropriate for religious tribunals—the chancels of churches, or the chapter houses or consistories of cathedrals.[1] Each court had usually one accustomed place for transacting its business and here alone would its sessions be held.

From the beginning of its life, it seems, the Court of Delegates stood rather outside this system. Special considerations governed the choice of its meeting places (in particular, the employment as commissioners of persons such as bishops, peers and common lawyers, who were not drawn from the usual ranks of civilian judges); it came to be recognized that the Delegates had 'the power of fixing upon the place of their sittings',[2] and the records suggest that this power was exercised to suit the convenience of whichever judges attended a particular session, so that hearings before civilians alone usually occurred in places quite different from those at which common lawyers attended. Certain conventions slowly became established, and the place to which the hearing of a cause was assigned came to depend upon the nature of the business to be transacted and the type of judge who was likely to transact it. The result of these conventions, in the distribution of the court's business throughout various parts of London, must now be briefly considered.

The opening session of a cause before the Delegates, when the commission was presented and the inhibition and citation decreed, was attended with some informality and for a long time it might be held anywhere. This stage of proceedings usually occurred before civilians alone and as most of the advocates had chambers in Doctors' Commons it was there that the appellant's proctor would usually seek them. The Act Books make it clear, however, that any other place would serve as well; commissions might be

[1] Some of the more important civilian courts which sat in London held their sessions in public rooms of Doctors' Commons until that college was demolished; see *F.E.L.*, App. VIII.

[2] *F.E.L.*, App. VIII (5).

presented in a church,[1] a private house,[2] a court of law[3] or even in the open air,[4] while often the entry merely states that the judges accepted the commission somewhere 'infra Civitatem London'.[5] If, as sometimes happened, a common law judge chose to take part in the opening session, the appellant's proctor would wait upon him in his chambers,[6] while if the cause was a weighty one and many judges chose to attend, they might assemble at a convenient place in Westminster or Whitehall.[7]

The variety of practice described above is shown by the records to have continued for about 130 years; by the Restoration, however, the custom of presenting commissions at Doctors' Commons, which had always been common, seems to have hardened into a fixed rule and presentations elsewhere become very infrequent.[8]

Between the opening session at the beginning of a cause and informations and sentence at the end there intervened various hearings, in the course of which the usual procedural steps were taken—the tendering of pleadings, the production of witnesses, the promulgation of decrees for commissions *ad partes* and the like. Most of this business was sped on the formal court days,[9] and what was left over was dealt with in subsidiary sessions held between one court day and the next. The ecclesiastical Delegates had begun the practice of using St Paul's Cathedral for sittings on court days and it appears from the entries in the earliest surviving Act Book that in the first decade of the court's life various places

[1] e.g. *Blades* v. *Warde* (1604), DEL 4/2/323 (St Mary le Bow); *the Bishop of Bristol* v. *the Bishop of Worcester* (1617), DEL 4/7/143 (Westminster Abbey).

[2] e.g. *Killett* v. *Grigges* (*in the principal cause*) (1603), DEL 4/2/203 (the house of Dr Creake in the parish of St Gregory).

[3] e.g. *Reynolds and others* v. *Waltham and others* (1603), DEL 4/2/217 (the Court of Requests Chamber).

[4] e.g. *Kinsbeare* v. *Kinsbeare* (1607), DEL 4/4/137 (the cemetery of St Paul's by the gate of the bishop's palace); *Wynche* v. *Wynche* (1607), DEL 4/4/57 (the garden of Doctors' Commons).

[5] e.g. *Cowlstock* v. *Cowlstock* (1606), DEL 4/3/183.

[6] e.g. *Muffett* v. *Fletcher* (1605), DEL 4/3/77; the commission was presented to Sir William Daniel, a judge of the Common Pleas, in his chambers in Serjeants' Inn.

[7] e.g. *the Earl of Hertford* v. *Lord Mounteagle* (1605), DEL 4/3/65; a group of ten judges met for this purpose 'in conclavi sive Camera prope Cameram Stellatam apud Westemonasterium' [*sic*].

[8] Presentations might still be made in an Inn of Court to a common law judge; e.g. entry for 31 August 1716 (DEL 6/34/pt. A/8) (a presentation was made at Serjeants' Inn, Fleet St., to Dr Strahan and Sir Robert Tracy, K.B.J.).

[9] For these, see p. 94 *ante*.

in the cathedral were used, in particular the consistory, the north isle, the vestry and the long chapel (*longa capella*).[1] When a single Court of Delegates came into existence this arrangement continued, although by now sittings were held only in the consistory. The court remained faithful to the cathedral until 1642; in that year (as a result, apparently, of disturbances caused by the outbreak of the Civil War)[2] sessions occurring on court days were transferred to Doctors' Commons where they continued to be held, either in the *aula publica* or the *cenaculum*, until the end of the court's life.[3]

Practice governing the choice of a meeting place for subsidiary sessions was rather more flexible, at least in the earlier period. When only civilians attended these sessions (which was the usual rule) they met for the most part in Doctors' Commons, either in chambers or in a public room. If common law judges chose to be present, the sitting would most often be held in one of the Serjeants' Inns,[4] or in some other place convenient for them.[5] If some considerable personage, an archbishop or the like, was to take part in proceedings, his preferences might be consulted beforehand.[6] Sittings at which the Archbishop of Canterbury attended were almost always at Lambeth Palace,[7] while, if a number of people

[1] See Act Book 1538–44 (DEL 4/1), entries for 5 February, 12 February, 20 March (1539) and 15 June (1540).

[2] Because of unsettled conditions in London, St Paul's had become unsafe for the conduct of judicial business. Archbishop Laud had tried the experiment of transferring sessions of the High Commission from Lambeth Palace to the cathedral with untoward results, as a sitting held there in October 1640 had been broken up by a riotous mob (H. R. Trevor-Roper, *Archbishop Laud 1573–1645* (London, 1962), p. 396).

[3] The last session held in St Paul's was the final session of the Trinity term, 1642 (DEL 4/18/25).

[4] e.g. *Aldebroughe* v. *Brakenburye and Graye* (1605), DEL 4/3/71; the session was held in the hall of Serjeants' Inn in Fleet St., two common law judges being among the Delegates.

[5] The Court of Requests Chamber was sometimes used for this purpose in the early seventeenth century; e.g. *Reynolds and others* v. *Waltham and others* (1603), DEL 4/2/223. It was within the Palace of Westminster and was, presumably, a convenient place for the common lawyers to attend.

[6] e.g. *Wandeford* v. *Wandeford* (1606), DEL 4/3/249; when it was proposed that the Archbishop of York should attend a hearing of this cause, some of the other judges on the commission instructed 'the sayd parties...to give their attendance on the most reverend my Lord Archbishopp of York his grace to knowe what time and place his Lordship will be pleased to appoint in that matter at what time and place (if it please his grace to appoint any) the sayd Judges delegate will be ready to attend him'.

[7] e.g. various hearings of *the Earl of Hertford* v. *Lord Mounteagle* recorded in Act Book 1605–7 (DEL 4/3/93, 95, 103).

of importance in church and state sat together as judges, the place selected for their meeting was usually some *aula* or *camera* in Westminster or Whitehall.[1]

After the Restoration, the occasions when commissioners other than civilians attended any sitting of the court prior to informations became very infrequent and the subsidiary sessions were held, almost without exception, at Doctors' Commons.[2]

The choice of meeting places for informations and sentence in a cause before the Delegates resulted in the creation of a pattern not dissimilar to those already discussed. There was, however, one significant difference. At no period of the court's life was the presence of common law judges at sittings prior to informations customary and indeed, until about the middle of the seventeenth century, they did not often serve on commissions of delegacy. When they were appointed as Delegates, the quorum clause would always require that at least one of them should be 'present and consenting' at sentence and this requirement resulted in a conflict between the civilians and the common lawyers as to whose convenience should be served when sittings for this purpose were held.

The problem cannot have arisen in a very acute form until the seventeenth century was well advanced, as civilians made up the entire commission in the great majority of causes and sat for informations and sentence in St Paul's Cathedral or Doctors' Commons. When common lawyers were joined with civilians, their relations at first were sufficiently amicable to make possible concessions on each side. Sometimes sittings for informations and sentence would take place at one of the Serjeants' Inns where the judges had their chambers,[3] but the civilians did not always defer in this way and other causes may be found in which the common

[1] Thus one hearing of *the Earl of Hertford* v. *Lord Mounteagle* was held 'in interiori Camera prope domum vocatum the Parliament House viz the higher house', another 'in loco vocato the Dutchie Court infra Aulam Westmonasterium' and a third 'in porticum prope ascensum in Cameram Stellatam infra palaciam Westmonasterium' (*supra*, at ff. 167, 203, 239). Among those who attended one or more of these hearings were the Archbishop of Canterbury, the Bishop of London, the Earl of Northampton and the Dean of St Paul's.

[2] An exception arose when the court sat to hear petitions presented to all the judges-delegate in a cause; these seem usually to have been directed against decisions of the civilian condelegates on interlocutory matters. If common law judges attended, sittings would be held at one of the Serjeants' Inns; *Greenhill* v. *Thomas* (1679), DEL 6/20/13, is apparently an example of such a sitting.

[3] e.g. *Aldebroughe* v. *Brackenburye and Graye* (1606), DEL 4/3/291; the court assembled in the hall of Serjeants' Inn in Fleet St.

lawyers came to Doctors' Commons.[1] Nevertheless, examples of the latter sort were never very common and by 1640 the attendance of civilians upon their colleagues of Westminster Hall for the purpose of sentence in Delegates' causes had become sufficiently tedious to provoke a formal complaint. Sir John Lambe, the Dean of the Arches, in a letter to Archbishop Laud which bears date 18 January of that year, set out several ill effects, as he saw it, of allowing common lawyers to assist in Delegates' business. Not the least among these was the inconvenience to the practitioners of the civil law in sessions held at the Serjeants' Inns: 'To attend at Sergeant's Inn was to the great trouble and extreme charge of the subject, in carrying down the proctors, advocates, registrars, and judges thither'.[2]

The letter bears an endorsement in Laud's hand suggesting that some of the complaints mentioned in it were to be attended to, but about this matter at least nothing seems to have been done. From the Restoration, more and more commissions were issued which contained common lawyers and in all the causes examined after that date not a single example has been found of their attendance at Doctors' Commons. Ill-feeling must have become steadily more acute and the matter came to a head in 1682 during the hearing of *Hyde* v. *Emerton*[3] when an attempt by the civilian condelegates to reverse the rule, by now well-established, that the judges of the common law should not be required to sit outside the Serjeants' Inns, was thought significant enough by Sir Thomas Raymond to deserve a place in his reports. It seems that on 16 December of that year a warrant was circulated among the commissioners appointing a time for informations and sentence in the Council Chamber at Whitehall; the document was signed by Sir Leoline Jenkins, two other doctors and two officers of state, but by none of the common law judges. Six of the latter promptly went in a deputation to the Lord Keeper to make objection; they pointed out that the proposed arrangement ran counter to established precedent and was in any case impolitic: 'because the Judges are constantly imployed in the publick Affairs of the Kingdom, in the Business

[1] e.g. *Dawson* v. *Dawson* (1607), DEL 4/4/17; sentence was given in the *cenaculum* in the presence of one justice of the King's Bench and one of the Common Pleas. See also *Gardner* v. *Gardner* (1605), DEL 4/3/147, and *Muffett* v. *Fletcher* (1607), DEL 4/4/43, which are also of this character.

[2] *C.S.P.D.*, 1639–40, p. 350.

[3] (1682), Raym. T. 475.

in their several Courts, and other Things which cannot be done so conveniently for the Subjects elsewhere'.[1]

The Lord Keeper advised them to attend on this occasion as the warrant directed but assured them that 'the ancient Course' would be observed in future.[2] Raymond ends his report by referring to the rumour circulating at the time that the judge of the Admiralty was behind the whole business: 'This (*ut dicitur*) did now arise from the Promotion of Sir *Leolin Jenkins*, who is a Civilian, and would favour his Profession as much as might be'.

Any later complaint which the civilians may have made about the rule confirmed by *Hyde* v. *Emerton* must have been ineffectual, as no example has been found after that date of a cause in which the common lawyers served where sentence was not given in a Serjeants' Inn or another Inn of Court.[3]

It is clear from what has been said above that, although the court sat in many different places, more frequent use was made of Doctors' Commons than of any other venue, and by the time of the Restoration, the Delegates transacted most of their business there. This ordered pattern was temporarily disturbed, however, when Doctors' Commons was destroyed by fire, for on 2 September 1666 the Great Fire broke out, and all the buildings in the College of Advocates were burnt to the ground.[4] Exactly one month later, the court began to sit again and a commission was presented in rooms occupied by Dr Merrick 'sub Signo Capitis Tauri in vico vocato Le Strand'.[5] Soon after the loss of their old home, the advocates migrated to Exeter House in the Strand,[6] and here they carried on the business of the Delegates (and no doubt of other civilian tribunals which had formerly been housed at Doctors' Commons).

[1] *Hyde* v. *Emerton*, *supra*, at 476. Another passage in the same report makes it clear that in Sir Henry Martin's time there had been an attempt of the same nature which had been thwarted by the king himself (Martin was admitted to Doctors' Commons in 1596 and died in 1641).

[2] The judges had their way a few days later; there survives among the cause papers a warrant in the cause dated 9 January 1683, which reads (in part): 'and Wee the Lords of the Counsel that are Delegated in this Commission takeing into Consideracion the business & convenience of the Judges of the Land are pleased for this time to appoint the place for the determinacion of ye Same to be the Common hall of Sergeants Inne in Fleet Street' (DEL 2/105/2).

[3] e.g. *Miller* v. *Walton and others* (1765), DEL 6/45/95 (the hall of the Inner Temple); *Oswald* v. *Lord Everard* (1702), DEL 6/30/39 (the library of the Inner Temple).

[4] Burn, *Ecclesiastical Law*, vol. 2, p. 194.

[5] *Uncles* v. *Uncles* (1666), DEL 4/21/48.

[6] Senior, *Doctors' Commons and the Old Court of Admiralty*, p. 100.

References in the Act Books show that chambers were assigned to members of the College,[1] and judicial business was conducted in rooms which bore the old titles of *cenaculum* and *aula publica*.[2]

Judicial sessions continued to be held with their usual regularity and the displacement of the court and its records seems to have had surprisingly little effect upon the conduct of proceedings. Nevertheless, there was some inconvenience; a number of litigants were caught unawares by the transfer of business to Exeter House,[3] and some causes were delayed by the destruction of documents.[4]

The advocates remained at Exeter House, and the Court of Delegates continued to sit there, until Doctors' Commons was rebuilt *prope ripam Paulinam* several years later; the Delegates held their first sitting there on 25 March 1672.[5]

Little information survives concerning the appearance of the public rooms in Doctors' Commons which were used for the conduct of judicial business by various civilian tribunals, including the Court of Delegates. In the course of this investigation, nothing has been found which relates to the old buildings, destroyed by the Great Fire, but there is a drawing by Rowlandson which shows how one of the rooms (presumably the *aula publica* or the *cenaculum*) had been fitted up by the latter half of the eighteenth century, and it was here that the Delegates must often have sat. The hearing depicted by Rowlandson took place in a wide recess at one end of the room.[6] This contained a high, horseshoe-shaped enclosure within which the advocates sat, with the judge presiding at the rear; below this and surrounded by it was a table for the proctors.[7]

[1] e.g. *Bee* v. *Moore* (1666), DEL 4/21/86, was heard by Jenkins and Sweit 'in Camera Doctoris Sweit'.

[2] e.g. *Butler and Corke* v. *Arkinstall* (1666), DEL 4/21/85 (*aula publica*); *Archdale* v. *Archdale* (1667), DEL 4/21/110 (*cenaculum*).

[3] e.g. *Cook and Sparke* v. *Carkeet* (1666), DEL 4/21/48; a mandate lapsed 'racione mutationis loci judicialis in hac Curia'.

[4] e.g. *Dillington* v. *Gorges* (1666), DEL 4/21/54; the process in the lower court had almost been written out when it was burnt. The displacement or destruction of records of the Prerogative Court (which provided a substantial amount of appellate business) caused the Delegates some trouble; it appears from *Butler* v. *Staines* (1666), DEL 4/21/60, that the Prerogative registry was still out of order in December 1666.

[5] DEL 4/21/471.

[6] It is unlikely to have been a hearing of the Court of Delegates as only one judge is shown presiding over it.

[7] The drawing is reproduced in R. Ackermann, *Microcosm of London* (London, 1808–11), and it serves as the frontispiece to Roscoe, *History of the English Prize Court*. There is a lively description of a sitting there in *David Copperfield*, ch. 23, and another in *Sketches by Boz* (*Doctors' Commons*).

Unlike other tribunals, the Court of Delegates does not seem to have been driven from its usual meeting places by outbreaks of plague. By the first half of the seventeenth century (which is the earliest date for which evidence on the matter survives) its usual practice, when the plague in London became too severe to permit the continuation of business, was merely to suspend sittings; when, for example, there was an epidemic of plague in the Michaelmas term 1636, the Act Book records that during that period 'propter sevientem in Civitate London et suburbijs eiusdem pestem nihil actum est in causis in hac Curia pendentibus'.[1]

[1] DEL 4/15/129. Surprisingly, there was no adjournment during the Great Plague, although the area around Doctors' Commons was particularly affected by it (*C.S.P.D.*, 1665–6, p. 80); the usual sessions were held, although business was often delayed 'ratione pestis' when witnesses could not appear and the like.

CHAPTER XII

THE RECORDS OF THE COURT OF DELEGATES

In this chapter it is proposed to examine the records of the Court of Delegates. Two justifications for a detailed study may be advanced: first, this account of the court has been based (to a greater extent than is usual in investigations of this kind) upon the manuscript records and it follows that the form and function of these records deserve consideration; secondly, no similar account exists, as far as is known, and it is believed that a minute analysis of a typical civilian archive may be of value.[1] Three matters are touched upon: the history of the records, the language in which they were written and the form and function of the various categories into which the surviving documents fall.

THE HISTORY OF THE RECORDS

It seems desirable to give some account of the various repositories in which the documents have been housed (as far as this can be established), partly in order that this investigation of the court may be made complete and partly because such an account will throw interesting light upon the hazards to which judicial archives might be subjected.

Convenience demands that the records of a law court shall be kept together in a registry, where the documents themselves may be cared for and where they may be accessible to those who have occasion to consult them. It is possible that the Delegates' archives were originally housed in St Paul's Cathedral, for it was there that the formal sessions of the court were held upon court days until the time of the Civil War.[2]

Doctors' Commons, however, where advocates and judges had

[1] Squibb's account of the records of the Court of Chivalry (*H.C.C.*, App. 1) is necessarily succinct as so little material survives. The attention devoted by Marsden to the records of the Court of Admiralty is limited (Marsden (ed.), *Select Pleas in the Court of Admiralty*, vol. 1, pp. lxi-lxiv), and the same objection can be made to Rothery's comments on the Delegates' archives (*R.R.*, pp. xii–xviii).

[2] For the various places where the Delegates sat, see pp. 201–8 *ante*.

their chambers and where the judicial business of the Delegates was also transacted not infrequently, must have seemed even more suitable and by the early seventeenth century (the earliest period for which evidence is forthcoming) the registry of the court was situated there. It was to the office of the registrar 'situatum in Knightrider Streete' that litigants would come if they wished to see to the entering of judges' certificates in the Act Books,[1] and it was here that officials of other courts would deposit documents which were exhibits in causes before the Delegates.[2]

It is impossible to tell for how long the records of the various civil law Delegates had been kept there before *c.* 1600 and the arrangement may have been made very much earlier than this. It is clear, however, that although the registry was always reasonably close to Doctors' Commons (as the needs of the court itself and of the litigants must have made necessary) it underwent several changes of location, dictated partly by the exigencies of war or natural disaster and partly, no doubt, by the convenience of those who were charged with its care. The evidence for these changes is notably meagre, but with such information as is available the main outlines of the story can be traced.

By the third decade of the seventeenth century, the records had apparently been transferred from Knightrider Street to Carter Lane, for in *Salter and Prestland* v. *Salter*[3] the 'officium Registrariatus' is said to be situated there. It is possible that some of them at least were taken to Oxford when the king withdrew there at the beginning of the Civil War; it seems that the records of the Prerogative Court (from which many appeals to the Delegates came) were taken there,[4] and on at least one occasion a sitting of the Delegates was held in an Oxford church.[5] No further information about the archives is available until the year of the Great Fire; numerous entries relating to this disaster occur in the Act Book for 1666 and some of these make it clear that many of the court's

[1] e.g. *Reynolds and others* v. *Waltham and others* (1607), DEL 4/4/16.

[2] e.g. *Freak* v. *Whitehall* (1607), DEL 4/4/49.

[3] (1637), DEL 4/15/247. Carter Lane was immediately to the North of Knightrider Street; see the map in J. Stow, *A Survey of London* (Oxford, 1908).

[4] In *Greaves* v. *Babington* (1646), DEL 4/18/121, the registry of that court was stated to have been at Oxford 'sub ditione et potestate exercitium domini Regis' for several years.

[5] For a full account of the Court of Delegates, both in London and Oxford, during the Civil War, see pp. 19–21 *ante*.

records were burnt or mislaid,[1] while those surviving were taken for safe custody from the registry (the precise location of which is not stated) to the house of John Oughton, the deputy registrar, at Putney.[2]

For about the next hundred years, nothing at all is known of the whereabouts of the records, while such evidence as is available for the later period is scanty. A Disbursements Account Book for the years 1760–90 records payments to various persons of rent for storage space,[3] without always stating the precise situation of the rooms which had been hired for this purpose.[4] Other entries in this book make it clear that by this time at least the records were not kept together; the processes are spoken of as housed apart from the other records in 1778,[5] and they were shifted in that year and again in 1782.[6] The custody of the archives at the end of the court's life and their subsequent fate was considered by the Royal Commission on the Public Records, whose second report (embracing the Court of Delegates among others) appeared in 1914.[7] The account of the matter given in this document is a rather confused one, and it is apparent that the commission was unable to discover in any detail what happened to the records from the abolition of the court until the time, many years later, when they passed into the keeping of the Master of the Rolls.

Since the jurisdiction of the Court of Delegates was transferred to the Privy Council, it was to be expected that the records would

[1] e.g. *Bainbrig* v. *Goodson and others* (*in the principal cause*) (1666), DEL 4/21/68; the appellant's proctor referred to a schedule which he had previously deposited in the registry and which 'in nuper infelicissima conflagracione Civitatis London combustam sive per aliam infortunam emissam & non esse inveniendam seu producendam'.

[2] This is referred to in *Goddard* v. *Dyde* (1666), DEL 4/21/52.

[3] There was a payment in 1761 to Isaac Miller 'for two years Rent of the Record Rooms', a similar payment to Richard Pailthorp in 1766 and several to Mrs Mary Boyd between 1767 and 1771 (DEL 8/41/2,5,7–15). None of these persons can be identified but it is possible that the 'Mr. Bishop' to whom rent was paid for the use of two rooms for storing records from 1773, was the then deputy registrar, Nathaniel Bishop.

[4] An entry of 10 September 1772 merely refers to the removal of the records 'from Mr. Stevens's to Mr. Bishop's,' while on 6 July in the following year there was a similar removal from Cheslyn's house in Carter Lane to the Admiralty office (DEL 8/41/unfoliated).

[5] *Ibid.*, entry of 25 March 1778.

[6] *Ibid.*, entries of 25 March 1778 and 31 December 1782. Removals such as these (which in one case at least were carried out by workmen liberally supplied with beer; see *ibid.*, entry for 10 September 1772) may help to explain the gaps in the records.

[7] *Public Records*. R. Com. 2nd. Rep.; 1914 Cmd. 7544, XLVI, 189.

have come under the control of that body; the persons in charge of the Privy Council office, however, insisted that none of the records were in their hands when the Royal Commission made its enquiries and an account of their history after the abolition of the court has to be sought for elsewhere.[1]

H. C. Rothery, in his introduction to the *Return of all Appeals in Causes of Doctrine or Discipline made to the High Court of Delegates*, made in 1868, spoke of the Delegates' archives as having come under his control about fourteen years before. This was about the time when Rothery became registrar of the Court of Admiralty,[2] and there can be little doubt that it was in this capacity that he received them; the two tribunals had shared the same registrar for a considerable time before 1832 and when the Court of Delegates was swept away it may have seemed best to all concerned that its records should remain, together with those of the Admiralty in joint custody.[3]

Most of the Delegates' records were transferred from the Admiralty registry into the control of the Master of the Rolls in 1863, at Rothery's suggestion.[4] One consignment (consisting very largely of testamentary documents) found its way into the principal Probate registry at Somerset House;[5] here it remained until 1962 when it was re-united with the rest of the archives in the repository of the Public Record Office at Ashridge. The documents

[1] Despite this disclaimer, the Royal Commission was of opinion that 'cognate or subsidiary records' relating to the Delegates might be discovered among the archives of the Judicial Committee (*Public Records Rep.* (1914), p. 91).

[2] His tenure of that office began in 1853 (Main Thompson, *Admiralty Registrars*, p. 19).

[3] It may seem a little surprising that the officers of the Judicial Committee, into whose 'nominal custody', as the Royal Commission put it, the records had passed, should have taken no steps to assert their control; the report of the Royal Commission plausibly suggests that the registries of the Delegates and the Admiralty may not have been kept properly distinct and it quotes a letter from the Admiralty Registrar to the Master of the Rolls admitting that the registries were in 'a great state of confusion' (Rolls House Correspondence, 7 October 1863). This confusion may well have been so great that the persons charged with the custody of the Privy Council records were disinclined to interfere.

[4] Rolls House Correspondence, 7 October 1863.

[5] The Royal Commission on the Public Records in its second report (*Public Records Rep.* (1914), p. 91) speaks of 'an official tradition' that the Probate and Admiralty registries had disputed the right to control the Delegates' archives, the former basing its claim on the terms of 6 & 7 Vict., c. 38 and on a legal opinion. The transfer of the testamentary material to the Probate registry (when all the other Delegates' records passed into the hands of the Public Record Office) may well represent a compromise of this claim.

housed there comprise almost all those that are known to exist,[1] and it seems unlikely that more will come to light. The Royal Commission's second report, in a rather muddled account of the dispersal of ecclesiastical records in the course of the nineteenth century, implies that some might still be found in the Privy Council office, in the archives of St Paul's Cathedral and in the Lambeth Palace Library, but enquiries which have been made in the course of this investigation suggest that no discoveries can be hoped for from these sources.[2]

THE LANGUAGE OF THE RECORDS

For the greater part of the court's life, Latin (and not English or law French) was the language in which most of the records were written. The Act Books, which contained a formal account of the court's proceedings, were always in Latin, except when English documents or statements by witnesses, process-servers and the like were quoted in the body of an act. The Assignation Books, from which the Act Books were written up, were of a mixed character; they were for the most part in Latin, but they lapsed not infrequently into English, a circumstance which is sufficiently explained by the fact that they were written at speed during sittings of the court. Documents embodying the examination of witnesses were written in the same manner; the formal introduction to each set of depositions was in Latin but the evidence itself was in the native tongue of the witness, and the same arrangement prevailed for taking personal answers from the parties.[3] Commissions of

[1] There are a few scattered among the State Papers Domestic and some have been mistakenly filed among the records of the Court of Admiralty (for these, see the Delegates' class list, facing pp. 1 and 13).

[2] The only document belonging to the Court of Delegates which was held by any of these repositories in recent years is the process in *Ball* v. *Walkeden* (1687), which was transferred from the Lambeth Palace library to the Public Record Office in 1963.

[3] The pleadings upon which the depositions and personal answers were based were in Latin and this could occasionally cause trouble if the person conducting the examination was careless or, perhaps, deliberately deceitful. Thus in *Graye* v. *Barrowe* (1633), DEL 4/14/97 & 101, the appellant came before the Delegates and petitioned for leave to retract the personal answers he had given to the respondent's libel at first instance. His petition declared: 'That he was and is a Cuntryman and did not nor doth understand the latine tonge. And that he that writt his answer made to the libell and schedule given in the first instance of this cause in writinge...erred therein. And he the sayd William Graye not understandinge the same was deceyved and erred therein.' Despite the argument of the respondent's proctor that Graye fully understood his answers before he acknowledged them, the court allowed retraction.

delegacy and all the mandates of the court, inhibitions, citations, monitions and the like, were entirely in Latin, as were those formal documents for the drafting of which the parties themselves were responsible, such as libels, sentences, bills of costs and so on.

The first breach of this rule occurred during the Interregnum. Among the reforms made by the usurping power in the administration of justice was the prohibition of Latin and law French and an Act prescribing the use of English for all legal records was passed by Parliament on 22 November 1650 to come into operation on the first of January following.[1] Not many of the Delegates' records have survived from this period, but it appears from those remaining that the rule was strictly adhered to, except in the Assignation Books where the shortness of many of the Latin formulae employed in them, compared with the rather clumsy English equivalents, must have made it convenient, very often, to adhere to the older language. For the Court of Admiralty there was a statutory reversion to Latin (although of a limited extent); it was soon found inconvenient for that tribunal to communicate with foreign courts in English and an amending statute provided that the earlier Act 'shall not extend to the certifying beyond the Seas any Case or Proceedings in the Court of Admiralty; but that in such cases the Commissions and Proceedings may be certified in Latin, as formerly have been'.[2] This rule was presumably followed by the Court of Delegates for marine appeals (which provided the bulk of the court's business during this period).

The Restoration brought with it a reversion to old ways; the statute which had abolished Latin lost its validity and at the head of the Act Book begun within a few weeks of the king's return there is a pleasant flourish, which links together as twin blessings the restoring of his Most Sacred Majesty to the throne of England and

[1] An Act for turning the Books of the Law, and all Proces [*sic*] and Proceedings in Courts of Justice, into English (Firth and Rait, *Acts and Ordinances*, vol. 2, pp. 455–6).

[2] *Ibid.*, pp. 510–11; an Additional Act concerning the Proceedings of the Law in English (Stat. 9 April 1651). The side note is careful to add: 'This Act not to extend to Proceedings in the Court of Admiralty', and it is clear that the use of Latin was sanctioned only for certificates and the like sent abroad, while all the records preserved in the court's archives were still to be in English. Inderwick's rather ambiguous comment on this provision must not, therefore, be understood to mean that there was a universal restoration of Latin in the Court of Admiralty (Inderwick, *The Interregnum*, p. 204).

the revival of Latin as the language of the court.[1] The old tongue, thus reinstated, remained in use for the next seventy-odd years, but by the eighteenth century there arose an increasing opposition to its employment in legal records which culminated in 1733 in its total abolition.[2] The relevant Act imposed a general prohibition which applied as much to the civilian tribunals as to others and from that year until the end of its life all the records of the Court of Delegates were in English.

ANALYSIS OF THE RECORDS

The Delegates' records now housed in the Ashridge repository are divided into eleven categories (until recently only eight groups were kept there, but the transfer of material from Somerset House has resulted in the addition of three more). The surviving mass comprises 1114 separate volumes or bundles. Their physical condition is naturally very uneven and the state of the documents surviving in each category will be commented on when that category is described. The records are now well cared for; loose bundles and the more fragile bound volumes are kept in cardboard boxes for the most part (with a few in brown paper parcels), while the remaining books stand free on the stacks. Some of the older books have been repaired and it is understood that others which stand in need of repair will receive it in due course.

It is much to be regretted that no attempt has been made to provide a more detailed classification of the documents than that described above. Without it, the cause papers especially have proved difficult to handle; as there is no identifying number upon each document, it has been impossible to provide a more precise reference to the many cause papers cited than the number of the bundle within which each is contained. It is difficult to conceive of a more unsatisfactory system of citation, as each bundle holds many documents which are often arranged in no perceptible order.

The analysis which follows is intended to provide as detailed an

[1] 'PRIMO die mensis AUGUSTI Anno Dmi. Millesimo sexcentesimo sexagesimo, Anno scilicet Jubilaeo non solum linguae Latinae feliciter restitutae, sed et Illustrissimi Principis CAROLI secundi, a populo suo diu per proditores depulsi, nunc miranda dei providentia restaurati, quem D. Opt. Max. diutissime servet incolumem' (DEL 4/20/1).

[2] By 4 Geo. II, c. 26. The translation of technical terms into English proved to be inconvenient and a later Act (6 Geo. II, c. 14, s. 5) permitted the retention of Latin for these.

account of each category of documents as is necessary for an understanding of it. It embraces the physical condition of the documents in that group, together with a description of their form and function (to the extent that this has not already been touched on in the chapters on procedure), their number, their chronological range and their relationship to other groups in the archive.[1]

(i) *Processes*

The process in the usage of the Court of Delegates was a full summary of proceedings in the courts below relating to a cause which had come to the Delegates on appeal. It was usually prefaced by a certificate, announcing receipt of the monition for process and compliance with its terms.[2] Then followed the process itself, consisting of copies of all the documents which had been drawn up (in each of the courts through which the cause had already passsed) either by the courts themselves or by the parties; pleadings, personal answers, depositions, interrogatories, exhibits, courts decrees and the like. At the end there was a certificate, signed by the registrar or other official of the *judex a quo*, to the effect that the process had been collated with the original papers; to this was usually affixed the notarial sign of the official concerned or the seal of his court. Below was endorsed a note of the sum at which the process was taxed, signed by those of the Delegates responsible for its taxation.

The processes form the most considerable category of the Delegates' records in point of bulk, comprising 727 volumes.[3] They were all loose until, in about 1853, they came into the custody of the Admiralty registrar, who described them as being for the most part 'in a very dilapidated condition', at that time;[4] under his direction, they were all securely bound (apart from those, already referred to,

[1] For a concise description of the records, see M. S. Giuseppi, *Guide to the Contents of the Public Record Office* (London, 1963), vol. 1, pp. 163–4; the latest edition contains no account of the material recently transferred to the Ashridge repository from Somerset House. There is a rather more detailed analysis in *R.R.*, pp. xii–xviii; this also omits the Somerset House material.

[2] For the monition for process, by which the Delegates directed that the process should be sent up to them, see pp. 106–7 *ante*.

[3] When they were first bound, there were 736 volumes, but nine of these are now missing (for a list of the missing numbers, see the P.R.O. class list, p. 124). There are also a number of processes, both bound and unbound, scattered among the cause papers.

[4] *R.R.*, p. xxiii.

filed among the cause papers) and they are now, on the whole, in excellent condition.[1]

The earliest, the process for *Bulbroke* v. *Norton and Piper*, dates from 1609 and only nine survive from the period before 1650. The preservation of processes for the latter half of the seventeenth century seems to have been somewhat erratic, but a substantial number remain from the century following, and for the last thirty odd years of the court's life the collection seems to be almost complete.

The importance of the processes to a student of the civil law can hardly be overrated, as they illustrate, within the compass of a single set of records, the workings of almost every type of civilian court (both ecclesiastical and secular) which has functioned in this country from the seventeenth century onwards. Documents which illumine the procedure and substantive law of tribunals which have long since ceased to exist,[2] or which no longer actively function,[3] may be found here and anyone concerned to make a comparative study of these courts may have convenient access to records which would otherwise have to be searched for among many different archives.

Their importance to practitioners, who might have occasion to search for precedents, was recognized towards the end of the court's life and Dr Jesse Addams, a prominent civilian, made an examination of them and compiled a reasonably full account of their contents;[4] this catalogue gives some indication of the nature of each cause and such other details as seemed of interest or importance to the compiler.

(ii) *Miscellaneous Cause Papers*

These comprise a great mass of documents of every sort relating to causes heard by the Delegates which have not been filed elsewhere.

[1] It has not been possible to examine more than a few of these volumes for the purpose of this investigation but no process has been found which is entirely illegible; the earlier ones are naturally in the most fragile state.

[2] e.g. the Court of Audience; appeals from this tribunal were frequent before the Civil War.

[3] e.g. the Court of Chivalry, which has sat only once since 1737. Addams lists four of its processes in his *Catalogue* (for which see note 4 *infra*).

[4] *A Catalogue of Processes in the Registry of the High Court of Delegates, from 1609 to 1823* (London, 1823). This catalogue is now exceedingly rare; there are no copies in the Univesity Library of Cambridge, the Bodleian Library or the British Museum and the only three which have been discovered in the course of this investigation are in the departmental library of the Public Record Office, the library of the Admiralty Registry and the library of the Society of Antiquaries.

Some cause papers, such as sentences, bills of costs, depositions and personal answers have been separately filed in a fairly consistent manner, but no uniform system was employed and examples of all these documents are also to be found in this category; personal answers are common and so are depositions taken by commission (the depositions in a separate group (DEL 3) are apparently confined to those taken in London). It should be noted that thirteen bundles of documents included among the Miscellanea (DEL 8/74–86) are also cause papers of precisely the same character as those to be found in the group now under consideration.

There are 119 bundles in all, the first 97 being arranged alphabetically,[1] while the remaining 22 are in no apparent order. The arrangement of the papers leaves much to be desired; in many cases, all the loose documents surviving in a cause have been tied together in a single parcel but this is not always so, and the haphazard system of filing has sometimes resulted in the papers in a cause being scattered throughout several parcels in a bundle or even through several bundles.[2] Moreover, the practice of maintaining separate files for certain documents, such as sentences and bills of costs, while at the same time including some of them among the cause papers, means that the task of assembling all the documents in a particular cause is wellnigh impossible. The papers are usually loose or tied into parcels with tape or string; a few are in files or bound volumes.[3]

Many of the cause papers are in surprisingly good condition, although those in the unclassified bundles (98–119) do not seem to have been preserved with the same care as the others, and the greater part of those which have been irretrievably damaged by damp or careless handling are to be found in this group. The papers filed among the Miscellanea (DEL 8/74–86) are in an even worse state, for the most part. All the cause papers, even those which are well preserved, are dirty and unpleasant to handle.

These documents have been of great value in the course of this investigation as they are by far the most varied category available in the archives of the court, and they explain and illustrate

[1] This is true only of the order of the bundles as a whole; within each bundle the arrangement of the documents is neither alphabetical nor chronological.

[2] Thus some of the papers in *Banks and others* v. *Finch and others* are to be found in DEL 2/9, some in DEL 2/100/2 and some in DEL 2/101/1.

[3] e.g. *Shaw* v. *Brathwate* (1730), DEL 2/83; copies of several wills, tendered in evidence in this cause, are bound into a single volume.

its operations better than the more formal records, such as Act Books and Assignation Books. It is all the more regrettable, then, that only a few cause papers have survived which are anterior to the first decade of the eighteenth century; there are only a few extant from an earlier date and most of these belong to the period 1660–1700 with a very small number from the Commonwealth and before.[1]

(iii) *Depositions and Personal Answers*

As has been seen, witnesses who gave evidence in causes heard by the Delegates were usually examined privately and their depositions committed to writing.[2] If witnesses appeared before commissioners *ad partes*, the record of their evidence was sealed up with the other documents relating to the commission and filed among the cause papers. If they were examined in London, their depositions were often taken down on loose sheets of paper which are also to be found among the cause papers. Sometimes, however, the evidence was written out in books (or on sheets later bound in book form) and these are now separately filed.

Fifteen of these books survive, together with one unbound bundle. Apart from the first,[3] they are all of the seventeenth century, forming a largely continuous series from 1634 to 1685. The volumes are bound in vellum or leather and are for the most part in good condition. They are not, however, easy to use; most of the books are unindexed and unfoliated and the depositions relating to a particular cause are not always together, as they were set down in chronological order and might be spread over a period, with depositions in other causes intervening.

It has been impossible to devote much attention to the series in the course of this investigation, but it seems likely that a more detailed study would bring to light much information of value

[1] Most of the papers prior to 1700 are filed among the Miscellanea (DEL 8/74–86.) The earliest cause papers noted in the course of the investigation of this category are a set of depositions of the year 1636, although it appears from the class list that there are some documents of *c.* 1600.

[2] For a detailed account of this, see pp. 114–55 *ante*.

[3] It is doubtful whether this volume was properly included among the Delegates' records. The greater part of the book is taken up with proceedings at first instance and upon appeal before judges-delegate in a marine cause (possibly prize) heard in the reign of Philip and Mary. There are also depositions and personal answers in various causes from 1564 to 1568; these all appear to relate to marine business, the last being concerned with a cause heard before commissioners of depradations.

about social conditions in the period to which the depositions relate.[1]

As well as depositions, this category contains a short series of personal answers.[2] These might also be taken by commission or in London and many examples are to be found among the cause papers.

There are seven bound volumes of personal answers. The first covers the period 1655–6, while the remaining six books form a series running from 1668 to 1711 (with one gap from 1679 to 1684). Like the depositions, they are bound in vellum or leather and are largely in good condition.

(iv) *Act Books*

The acts of the Court of Delegates (as of any other civilian court) enshrined the various stages through which a cause passed in the course of its hearing; they were entered into Act Books and the entries in an Act Book relating to a particular cause made up the history of that cause.[3]

In the conventional practice of the civil law, however, an act was preceded by an assignation. The court would make an assignation in a cause, i.e. direct that certain business should be transacted in that cause when it was next heard; a note of the assignation would be entered in an Assignation Book,[4] and below this note was written, when the hearing took place, a brief summary of the business actually done. Later this entry, which embodied the act of the court relating to that cause, was entered in a fair copy in the Act Book.[5]

The form in which an act was drafted remained substantially

[1] On the historical value of the depositions preserved among the records of this and other civilian courts, see the interesting comments of F. W. X. Fincham, superintendent of the literary search department of the principal Probate registry in 1913 (*Public Records Rep.* (1914), pp. 92–3). He suggested, for example, that 'a fairly complete list' of ancient London taverns might be constructed from such records and he also referred to the more general value which depositions, personal answers and the like might have for the historian.

Squibb has also drawn attention to the fact that depositions taken in the Court of Chivalry are rich in biographical and genealogical material (*H.C.C.*, p. 203).

[2] For the function of these, see pp. 102–6 *ante*.

[3] C. C. Langdell, 'The Development of Equity Pleading from Canon Law Procedure', *Select Essays in Anglo-American Legal History* (Cambridge, 1908), vol. 2, p. 773.

[4] For these, see pp. 225–6 *post*.

[5] This sytem continued in the Court of Delegates until the last decade of the seventeenth century when the practice of keeping separate Act Books was abandoned; see p. 226 *post*.

the same throughout the whole period during which Act Books were kept. Each book was divided into terms, which were the same as those of the common law courts, and the entries are arranged under the various court days (or sessions following court days) when the Delegates sat;[1] the books also record any business transacted outside the formal sittings, whether during term or vacation. Each entry begins with the names of the parties written above the names of their proctors;[2] the body of the entry usually consists of a summary of the assignation followed by a statement of the business done.

Although largely confined to a formal account of business transacted in particular causes, the Act Books were also used to record other information which affected the workings of the court, such as the death of the reigning monarch,[3] the text of *Monitiones Generales* (i.e. orders to proctors exercent in the court),[4] receipts for the payment of money or the transfer of documents and the like.[5]

This category of the records contains twenty-six items; twenty-four bound volumes and two bundles. The first volume is the oldest document in the collection, a fragile leather-covered book in surprisingly good condition.[6] Its contents are miscellaneous: acts in various causes from 1538 to 1545, some fragments which seem to have belonged to an early Repertory Book and several pages which are apparently rough drafts of the second surviving Act Book of the Court of Admiralty. The second item in the series covers the years 1601 to 1605 and consists entirely of acts of the Court of Delegates; this book and the next seventeen volumes make up a continuous series of acts to 1650 (with one gap from the Easter term, 1609 to the Hilary term, 1611). No Act Books survive for

[1] For court days, see p. 94 *ante*.

[2] The names of advocates were not given here; they can be discovered only by consulting documents in the cause which they have signed, such as bills of costs, libels or sentences.

[3] e.g. DEL 4/2/177 (death of Elizabeth I).

[4] e.g. DEL 4/2/252.

[5] e.g. *Clerk* v. *Stapleton* (1605), DEL 4/3/21 (payment of money); *Dumbell* v. *Townes* (1605), DEL 4/3/15 (transfer of document).

[6] Although it has been suggested that this book may be a seventeenth-century copy (Brodrick and Fremantle, *A Collection of the Judgments of the Privy Council*, p. li), there is good reason to believe that it is original. It is smaller than folio size and consists of loose sheets of paper stitched together, which is precisely the form of the Act Books of the Court of Admiralty in the earlier part of the sixteenth century (Marsden (ed.), *Select Pleas in the Court of Admiralty*, vol. 1, p. lxii); moreover, the script of the entries, as far as the present writer can judge, belongs to that period.

the Interregnum,[1] but the series recommences shortly after the Restoration and five volumes provide a further set of acts which extend (with some intermissions) from 1660 to 1692. At this point, the bound volumes end but there are two bundles of acts on loose sheets from the eighteenth century, the first (DEL 4/25) covering the years 1708–9 and the second (DEL 4/26) the years 1716–56.

With the exception of the first, the bound Act Books are all of folio size and in a variety of bindings, leather, vellum or boards. The first volume from the seventeenth century is in a precarious state, but the others are in good condition (apart from several whose opening and closing pages have been affected by damp). Most of the books are foliated and have an index, which in some cases was supplied by Rothery, when he examined them for the purpose of making his return. They are in consequence easy to consult and the only difficulty in their use derives from the way in which they were written in the first four decades of the seventeenth century; the crabbed handwriting and the continual abbreviations of words have first to be mastered before the most important of the Act Books become accessible. The writing of the post-Restoration books, however, presents no such difficulty.

As the account given above of the function performed by Act Books will have suggested, their importance to a student of the court's workings lies in the full statement of procedure they contain, and a comprehensive examination has been made of the Act Books written up in the first two decades of the seventeenth century. Those belonging to the post-Restoration period are perhaps of rather less value for the purpose of procedural study, as the style in which acts were written had achieved by that time a rather arid formality, and they provide little useful detail.

(v) *Sentences*

The practice of porrecting sentences, which the Court of Delegates followed, like most other civilian tribunals,[2] until the latter

[1] There may have been Act Books which were subsequently lost, but it is possible that the writing up of Act Books from Assignation Books was dispensed with, as an anticipation of the reform which was made many years later; see p. 226 *post*.

[2] The way in which the rule was usually expressed implied that there were no exceptions to it (e.g. *F.E.L.*, CLV/1), but there is reason to believe that, in the early seventeenth century at least, it was not universal. There is an interesting statement by the respondent's proctor in *Stevenson* v. *Watson* (1604), DEL 4/2/332, in which he alleges that the practice in the Exchequer Court at York 'et

part of the eighteenth century, has already been fully described.[1] The sheets of parchment on which the sentences were engrossed are sometimes to be found among the cause papers, but most of the surviving examples are in a separate group.

Today there are thirty-five bundles of sentences in the archives. Although in some of the later bundles the sheets are loose, most consist of a single file, containing several years' sentences arranged in roughly chronological order and numbered.[2] The greater part of the sentences surviving are those porrected by the successful party to a cause, although in some cases sentences which were rejected by the court have also been kept.[3] The first two parcels in the series contain sentences from 1585 to 1593 and from 1594 to 1601 respectively; these are among the earliest records of royal judges-delegate extant. The next twenty-seven bundles extend over almost the whole of the seventeenth century, from 1601 to 1698, while there are three further bundles which cover the period from 1702 to 1757.[4] Within the chronological limits laid down above, the sentences porrected by successful parties seem to form a fairly complete series, although the condition of many of them makes a thorough check against the record of sentences entered in the Act Books impossible.

The condition of the sentences varies a great deal, as might be expected when their number and chronological range is borne in mind.[5] Perhaps two-thirds are in fair to good condition, but many of the others have been badly damaged by damp or by fire and some have been torn by careless handling. A number of the files have been folded vertically and then compressed (perhaps

in aliis Curiis ibinc', in testamentary causes if not in others, was to allow written or unwritten sentences: 'Judices quandoque in scriptis quandoque sine scriptis sententias ferre solent et tulerunt. Quodque sententie sine scriptis late perinde valent & valere solent atque si in scriptis pronunciate fuissent.'

[1] See pp. 162–4 *ante*.

[2] The documents were filed by making an incision in the left hand margin through which was threaded a stout piece of tape or string, which might be strengthened with metal tags at each end, so that it resembled the modern shoe lace. This method of filing was used by other civilian courts (*H.C.C.*, p. 226).

[3] Examples are to be found in bundles 20, 24 and 27.

[4] The regular practice of porrecting sentences seems to have ceased about this time.

[5] Only an approximate total can be given, as some of the bundles are unnumbered while several of the numbered files are in so bad a condition that the size of the file can only be guessed at; a reasonable conjecture would put the number of sentences preserved at between three and four thousand.

to fit them into available storage space); this has not improved them.

The system of porrecting sentences can never have been satisfactory. It involved the parties in unnecessary expense, as each had to pay for the drafting and engrossing of a sentence although only one was to be accepted; moreover, if the terms of the sentence porrected by the successful party were not precisely the same as those which the judges were prepared to allow, the sentence might require considerable alteration.[1] In the Court of Delegates, the practice continued until the second half of the eighteenth century.[2] It then became the rule for the proctor of each side to state the nature of the relief sought in a prayer, apparently addressed to the judges in open court, and the Delegates would find for one party or the other by a 'final decree or sentence' or an 'interlocutory decree having the force of a definitive sentence in writing', which embodied as much of the successful party's prayer as the court thought fit to grant. Throughout this period, the only record of the sentence readily available is the brief statement of its contents in the Assignation Book;[3] sometimes, however, for reasons which do not now appear, the sentence was engrossed.[4]

It is, perhaps, worthy of notice that the sentences were the only documents drafted in the course of an action before the Court of Delegates whose physical appearance sometimes preserved the lingering traditions of medieval penmanship. The initial letter of the earliest examples was often ornately drawn, sometimes with great elaboration; among the more striking instances is *Warfeld and Brokebanck* v. *Butler*,[5] a pen and ink drawing of a dog against

[1] A typical example of such a sentence is one porrected in *Beare* v. *Collins* (*in the grievance*) (1633), DEL 5/9/26; the sheet has been so drastically amended that it is barely decipherable. Sometimes the problem was solved by a decree for a fair copy; thus in *Bovey* v. *South and others* (1651), DEL 6/4/80, the sentence promulgated by the Delegates was so 'full of erasures, interlineacions and obliteracions' that the judges found it necessary to order that it should be 'fayrely Registred in a booke to remayne in ye Registry'.

[2] The practice of porrection ceased to be common *c.* 1755, but a few sentences survive from 1760 to 1776 in DEL 5/34.

[3] In addition, a number of prayers and sentences, written on loose sheets of paper, are to be found in DEL 5/34. From 1796 to 1802 the substance of sentences promulgated by the court was entered in a book kept solely for this purpose (DEL 5/35).

[4] e.g. *Thue* v. *Pechell* (1813), DEL 6/54/183; *Dalrymple* v. *Dalrymple* (1814), DEL 6/54/195.

[5] (1587), DEL 5/1/67.

a background of flowers and bunches of grapes, *Lord Howard* v. *Lady Howard*,[1] an abstract design with flowers, partly coloured and *Lucas* v. *Burgoyne*,[2] a similar design, fully coloured.

(vi) *Assignation Books*

These books were used for the purpose of entering assignations for causes before the court, i.e. orders by the Delegates that certain business should be transacted in those causes when they were next heard. The relationship between these books and Act Books has already been explained.[3]

The form of an entry in an Assignation Book closely resembled that of an act. When the court made an assignation in a cause, the names of the parties and their proctors and a brief note of the business assigned were written out on a page in the Assignation Book allotted to the appropriate day. Below this entry was left a blank space in which an account of the business actually done on that day was entered when the court sat.

The Assignation Books form the largest consecutive series of documents remaining in the Delegates' archives; fifty-six of these books survive,[4] extending from June 1650 to February 1829 with only one small gap.[5] It seems that at one time the series extended beyond the *terminus a quo* of 1650 as an Assignation Book of 1640 is known to have existed,[6] and as the practice of writing up acts from Assignation Books was apparently general in civilian tribunals, such books may well have been kept from the earliest days of the court's life.

The Assignation Books which survive are in good condition, although the pages of several written up during the Interregnum are rather ragged.[7] With one exception,[8] they have been uniformly

[1] (1588), DEL 5/1/76. [2] (1588), DEL 5/1/80. [3] See p. 220 *ante*.

[4] There were two additional Assignation Books among the Delegates' records kept in Somerset House until 1962 (*Public Records Rep.* (1914), p. 202) but these seem to have been lost.

[5] Volume 34 ends in May 1716 and volume 35 begins in May 1720. As the numeration of the volumes is continuous, it appears that the pages comprising one volume must have been lost before they were bound in their present form.

[6] See the *Appendix to the Schedule of Admiralty Registry Records* (1878), p. 66, preserved in the Public Record Office.

[7] It should be noticed that the forty-two folios comprising volume 3, which contains entries running from January 1651 to May 1654, have been bound together by mistake; they should have been distributed among volumes 2, 4, and 5 which contain the remaining entries for that period.

[8] Volume 15, which is in the original vellum binding.

bound in half leather. They are not easy to consult; most of the seventeenth-century examples have no index, and the speed with which the business transacted in a cause had to be noted in the Assignation Book at the time when it occurred meant that they were often roughly and carelessly written, with many obliterations and interlineations.

The formal distinction between Assignation Books and Act Books was preserved until the end of the seventeenth century. It must then have been decided to dispense with the latter, a reasonable reform as the acts were no more than copies of entries in the Assignation Books. The last bound Act Book ends in 1692 and from about that time the Assignation Books are all equipped with an index, which makes their contents readily accessible.

(vii) *Appeal Case Books*

Throughout the greater part of the court's life, the only account of earlier proceedings in an appealed cause which was available for perusal by the judges-delegate and by the advocates who appeared before them was the process, a single handwritten copy of which was transmitted by the *judex a quo* at an early stage of proceedings upon appeal.[1] The existence of no more than one copy of the process was clearly inconvenient, and it is a little surprising that no steps seem to have been taken to provide supplementary documents until the very end of the eighteenth century.

It was apparently in 1796 that the Delegates first required such documents (which became known as appeal cases) to be printed and this practice continued until the end of the court's life.[2] The papers were printed loose,[3] separate copies being doubtless provided for each of the judges sitting in a cause and for the parties' counsel, but one complete set was bound for preservation among the records and is still available in the archives.

The manner in which appeal cases were drafted was not rigidly uniform but they all adhered to the same general pattern.[4] The

[1] See pp. 216–7 *ante*.

[2] The idea may have been borrowed from the practice of the House of Lords, where printed cases had been employed from a much earlier period; see the standing order of 19 April 1698, quoted in Palmer, *The Practice in the House of Lords on Appeals etc.*, p. 53.

[3] Many of them are to be found among the cause papers.

[4] A court order made at the beginning of the third session of the Trinity term, 1801, directed that each appeal case was to be approved by the counsel on both sides and printed at the joint expense of the parties (DEL 6/52/facing f. 1).

document began with the names of the parties and a brief statement of the nature of the cause and the court or courts through which it had passed; then followed a full account of the pleadings on both sides and (briefly) the judgment of the *judex a quo* and the course of proceedings before the Delegates as far as informations. This section of the appeal case usually ended with the prayers of the appellant and respondent, setting out the nature of the relief they sought and the names of their counsel; below this is a handwritten note of the Delegates' judgment.[1] When necessary, a printed appendix was added to the appeal case, containing exhibits tendered below and a full summary of any evidence taken, personal answers and the like; other documents might also be included on occasions.[2]

The bound set of appeal cases comprises twelve volumes and an index (printed separately). The series begins in 1796 and ends in 1834; all the causes heard by the court over this period seem to have been included, except for a few where proceedings terminated prematurely and it was found unnecessary to print a case.[3] Most of the volumes have at some time been roughly handled and the covers are loose, but this defect apart, they are easy to use.

(viii) *Miscellanea*

This is a residual category, comprising groups of documents which could not be conveniently assigned elsewhere. It embraces commissions of delegacy, several imperfect processes, protocols of appeal, account books of various sorts, bills of costs, inventories of estates, draft instruments, inhibitions, monitions, interlocutories, returns,[4] Repertory Books and a group of thirteen bundles described merely as 'Various', which in fact contain documents identical with those filed among the Miscellaneous Cause Papers.[5]

[1] If the court decided to retain the principal cause, proceedings in that cause following retention would also be given; e.g. *Jenner and others* v. *Tyrell* (1830), DEL 7/13/71.

[2] e.g. *Clark and Clark* v. *Dew* (1826), DEL 7/12; bound into the volume is a copy of Sir John Nicholl's judgment at first instance in the Prerogative Court, a newspaper report of the Lord Chancellor's decision on the application for a commission of review in the cause and a copy of a petition by one of the appellants to the House of Commons.

[3] e.g. *Robson* v. *Rocke and others* (1823), DEL 2/71; the warrant is endorsed: 'No Printing or Papers in this case. The Decree will not be opposed, but Costs will be prayed against the Appellant.'

[4] These are rough drafts upon which was based Rothery's *Return of all Appeals in Causes of Doctrine or Discipline made to the High Court of Delegates*, made to the House of Commons in 1868.

[5] See pp. 217–19 *ante*.

Most of these documents require no further comment, but something must be said about the Repertory Books, as they comprise an important group which has yielded much useful information. As their name implies, they seem to have been intended as an accessible source of certain facts about the causes which came before the court and as a species of key to the records as a whole. Each book is fully indexed, so that an enquirer equipped with nothing but the name of the appellant in a cause could easily find the reference to it in the appropriate Repertory Book, from which he would be directed to the Act Book or Assignation Book where proceedings were fully set out. Each entry in the Repertory Books contains the names of the parties to the cause, and the date when it was introduced into the court, the names and styles of the judges, the date of the commission, the details of the quorum clause, the name of the court from which the appeal came up and (when necessary) the fact that one or both of the parties was a pauper, that the commission was one of adjuncts or review or that judges whose names had been placed on the commission had later refused to act. From 1771, it became the practice to add a note (sometimes lengthy) on the judgment appealed from.[1]

There are four Repertory Books surviving,[2] running in an unbroken series from 1619 to 1789; each book is divided into several parts (there are seven in all) which are separately indexed. The books are uniformly bound in vellum; they are in good condition, although the pages in the first two parts are ragged and the writing very crabbed.

(ix) *Muniment Books*

When documents were produced in the course of a hearing, the court would often direct that copies should be made so that the originals could be returned to their owners; the books in which these copies were entered were known as Muniment Books.

The documents they contain are of a heterogeneous character; they are mostly testamentary, but there are in addition copies of petitions,[3] letters,[4] indentures[5] and any other sort of document which might be tendered in evidence. There are also copies of documents which related in some way to the work of the court,

[1] e.g. *Key* v. *Clay* (1775), DEL 8/73/pt. 3/47.

[2] Some fragments which apparently belonged to an early Repertory Book are to be found in DEL 4/1; see p. 221 *ante*.

[3] e.g. DEL 9/1/134–5. [4] e.g. DEL 9/7/170–5. [5] e.g. DEL 9/7/122–34.

such as Letters Patent appointing registrars,[1] instruments appointing deputy registrars[2] and orders made by the judges and advocates of Doctors' Commons relating to the conduct of business in the civilian tribunals.[3]

Nine Muniment Books survive;[4] the documents copied into them bear dates from 1651 to 1839. They are cloth bound (the original binding being vellum) and are all in good condition. Each book is foliated and provided with an index.[5]

The Muniment Books contain little information of value but there is one series of entries sufficiently important to deserve mention. In the first volume are copies of several letters written by Sir Maurice Eustace, Lord Chancellor of Ireland for several years after the Restoration, to his nephew who was then a student at Lincoln's Inn. They provide much curious information about student life in the Inns of Court at that time and about methods of reading law then in vogue.[6]

(x) *Wills etc.*

This category consists of wills or related documents (draft copies, bonds and the like) which were brought into court in connection with testamentary appeals. They extend from 1636 to 1857 (the later papers relating to appeals which were heard by the Judicial Committee of the Privy Council). There are nine bundles, containing 188 separate items.

An elaborate analysis of this category has recently been made by Mr Conway Davies, the typescript of which may be consulted.

[1] e.g. DEL 9/5/53–8.

[2] e.g. DEL 9/6/11.

[3] e.g. DEL 9/7/84–5.

[4] It was stated by the Royal Commission on the Public Records (*Public Records Rep.* (1914), p. 202) that there were ten Muniment Books housed in the principal Probate registry in 1914, but it seems that one has been lost between that date and 1962, when these records were transferred to the Ashridge repository.

[5] As the current class list of the Delegates' records contains no reference to this category, an analysis is provided below:

DEL 9/1	1651–70	DEL 9/5	1707–20
DEL 9/2	1670–80	DEL 9/6	1720–33
DEL 9/3	1681–95	DEL 9/7	1733–52
DEL 9/4	1695–1707	DEL 9/8	1752–94
		DEL 9/9	1794–1839

[6] These letters have been published in *E.H.R.*, xxxv (1920), pp. 251–9.

(xi) *Additional Miscellanea*

There are six items in this category. One is a copy of Rothery's *Return of all Appeals in Causes of Doctrine or Discipline made to the High Court of Delegates*; the other documents are of no interest.

NOTE ON PUBLISHED ACCOUNTS OF THE COURT OF DELEGATES

Return of the Composition of the Court of Delegates, as Shown by the Commissions issued under the Great Seal at various Periods, from the earliest to the most recent Dates, Particularly noticing Commissions in Cases of Heresy or Unsound Doctrine, and, as far as appears from the Records, the Commencement and Results of such Cases. (Return to an Address of the Honourable the House of Commons, dated 25 June 1850).

This document was prepared by H. B. Swabey, formerly a deputy registrar of the Court of Delegates. It embraced twenty-five causes and provided for each cause the date of the commission, the names of the parties and the court appealed from and the names and styles of the judges. In a few cases, the nature of the cause and brief details of its progress before the Delegates are also given.

Return of all Appeals in Causes of Doctrine or Discipline made to the High Court of Delegates, from its Erection by the 25 Hen. 8, c. 19, A.D. 1533, until its Abolition by the 2 & 3 Will. 4, c. 92, A.D. 1832; specifying,

1 The Date of the Cause
2 The Names and Descriptions of the Parties
3 The Court appealed from
4 The Nature of the Cause
5 The Names and Descriptions of the Delegates or Condelegates, distinguishing whether appointed under the Great Seal or Half Seal
6 The Nature of the Sentence, or whether the Cause was otherwise settled or abandoned
7 The Date of the Sentence

(Return to an Address of the Honourable the House of Commons dated 5 July 1856).

This return was made by H. C. Rothery, the Registrar of the Court of Admiralty, and is a full and painstaking piece of work. The causes which Rothery was able to identify as falling within the terms of the order are set out in tabular form; the information required by the order is given whenever possible, together with such observations upon each cause as Rothery thought might be useful. Appeals in doctrinal and disciplinary matters formed only a small part of the Delegates' jurisdiction, and had the return been confined to this it would have been of little interest; fortunately, Rothery thought it desirable to set the return in an explanatory context, and in a long introduction he touches on the court's jurisdiction, procedure and records, while in several appendixes he discusses appeals to the Delegates from the secular civilian courts and from Ireland, and gives some account of the Courts of Audience and Arches and the practice relating to the *ex officio* oath and canonical purgation. There is also a curious account of the ecclesiastical courts drawn up by Sir John Lambe in 1636 and never previously printed.[1]

[1] This document is briefly calendared in *C.S.P.D.*, 1636–7, p. 521.

APPENDIX I

PETITION OF APPEAL

To the right honorable the Lord Chancellor of England
The humble petition of Francis Crumpe alias Hinckley
Sheweth

That there was lately a Cause depending before the then Judges of the Court for probate of wills and granting Administrations betweene James and Simon *Hinckley* on the one parte and yor petitioner on the other parte concerning the granting of adcon with the will annexed of *Richard Quested* deceased wherein the said Judges did unduely reject an allegation offered on yor peticoners parte and did alsoe in fact decree the said adcon unto the foresayd James and Simon Hinckley and did otherwise proceed to the great greivance and damage of yor peticonr. From which yor petitioner hath by advise of Councell duely appealed.

May it therefore please yor honor to grant unto your petiticoner [*sic*] a Comission of Appeale directed according to the usuall manner heretofore observed to doctors of the Lawes or to referre the nomination thereof to his majesties advocate generall as hath beene alwayes accustomed To heare and determine this businesse:

And as in duty bound yor peticoner shall pray &c.

Third of July 1660
Let doctor Wyseman the Kings Advocate name the Judges for this Appeale as alsoe for other Appeales for the future except I be specially moved to name them myselfe.

Edw. Hyde.

[DEL 9/1]

APPENDIX II

COMMISSION OF DELEGACY

GULIELMUS ET MARIA Deo gratia Anglie Scocie Francie & Hibernie Rex & Regina fidei Defensores &c. DILECTIS nobis in Christo Reverendis in Christo Patribus ac Dominis Dominis Willielmo permissione divina Sancti Asaphen' Episcopo Edwardo eadem permissione Wigorn' Episcopo & Simoni eadem permissione Cicestren' Episcopo Edwardo Nevill militi uni Baronum Scaccarij nostri Johanni Powell militi uni Justitiariorum nostrorum de Banco & Willielmo Gregory militi uni Justitiariorum nostrorum ad placita coram nobis tenenda assignatorum Ricardo Raines militi Curie Prerogative Cantuar' magistro Custodi sive Commissario legitime constituto Johanni Edisbury legum Doctori supreme nostre Curie Cancellarie Anglie magistrorum uni Fishero Littleton Henrico Newton & Stephano Waller legum respective Doctoribus Salutem OSTENSUM EST nobis in suprema Curia nostra Cancellarie ex parte discreti subditi nostri Philippi Maddocks Clerici senioris Vicaris Choralis Ecclesie Cathedralis Landaven' Provincieque nostre Cant' quod ipse sentiens se ex quadam pretensa sententia definitiva ac ab iniqua & iniusta prolacione eiusdem alijsque gravaminibus nullitatibus iniquitatibus iniurijs & iniustitijs ac processus erroribus contra eum in quadam causa appellacionis & querele que coram dilecto nostro venerabili & egregio viro Georgio Oxinden legum Doctore Alme Curie Cantuar' de Archubus [*sic*] London Officiali principali utcunque constituto eiusve Surrogato pretenso inter prefatum Phillippum Maddocks partem appellantem & querelantem ex una & Reverendum in Christo Patrem ac Dominum Dominum Willielmum permissione divina predict' Landaven' predictum Episcopum partem ream & querelatam partibus ex altera nuper vertebatur & pendebat indecisa per dictum venerabilem virum Georgium Oxinden legum Doctorem & Judicem pretensum predictum ad peticionem partis prefati Reverendi Patris Landaven' Episcopi predicti utcunque latis & promulgatis habitis factis & inflictis ac ab omnibus & singulis adversus eum in dicta pretensa sententia utcunque pronunciatis decretis declaratis & condemnatis ac ab omnibus & singulis exinde sequentibus indebite lesum gravatum & iniuriatum fuisse & esse ac timens in futuro enormius ledi &

gravari posse ab eisdem & eorum quolibet AD Curiam nostram Cancellarie Anglie & ad nos in eadem Curia rite & legitime appellavit deque nullitate & iniquitate premissorum omnium & singulorum eque principaliter dixit & querelatus est ac deinde NOBIS supplicari fecit quatenus huiusmodi appellacionis & querele suarum causam & causas & post & contra eas attentatorum & innovatorum quorumcunque & quorumvis aliorum omnium & singulorum per dictum venerabilem virum Georgium Oxinden Judicem pretensum predictum eiusve pretensum Surrogatum in dicta pretensa causa in ipsius partis appellantis & querelantis preiudicium non modicum & gravamen quomodolibet gestorum necnon totius cause sive negotij principalis predicti cum suis incidentibus emergentibus dependentibus annexis & connexis quibuscunque aliquibus probis viris committere opportunumque remedium super hijs providere de Clementia nostra dignaremur NOS vero huiusmodi supplicacioni favorabiliter inclinati ac iustitie Complementum eque in premissis ministrari volentes VOBIS de quorum sana doctrina ac industria plurimum in hac parte confidimus per hec scripta nostra committimus & mandamus quatenus vos omnes aut duo vestrum ad minus in omnibus actis ordinarijs usque ad sententie definitive prolacionem in hoc negotio exclusive ferendis in ferenda vero sententia quatenus vos omnes aut tres vestrum ad minus Quorum vos prefatos Reverendos Patres Willielmum Sancti Asaphen' Episcopum Edwardum Wigorn' Episcopum & Simonem Cicestren' Episcopum vestrumve unum Edwardum Nevill Militem Johannem Powell & Willielmum Gregory militem vestrumve unum presentes & consentientes esse volumus in causa & causis appellacionis & querele nullitatis predicte necnon post & contra eas attentatorum & innovatorum quorumcunque totiusque cause sive negotij principalis predicti cum suis incidentibus emergentibus dependentibus annexis & connexis quibuscunque vocato primitus coram vobis prefato Reverendo Patre Willielmo Landaven' Episcopo predicto in specie ac omnibus alijs qui de Jure in hac parte fuerint evocandi sumarie & de plano & sine strepitu & figura Juditij sola rei veritate inspecta ac mera equitate attenta procedatis auditisque huicinde propositis & proponendis quod iustum fuerit & equum in premissis decernatis facientes quod & que in premissis decreveritis per legitima Juris remedia firmiter observari IN CUIUS rei testimonium has litteras nostras fieri fecimus Patentes TESTIBUS nobis ipsis apud Westmonasterium Nono die martij Anno Regni nostri Tertio.

[DEL 8/5] SEYMOUR

APPENDIX III

COMMISSION OF ADJUNCTS

ANNA Dei gratia Anglie Scotie Francie & Hibernie Regina fidei defensor &c.[1] PREDILECTO & preterquamfideli Consanguineo & Consiliario nostro Carolo Comiti de Manchester predilecto & preterquamfideli Consanguineo nostro Johanni Comiti de Anglesey predilecto & preterquamfideli Consanguineo & Consiliario nostro Mountagu Comiti de Abingdon predilecto & preterquamfideli Consanguineo nostro Carolo Vicecomiti Townshend predilecto & preterquamfideli nostro Francisco Domino Guilford predilecto & preterquamfideli Consiliario nostro Johanni Domino Granville predilecto & preterfideli Consiliario nostro Thome Trevor Militi Capitali Justicio nostro de Banco DILECTIS & fidelibus nostris Edwardo Ward Militi Capitali Baroni Scaccarij nostri Roberto Tracy Armigero uni Justiciorum nostrorum de Banco Roberto Price Armigero uni Baronum Scaccarij nostri Ricardo Raines Militi & legum Doctori Curie Prerogative Cant' Magistro Custodi sive Commissario legitime constituto Henrico Newton Ricardo Pagitt Johanni Harwood & Gulielmo Clements legum respective Doctoribus Salutem CUM Nos Literas nostras Commissionales Magno Sigillo nostro Anglie communitas nuper concesserimus sub tenore verborum sequentium videlicet ANNA Dei gratia Anglie Scotie Francie & Hibernie Regina fidei defensor &c. Clarissimis Consanguineis nostris Mountagu Venables Comiti de Abingdon Henrico Vicecomiti Longueville & predilecto & fideli nostro Francisco Domino Guilford & dilectis & fidelibus nostris Thome Trevor Militi Capitali Justicio nostro de Banco Edwardo Ward Militi Capitali Baroni Scaccarij nostri Roberto Tracy uni Justiciorum nostrorum ad placita coram Nobis tenenda assignatorum Ricardo Raines Militi Curie Prerogative Cant' Magistro Custodi sive Commissario legitime constituto Henrico Newton Ricardo Pagitt Johanni Harwood & Gulielmo Clements legum respective Doctoribus Salutem OSTENSUM est Nobis in Suprema Curia nostra Cancellarie Anglie per appellacionem quandam ex parte Subditi nostri Gregorij King Lancaster-Heraldi

[1] Two 6*d.* stamps were affixed in the margin against the preamble.

in hac parte interpositam quod ipse sentiens se ex quibusdam gravaminibus nullitatibus & iniurijs per prenobilem & honorandum virum Carolum Dominum Comitem Carlisle Dominum Comitem Mareschallum Anglie eiusve Surrogatum in quodam pretenso negotio sive pretensa causa pro correctione sive Castigacione vel punicione prefati Gregorij King Lancaster-Heraldi quod coram eo in Judicio inter prenobilem & honorandum virum Thomam dominum Comitem Coventrie partem dictum pretensum negotium sive dictam pretensam causam promoventem ex una Et prefatum Gregorium King Lancaster-Heraldum partem contra quam idem pretensum negotium sive dicta pretensa Causa promovebatur partibus ex altera nuper vertebatur & pendebat indecisum nulliter tam ex Officio suo pretenso quam ad instanciam peticionem procuracionem & sollicitacionem prefati prenobilis & honorandi viri Thome Domini Comitis Coventrie seu eius partis subdolas iniquas & iniustas in quo quidem pretenso negotio sive pretensa Causa libellus pretensus sive Articuli pretensi sunt sive fuerunt exhibiti & admissi & lis contestata desuper negative premissis tamen non obstantibus pars prefati prenobilis & honorandi viri Thome Domini Comitis Coventrie minus tamen iuste petijt prefatum Gregorium King responsum positionibus sive Articulis pretensis dicti pretensi libelli continentis Crimina pretensa sive Delicta pretensa animo & intentione eum corrigendi & puniendi datis vigore Juramenti sui Corporalis dari (Cum de Jure vigore Juramenti sui Corporalis non astrictus vel obligatus fuit) prefatus tamen prenobilis & honorandus vir Carolus Dominus Comes Carlisle Dominus Comes Marescallus Anglie ad instanciam instigacionem procuracionem & peticionem partis prefati prenobilis & honorandi viri Thome Comitis Coventrie minus Juste (eius honore semper salvo) procedens [per] prefatum Gregorium King [responsum] vigore juramenti sui Corporalis positionibus sive Articulis pretensis dicti pretensi libelli dari decrevit a quoquidem pretenso Decreto protestationem fecit de gravamine & de Appellando infra tempus de Jure indultum premissis tamen non obstantibus prefatus prenobilis & honorandus vir Dominus Comes de Carlisle Marescallus Anglie ad similem instanciam instigacionem procuracionem et peticionem partis prefati prenobilis & honorandi viri Thome Comitis Coventrie ad ulteriora minus Juste (eius honore semper salvo) processit & monuit & mandavit prefatum Gregorium King ad prestandum Instrumentum Corporale de fideliter respondendo dicto libello sive Articulis dicti pretensi libelli primo secundo & tercio Et prefatus Gregorius King sic monitus & mandatus protestatus est de gravamine continuato & de Appellando infra tempus de Jure indultum sed sub metu suspensionis ab officio suo & sub protestatione de non recedendo a protestationibus predictis manum suam super libello posuit & prenobilis & honorandus vir Dominus Comes de Carlisle Dominus Comes Marescallus Anglie detulit ei Juramentum de fideliter respondendo Articulis pretensis dicti pretensi libelli & monuit eum ad dandum responsa sua personalia vigore Juramenti sui in vel ante proximum diem Juridicum videlicet in vel ante duodecimum diem instantis Junij in omnibus (eius honore semper salvo) minus Juste monitum & inflictum indebite ledi & gravari ac lesum & iniuriatum fuisse & esse ac timens se ex eisdem enormius ledi & gravari posse in futurum ab eisdem et eorum quolibet & presertim a decernendo eum vigore Instrumenti sui Corporalis ad respondendum dicto libello sive Articulis pretensis dicti pretensi libelli & a deferendo ei Juramentum ad respondendum eidem sive eisdem & a monendo eum ad dandum responsa sua personalia in vel ante duodecimum diem Instantis Junij & ab omnibus & singulis exinde sequentibus ad supremam Curiam nostram Cancellarie & ad Nos in dicta Curia nostra rite & legitime Appellavit deque nullitate & iniquitate premissorum omnium & singulorum & ab omnibus & singulis inde sequentibus eque principaliter dixit & querelatus est Nosque humiliter supplicari fecit quatenus de remedio sibi in hac parte providere de Clementia nostra regia...dignaremur opportuno NOS huiusmodi supplicacionibus favorabiliter inclinate ac Justitiam & eius complementum eque in premissis ministrari volentes VOBIS de quorum sana Doctrina Conscientie puritate & in rebus gerendis dexteritate plurimum in hac parte confidemus per hec scripta nostra committimus & mandamus quatenus vos omnes aut duo vestrum ad minus in omnibus actis ordinarijs in dicta causa ante prolacionem sententie definitive exclusive expediendis in sententia vero definitiva ferenda quatenus vos omnes aut tres vestrum ad minus Quorum vos Mountagu Venables Comitem de Abingdon Henricum Vicecomitem Longueville Franciscum Dominum Guilford vestrumve unum unum esse volumus Necnon vos prefatum Thomam Trevor Militem Edwardum Ward Militem & Robertum Tracy vestrumve unum unum etiam esse volumus presentem & consentientem in Causa & Causis Appellacionis &

querele nullitatis huiusmodi necnon post et contra eas attentatorum & innovatorum quorumcunque & quorumvis totius negotij principalis unacum suis incidentibus emergentibus dependentibus annexis & connexis quibuscunque vocato primitus coram vobis dicto prenobile & honorando viro Thoma Domino Comite Coventrie atque alijs de Jure in hac parte vocandis sumarie & de plano & sine strepitu & figura Judicij sola rei veritate inspecta meraque equitate attenta rite et legitime procedatis Inditisque huicinde propositis & proponendis quod Justum fuerit & equum in premissis decernatis per legitima Juris remedia firmiter in hac parte observari IN CUIUS rei Testimonium has literas nostras fieri fecimus Patentes TESTE meipsa apud Westmonasterium septimo die Julij Anno regni nostri Primo NUNC vero ex certis Causis Nos in hac parte specialiter moventibus ad peticionem prefati prenobilis & honorandi viri Thome Comitis Coventrie Nobis in Curia Cancellarie predicta (inter alia) monstrantem antedictum Henricum vicecomitem Longueville citra concessionem dictarum literarum nostrarum Commissionalium sub magno sigillo nostro Anglie munitarum esse demortuum Necnon honorabilem virum Robertum Tracy Armigerum unum Justiciorum nostrorum de Banco per Titulum erroneum unius scilicet Justiciorum nostrorum ad placita coram Nobis tenenda assignatorum in Commissione nostra prerecitata utcunque nominatum & inscriptum esse Ideoque Onus execucionis dicte Commissionis in se non suscepisse Errorem igitur in Commissione nostra priori rectum esse volumus prefatoque Roberto Tracy Armigero uni Justiciorum nostrorum de Banco committimus & mandamus prout in tenore Commissionis nostre predicte (ac si Titulo proprio in eadem descriptus fuerat) commissimus & mandavimus Vosque prefatum Carolum Comitem de Manchester Johannem Comitem de Anglesey Carolum Vicecomitem Townshend Johannem Dominum Granville Teque prefatum Robertum Price Armigerum vobis prefato Mountagu Comiti de Abingdon Francisco Domino Guilford Thome Trevor Militi Edwardo Ward Militi Roberto Tracy Armigero uni Justiciorum nostrorum de Banco Ricardo Raines Militi Henrico Newton Ricardo Pagitt Johanni Harwood & Gulielmo Clements legum Doctoribus duximus adiungendos fore & adiungimus per presentes MANDANTES quatenus assumentes Causam & Causas huiusmodi in statu quo nunc sunt vos omnes aut duo vestrum ad minus in omnibus Actis ordinarijs in dicto negotio sive Causa expediendis usque ad prolacionem sententie vestre definitive exclusive in ferenda vero sententia definitiva quatenus vos omnes aut tres vestrum ad minus Quorum vos prefatum Carolum Comitem de Manchester Johannem Comitem de Anglesey Mountagu Comitem de Abingdon Carolum Vicecomitem Townshend Franciscum Dominum Guilford Johannem Dominum Granville vestrumve unum unum esse volumus Necnon vos prefatum Thomam Trevor Militem Edwardum Ward Militem Robertum Tracye Armigerum & Robertum Price Armigerum vestrumve unum unum etiam esse volumus presentes & consentientes esse volumus in Causa sive negotio principali unacum suis incidentibus emergentibus dependentibus annexis & connexis quibuscunque sumarie & de plano & sine strepitu seu figura Judicij sola rei veritate inspecta meraque equitate attenta secundam tenorem literarum nostrarum Commissionalium predictarum & literarum Commissionalium Adiunctorum huiusmodi procedatis Auditisque huicinde propositis & proponendis quod Justum & equum fuerit in eisdem decernatis facientes quod & que in eisdem decreveritis per legitima Juris remedia firmiter in hac parte observari IN CUIUS rei Testimonium has literas nostras fieri fecimus Patentes TESTE meipsa apud Westmonasterium octavo die Maij Anno Regni nostri Tercio.

SEYMOUR

[DEL 2/102/pt. 1]

APPENDIX IV

GENERAL PROXY

WHEREAS the worshipfull John Bettesworth Doctor of Laws & Judge of the Prerogative Court of Canterbury in a Cause lately brought before him by me the underwritten Nathanaell Austin the naturall & lawfull Son of Catharine Austin late of Longbridge in the County of Warwick widow dec'ed against Catharine Cock (the wife of William Cock) prtended administratrix with ye prtended Schedules Testamentary annexed of the Goods Chattells & Creditts of the said deceased annexed and whereas the said Judge hath given a Sentence definitive against me in the said Cause on the part & behalf of the said Catherine Cock.

NOW KNOW all men by these presents That I the said Nathanael Austin do hereby constitute & appoint Charles Garrett Notary Publick one of the Procurators Generall of the Arches Court of Canterbury my true & lawfull Proctor for me & in my name to interpose and bring an Appeal from the said Sentence & to prosecute the same & cause ye said Cause to be heard & tryed in the Court of Delegates & if occasion be to propound & plead any new Matter before the Judges of the said Cause that may be materiall for me in the said Cause and to do all other things requisite & necessary to be done therein and I do hereby promise to ratify & confirm what my said Proctor shall act or do therein Witness my hand & Seal this first Day of February in the year of our Lord 1722.

Signed Sealed & Delivered
in the presence of us. NATH AUSTIN (L.S.)

ELIZ. AUSTIN
MATH: PAGE

[DEL 2/3]

APPENDIX V

SPECIAL PROXY

Whereas there is a Cause of Appeal, now depending in the High Court of Delegates, between the undersubscribed Elizabeth Wiat, the wife of Francis Wiat of Charterhouse yard, London, Merchant, the Natural & lawfull sister of John Mead late of the Parish of St Andrew Holborne in the County of Midd'x Batchelor, dece'd the party Appellant on the One part, and Richard Mead of London, Merchant, the Natural and lawful Brother of the sd dece'd the Party Appellate on the other part, concerning several Proceedings made by the Judge of the Prerogative Court of Canterbury, in a Cause lately depending before him, between the said Parties, and that such Cause of Appeal, and suit in ye Prerogative Court of Canterbury, is lately agreed by and between us the sd Partys to be executed. Now KNOW, all men by these presents that I the said Elizabeth Wiat, Do (with the Consent of my said Husband testify'd by his subscribing himself as Witness to these presents) for divers good Causes & Considerations me Hereunto moveing to all Intents and purposes in law Renounce the Appeal Enter'd or Interpos'd on my behalf in the say'd Cause, and Consent and Agree that the Judges in the Said Cause or any two or more of them may Remitt the same to the aforesaid prerogative Court of Canterbury, and in Order that this my Proxy of Revon & consent may be admitted and have its due Effect in Law I do hereby order, direct, authorise and Impower Mr George Sayer Notary Publick my proctor in the said Cause to appear before the sd Judges delegates or any two or more of them, and for me and in my name to pray and procure the same to be admitted & enacted and do all other Acts & deeds requisite & necessary to be done in and about the same as fully & amply as I might or could do if Personally prest, in Witness whereof I have hereunto Sett my hand & seal this Eigth day of February one Thousand Sevenhundred & twenty One

ELISABETH WIAT (L.S.)

Signed Sealed and Deliver'd in the Presence of us
Francis Wiat Richard Wiat Hen' Steer
[DEL 2/90]

APPENDIX VI

INHIBITION AND CITATION

GULIELMUS Tertius, Dei gratia Anglie, Scotie, Francie, et Hibernie Rex fidei Defensor UNIVERSIS et singulis Clericis, et Literatis quibuscumque in et per totum nostrum Anglie Regnum ubilibet Constitutis SALUTEM Cum Nos Literas nostras Commissionales magno Sigillo nostro Anglie Communitas nuper concesserimus, sub tenore Verborum Sequentium Videlicet GULIELMUS Tertius Dei gratia Anglie, Scotie, Francie, et Hibernie, Rex fidei Defensor &c. Dilectis Subditis nostris Johanni Powell Militi uni Justitiariorum nostrorum de Banco, Johanni Powell Militi uni Baronum Scaccarij nostri Samueli Eyres Militi uni Justitiariorum nostrorum ad placita coram Nobis tenenda assignatorum, Georgio Oxenden, Legum Doctori Alme Curie Cantuariensis de Archubus [*sic*] London Officiali principali, Fishero Littleton, Stephano Waller, Johanni Harwood, et Gulielmo King Legum respective Doctoribus SALUTEM Ostensum est Nobis in Suprema Curia nostra Cancellarie Anglie per appellacionem ex parte subditi nostri Thome Thwaites fratris naturalis et legitimi et proximi Consanguinei Marie Thwaites Solute nuper de Low-Burton in provincia Ebor' defuncte, interpositam Quod ipse sentiens se ex quibusdam gravaminibus nullitatibus iniquitatibus injustitijs et injurijs per venerabilem Virum Richardum Sterne Armigerum et Artium Magistrum, Scaccarij et Curie Prerogative Domini Archiepiscopi nostri Ebor' Commissarium sive Custodem generalem, seu per ejus Surrogatum in quodam negotio pretenso probacionis Testamenti pretensi sive ultime pretense voluntatis dicte Marie Thwaites defuncte quod Coram Eo in juditio inter Joshuam Smith Executorem pretensum in dicto Testamento pretenso nominatum partem dictum pretensum negotium promoventem ex una, et se prefatum Thomam Thwaites fratrem naturalem et legitimum et proximum Consanguineum dicte defuncte partem contra quam idem negotium promovebatur partibus ex altera vertebatur nuper et pendebat indecisum, sibi ad peticionem partis dicti Joshue Smith latis, illatis, et inflictis, indebite pergravari, ac lesum, gravatum, et injuriatum fuisse et esse, ac timens in futuro enormius ledi, et gravari posse ab eisdem et eorum quolibet, et presertim a quadam Sententia pretensa diffinitiva contra eum in dicto negotio utcunque lata, ejusque asserta prolacione, ac ab omnibus inde sequentibus ad supremam Curiam nostram Cancellarie Anglie et ad Nos in dicta Curia nostra, rite et legitime in Scriptis appellavit, deque nullitate et iniquitate premissorum &c. principaliter dixit, querelatus et conquestus est ac deinde Nobis humiliter suplicatum [*sic*] ecit QUATENUS hujusmodi sue appellacionis et querele nullitatis et iniquitatis predicte causam et causas, ac post et contra Eas temere attentatorum et innovatorum quorumcunque, et quorumvis aliorum et per Judicem antedictum in prejudicium dicte partis appellantis et querelantis quomodollibet [*sic*] gestorum, totamque causam sive negotium principale, Unacum suis incidentibus, emergentibus, dependentibus, annexis et connexis quibuscunque, aliquibus probis viris committere, oportunumque remedium sibi in premissis providere de Clementia nostra regia dignaremur Nos igitur huiusmodi supplicationibus favorabiliter inclinati ac justitie Complementum &c. in premissis fieri volentes NOBIS (de quorum sana Doctrina Conscientie puritate et in rebus gerendis dexteritate plurimum in hac parte confidimus) per hac Scripta nostra committimus et mandamus QUATENUS vos omnes octo, septem, sex, quinque, quatuor, tres, aut duo vestrum in omnibus actis ordinarijs in dicto negotio expediendis usque ad prolacionem sententie diffinitive in eodem ferende exclusive: In ferenda vero sententia diffinitiva Quatenus vos omnes octo, septem, sex, quinque, quatuor aut tres vestrum ad minus (quorum vos prefatos Johannem Powell Militem et Justitiarium nostrum antedictum, Johannem Powell Militem Baronem nostrum antedictum et Samuelem Eyres Militem, vestrumve unum presentes et consentientes esse volumus) In causa et causis appellacionis et querele nullitatis et iniquitatis predicte, ac post et contra Eas temere attentatorum, et innovatorum quorumcunque et quorumvis aliorum nec non in causa sive negotio principali, Unacum suis incidentibus, emergentibus, dependentibus, annexis, et connexis quibuscunque, vocatis primitus coram Vobis prefato Joshua Smith alijsque de jure in hac parte vocandis, Summarie, et de plano, ac sine Strepitu, et figura Juditij, sola rei veritate inspecta, meraque equitate attenta, procedatis auditisque hic inde propositis, et proponendis quod Justum, et equum fuerit in eisdem decernatis facientes quod et que in premissis decreveritis per legitima juris remedia firmiter observari In Cuius rei Testimonium has Literas nostras fieri fecimus patentes, Teste Meipso apud Westmonasterium Nono Die Mensis Januarij Anno Regni nostri Sexto CUMQUE Dilecti Nostri Georgius Oxenden, Stephanus Waller & Johannes Harwood Legum doctores Judices (inter alios) Delegati nostri antedicti Onus Executionis dictarum nostrarum Literarum Commissionalium in se acceptaverint, ac inhibicionem et citacionem infrascriptas, ad peticionem partis dicti Thome Thwaites decreverint, Justitia mediante, VOBIS Igitur conjunctim et divisim comittimus ac firmiter injungendo mandamus quatenus inhibeatis seu inhiberi faciatis peremptorie prefato venerabili viro Richardo Sterne Artium Magistro Judici a quo extitit in hac parte appellatum et querelatum ejusque Surrogato ac Registrario seu Actorum Scribe seu Scribis prefatoque Joshue Smith in specie ac omnibus et singulis alijs quibus jus exigit in hac parte inhiberi in genere NE ipsi seu eorum aliquis pendente coram Delegatis nostris antedictis eorumve Condelegatis huiusmodi appellationis et querele nullitatis et iniquitatis negotio indiscusso quicquam in prejuditium dicte partis appellantis et querelantis litisve pendentis aut Juris et jurisdictionis nostre...quominus dicta pars appellans liberam habeat dicte sue appellationis et querele nullitatis et iniquitatis negotium prosequendi facultatem quovismodo attentent seu attentari faciant vel attentat seu attentari faciat sub pena juris et Contemptus. CITETIS insuper seu citari faciatis peremptorie prefatum Joshuam Smith quod compareat coram Delegatis nostris antedictis eorumve Condelegatis In Aula Communi infra Hospitium Dominorum Advocatorum London locoque Judiciali ibidem Octavo die post Citacionem hujusmodi ei in hac parte factam Si Juridicus fuerit alioqui proximo die juridico ex tunc proxime sequente Horis Causarum ibidem ad jura reddarum [*sic*] Consuetis prefato Thome Thwaites in dicto sue appellacionis et querele nullitatis et iniquitatis negotio de Justitia responsurus ulteriusque facturus et recepturus quod Justum fuerit in hac parte Et quid in premissis feceritis Delegatos nostros antedictos Eorumve Condelegatos debite Certificetis Unacum presentibus DATIS Sub Sigillo supreme Curie nostrorum Delegatorum decimo Nono die Mensis Januarij Anno Regni Nostri Sexto.

THO: OUGHTON REGISTRARIUS REGIUS

[endorsed]

This Inhibition was psonally Served Upon Mr Robert Oates Deputy Register & a true Copy thereof left with him the 29th day of January (94) And also Upon ye Rt Worpll Dr Henry Watkinson Surr to the withinnamed Richard Sterne Esq this 30th day of January 1694 by me

Jacob Costebadie

[DEL 8/64]

APPENDIX VII

LIBEL

IN DEI NOMINE AMEN Coram vobis prehonorandis viris Roberto Tracy Armigero uno Justiciariorum de communi Banco Serenissimi Domini Nostri Georgij Regis &c. Johanne Fortescue Aland Milite uno Justiciariorum ad Placita coram dicto Serenissimo Domino nostro Rege tenenda assignatorum et Francisco Page Milite uno Baronum Scacarij dicti Serenissimi Domini Nostri Regis Nathanaele Lloyd Milite Legum Doctore Carolo Heriot, Roberto Wood, Georgio Paul, et Gulielmo Bramston Legum respective Doctoribus in Causa infrascripta atque inter partes inferius nominatas Judicibus Delegatis Regis pars cuiusdam descrete femine Susanne Charlton vidue Relicte et Executricis unice in Testamento vero ultimo et Originali sive ultima Voluntate in Scriptis Johannis Charlton nuper de Yarmouth Magna in Comitatu Norfolcie et ad Navem Mercatoriam le Pheasant spectantis defuncti gerente Datum decimo sexto die mensis Februarij Anno Domini millesimo septingentesimo vicesimo secundo nominate contra Richardum Charlton fratrem naturalem et legitimum et Executorem pretensum Testamenti pretensi sive ultime voluntatis pretense dicti defuncti gerentis (uti pretenditur) Datum primo die mensis Augusti Anno Domini millesimo septingentesimo vicesimo tertio ac contra et adversus quemcunque alium sive alios quoscunque pro Eo in Judicio coram vobis legitime intervenientes per viam Appellationis et querele omnibus melioribus et efficacioribus via modo et Juris forma necnon ad omnem quemcunque Juris Effectum dicit allegat et in hijs Scriptis in Jure proponit articulatim prout sequitur videlicet

I INPRIMIS quod coram venerabili et Egregio viro Johanne Bettesworth Legum doctore Curie Prerogative Cantuarien' Magistro Custode sive Commissario legitime constituto ejusve Surrogato pretenso quoddam Negotium Testamentarium sive probationis [*sic*] per Testes dicti Testamenti sive ultime voluntatis dicti defuncti gerentis (ut prefertur) Datum decimo sexto die mensis februarij predicti necnon Schedule Testamentarie dicti defuncti gerentis Datum vicesimo secundo die mensis Aprilis Anno

Domini millesimo septingentesimo vicesimo quarto inter prefatam Susannam Charlton[1]... hujusmodi Negotium promoventem ex una et dictum Richardum Charlton partem contra quam idem Negotium promovebatur partibus ex altera vertebatur nuper et pendebat indecisum Et ponit pars ista proponens conjunctim divisim et dequolibet.

2 Item quod dictus venerabilis et egregius vir Johannes Bettesworth Legum doctor Judex antedictus ejusve Surrogatus pretensus perperam nulliter et inique (ejus Reverentia semper salva) in dicto Negotio utcunque procedens partique dicti Richardi Charlton plus justo favens Jurisque et Judiciorum Ordine in ea parte requisito minime observato sed penitus spreto et postposito Sententiam in Scriptis (uti pretenditur) definitivam omnino tamen nullam et de Jure prorsus invalidam pro parte et in favorem dicti Richardi Charlton ac contra et adversus eandem Susannam Charlton in dicto Negotio contra omnem Juris ordinem ac sine probationibus sufficientibus et legitimis in ea parte prius habitis et factis utcunque nulliter legit tulit et promulgavit per quam inter alia dictam Susannam Charlton in Expensis pretensis litis ex parte et per partem antedicti Richardi Charlton in eodem Negotio (uti pretenditur) factis et faciendis condemnavit in omnibus minus juste nulliter de facto et inique tam ex Officio suo pretenso quam ad Instantiam Instigationem petitionem procurationem Sollicitationem et persuasionem prefati Richardi Charlton seu partis sue subdolas iniquas et injustas in dicte Susanne Charlton prejudicium non modicum et Gravamen Et ponit ut Supra.

3 Item quod fuit et est ex parte et per partem prefate Susanne Charlton sentientis se ex premissis Gravaminibus Nullitatibus Iniquitatibus Injustitijs et Injurijs omnibus et singulis indebite pergravari ac lesam gravatam et injuriatam fuisse et esse ac juste timentis se in futurum enormius ledi et gravari posse ab eisdem et eorum quolibet Et presertim a dicta pretensa Sententia in Scriptis (uti pretenditur) definitiva in dicto Negotio (ut prefertur) lecta lata et promulgata ejusque asserta prolatione ac a Condemnatione pretensa dicte Susanne Charlton in dictis Expensis pretensis Litis predicte ac ab omnibus et singulis exinde sequentibus seu sequi valentibus ad Serenissimum Dominum in Christo Principem ac Dominum Dominum Georgium Dei Gratia Magne Britannie Francie et Hibernie Regem Fidei Defensorem &c. et ad ejus

[1] The following word is illegible.

Supreme Curie [*sic*] Cancellarie Magne Britannie rite et legitime appellatum deque nullitate et iniquitate omnium et singulorum premissorum eque principaliter dictum querelatum et conquestum est Et ponit ut supra.

4 Item quod prefatus Serenissimus Dominus Noster Rex ad petitionem partis dicte Susanne Charlton per literas suas patentes Magno Sigillo Magne Britannie communitas auditionem et determinationem hujus Cause unacum suis incidentibus emergentibus dependentibus annexis et connexis quibuscumque vobis Judicibus delegatis Regijs antedictis cum ista Clausula quatenus vos omnes aut duo vestrum ad minus in omnibus Actis ordinarijs in hujusmodi Negotio expediendis ad prolationem Sententie definitive in eodem exclusive inferenda vero Sententia definitiva quatenus Vos omnes aut tres vestrum ad minus (Quorum vos prefati Robertus Tracy Armiger Johannes Fortescue Aland miles et Franciscus Page miles eorumve unus presentes et consentientes sitis) commisit prout per dictas Literas Patentes plenius liquet et apparet Et ponit ut supra.

5 Item quod Vos domini Judices delegati Regij antedicti vestrumve duo onus Executionis dictarum Literarum Patentium et Comissionalium in vos acceptatis ac juxta tenorem et effectum earundem procedendum fore decrevistis Et ponit ut supra.

6 Item quod prefatus Richardus Charlton fuit et est hujus incliti Regni Magne Britannie subditus eoque intuitu ac ratione appellationis et querele ex parte dicte Susanne Charlton in hac parte debite facte et interposite Jurisdictioni hujus Curie notorie subditus et subjectus Et ponit ut supra.

7 Item quod premissa &c.

[DEL 2/15]

APPENDIX VIII

DECREE FOR PERSONAL ANSWERS

GEORGE The Second by the Grace of God of Great Britain France and Ireland King Defender of the Faith and so forth To all and singular Clerks and literate persons in and throughout Our Kingdome of Great Britain whomsoever and wheresoever GREETING[1] Whereas Our beloved the Worshipfull Edward Kinaston, William Bramston, and Stephen Cottrell respectively Doctors of Laws in the Busyness hereafter described and between the Partyes hereunder named Our Judges (among others) Delegates in a certain Cause of Appeal and Complaint now depending before them in Judgment between the Worshipfull Peregrine Gastrell Esq Batchelor of Laws Vicar General and Official principal to the Right Reverend Father in God Samuel by Divine Permission Lord Bishop of Chester, lawfully constituted, and Henry Hand the Partyes Appellants and Complainants on the one part, and Robert Herbert, Jeoffry Moulding, and John Parry Procurators General of the Consistory Court of Chester the Partyes complained of on the other part rightly and lawfully proceeding against the said Robert Herbert, Jeoffry Moulding, and John Parry as the Partyes principal, for that they are the more lawfull persons from whom the truth in this behalf may be better drawne and inquired into, than from their proctor appearing for them in this Busyness, have decreed at the petition of the proctor of the said Peregrine Gastrell Esq and Henry Hand, the said Robert Herbert, Jeoffry Moulding, and John Parry to be cited and called into Judgment, and to appear the day time and place hereunder written, and in the manner and form hereafter described (Justice so requiring) Therefore We impower and by injoyning strictly command You joyntly and severally That you cite or cause to be cited peremptorily the said Robert Herbert, Jeoffry Moulding, and John Parry by the Execution of these presents on Mr Sandford Nevile their proctor That they appear before Our Judges Delegates aforesaid, or their Condelegates in the common Hall of Doctors Commons situate in the Parish of St Benedict near Pauls Wharfe

[1] Three 6*d*. stamps were affixed in the margin against the preamble.

London and Place of Judicature there on Friday the twenty third of this instant November between the hours of three and five in the Afternoon, then and there to answer by virtue of their Corporal oaths to the several positions or Articles of a certain allegation given in, and as it stands admitted in this Cause on the part and behalf of the said Peregrine Gastrell Esq and Henry Hand under pain of the Law and Contempt thereof and further to do, and receive as unto Law and Justice shall appertain, and whatsoever You shall do in the premisses that You certifye the same to Our Delegates aforesaid, or their Condelegates together with these presents Dated at LONDON Under the Seal of our High Court of Delegates the fourteenth day of November in the Year of Our Lord One thousand Seven hundred thirty three and in the Seventh Year of Our Reigne.

EDWARD SMITH Deputy Register of
His Mat'yes High Court of Delegates.

[Endorsed]

This Citation was Duly Executed by shewing this original to the within named Mr Sandford Nevile Proctor by Delivring to Him a Copy hereof on the 20 day of November 1733

by me Peter Powell.

[DEL 2/32]

APPENDIX IX

MONITION FOR PROCESS

ANNA Dei gratia Anglie Scotie Francie et Hibernie Regina fidei Defensor &c.[1] UNIVERSIS et Singulis Clericis et Literatis quibuscunque per totum Nostrum Hibernie Regnum ubiquolibet constitutis Salutem Cum Dilecti Nostri Johannes Cook Miles et Legum Doctor Alme Curie Cantuar' de Arcubus London Officialis principalis legitime constitutus et Georgius Bramston Legum etiam Doctor in Negotio infrascripto atque inter partes inferius nominatas Judices (inter alios) Delegati Nostri in quadam Causa Appellationis et querele que coram eis in Judicio inter Reverendum Johannem Clayton Clericum Prebendarium Sancti Micharis Canonicum Ecclesie Cathedralis Sancte Trinitatis alias Christ Church Dublin' partem appellantem et querelantem ex una et Reverendissimum in Christo Patrem Gulielmum Providentia divina Dublin' Archiepiscopum Hibernie Primatem et Metropolitanum partem appellatam et querelatam partibus ex altera vertitur et pendet indecissa rite et legitime procedentes Decretum Eorum Interlocutorium pro toto et integro processu Judicis a quo extitit in hac parte appellatum et querelatum eis in forma Subscripta transmittendo ad petitionem partis dicte partis appellantis interposuerint (Justitia mediante) Vobis igitur conjunctim et divisim comittimus ac firmiter injungendo mandamus quatenus (authoritate Nostra) moneatis seu moneri faciatis peremptorie Dilectum Nostrum Gulielmum Providentia divina Dublin' Archiepiscopum Hibernie Primatem et Metropolitanum predictum Judicem a quo extitit in hac parte appellatum et querelatum ejusque Surrogatum et Registrarium sive actorum Scribam Seu Scribas in Specie Necnon omnes et Singulos alios penes quos aliqua acta inactitata Exhibita munimenta instrumenta et processus hujusmodi Negotium qualitercunque concernentia remanent sive existunt in genere (quos Nos etiam tenore presentium sic monemus) quatenus ipsi Ultima Sessione Termini Sancti Michaelis proximi post datum presentium futuri aut citra omnia et singula acta inactitata exhibita munimenta instrumenta totumque

[1] Two 6*d*. stamps were affixed in the margin against the preamble.

et integrum processum hujusmodi Negotium qualitercunque concernentia seu tangentia et penes eos remanentia sub debita atque authentica forma vel in eorum formis originalibus unacum Exemplaribus fideliter collatis Sigilloque authentico Sigillatis ita quod plena fides eisdem tam in Judicio quam extra merito valeat exhiberi Delegatis Nostris antedictis Eorumve Condelegatis ad locum Judicialem in Aula communi Hospitij Dominorum Advocatorum infra parochiam Sancti Benedicti prope Ripam Paulinam Lond' notorie situati plene plane integre et fideliter transmittant seu transmitti faciant cum effectu Sub pena juris et Contemptus Et quid in premissis feceritis Delegatos Nostros antedictos Eorumve Condelegatos debite certificetis unacum presentibus Datis Sub Sigillo Supreme Curie Nostre Delegatorum Regiorum decimo quarto die mensis Octobris Anno Domini Millesimo Septingentesimo Tertio Regnique Nostri Secundo.

THO: OUGHTON REGISTRARIJ REGIJ DEPUTATUS

[Endorsed]

On the twenty ninth day of October 1703 This Monition was then psonally served on John Sale Esq. Register to the Archbishop of Dublin by sheweing to him ye same under seale and leaveing with him a Coppy thereof and Likewise fifteene shillings towarde transmitting ye processe by me

JOHN HOLMES

on the 18th of Novr 1703 John Holmes came psonally before me & made oath that the above written certificate is true.
John Page Maior of Dublin
1703

[DEL 2/16]

APPENDIX X

INSTRUMENT OF APPEAL

IN THE NAME OF GOD AMEN[1] Before you the Notaries Public here present approved and allowed of by Authority, I George Buckton Notary Public one of the Procurators General exercent in His Majestys High Court of Admiralty of England and as such and under that denomination do exhibit as Proctor and make myself a party for John Campbell of White Lion Court Cornhill London Merchant in a certain cause of Bottomree civil and Maritime with a design and intent to appeal from and complain of all and singular the nullities iniquities injustices injuries grievances and errors in the proceedings hereinafter mentioned promulged by the Judge hereinafter named on the twelfth day of July instant and equally and alike principally complaining of them do by this Writing say allege and in Law propound That a certain cause of Bottomree Civil and Maritime was lately depending in Judgment Before the Right Honorable William Baron Stowell Doctor of Laws Lieutenant of His Majestys High Court of Admiralty of England and in the same Court Official Principal Commissary General and special and president and Judge thereof lawfully constituted or his lawful Surrogate between Messieurs Phillips and King of London Merchants the alleged legal holders of a Bond of Bottomree on a Ship or Vessel called the Nelson her Tackle Apparel and Furniture and the Freight due for the transportation of the Cargo lately on board her the parties promoting the said Cause or business on the one part against the said Ship and Freight and also against the aforesaid John Campbell the sole owner thereof intervening the party against whom the said Cause or business was promoted on the other part and That the said Judge unduly and injustly proceeding in the said Cause or business and (saving all reverence due to him) favoring and countenancing more than by Law he ought to have done the part of the said Messieurs Phillips and King and not in the least regarding the requisites and points of Law and other Judicial proceedings did in fact though unduly on the said twelfth day of July Instant make give pronounce and interpose

[1] A £15 stamp was affixed in the margin against the preamble.

a certain pretended Interlocutory order or decree having as pretended the force and effect of a definitive Sentence in writing and did thereby pronounce decree and declare for the force and validity of the pretended Bottomree Bond proceeded on in the said Cause and did condemn the said John Campbell and the Bail given in the said Cause on his behalf in the amount thereof and costs against right and Justice and without any sufficient or lawful proof in that behalf had and made acting in all things Nully and unjustly as well by virtue of his pretended office as at the unjust instance instigation solicitation procurement and petition of the said Messrs. Phillips and King or of their Proctor to the very great detriment and prejudice of the said John Campbell WHEREFORE I the Proctor aforesaid looking upon and believing him the said John Campbell to be very much injured and aggrieved by all and singular the grievances Nullities iniquities injustices injuries and errors in the proceedings aforementioned and justly fearing that my said party may be further injured and aggrieved thereby have rightly and duly appealed from them and every of them and more especially from the said pretended Interlocutory Order or decree having as pretended the force and effect of a definitive Sentence in Writing made given interposed and pronounced by the said Judge on the said twelfth day of July instant whereby he did amongst other things pronounce decree and declare for the force and validity of the said pretended Bottomree Bond proceeded on in the said Cause and condemned the said John Campbell and the Bail given in the said Cause on his behalf in the amount thereof and Costs and from the said Judge not having pronounced against the force and validity of the said pretended Bottomree Bond and not having dismissed the said John Campbell and his Bail from the said Suit and all further observance of Justice therein with Costs Therefore unto the most Serene Prince George the Fourth by the Grace of God of the United Kingdom of Great Britain and Ireland King Defender of the Faith and so forth and to his High Court of Chancery of Great Britain and to him in the said Court and hath equally and alike principally complained of all and singular the Nullities iniquities injustices injuries grievances and errors of proceeding before mentioned and I do three times severally and most earnestly pray Letters dimissory in this behalf to be made out and directed to me or my aforesaid Party AND LASTLY I do protest and reserve to myself full power of correcting and reforming this my Appeal and complaint by adding thereto or subducting therefrom and of reducing the same into a better and more competent form and of intimating the same to every person whom by Law I ought as the Law shall require and Counsel advise at time and place convenient according to Law Style and Custom

UPON all and Singular which premises the said George Buckton the Proctor aforesaid desired and requested me the Notary Public hereunto written to draw up from thence for him one or more Public Instrument or Instruments and the Witnesses subscribed to attest the same. THIS APPEAL was interposed on Tuesday the twenty second day of July in the Year of Our Lord one thousand eight hundred and twenty three in the office of me the Undersigned Notary situate in Great Knight Rider Street Doctors Commons London by the aforesaid George Buckton who then and there appealed protested prayed Letters dimissory and did in all things as in the aforegoing Appeal is contained there being then and there present with me the Notary Public subscribed Thomas Poynter also Notary Public approved and allowed by Authority especially requested to Witness the same.

Which I attest
Stanley Stokes
Not'y Public

Witness
Th. Poynter
Not: Pub.
[DEL 2/16]

APPENDIX XI

COMPULSORY

GEORGE the second by the Grace of God of Great Britain France and Ireland King Defender of the Faith and so forth To all and Singular Clerks and literate Persons in and throughout our Kingdom of Great Britain whomsoever and wheresoever Greeting[1] Whereas our beloved the Worshipfull Thomas Walker Edward Simpson & Robert Chapman respectively Doctors of Laws our Judges (among others) Delegates in a certain Cause of Appeal & Complaint of Nullity now depending before them in Judgment between William Adams of the Town of Monmouth in the County of Monmouth the Party Appellant & Complainant of the one Part and Jane Bellamy Elizabeth Roberts & Mary Roberts the Partys appellate & complained of on the other Part rightly & lawfully proceeding at the Petition of the Proctor of the said Jane Bellamy Elizabeth Roberts and Mary Roberts have decreed John Bulbrick, Thomas Belchier, Roger Hughes Elizabeth Hughes (wife of Thomas Hughes) Thomas Middleton & James Mercer Witnesses (as asserted) very necessary to prove the Contents of a certain Allegation & Exhibits thereto annexed given in and as it stands admitted in this Cause on the Part and Behalf of the said Jane Bellamy Elizabeth Roberts and Mary Roberts who being required and having their travelling Expences offered them have refused to come without being compelled (as it stands alledged before them in this Behalf) to be cited and called into Judgment to appear on the Day and at the Time & Place & for the Purposes hereafter described (Justice so requiring) Therefore we impower & by enjoining strictly command you jointly and severally that you cite or cause to be cited peremptorily the said John Bulbrick Thomas Belchier Roger Hughes Elizabeth Hughes (wife of Thomas Hughes) Thomas Middleton & James Mercer that they and each of them personally appear before Commissioners lawfully appointed in this Behalf in the Parish Church of Monmouth in the County of Monmouth on the twenty third twenty fourth and twenty fifth Days of April instant or at such other Time and Place to which the

[1] Two 6*d*. stamps were affixed in the margin against the preamble.

further Execution of the said Commission shall be adjourned then and there to take the Oath usually taken by witnesses according to the Exigency of the Law and to give their Testimony of the Truth which they know in this Behalf under Pain of the Law and Contempt thereof and further to do and receive as unto Law & Justice shall appertain And whatsoever you shall do in the Premisses you shall duly certify to our Judges Delegates aforesaid or their Condelegates together with these Presents. Dated at LONDON under the Seal of our High Court of Delegates (as to the affixing the Seal) the third Day of April in the Year of our Lord one thousand seven hundred and forty seven and in the twentieth Year of our Reign.

EDWD RUSHWORTH Deputy Register of His Majestie's High Court of Delegates.

[endorsed]
15 Aprill 1747 served Mr Bulbrick
Roger Hughes, Thos Middleton.
16 Aprill servd Mr Belchier and
Elizabeth Hughes all in p'son
p' G: C
James Mercer dead.
[DEL 2/2]

APPENDIX XII

COMMISSION *AD PARTES*

JACOBUS SECUNDUS Dei Gratia Anglie Scotie Francie et Hibernie Rex Fidei Defensor &c. DILECTIS Nobis in Christo Henrico Greswold Rectori de Soleyhall Gulielmo Malines Vicario de Tanworth Benjamino Milward Rectori de Baldesent in Comitatu Warwici et David Bondell Rectori de Beeley in Comitatu Wigorn' necnon Samueli Gemmatt Richardo Chamberlane Johanni Edes et Samueli Lawrence Clericis SALUTEM Cum dilecti nostri Richardus Raines miles legum Doctor Georgius Bramston et Matheus Tindall legum etiam Doctores Judices Delegati nostri in quadam causa appellationis et querele que coram eis in judicio inter Andream Archer armigerum partem appellantem et querelantem ex una et Thomam Wagstaffe Thomam Hicks et Thomam Everton alias Overton partes appellatas et querelatas partibus ex altera vertitur et pendat indecisa legitime procedentes Comissionem fieri ad partes pro receptione admissione juramenti prestatione et examinatione testium quorumcunque ex parte et per partem dicti Andree Archer armigeri de et super positionibus sive articulis allegationis articulate ex parte sua in hac causa date et admisse presentibusque annexe producendorum decreverint ac potestatem subscriptam sub modo et formis inferius descriptis Vobis seu aliquibus vestrum duobus vel pluribus comisserint justitia mediante ad recipiendum igitur admittendum et in debita juris forma jurari faciendum testes quoscunque ex parte dicti Andree Archer super positionibus sive articulis dicte allegationis presentibus ut prefertur annexe in ecclesia parochiali Sancte Marie in oppido Warwici nono decimo et undecimo respective diebus mensis Januarij proximi cum continuatione et prorogatione dierum et loci ex tunc proximi sequentis si oporteat fieri in presentia magistri Francisci Nixon Notarij Publici procuratoris originalis dictorum Thome Wagstaffe Thome Hicks et Thome Everton alias Overton ad tunc et ibidem interessendum si suum putaverit interesse alias judicialiter moniti seu minus in ipsius contumacia coram vobis producendi ipsosque testes sic receptos admissos et juratos de et super allegatione articulata predicta presentibus ut prefertur annexa necnon super interrogatorijs ex adversa parte ministrandis si que eadem pars ministrari curaverit secrete et diligenter examinandos et interrogandos testesque hujusmodi si se gratia odij lucri vel favoris vel alia quacunque de causa testimonium veritati perhibere recusaverint per legitima juris remedia cogendos et coercendos ASSUMPTO vobis omnibus seu aliquibus vestrum duobus vel pluribus Thoma Oughton Notario Publico Supreme Curie nostre Delegatorum Registrario principali vel alio quocunque Notario per eum substituendo in actorum vestrorum in hac parte scribam seu Registrarium ceteraque omnia et singula alia faciendum exercendum et expediendum que in premissis aut circa ea necessaria fuerint seu quomodolibet opportuna vobis de quorum fidelitate et industria plurimum in hac parte confidimus per presentes authoritatem comittimus cum cujuslibet coertionis Potestate Mandantes quatenus hujusmodi examinatione completa dicta et depositiones testium predictorum totumque et integrum processum coram vobis vel aliquibus vestrum duobus aut pluribus habitum et factum Judicibus Delegatis antedictis seu eorum condelegatis ad locum judicialem in aula publica hospitij Dominorum Advocatorum London prima sessione proximi termini authentice et clause sigillatum unacum presentibus transmittatis seu sic transmitti faciatis cum effectu Datum sub sigillo Supreme Curie nostre Delegatorum vicesimo quinto die mensis Novembris Anno regni nostri tertio.

THO: OUGHTON REGISTRARIUS REGIUS

[endorsed]

> Ego Thomas Oughton notarius Publicus antedictus varijs negotijs impeditus dilectum mihi in Christo Willelmum Walmisley Notarium Publicum pro expeditione hujusmodi Comissionis vice et loco meis nomino et constituo per presentes datum 22 Decembris 1687.
>
> THO: OUGHTON NOTARIUS PUBLICUS

[DEL 2/4]

APPENDIX XIII

COMMISSION *PRO SCRUTINIO*

GEORGIUS Dei Gratia Magne Britannie Francie et Hibernie Rex Fidei Defensor &c. DILECTIS Nobis in Christo Venerabili Viro Johanni Senior Legum Baccalaureo Uno Advocatorum in Curia Domini Archiepiscopi Ebor' et reverendis Viris Gulielmo Herbert Clerico Artium Magistro Curato Ecclesie Sancti Sampson' in Civitate Eboracen' et Thome Moseley seniori Clerico in Artibus Magistro Rectori de Skelton in Comitatu Ebor' et Darcy Preston Generoso Necnon Venerabili Viro Gulielmo Ward Legum Doctori Francisco Tayler Richardo Mawhood et Richardo Brathwait Generosis SALUTEM Cum Dilecti Nostri Robertus Wood et Edvardus Kinaston Legum Doctores in Negotio infrascripto atque inter partes inferius nominatas Judices inter alios Delegati Nostri in quadam Causa Appellationis et Querele Que coram Eis in Judicio inter Leneve Boughton Clericum unum Vicariorum Choralium Ecclesie Cathedralis Sancti Petri Ebor' partem appellantem et querelantem ex una Et Dominos Decanum et Capitulum dicte Ecclesie Cathedralis Sancti Petri per honorabiles et reverendos Viros Henricum Finch Decanum et Edvardum Finch et Samuelem Terrick prebendarios Residentiarios Eorum Syndicos Vel Procuratores agentes partes appellatas et Querelatas partibus ex altera Vertitur et pendet indecisa legitime procedentes ad petitionem partis dictarum partium appellatarum et querelatarum allegantium Diversos Libros Munimenta Actus Capitulares Statuta et alia Instrumenta hujusmodi Causam concernentia penes Registrum Decani et Capituli Ecclesie Cathedralis Sancti Petri Ebor' remanere COMISSIONEM fieri ad partes pro Scrutinio in Recordis Libris publicis et Archivis Registri Decani et Capituli predicti fiendo ac potestatem subscriptam sub modo et forma inferius descriptis committendam fore decreverint et comiserint (Justitia mediante) AD Scrutandum igitur investigandum et inspiciendum in Recordis Libris publicis et Archivis dicti Registri Reverendorum Dominorum Decani et Capituli Ecclesie Cathedralis Sancti Petri Ebor' predicte pro Libris Munimentis Instrumentis Actis et Recordis hujusmodi Causam qualitercunque concernentibus in dicto Registro seu Archivo publico dictorum Reverendorum Dominorum Decani et Capituli vel Domo Capitulari Ecclesie Cathedralis Sancti Petri Ebor' predicte Decimo quarto, decimo quinto, et decimo sexto respective Diebus mensis Maij proximi post datum presentium futuri cum continuacione et prorogatione Dierum et Loci ex tunc proximi sequentis (si opporteat [*sic*] fieri) in presentia Magistri Roberti Peirson Notarij publici procuratoris Originalis dicti Lenere Boughton ad tunc et ibidem interessendum si suum putaverit interesse alias judicialiter moniti seu minus in Ipsius contumacia coram Vobis seu aliquibus Vestrum duobus vel pluribus producendi et ostendendi Verasque Copias Munimentorum Instrumentorum Actorum et Recordorum predictorum qualitercunque hujusmodi Causam concernentium per Vos Scrutatorum et compertorum extrahi et excribi [*sic*] faciendum ac illas sic extractas cum ipsis Originalibus sive Registratis conferri et examinari Videndum ASSUMPTO Vobis seu aliquibus Vestrum duobus vel pluribus Thoma Oughton Notario publico Supreme Curie Nostre Delegatorum Regiorum Registrarij Deputato vel alio quocunque Notario publico per Eum substituendo in actorum Vestorum [*sic*] in hac parte Scribam seu Registrarium Ceteraque Omnia et Singula alia faciendum exercendum et expediendum que in premissis aut circa Ea necessaria fuerint seu quomodolibet opportuna VOBIS de quorum fidelitate et industria plurimum in hac parte confidimus seu aliquibus Vestrum duobus vel pluribus Vices et Authoritatem nostras comittimus per presentes cum legitime Coercionis potestate MANDANTES quatenus hujusmodi Scrutinio finito Veras Copias Munimentorum Instrumentorum Actorum et Recordorum predictorum per Vos[1] ... extractas et cum ipsis Originalibus seu Registratis fideliter collatis et totum et integrum processum coram Vobis seu aliquibus Vestrum duobus vel pluribus habitum et factum (authentice et clausim Sigillatum) Judicibus Delegatis Nostris antedictis Eorumve Condelegatis in aula publica Hospitij Dominorum Advocatorum in parochia Sancti Benedicti prope Ripam Paulinam London notorie Situati prima Sessione Termini Sancte Trinitatis proximi post Datum presentium futuri aut citra transmittatis seu debite transmitti faciatis unacum presentibus

[1] The following word is illegible.

DATIS Londini Sub Sigillo Supreme Curie Nostre Delegatorum Regiorum Vicesimo Octavo die mensis Aprilis Anno Domini Millesimo Septingentesimo decimo sexto Regnique Nostri Anno Secundo

THO: OUGHTON REGISTRARIJ REGIJ DEPUTATUS

[endorsed]

Et Ego Thomas Oughton Notarius publicus Registrarij Regij Deputatus Supra Nominatus Varijs Negotijs impeditus Dilectum Mihi in Christo Thomam Jubb Notarium publicum pro Expedicione hujusmodi Commissionis Vice et loco meis Nomino et constituo per presentes Datum ut supra.

THO: OUGHTON N.P.

[DEL 2/10]

APPENDIX XIV

REQUISITION

GEORGE the Second by the Grace of God of Great Britain France and Ireland King Defender of the Faith and so forth To Our beloved in Christ the Honourable and Right Worshipful the Auditor General of the Civil Court or the Judge of the Justifications of the City of Saint Salvador in the Bay of All Saints in the Brazills, and the Territorys thereto belonging, and to the Judges of the several Courts of Judicature there in General, and to every one of them in particular to whom it may belong Greeting[1] Whereas our beloved Charles Pinfold, William Strahan and John Audley Doctors of Laws Our Judges (among others) Delegates in a certain Cause of Appeal and Complaint now depending before them in Judgment between Isabella Lopes da Rosa and Catharina da Rosa the natural and lawful Daughters of Isabella Louisa de Pinna late at the Brazill in America Widow deceased the Partys Appellant and Complainant on the one part and Isaac Lusitano de Pinna the Husband of Mary Ayres de Pinna the natural and lawful daughter of the said Deceased, and the said Mary Ayres de Pinna the Partys complained of on the other part, rightly and lawfully proceeding have at the petition of the Proctor of the said Isabella Lopes da Rosa and Catharina da Rosa alledging his Clients to be in parts beyond the Seas decreed a Commission or Requisition to be made to You jointly or severally for administring an Oath to the said Isabella Lopes da Rosa and Catharina da Rosa and also to Manuel de Vargas Silveira, and Joseph Henriques Sequeira their Husbands faithfully to answer to the Positions or Articles of a certain Allegation annexed to these Presents given in and admitted in this Cause on the part and behalfe of the said Isaac Lusitano de Pinna and Mary Ayres de Pinna and for receiving their Personal Answers to the truth of the said Allegation and also decreed that their Power and Authority should be committed to You jointly and severally in the manner and form following (Justice so requiring) We therefore in Aid of the Law and under promise of the like Assistance earnestly desire and

[1] Two 6*d*. and two 2*s*. stamps were affixed in the margin to the preamble.

request You jointly and severally to call the said Isabella Lopes da Rosa and Catharina da Rosa and Manuel de Vargas Silveira and Joseph Henriques Sequeira before you jointly or severally in any convenient place and on any Day or Days before the first Session of Trinity Term One Thousand seven hundred and thirty nine and not further or longer (Sundays excepted), and to administer an Oath to them faithfully to answer to the said Allegation annexed to these Presents as aforesaid and to receive their Personal Answers in your presence reduced into Writing to the said Allegation by Vertue of the Oath so given taking to Yourselves jointly and severally any Publick Notary indifferent to the Partys in this Cause to be your Scribe or Actuary in this behalfe and to do, perform and expedite all and singular other matters which in or concerning the Premisses shall be necessary or in anywise convenient Committing by these Presents Our Authority to you jointly and severally in whose eminent Learning and Skill in Business We very much confide Requesting You that the Oath being administred and the Answers taken, You transmitt or Cause to be transmitted together with these Presents your Proceedings in this behalfe had, taken, drawn and reduced into a publick and authentick form closed and sealed up to our Judges Delegates aforesaid or their Condelegates at the place of Judicature the Common Hall of Doctors Commons situate in the Parish of Saint Benedict near Pauls Wharfe London on or before the first Session of Trinity Term which shall be in the Year of Our Lord One Thousand Seven Hundred and thirty nine, promiseing the like return when Affairs shall so require Given at London under the Seal of Our High Court of Delegates (as to the fixing the Seal), the fourth Day of March In the Year of Our Lord One Thousand Seven Hundred and thirty seven and in the eleventh Year of Our Reign.

Edward Smith Deputy Register
of his Majesty's High Court of Delegates.

[Endorsed in Portuguese]
[DEL 2/69]

APPENDIX XV

WARRANT

PLAXTON contra THORPE
Nevile Greenly

WE do appoint to hear and determine this Cause on Thursday the Thirteenth day of May instant between the hours of Three and Five in the afternoon in the Common Hall of Serjeants Inn in Fleetstreet London and do require the Proctors on both sides to attend with their Council accordingly Dated this Eighth day of May One Thousand Seven Hundred and Thirty One.

Hay
J Bath & Wells
Jo. Oxford
Fortescue
Wm Thomson
W Lee
Jno: Bettesworth
Hum: Henchman
Ex: Sayer
J. Isham

[endorsed]
This warrant was duly executed by shewing this original to Mr. Sandford Nevel Procter [*sic*] and by delivering to him a copy hereof on the Eighth day of May 1731.

by me Peter Powell

[DEL 2/95]

APPENDIX XVI

SENTENCE (TESTAMENTARY CAUSE)

IN THE NAME OF GOD AMEN

We Sr Lawrence Carter Knight One of the Barons of His Ma'tyes Court of Exchequer, William Strahan, John Audley and George Lee Doctors of Laws Judges (among others) Delegates lawfully appointed by Virtue of Letters Patent and Commissional under the Great Seal of Great Britain in the underwritten Cause or Business rightly and duely proceeding Having heard seen and understood and fully and maturely discussed the Merits and Circumstances of a certain Cause or Business of Appeal and Complaint which lately depended in Judgement between MARTHA COLLINS Widow the Relict and sole Executrix named in the Last Will and Testament in writing of JONATHAN COLLINS Esquire late of the Parish of St Saviour Southwark in the County of Surry deceased the party appellant and complainant on the one part and ELIZABETH MOLYNEUX (Wife of Thomas Molyneux) the natural and lawfull daughter of the said deceased the party appellate and complained of on the other part, but now depends and remains undetermined in Judgement before Us between WILLIAM TILLETT the Administrator (with the Will annexed) of all and singular the Goods Chattells and Credits of the said Martha Collins deceased appearing for his Interest in the said Cause or Business on the one part and the said Elizabeth Molyneux (Wife of Thomas Molyneux) the party appellate as abovementioned on the other part, and the parties aforesaid lawfully appearing before us in Judgment by their Proctors respectively and the Proctor of the said William Tillett praying SENTENCE to be given for and Justice to be done and administred to his party and the Proctor of the said Elizabeth Molyneux praying... *Justice*...to be done to his party And We having first carefully and diligently searched into and well weighed and considered the Proceedings had and done before Us in this Cause and having observed all and singular the matters and things that by Law in this behalf ought to be observed We have thought fit and do thus think fit to proceed to the giving our Definitive Sentence or Final

Decree in this Cause in manner following to wit FORASMUCH as We have by the Acts enacted deduced alledged exhibited propounded proved and confessed in this Cause found and clearly discovered That the Proctor of the said Martha Collins now deceased has sufficiently and fully founded and proved the Intentions of his said party deduced in a certain Appeal and other Pleadings and Exhibits heretofore given in exhibited and admitted in this Cause on the part and behalf of the said Martha Collins (which Appeal and other Pleadings and Exhibits We take and will have taken as if here rede and inserted) And that nothing at least effectual in Law hath on the part and behalf of the said Elizabeth Molyneux been excepted deduced alledged exhibited propounded proved or confessed in this Cause which may or can in anywise weaken or defeat the Intention of the said Martha Collins THEREFORE We the Judges Delegates aforesaid first calling upon God and setting him alone before our Eyes and having heard Council thereupon Do pronounce decree and declare for the force and validity of the Appeal and Complaint interposed on the part and behalf of the said Martha Collins to our Sovereign Lord GEORGE THE SECOND by the Grace of God of Great Britain France and Ireland King Defender of the Faith and so forth and to his High Court of Chancery of Great Britain and to him in his said Court and that the Appeal and Complaint were and are true just and lawfull and for true just and lawfull Causes made and interposed and for our Jurisdiction or rather that of our said Sovereign Lord the King in this behalf to all Intents and purposes in Law whatsoever And We do revoke annull and make void and pronounce decree and declare for null and void to all Intents and purposes in Law whatsoever the Interlocutory Decree (having the Force and Effect of a Definitive Sentence) appealed from and complained of in this behalf and We do further pronounce decree and declare that the said Jonathan Collins the Testator aforesaid deceased whilst living and of sound Mind and Memory duely made and executed his Last Will and Testament in writing now remaining in the Registry of the Prerogative Court of Canterbury bearing date the eighteenth day of August in the Year of our Lord one thousand seven hundred and twenty nine and therein named and appointed the said Martha Collins sole Executrix and did give will bequeath dispose and do in all things as in the said Will is contained (which Last Will and Testament We take and will have taken as if here read and inserted) and do likewise pronounce for the Force and Validity of the said Will and do approve of and receive the same And We do decree Letters of Administration (with the said Will annexed) of all and singular the Goods Chattells and Credits of the said Jonathan Collins deceased as they were and are left unadministred by the said Martha Collins deceased to be committed and granted to the said William Tillett the Administrator (with the Will annexed) of all and singular the Goods Chattells and Credits of the said Martha Collins deceased as abovementioned who while living was the sole Executrix and Universal Legatary named in the said Will of the said Jonathan Collins deceased under sufficient Security and We do accordingly commit the same by this our Definitive Sentence or Final decree which We read and promulge by these presents.

J. ANDREW

Law Carter.
Will: Strahan.
Joh: Audley.
Geo Lee.

[DEL 5/32]

APPENDIX XVII

SENTENCE (DEFAMATION CAUSE)

IN DEI NOMINE AMEN Auditis visis et intellectis ac plenarie et mature discussis per Nos Nathaniele Brent militem et legum doctorem iudicem et Delegatum regium unacum venerabilibus viris Thoma Rives et Basilio Wood legum respective doctoribus Meritis et circumstantijs cuiusdam cause appellationis sive querele (quoad causam principalem) que coram nobis in iuditio virtute Delegacionis regie magno Sigillo Anglie sigillate inter Franciscum Coppinger partem appellantem et querelantem ex una et Johannem Jegon Clericum partem appellatam et querelatam partibus ex altera nuper iudicialiter controvertebatur et pendebat vertiturque adhuc et pendet indecisa rite et legitime procedentes partibusque predictis per earum procuratores coram nobis in iuditio legitime comparentibus parteque antedicti Johannis Jegon Sententiam ferri ac iustitiam fieri pro parte sua, Parte vero memorati Francisci Coppinger... *Justitiam*...etiam fieri pro parte sua instanter respective postulantibus et petentibus Rimatoque primitus per Nos toto et integro processu coram nobis in huiusmodi causa habito et facto ac diligenter recensito, servatisque per Nos de iure in hac parte servandis, ad nostre sententie diffinitive sive nostri finalis decreti prolacionem in huiusmodi causa ferendi sic duximus procedendum fore et procedimus in hunc qui sequitur modum QUIA per acta inactitata, deducta, exhibita, allegata, proposita et probata pariter et confessata in huiusmodi causa comperimus luculenter et invenimus partem prefati Johannis Jegon intencionem suam in quodam libello suo alias coram nobis in huiusmodi causa dato et oblato, deductam, Cuius quidem libelli tenor sequitur et est talis In Dei nomine Amen Coram vobis venerabilibus et egregijs viris dominis Nathaniele Brent, Carolo Cesar militibus, Thoma Rives, et Basilio Wood...legum respective doctoribus in causa infrascripta atque inter partes inferius nominatas Judicibus delegatis regijs auctoritate regia legitime constituta &c. Quem quidem libellum pro hic lectum et insertum habemus et haberi volumus sufficienter et ad plenum (quoad hic inferius pronuntianda) fundasse pariter ac probasse, nihilque omnino seu saltem effectuale ex parte aut per partem dicti Francisci Coppinger in hac parte exceptum, deductum, allegatum, exhibitum, propositum, probatum, aut confessatum fuisse aut esse quod intencionem prefati Johannis Jegon in hac parte elideret seu quomodolibet enerraret. IDCIRCO Nos Nathaniel Brent Judex et delegatus regius antedictus...Tho: Rives, Basilius Wood, legum respective doctores Christi [nomine] primitus invocato ac ipsum solum Deum oculis nostris proponentes et habentes deque et cum consensu et assensu prefatorum venerabilium virorum Collegorum nostrorum iudicum delegatorum regiorum una nobiscum sedentium et procedentium, deque et cum Consilio Jurisperitorum cum quibus in hac parte communicavimus matureque deliberavimus prenominatum Franciscum Coppinger Annis mensibus et loco in hac parte libellatis vel eorum uno sive aliquo publiciter nequiter et malitiose dictum Johannem Jegon diffamasse, ac nonnulla verba scandalosa, vilipendiosa, convitiosa, et diffamatoria in hac parte libellata, ad infamiam, lesionem, et diminucionem status, nominis, et bone fame prefati Johannis Jegon sonantia et tendentia contra bonos mores eiusdem seu de eodem Johanne Jegon publiciter, nequiter, et malitiose dixisse, protulisse et predicasse pronuntiamus decernimus et declaramus, Eundem igitur Franciscum Coppinger pro tanto temeritatis et petulentie sue excessu in premissis perpetrato ad reclamacionem verborum hujusmodi diffamatorum iuxta Juris exigentiam et quatenus Jura ferunt cogendum et compellendum fore de Jure debere pronuntiamus, decernimus et declaramus, necnon Eundem Franciscum Coppinger in expensis legitimis ex parte et per partem dicti Johannis Jegon in hac parte factis et faciendis eidemque vel parti sue solvendis, Condemnandum fore de iure debere insuper pronuntiamus et Condemnamus per hanc nostram sententiam diffinitivam sive hoc nostrum finale decretum, quam sive quod ferimus et promulgamus in hijs scriptis, Taxacionem vero sive moderacionem expensarum hujusmodi nobis aut alijs Judicibus Condelegatis nostris reservando, reservamus.

Arth: Ducke

Na: Brent
T. Rives
Basill Woodd

[endorsed]

Lecta lata et promulgata fuit Sententia retroscripta per Judices in eadem descriptos in loco Consistorio infra ecclesiam Cathedralem divi Pauli London 3 die iuridico post festum Ascensionis domini xiiij viz die Maij Anno domini 1632 Regnique domini nostri Caroli Regis &c. Octavo inter horam 2am et 4am post meridiem eiusdem diei in presencia mei Willielmi Barker notorij publici deputati Georgij Paule militis Regie majestatis Registrarij ac testium in actis desuper factis nominatorum.

Gulielmus Barker
notarius publicus

[DEL 5/7]

APPENDIX XVIII

SENTENCE (SIMONY CAUSE)

IN DEI NOMINE AMEN Auditis visis et Intellectis ac plenarie et mature discussis per Nos Hugonem Wyndham militem unum Justiciariorum Domini nostri Regis de Banco Robertum Atkins militem de Balneo alterum Justiciariorum Domini nostri Regis de Banco Gulielmum Ellys militem alterum Justiciariorum Domini Regis de banco Mondefordum Bramston & Edvardum Lowe milites & Legum doctores Henricum Alworth Thomam Pinfold Gulielmum Oldys et Robertum Thompson...Legum respective Doctores, in Causa Infrascripta atque inter partes inferius nominatas (inter alios) vigore Comissionis magno Sigillo Anglie Comunite Judices legitime constitutos Meritis et Circumstantijs Cujusdam Cause Revisionis, Que Coram Nobis in Judicio inter Henricum Jackson Clericum Vicarium se pretendentem Vicarie perpetue et Ecclesie parochialis de Inkbarrow in Comitatu et Diocesi Wigorniensi partem Supplicantem ex una, et Henricum Mugg Clericum partem contra Quam in hac parte Supplicatum est, partibus ex altera nuper vertebatur et pendebat, vertiturque adhuc et pendet indecisa rite et legitime procedentes, partibusque predictis per earum respective Procuratores Coram Nobis in Judicio legitime Comparentibus, Parteque prefati Henrici Mugg Sententiam ferri et Justiciam fieri pro parte sua Parte vero Memorati Henrici Jackson...*Sententiam*...etiam pro parte sua respective et Instanter postulante et petente, RIMATOQUE etiam primitus per Nos toto et integro Processu in hac Causa coram Nobis habito et facto ac diligenter recensito, Servatisque per Nos de Jure in hac parte Servandis, ad nostre Sententie Definitive sive nostri finalis Decreti prolationem in hac Causa ferende sic duximus procedendum fore, et Procedimus in hunc qui sequitur Modum QUIA per Acta inactitata deducta allegata exhibita proposita et probata in hac Causa Comperimus luculenter et invenimus partem prefati Henrici Mugg Intentionem suam in Quibusdam Articulis ex parte sua contra dictum Henricum Jackson in prima hujus Cause Instantia alijsque propositis ex parte sua in secunda hujus Cause Instantia datis exhibitis et Admissis, ac penes Registrum hujus Curie remanentibus deductam (Quos quidem Articulos et proposita pro hic lectis et insertis habemus et haberi volumus) sufficienter et ad plenum quoad hic inferius pronuntianda fundasse pariter et probasse, Nihilque Effectuale ex parte aut per partem prefati Henrici Jackson in hac parte exceptum deductum allegatum exhibitum propositum aut probatum fuisse aut esse, Quod Intentionem prefati Henrici Mugg in hac parte elideret seu quomodolibet enervaret IDCIRCO Nos Judices Delegati antedicti Christi Nomine primitus Invocato, ac ipsum Solum Deum Oculis nostris preponentes et habentes, deque et cum Consilio Jurisperitorum cum Quibus in hac parte Communicavimus, maturequе deliberavimus, prenominatum Henricum Jackson Clericum Annis et Mensibus in hac parte Articulatis, eorumve uno sive aliquo, et ante ejus pretensam presentationem ad vicariam de Inkbarrow predictam, et pro ejus pretensa presentatione ad eandem, cum Quodam Johanne Latham patrono ejusdem pro ista vice, pro quadam pecunie Suma contraxisse, et contractum plane Simoniacum inijsse, Dictamque pecunie Sumam de qua Convenerat, pro pretensa presentatione Persone sue ad eandem Vicariam de Inkbarrow dedisse Numerasse et Simoniace exolvisse [*sic*] et Numerari Simoniace exolvi [*sic*] curasse, Eundemque igitur Henricum Jackson clericum fuisse et esse Simoniacum, et ad vicariam predictam de facto licet Simoniace tamen et nulliter presentatum et promotum, et ob Simonie Labem a se ut prefertur contractam, ab eadem Vicaria et Ecclesia parochiali de Inkbarrow cum suis Juribus Membris et pertinentijs Privandum et Amovendum fore, juxta juris in hac parte exigentiam pronuntiamus decernimus et declaramus Sicque eum Deprivamus et Amovemus, dictamque Vicariam et Ecclesiam parochialem de Inkbarrow vacuam et pro vacua et vacante ad omnem Juris Effectum reputandam et censendam esse pronuntiamus decernimus et declaramus, Dictumque Henricum Mugg citra Presentationem et Promotionem prefati Henrici Jackson per Literas Patentes Domini nostri Regis magno Sigillo Anglie communitas, datas Vicesimo Octavo die Mensis Octobris Anno Regni Regis Caroli Secundi Decimo Sexto, ad dictam Vicariam et Ecclesiam parochialem de Inkbarrow rite et legitime presentatum fuisse etiam pronuntiamus decernimus et declaramus, sententiamque alias per Dominos Judices Delegatos in Secunda hujus Cause Instantia latam et promulgatam ac Taxationem Expensarum in eadem Instantia factam ad omnem Juris Effectum ratificamus et confirmamus, Executionem tamen tam dicte Sententie in Secunda, quam Sententie modo late, Nobis aut alijs Judicibus in hac parte Competentibus retinendo retinemus, Dictumque Henricum Jackson in Expensis legitimis ex parte et per partem prefati Henrici Mugg in hac Instantia factis et faciendis Condemnamus per hanc nostram Sententiam definitivam sive hoc nostrum finale Decretum, Quam sive Quod ferimus et promulgamus in hijs Scriptis. Taxationem vero sive Moderationem hujusmodi Expensarum, Nobis, nostrumve Condelegatis, aut alijs Judicibus in hac parte Competentibus Reservando et Reservamus.

Tho: Exton
Edw: Masters

Hugh Wyndham
Robt. Atkyns
Willm Ellys
Mo: Bramston
E. Lowe
Hen Alworth
Tho: Pinfold
Wlm: Oldys
Robt Thompson

[endorsed]
Lecta lata et promulgata fuit hujusmodi Sententia retroscripta per Judices Delegatos intra-nominatos vicesimo tertio Junij anno domini 1675 in aula hospitij dominorum Servientum ad legem in vico vocato Fleet-street Lond' inter horas quartam et sextam [*sic*] postmeridianas in presentia mei Tho. Oughton notarij publici ac testium in actis desuper factis nominatorum

Ita testor
T Oughton
notarius publicus
Registrarij Regij
deputatus.

[DEL 5/8]

APPENDIX XIX

BILL OF COSTS (*RETARDATI PROCESSUS*)

EXPENSE retardati Processus facte et faciende ex parte, et per partem Elizabeth Ellis in Quadam pretensa Causa Appellationis et Querele contra Eam per quendam Thomam Day ubicunque mota, et prosecuta sequuntur videlicet

Termino Michaelis 1679

	s	d
IMPRIMIS pro Copia petitionis per dictum Day facte pro Comissione Appellationis	ij	vj
ITEM pro feodo procuratoris bis attendentis apud Lincolns Inn ad procurandum dictam Copiam	vj	viij
ITEM pro Conceptione et ingrossatione Certificatorij quod Comissio Appellationis non fuit presentata Judicibus Delegatis	v	
ITEM feodis Dominorum Judicantium subscribentium dictum certificatorium	x	
ITEM pro Conceptione et ingrossacione peticionis Domino Cancellario ad supersedendum dictam Comissionem	vj	viij
ITEM pro feodo procuratoris bis attendentis dictum Cancellarium cum dicta peticione	x	

	l	s	d
ITEM pro feodis Advocati bis informantis	l j		
ITEM pro Concepcione et ingrossatione hujus bille		s vj	d viij
ITEM pro taxatione ejusdem		s iiij	
ITEM pro feodo procuratoris attendentis die Extraordinario et Actis		s iiij	d viij
Summa totalis hujus Bille	l iij	s xvj	d ij

Tho: Exton

Taxamus hanc billam
ad Summam triginta solidorum
preter &c.
Hen: Fauconberge
Hen: Newton

[DEL 8/53/pt. 1]

APPENDIX XX

BILL OF COSTS (*EXPENSAE LITIS*)

EXPENSE litis facte et faciende
ex parte et per partem Anne Wright in quadam
causa Appellationis et Querele per eam
contra Richardum Sessions mota et prose
-quuta sequuntur

Termino Michaelis 1678 et Vacacione procedenti	l	s	d
Pro conceptione peticionis pro Commissione Appellationis	00	05	00
pro Responsis ad dictam peticionem	00	12	06
pro conceptione Commissionis Appellationis	00	06	08
pro Solicitacione super obtentu dicte Commissionis	00	10	00
pro feodo Commissionis et Domino Rege	02	15	00
pro conceptione Inhibitionis et acceptacione Dominorum Judicum super prima presentacione Commissionis Appellationis	01	00	00
pro Sigillo Inhibitionis et Registrario	00	13	04
pro feodo Procuratoris presentantis Commissionem Appellationis et procurantis	00	04	08
pro Monicione pro processu Judicis a quo et copia ejusdem	00	08	00
pro presentacione Commissionis Appellationis tribus alijs Judicibus Delegatis legum Doctoribus	00	10	00
pro feodo Procuratoris presentantis	00	03	04
pro Actis Curie	00	01	08
Termino Michaelis 1678	05	10	02 [*sic*]
Pro feodo Advocati	01	00	00
pro feodo procuratoris	00	03	04
pro Certificatorijs Inhibitionis et Monicionis pro processu	00	02	08
pro conceptione et ingrossatione Libelli	00	10	00
pro actis Curie	00	03	04

pro Execucione Monicionis pro processu	00 01 00
pro feodo transmissionis processus Judicis a quo et compositione pro eodem	03 00 00
pro salario procuratoris perlegentis et abbre viantis processum Judicis a quo &c.	00 05 00
pro solicitacione	00 06 08
Termino Hillarij 1678°	05 12 04 [*sic*]
Pro feodo Advocati et Procuratoris	01 03 04
pro actis Curie	00 03 08
pro conceptione Brevis et copia ejusdem	00 10 00
pro feodo procuratoris sepius attendentis tempore Informacionum	00 06 08
pro Precone	00 02 06
pro Warranto pro auditione Cause et procuracione ejusdem	01 00 00
pro Execucione dicti Warranti	00 01 00
pro conceptione et Ingrossatione Sententie	00 10 00
pro feodo Advocati attendentis tempore late Sententie et Informacionum	02 00 00
pro Registrario attendenti tempore Informacionum	00 03 04
pro Curriculis	00 03 00
pro feodis Judicum	00 04 00
pro eorum Famulis	00 15 00
pro feodo Sententie	00 13 10
pro Salario Procuratoris attendentis apud Hospitium Servientium ad legem	00 06 08
pro Ostiatore Servientium ad legem	00 06 00
pro Ostiatore Dominorum Advocatorum	00 05 00
pro Magistro Welham attendenti cum Sententia e Curia Prerogativa	00 03 04
pro Solicitacione	00 13 04
Termino Pasche 1679°	09 17 04 [*sic*]
Pro feodo Advocati et Procuratoris	00 13 04
pro actis Curie	00 00 08
Termino Trinitatis 1679°	00 14 00
Pro feodo Advocati et Procuratoris	00 13 04
pro actis Curie	00 01 04
pro conceptione et ingrossatione bille Expensarum	00 06 08
pro taxacione	00 05 00

pro feodo Advocati subscribentis	00 10 00
pro feodo procuratoris attendentis tempore Informacionum	00 03 04
pro Monicione ad solvendum	00 07 00
pro copia et Execucione dicte Monicionis	00 02 06
pro Solicitacione	00 06 08
	02 15 10
Summa totalis	24 09 08

Guil: Trumbull.

Taxamus ad summam
quindecim librarum legalis &c.
preter &c.

Hen: Fauconberge
Ri: Raines

[DEL 8/53/pt. 1]

APPENDIX XXI

SCHEDULE OF EXCOMMUNICATION

[POOR][1] In the Name of God Amen Whereas the Honorable and Reverend Sir Michael Foster Knight one of the Justices of the Court of Kings Bench Sir Sydney Stafford Smythe Knight one of the Barons of the Exchequer the Worshipful Richard Smalbroke and Dennis Clarke Doctors of Laws respectively Judges among others by virtue of Letters patent and Commissional under the Great Seal of Great Britain rightly and duly proceeding in a certain Cause of Appeal and Complaint of Nullity now or lately depending in Judgment between Sarah Holmes Wife of Francis Holmes of the Parish of St Sepulchre London the party Appellant and Complainant of the one part and the said Francis Holmes her Husband the Party Appellate and Complained of on the other part did at the Petition of the procter [*sic*] of the said Francis Holmes read and promulge a Definitive Sentence in Writing whereby they did pronounce decree and declare that the said Francis Holmes and Sarah Holmes did at the time and place mentioned in the Libel given in and admitted in the first Instance of this Cause contract true pure and lawful Matrimony and did rightly and duly solemnize the same in the face of the Church according to the Rites and Ceremonies thereof and did afterwards consummate the same by Carnal Copulation and Mutual Cohabitation and did also pronounce decree and declare the said Francis Holmes and Sarah to be lawful Husband and Wife and did further decree the said Sarah Holmes to be monished to return to the said Francis Holmes her Husband and to cohabit with him as her lawful Husband and perform conjugal Rites with the said Francis Holmes her Husband and to demean herself towards him at Bed and Board with Conjugal Affection And Whereas the said Sarah Holmes hath in pursuance of such Sentence been duly monished to return to the said Francis Holmes her Husband and to cohabit with him as her lawful Husband and perform Conjugal Rites with the said Francis Holmes her Husband and to demean herself towards him at bed and board with Conjugal Affection under pain of the Law and

[1] This word appeared in the margin here and in the next two documents.

Contempt thereof And Whereas the said Sarah Holmes hath not returned to the said Francis Holmes her Husband nor cohabited with him as her lawful Husband nor performed Conjugal Rites with the said Francis Holmes her Husband nor in any wise obeyed such Monition but Contumaciously disregarded the same Therefore We Richard Smalbroke and Dennis Clarke Doctors of Laws Judges Delegates among others lawfully appointed at the like petition of the procter [*sic*] of the said Francis Holmes do by these presents Excommunicate the said Sarah Holmes

This Schedule of
Excommunication was read and
promulged on the Ninth
day of February in the year of
our Lord 1758

By us
R. Smalbroke
D. Clarke.

[DEL 2/36]

APPENDIX XXII

DECREE OF EXCOMMUNICATION

[POOR] GEORGE THE SECOND by the Grace of God of great Britain France and Ireland King Defender of the Faith and so forth TO all and singular Rectors Vicars Chaplains Curates Clerks and literate persons whomsoever and wheresoever in and throughout our whole Kingdom of Great Britain Greeting WHEREAS our beloved the Worshipful Richard Smalbroke and Dennis Clarke respectively Doctors of Laws our Judges (among others) Delegates in a certain Cause of Appeal and Complaint of Nullity now or lately depending before them in Judgement Between Sarah Holmes (Wife of Francis Holmes) of the parish of Saint Sepulchre London the party Appellant and Complainant on the one part and the said Francis Holmes her Husband the party Appellate and complained of on the other part rightly and duly proceeding at the petition of the proctor of the said Francis Holmes did pronounce the said Sarah Holmes contumacious for her manifest Contempt and Contumacy in not obeying a certain Monition duly served to return to the said Francis Holmes her Husband and cohabit with him as her lawful Husband and to demean herself towards him at Bed and Board with Conjugal Affection and for such her Contumacy and Contempt have decreed her to be excommunicated (Justice so requiring) We do therefore authorize and empower and strictly enjoyn you joyntly and severally that you in some or one of your parish Churches upon the Sunday or Festival Day next immediately following the Receipt of these Presents during the Time of divine Service whilst the greater part of the Congregation are present openly and publickly denounce and declare the said Sarah Holmes to be by our authority excommunicate under pain of the Law and Contempt thereof And whatsoever you shall do in the premisses you shall duly certify our Judges Delegates aforesaid or their Condelegates together with these Presents Given under the Seal of our High Court of Delegates the ninth Day of February in the year of our Lord one Thousand Seven Hundred and fifty Eight and in the Thirty first year of our Reign.

EDWD RUSHWORTH Deputy Register of his Majesties' high Court of Delegates.

[Endorsed]

THIS EXCOMMUNICATION was duly published in the Parish Church of Saint George in the County of Middlesex on Sunday the twenty sixth day of February in the Year of our Lord One thousand seven hundred and fifty eight during the time of Divine Service in the forenoon according to the Rubrick

by me

Wm Simpson Rector

of St. George's Middx

[DEL 2/36]

APPENDIX XXIII

DECREE OF SIGNIFICAVIT

[POOR] To the most Serene Prince in Christ and Our Sovereign Lord George the Second by the Grace of God of Great Britain France and Ireland King Defender of the Faith and so forth We your most humble & devoted Richard Smalbroke & Dennis Clarke Doctors of Laws your Judges (among others) Delegates in the Cause and between the Parties hereunder described with all Duty Reverence & Obedience due to so illustrious Prince and wishing Health and Prosperity here and hereafter in him by whom Kings reign & Princes bear Rule We do with all humble Obedience hereby signify and make known to your Royal Majesty That a Certain Cause of Restitution of Conjugal Rites was lately promoted by Francis Holmes of the Parish of St Sepulchre London against Sarah Holmes his Wife and did lately depend in the Consistorial & Episcopal Court of London before the Worshipfull Edward Simpson Doctor of Laws Vicar General of the Right Revd Father in God Thomas by Divine Permission Lord Bishop of London and Official Principal of the said Consistorial & Episcopal Court of London between the said Francis Holmes of the one Part & the said Sarah Holmes of the other Part That the said Edward Simpson the Judge aforesaid did on the sixth Day of July in the year of our Lord one thousand seven hundred fifty four admitt a certain Allegation in Writing given in on Behalf of the said Sarah Holmes, from the admission of which Allegation he the said Francis Holmes appealed to the Arches Court of Canterbury and to the Right Hon'ble Sr George [Lee] Knight Doctor of Laws Official Principal of the said Court And We do farther most humbly signify to your Royal Majesty That the said Sr George Lee Knight the Judge aforesaid rightly & duly proceeding in the said Cause of Appeal & Complaint so brought by the said Francis Holmes against the said Sarah Holmes did on the 25th Day of February in the Year of our Lord one thousand Seven hundred fifty five make & interpose an Interlocutory Order or Decree having the Force & Effect of a Definitive Sentence in Writing in Favour of the said Francis Holmes and against the said Sarah Holmes from which Decree she the said Sarah Holmes appealed to your Sacred Majesty in your

High Court of Chancery and that a Commission issued under the Great Seal of Great Britain for the hearing and determining the Merits of the said Appeal, And We do farther most humbly signify to your Royal Majesty That the Hon'ble Sr Michael Foster Knight one of the Justices of your Majesty's Court of King's Bench Sr Sydney Stafford Smythe Knight one of the Barons of your Majesty's Exchequer the Worshipfull Thomas Walker and We the Said Richard Smalbroke & Dennis Clarke respectively Doctors of Laws your Judges (among others) Delegates in the Cause of Appeal & Complaint so brot by the said Sarah Holmes against the said Francis Holmes rightly and duly proceeding did at the Petition of the Proctor of the said Francis Holmes by their Interlocutory Decree (having the Force of a Definitive Sentence in Writing) pronounce against the Force & Validity of the Appeal so made & interposed on the Behalf of the said Sarah Holmes but with the consent and at the Petition of the Proctor of the said Francis Holmes did retain the Principal Cause with all its Incidents Emergents Dependents and Things adjoined & connected thereto, That the said Sr Michael Foster Knight Sr Sydney Stafford Smythe Knight & we the said Richard Smalbroke & Dennis Clarke your Judges Delegates aforesaid rightly & duly proceeding in the said Principal Cause of Restitution of Conjugal Rites so brought by the said Francis Holmes against the said Sarah Holmes did at the Petition of the Proctor of the said Francis Holmes read and promulge a Definitive Sentence in Writing whereby they did pronounce decree & declare that the said Francis Holmes and Sarah Holmes did at the Time & Place mentioned in the Libell given in & admitted in the first Instance of the said Cause contract true pure and lawfull Matrimony and did rightly & duly solemnize the same in the Face of the Church according to the Rites & Ceremonies thereof and did afterwards consummate the same by Carnal Copulation & mutual Cohabitation and did also pronounce decree & declare the said Francis & Sarah to be lawfull Husband & Wife and did further decree the said Sarah Holmes to be monished to return to the said Francis Holmes her Husband and to cohabit with him as her lawfull Husband & perform conjugal Rites with the said Francis Holmes her Husband & to demean herself towards him at Bed & Board with Conjugal Affection under Pain of the Law & Contempt thereof (Justice so requiring) That afterwards a monition issued under the Seal of your Majesty's High Court of

Delegates against the said Sarah Holmes to return to the said Francis Holmes her Husband & to demean herself towards him at Bed & Board with Conjugal Affection under Pain of the Law & Contempt thereof & that such Monition hath been duly executed and that the said Sarah Holmes hath not returned to or cohabited with the said Francis Holmes her Husband or performed Conjugal Rites with him That We the said Richard Smalbroke & Denis Clarke your Judges Delegates aforesaid rightly and duly proceeding at the Petition of the Proctor of the said Francis Holmes did pronounce the said Sarah Holmes contumacious for not obeying the said Monition and for such her Contumacy & Contempt decreed her to be by your Majesty's Authority excommunicated. That the said Sarah Holmes was on Sunday the Twentysixth Day of February in the year of our Lord one thousand seven hundred & fifty Eight in the Face of the Parish Church of St George in the sd County of Midd'x in the Time of divine Service publickly denounced and declared excommunicate and that she the said Sarah Holmes hath obstinately and obdurately stood & perservered under such Sentence of Excommunication for the Space of forty Days and upwards since such Publication & Denunciation thereof and still doth stand & persevere under the same through an obstinate & incorrigible Disposition and in Contempt of your Majesty's Authority and Jurisdiction Ecclesiastical to the great Prejudice of her Soul's Health & the pernicious Example of others Good Christians And Whereas the Ecclesiastical Laws have no farther Power in this Behalf we therefore humbly supplicate & beseech your Majesty That in order to repress and correct the Contumacy and Contempt of the said Sarah Holmes so excommunicated by your Majestys Authority & so openly and publickly denounced excommunicate as aforesaid Your Majesty would vouchsafe pursuant to the Laws and Laudable Customs and Statutes of this Realm to extend the Aid of your Secular Arm and be graciously pleased to write to your Secular Officers to take & imprison the Body of the said Sarah Holmes that they whom the Fear of God will not reclaim from evil ways your Majesty's Animadversion may force & compell & may the Almighty long preserve your Majesty to the well governing your People in Testimony whereof We have caused the Seal of your Majesty's High Court of Delegates to be affixed to these Presents Dated the...Day of...in the year of our Lord one thousand Seven hundred & fifty Eight.
[DEL 2/36]

APPENDIX XXIV

PETITION FOR COMMISSION OF REVIEW

TO THE KINGS MOST EXCELLT MATIE.

The humble Peticon of Robert Prujean Esq. Grandchilde and heire of Sr Francis Prujean, Kt deceased, by and with his Curator Thomas Exton Doctor of Lawes.

Sheweth.

That the said Sr Francis Prujean made his will in writeing, and therein named the Lord Gorges, Doctor Stanly and Michael Pearse Executors, and gave them the Residue of his estate, after debts and legacies paid all in trust, and for the use, and during the minoritie of your peticoner, and did also give and bequeath to the Ladie Prujean his then Wife, since married to Sr John Maynard Baronet 2500 li in money and other legacies amounting in the whole to neare 5000 li in plaine and expresse words, over and above 2000 li in Gould that he freely gave her, after she was married unto him; all which several legacies so plainely given as aforesaid, the Executors long since paid and performed unto her.

But the said Ladie Prujean not being therewith contented, though she was not married to him above two yeares and foure moneths, and brought him no Issue, did commence a suit against the said Executors in the Arches Court of Canterburie for 550 li more, upon some general words of the will, and upon a Construction directly contrarie to the Law, and to the true intent and meaning of the Testator, as Sr Giles Sweit the Judge of the said Court, after a Solemne heareing by his diffinitive Sentence did adjudge and pronounce, acquitting the said Executors from payment of the said Legacie of 550 li.

But the said Ladie Prujean brought an Appeale from the said Sentence, and upon a Commission of Delegacy to her granted hath prevailed by a majority of Votes to get the said sentence given in the Arches Court to be reversed, and the executors to be condemned to pay the said Legacie of 550 li contrarie to the direct construction of Law, and to the true meaning of the Testator, and to the great damage of your peticoner, who hath the remainder given him not disposed by the said will.

Your peticoner therefore humbly beseecheth your Matie that in respect your peticoner hath no way to relieve himselfe but by a Commission of Review, whereby the Sentence of the Delegates may be reviewed, and if Justice so require be reversed your Matie would be graciously pleased to grant him the said Commission, and to order that nothing may be done, nor anie paiment of the said 550 libe made by the executors or anie of them, to the prejudice of your said peticoner in the meane time.

And your peticoner as ever bound shall pray &c.

[endorsed]

Att the Court att Whitehall

February 20th 1670/71

His Maty is Graciously pleased to referre it to the Rt Honble Sr Orlando Bridgeman Knt & Bart Lord Keeper of the Greate Seale of England, who is desired to informe himselfe of the nature of this matter, & what has been done in it, and to report to his Maty his Lopps opinion how fitt it may bee for his Maty to grant a Commission of Review, And then his Maty will declare his further Pleasure.

ARLINGTON

February 22: 1670/1

Lett Mr. Serjt Maynard & his Lady have notice of this Peticon and Lett all parties concerned attend mee at Essex house upon Saterday next being the 25th Instant at three of the clock in the afternoone that I may bee informed why the Comission of Review should not bee granted according as is desired by the Petr.

ORL BRIDGEMAN CS

March 15th: 1670/1

In obedience to yor Maties gracious reference to mee directed, having heard Councell on both Sydes, I doe humbly certify that I doe think it fitt to graunt a Comission of Review to the Peticonr, if yor Maty shall so bee pleased.

ORL BRIDGEMAN CS

[S. P. Cav, II, 29/287]

APPENDIX XXV

COMMISSION OF REVIEW

GEORGE THE THIRD BY THE GRACE OF GOD of Great Britain France and Ireland King Defender of the faith and so forth To our well beloved in Christ Samuel Lord Bishop of Rochester Charles Lord Bishop of Norwich Henry Reginald Lord Bishop of Exeter Lloyd Lord Kenyon Lord Chief Justice of our Court of Kings Bench William Lord Auckland Charles Lord Bayning Sir Archibald Macdonald Knight Lord Chief Baron of our Court of Exchequer Sir Giles Rooke Knight one of our Justices of our Court of Common Pleas Sir Soulden Lawrence Knight one of our Justices of our Court of Kings Bench Sir William Scott Knight Judge of our High Court of Admiralty James Henry Arnold and Christopher Robinson Doctors of Law respectively greeting WHEREAS it hath been represented and made appear to us by the humble petition of Richard Mathews of Leominster in the County of Hereford a Pauper that in a certain Testamentary Cause which lately depended before the Right Honorable Sir William Wynne Knight Doctor of Laws Master Keeper or Commissary of the Prerogative Court [of] John by Divine Providence Lord Archbishop of Canterbury Primate of all England and Metropolitan between the said Richard Mathews of the one part and Isaac Warner Esquire and others of the other part which said Cause was regularly called on for Sentence in the said Prerogative Court before the sd Right Honorable Sir William Wynne Knight Doctor of Laws Official Principal of the said Prerogative Court he the said Sir William Wynne pronounced a certain Interlocutory Decree having the force and effect of a definitive sentence in writing for the force and validity of a Testamentary Paper bearing date the second and sixth days of October one thousand seven hundred and eighty five purporting to be the last Will and Testament of William Mathews Esquire the party in the said Cause deceased Whereupon the said Richard Mathews rightly and duly appealed to our High Court of Chancery of Great Britain and to us in our said Court and we did by our two several Letters Patent bearing date respectively the twentieth day of June in the year of our Lord one thousand seven hundred and ninety four and in the thirty fourth year of our reign and the sixth day of April in the year of our Lord one thousand seven hundred and ninety six and in the thirty sixth year of our Reign commit the decision and determination of the said Cause of Appeal together with all its incidents Emergents Dependents and things adjoined and connected thereto to certain Judges Delegates therein named AND WHEREAS our said Judges Delegates or some of them by virtue of our said Letters Patent or Commission aforesaid proceeding in the said Cause of Appeal did pronounce a certain Interlocutory Decree having the force and effect of a definitive Sentence in writing on the part and behalf and in favor of the said Isaac Warner and against the said Richard Mathews by which Sentence they did amongst other things confirm the said Sentence so given read and promulged in the said Prerogative Court of Canterbury against the said Appeal and Complaint of the said Richard Mathews and for the force and validity of the said Testamentary paper of the second and sixth of October one thousand seven hundred and eighty five WHEREFORE the said Richard Mathews conceiving that he has been and is aggrieved and injured by the said pretended Interlocutory Order or Decree of our said Judges Delegates made and interposed in the said Cause and from all & every thing and things that do or may follow thereupon and that he was and is by the Laws and Statutes of this Kingdom of England deprived and excluded from all ordinary remedies by way of further Appeal hath humbly complained and petitioned unto us and our Person that we would be pleased by virtue of our Royal authority to provide him with some fit and meet remedy by way of Review WE THEREFORE being unwilling to deny our Royal favor to the said party intreating us by his petition and considering that the said petitioner was and is destitute and deprived of all other ordinary remedies by way of Appeal and Complaint AND WILLING NEVERTHELESS to provide him with a fit and convenient remedy by way of Review (as far as we can or may by Law) DO by these presents of our own meer motion and by virtue of our Royal Prerogative and the fullness of our power which we will shall not be called in question Commit to you in whose sound learning integrity judgment and skill in business of our own certain knowledge thereof We much confide in this behalf the Re-examination and Review of the whole proceedings in the said principal Cause lately depending before our said former Judges Delegates and in which they in fact made and interposed their said Interlocutory order or decree having the force and effect of a definitive Sentence in writing on the behalf and in favor of the said Isaac Warner Esquire together with all its incidents emergents and things whatsoever annexed and connected thereto AND we also commit to you the Re-examination of the said Decree and we reinstate the said Richard Mathews and our Will is that he be kept harmless and indemnified from and against the said pretended Decree...made and interposed against him the said Richard Mathews by our said Judges Delegates on the part and behalf of the said Isaac Warner Esqr until this Cause of Review be decided and determined by our said Judges Delegates in manner and form hereafter mentioned Commanding you that in all ordinary acts to be expidited in this Cause of Review until the giving the definitive Sentence exclusive all or at least two of you be present consenting but that in the giving the said definitive Sentence all or at least five of you of whom you the said Samuel Lord Bishop of Rochester Charles Lord Bishop of Norwich and Henry Reginald Lord Bishop of Exeter or one of you and of whom you the said Lloyd Lord Kenyon William Lord Auckland and Charles Lord Bayning or one of you and of whom you the said Sir Archibald Macdonald Sir Soulden Lawrence and Sir Giles Rooke or one of you we will shall be present and consenting CONVENING first before you the said Isaac Warner Esquire and all others by Law to be convened And that you re-examine and review the said final Decree of our former Judges Delegates and the whole and entire proceedings had and done before them in the said Cause with all the dispatch you can according to the exigency of the Law and having heard whatever on both sides is to be urged and insisted on you DO DECREE what shall be just and right in the said Cause and that you by your definitive Sentence finally determine the said Cause or Suit and that you decree the said final Decree made and interposed by our said former Judges Delegates and all and every thing or things that may or can follow thereupon to be revoked retracted made void annulled or otherwise to be confirmed in part or in the whole according to the exigency of the Laws as the Laws direct and that you make or give such other definitive Sentence or interpose such other Decree in the said Cause or Suit as according to Justice and as the Laws shall seem to you to direct require and demand notwithstanding our former Commission to our said former Judges Delegates amongst other things as aforesaid granted and the said final Decree made and interposed or other cause matter or thing whatsoever to the contrary had done promulged or interposed all and singular which matters and things of our own knowledge and of our own meer motion as touching and concerning the premisses we so far delegate to you by these presents AND that you furthermore Inhibit or cause to be Inhibited our said former Judges Delegates and every one of them and also the said Isaac Warner Esquire and all and singular others pretending a right title and interest in this behalf (whom we do also by these presents so Inhibit) that pending the Petition Re-examination Review and Complaint in this Cause undecided before you they do not proceed to the Execution of the said Decree and that they or either of them do not attempt to do any other thing or cause or procure any other thing to be done or attempted to the prejudice of the party petitioning Commanding by these presents all and singular our former Judges Delegates and also all and singular Registers and Actuaries of whatsoever Courts and Offices and all other our Officers and Ministers whatsoever that they peremptorily observe and obey you and your Decrees in and about the Premisses and touching and concerning all and every the premisses and whatsoever you shall Decree and promulge in or concerning the premisses or in any or either of them you shall duly cause to be put in Execution by fit remedies of Law IN TESTIMONY whereof we have caused these our Letters to be made Patent WITNESS ourself at Westminster the twenty seventh Day of July in the thirty ninth year of our Reign and in the Year of our Lord One thousand seven hundred and ninety nine.

BLACKSTONE

[DEL 8/32]

APPENDIX XXVI

APPOINTMENT OF DEPUTY REGISTRAR

Tenor Instrumenti Jacobum Pinfold Notarium Publicum Deputatum Samueli Hill Armigero Registrario Principali Supreme Curie Delegatorum Regiorum constituentis per prefatum Samuelem Hill, Die Extraordinario post Terminum Sancti Hilarij Episcopi finitum Die Lune Vicesimo Septimo scilicet de Mense Februarij Anno Domini Millesimo Septingentessimo Vicesimo Primo exhibiti.

WHEREAS, I Samuel Hill of the Inner Temple London Esq have been sometime and now am by Virtue of Letters Patent under the Great Seal of Great Britain bearing Date on or about the tenth day of December 1714, seized and possessed of the Office or Offices of Principal Register, and Clerk of the Ecclesiastical and Admiralty Courts of Delegates, and Keeper of the Books of Registers, Acts, and other Evidences to the said Office or Offices belonging, to hold by myself or my sufficient Deputy or Deputy's for and during the Term of my Natural Life AND WHEREAS I the said Samuel Hill did sometime ago. vizt since the Date of the said Letters Patent nominate constitute and appoint Thomas Oughton of Doctors Commons London Notary Publick to Exercise the said Office or Offices of Register and Clerk of the Ecclesiastical and Admiralty Courts of Delegates and Keeper of the Books of Registers, Acts and other Evidences, to the said Office or Offices belonging as my Deputy, AND WHEREAS I the said Samuel Hill have by an Instrument under my hand and Seal bearing even Date with, but executed before, these presents, for diverse good Causes and Considerations me thereunto moveing, Retracted, Revoked, and annulled, and declared null and void to all Intents and purposes whatsoever, the Constitution, Nomination and appointment by me made as aforesaid of the said Thomas Oughton to Exercise the Office or Offices aforesaid of Register and Clerk of the said Ecclesiastical and Admiralty Courts of Delegates and Keeper of the Books of Registers, Acts and other Evidences to the said Office or Offices belonging, as my Deputy, and have Revoked and Declared void all and all manner of Deputations, Grants, Covenants, Concessions, Powers, Faculty's, Profitts, Fees Pensions, Advantages, Emoluments, or Commodities, whatsoever touching or concerning the prmisses by me heretofore given, granted or made to the said Thomas Oughton either by word of mouth, act or acts of Court, or in writeing or writeings under my hand, or under my hand and seal or otherwise howsoever, as in and by the said Instrument relation being thereunto had may more fully appear NOW KNOW ALL MEN by these presents That I the said Samuel Hill do hereby Nominate Constitute and appoint JAMES PINFOLD of Doctors Commons aforesaid Notary Publick to Exercise as my Deputy the said Office or Offices of Register and Clerk of the Ecclesiastical and Admiralty Courts of Delegates, and Keeper of the Books of Registers, Acts and other Evidences to the said Office or Offices belonging (all Appeals about Causes of Reprisall and all things thereunto relateing only excepted) and to take into his Custody and possession all and singular the said Books of Registers, Acts, Records Muniments and other Evidences belonging to the said Office or Offices (Except as before Excepted) and to attend all Courts, Sessions, or Sittings, and take, make out, and draw and Sign as my Deputy all Minutes Acts and Instruments that shall be transacted in or any ways concern relate or belong to the said Office or Offices (except as before excepted) and to ask demand receive and take of and from all persons whom it may concern all the fees, advantages, Proffitts and Comodities of the said Office or Offices (except as before excepted) and finally to act, do, perform, and transact every thing relateing to the premisses, in as full and ample manner as I the said Samuel Hill could or might do, if I attended and Exercised the said Office or Offices in person And I do hereby promise to ratify and confirm whatever the said James Pinfold shall Lawfully do or cause to be Lawfully done as my Deputy in the premisses. IN WITNESS whereof I have hereunto set my hand and Seal the Twenty first day of February in the year of our Lord God One Thousand Seven Hundred and Twenty.

Signed Sealed and Delivered by the said Samuel Hill (being first trebly stamp'd) in the presence of — SAML HILL (L.S.)

ROBERT PEIRSON Notarij Publici
CHA: GARRETT Notarij Publici
EDW: GREENLY Notarij Publici

[DEL 9/6]

APPENDIX XXVII

LIST OF REGISTRARS OF THE DELEGATES

The following abbreviations are used:

adm.	admitted	pr.	promoted to office of principal registrar
app.	appointed		
app. rev.	appointment revoked	res.	resigned
d.	died	succ.	succeeded
occ.	occurs	surr.	surrendered

When a registrar is shown occurring on two different dates, these represent the earliest and latest references to him which have been found.

John ap Rice (or Price) occ. 1540.

In the first surviving Act Book of the ecclesiastical Delegates, he is said to have assisted at the hearing of *Thomas Butterwick's Case* and he is there described as 'registrarius regius', the usual title of the principal registrar of the court.[1] He is probably to be identified with the John ap Rice who was granted for life, by a patent of 1 September 1534, the office of 'clerk and assistant to the commissioners who shall from time to time be appointed in accordance with the act of parliament 25 Hen. VIII, [c. 21], for the visitation of religious places; and principal registrar and clerk to any other commissioners who are or shall be appointed in matters touching the spirituality and their laws, as visitations, elections and delegations';[2] the grant is widely enough phrased to include the registrarship of the ecclesiastical Delegates, as is the title 'registrar-general in ecclesiastical matters' given to the John ap Rice who figures in a petition dated 1 December of that year.[3]

It is also tempting to associate the Delegates' registrar with the John ap Rice who is the subject of an article in the *Dictionary of National Biography*;[4] the latter worked under Cromwell and was involved in the great visitation of the monasteries in 1535, to which the wording of the patent of 1534 would seem clearly to point. The difficulty in the way of this identification is that the John ap

[1] DEL 4/1/137. [2] *L. & P. Hen. VIII*, 1534, p. 474.

[3] *Ibid.*, p. 598.

[4] (London, 1885–1913), vol. 46, pp. 329–30.

Rice of the biographical note died *c.* 1573,[1] while the John ap Rice of the patent must have died by 1554.[2] The solution of the problem may lie in the fact that there are no less than three persons of this name noted in the *Dictionary of National Biography*, all of whom were alive in the first half of the sixteenth century and at least two of whom were in the service of the Crown;[3] such a coincidence clearly provides scope for confusion and it seems at least possible that the biographical note on John ap Rice combines references to more than one person.

William Say, app. 1554.

In 1554 he was appointed for life by patent as registrar for appeals in marine causes and also for appeals in ecclesiastical causes 'to be committed by the archbishop, his vicar-general, principal official or special commissary to his superior judges'.[4] It appears from a later patent that he was appointed upon John ap Rice's death.[5] Shortly after the grant to Say the Act 25 Hen. VIII, c. 19, was repealed, and for the rest of Mary's reign he cannot in strictness be regarded as registrar of the Court of Delegates but of those judicial bodies which replaced it. Upon Elizabeth's accession, however, the ecclesiastical Delegates were revived, and it is clear from a patent issued in 1562 that Say became their registrar.[6] There is no entry of a patent for this appointment in the Calendar of Patent Rolls and it is likely that Say continued to act throughout the whole of this period by virtue of the grant made by Mary.

William Say and Robert Say, app. 1562.[7]

By a patent of 28 August 1562, there was a grant and confirmation for life in survivorship of the registrarship of the ecclesiastical Delegates to William and Robert Say, the grant reciting that Robert had been trained to do the work by William 'as he is now growing old'.[8] This seems to be the first example of a joint appointment to the office.

[1] *D.N.B.*, vol. 46, p. 330.

[2] His death is referred to in a patent of 1562 (*C.P.R.*, 1560–63, p. 256).

[3] *D.N.B.*, vol. 46, p. 329. Two of the references are merely casual, as only one person of this name is accorded a full biography. The author of it had not consulted the Calendar of Patent Rolls and was thus unaware of the problem.

[4] *C.P.R.*, 1554–5, pp. 35–6.

[5] *C.P.R.*, 1560–63, p. 256.

[6] *Ibid.*

[7] *Ibid.*

[8] *Ibid.*

Robert Say, succ.?, d. 1584?

He presumably succeeded his father, and he may well have held the office until Edward Barker's accession.

Edward Barker, LL.B., occ. 24 May 1585;[1] occ. 17 May 1602.[2]

There are several references to him in the State Papers Domestic, of which the most interesting is a letter to Walsingham giving advice on a point of matrimonial law.[3]

John Plomer, adm. 2 June 1602;[4] occ. 22 June 1608.[5]

Nothing is known of Plomer, except that he was also registrar of the High Commission, jointly with Sir George Paule.[6]

Sir George Paule, occ. 27 April 1607;[7] occ. 18 February 1634.[8]

Paule was a man of some prominence in his period.[9] In his youth, he attached himself to Archbishop Whitgift and gradually rose in his service, becoming comptroller of his household in 1599; he retained a close association with the archbishop, attending him on his deathbed and later writing his biography. He was in addition employed in a variety of public services, being twice returned to Parliament and sitting on three occasions on the commission set up to examine the Duke of Buckingham's affairs; he was also, it seems, a Master of Requests. He obtained his first ecclesiastical registrarship in 1588, when the interest of Anthony Calton, registrar to the Bishop of Ely, was assigned to him; this he retained until 1600, when he transferred it to Sir John Lambe. On 16 May 1603 the office of registrar and clerk of the acts was granted to Paule and John Plomer;[10] the latter had already been admitted to the same office in the Court of Delegates and Paule must later have been joined with him as registrar of that tribunal also (the first

[1] DEL 5/1/3. He cannot have held the office for long before this, as a testimonial dated 11 November 1584 was sent to the Earl of Leicester by the advocates of Doctors' Commons in favour of his application for the registrarship (*C.S.P.D.*, 1581–90, p. 212).

[2] DEL 4/2/74.

[3] *C.S.P.D.*, 1581–90, p. 504; see also pp. 264, 360(?) and 563(?).

[4] DEL 4/2/79.

[5] DEL 4/4/192.

[6] *D.N.B.*, vol. 44, p. 79.

[7] DEL 4/3/301.

[8] DEL 4/14/255.

[9] This note is based on *D.N.B.*, vol. 44, pp. 79–80.

[10] This grant apparently refers to the High Commission, for if it is taken to refer to the Court of Delegates it is strange that Paule was not spoken of as its registrar in the Act Books until several years later.

reference to him in the records occurs on 27 April 1607). It seems that Paule held the office of Delegates' registrar alone from Plomer's death or retirement in 1608 until his own death in April 1635; he is last referred to in the records as registrar on 18 February of that year.

Although the routine business of the court was managed by deputies, Paule's wide experience of affairs gave him a sufficient interest in its workings to intervene on occasions, and there survives among the State Papers Domestic correspondence he conducted with various royal secretaries arising out of litigation before the Delegates.[1]

Sir John Oldbury, adm. 15 April 1635,[2] surr. December? 1672.[3]

Oldbury, like his predecessor, held together the registrarships of the Court of Delegates and the High Commission. He applied for admission to that office in the High Commission on 16 April 1635,[4] and was admitted the following day after agreeing to the terms of a decree in Chancery, which allotted three eighths of the profits to the widow and children of John Plomer.[5] At the time of his admission, he produced letters patent of 20 April 1627 which conferred both registrarships upon himself and one Francis Paule jointly after the death of Sir George Paule; but the entry in the Delegates' Act Book which records Oldbury's admission to that tribunal says nothing of Francis Paule nor does it mention any charge upon the revenues of the office; from the evidence of the Delegates' archives, he held the registrarship of that court alone and for his own benefit for the whole time that he enjoyed it.

It is clear from other sources, however, that the office soon became the subject of a long and rancorous dispute. Two years later Francis Paule presented a petition to Archbishop Laud, seeking his assistance in gaining admission to both registrarships;[6] the petition is endorsed with a reference to Sir John Lambe and Dr Ducke who appointed to hear it a few days later in the dining room at Doctors' Commons. They apparently found against Paule,

[1] *C.S.P.D.*, 1623–5, pp. 450 and 506.
[2] DEL 4/14/264.
[3] *C.S.P.D.*, 1672–3, p. 270.
[4] *C.S.P.D.*, 1635, p. 185.
[5] *Ibid.* pp. 187–8. The decree was based upon articles of agreement between Sir George Paule and Plomer, and the incident serves as an interesting illustration of the way in which a patentee could apparently use his right to dispose of the reversion to his office as a means of providing for his family after his death.
[6] *C.S.P.D.*, 1636–7, p. 459.

as in 1640 he presented a second petition to the House of Lords, claiming that he had been deprived of his rights through the opposition of Lambe.[1] Sir George Paule's widow then intervened on behalf of herself and her son and the dispute dragged on for several years, being still undecided in 1645.[2] The final issue of the dispute is obscure but it seems to have been resolved in Oldbury's favour; shortly after the Restoration, his name recurs in the records for a brief period with the title of principal registrar,[3] and an application for a reversionary grant of the office made towards the end of 1660 refers to him (but not to Paule) as the current patentee.[4] He still held the post in December 1672, when he surrendered in favour of his nephew John.[5]

No reference has been found to any principal registrar during the Interregnum, and the business of the court was conducted by John Oughton the deputy registrar.[6] Oldbury's interest may have lapsed because he was a Royalist (the fact that references to him recur immediately after the Restoration suggests this), but it is also possible that the legal right to the registrarship remained uncertain throughout the whole of this period and it was impossible to say who was entitled. If the office was filled during the Interregnum, Main Thompson's conjecture about the Court of Admiralty (that there was a series of short-term appointments by Parliament)[7] may also be applicable to the Court of Delegates.

Simon Rolleston, occ. December 1660.[8]

He is referred to in a petition as enjoying the office jointly with Oldbury at this time; no other reference to him has been found.

John Oldbury Junior, app. 12 December 1672.[9]

Thomas Oughton, occ. 17 January 1679;[10] occ. 15 August 1695.[11]

[1] H.M.C., App. to 4th Rep., p. 33.

[2] H.M.C., App. to 4th Rep., p. 47; H.M.C., App. to 6th Rep., p. 87.

[3] DEL 4/20/7 (5 October 1660); DEL 4/20/unfoliated (1 June 1661).

[4] *C.S.P.D.*, 1660–1, p. 446.

[5] *C.S.P.D.*, 1672–3, p. 270.

[6] See p. 303 *post*.

[7] Main Thompson, *Admiralty Registrars*, p. 9.

[8] *C.S.P.D.*, 1660–1, p. 446.

[9] *C.S.P.D.*, 1672–3, p. 270.

[10] DEL 6/19/99.

[11] DEL 6/27/104; he is here referred to as 'principal register recently deceased'.

Sir Richard Crawley, app. 15 August 1695;[1] d. 21 March 1712.[2]

Crawley had previously acted as deputy registrar of the Court of Admiralty,[3] and in September 1698 he was granted the principal registrarship of that Court from the death of Sir Orlando Gee.[4] From that date until the abolition of the Court of Delegates, the registrarships of both tribunals were always held together.

Richard Hill, succ. 1712?, surr. 23 October 1714.[5]

The office of principal registrar had been granted to Richard Hill in reversion by letters patent after the determination of Crawley's interest and to Sir Charles Hedges after the determination of Crawley's and Hill's interests.[6] Hill presumably succeeded Crawley upon the latter's death, but he surrendered the office on 23 October 1714 in favour of Samuel Hill; Hedges had already died,[7] and there was therefore no reversionary interest outstanding when the surrender occurred.[8]

Sir Samuel Hill, app. 3 December 1714;[9] d. 21 February 1758.[10]

No reversionary interest was created by the letters patent embodying his grant, but it is clear that at some later date further letters patent were issued, conferring the office on Godfrey Lee

[1] DEL 6/27/104. In a warrant to the Attorney-General authorizing him to prepare a patent in Crawley's favour, there is a reference to the prior interests of Thomas Oughton and of 'Charles Tucker, junior', both of whom were stated to enjoy such rights as they possessed in the office under a patent of 25 Charles II (*C.S.P.D.*, 1694–5, p. 14). Tucker's interest presumably determined by death or surrender before Crawley's appointment.

[2] DEL 6/33/126.

[3] Main Thompson, *Admiralty Registrars*, p. 10.

[4] *C.S.P.D.*, 1698, p. 396.

[5] DEL 9/5/71.

[6] DEL 9/5/53–8.

[7] DEL 9/5/71.

[8] The registrarship of the Court of Admiralty was granted to Crawley, with reversions to Richard Hill and Charles Hedges by letters patent under the seal of that court dated 27 November 1710 (Main Thompson, *Admiralty Registrars*, p. 10). Upon Crawley's death, Richard Hill succeeded to this office, which he also resigned in October 1714, being followed (as in the case of the Court of Delegates) by Samuel Hill. The Charles Hedges referred to in the Admiralty patent was thus passed over and the most likely explanation of this fact (which puzzled Main Thompson) is that he is to be identified with the Sir Charles Hedges of the Delegates' patent, who died before Richard Hill surrendered. The presence of Hedge's name in the patents may have some connection with a proposal made in 1695 to grant the registrarship of 'the Ecclesiastical and Admiralty Court' to his nephew, a Mr Smith, upon Crawley's death (H.M.C., Downshire MSS, vol. 1, p. 527). Nothing seems to have come of this, although an Edward Smith was deputy registrar of the Delegates from 1732 to 1741 (see p. 303 *post*).

[9] DEL 9/5/69–72.

[10] DEL 6/44/79.

Farrant after the death of Samuel Hill and of Henry Farrant.[1] The latter, the father of Godfrey Lee Farrant, predeceased him, dying in 1727;[2] although he never held office in the Court of Delegates, he was principal registrar of the Court of Chivalry from 1707 until his death and also (for a period) of the Court of Arches.[3]

Godfrey Lee Farrant, adm. 27 February 1758;[4] d. 9 August 1790.[5]

The Hon. Charles George Perceval (later Lord Arden), app. 23 June 1764;[6] adm. 11 August 1790.[7]

Arden's patent entitled him to the office 'after the decease, surrender, Forfeiture or other avoidance or determination of Godfrey Lee Farrant Esq.'.[8] There was also a reversion, after the determination of Arden's interest, in favour of his younger brother, the Hon. Spencer Perceval.[9] Arden remained registrar of the Court of Admiralty until 1840;[10] presumably he retained the registrarship of the Court of Delegates until its abolition in 1832.

1 *Ibid.* 2 *Ibid.* 3 *H.C.C.*, pp. 235 and 226.
4 DEL 6/44/79. 5 DEL 6/50/18.
6 *Cal. Home Off. Papers*, 1760–5, p. 496.
7 DEL 6/50/18. 8 *Ibid.*
9 *Cal. Home Off. Papers*, 1760–5, p. 496.
10 Main Thompson, *Admiralty Registrars*, p. 14.

APPENDIX XXVIII

LIST OF DEPUTY REGISTRARS OF THE DELEGATES

The abbreviations are the same as those used in the preceding list.

William Say, app. *c.* 1534; pr. 1554.

He is described in a patent of 1562 as having been deputy registrar under John ap Rice 'for about 20 years';[1] as ap Rice's tenure of that office apparently extended from 1534 to *c.* 1554, it is likely that Say acted as his deputy for the whole of that period. In the period covered by the Act Book 1538–44 he was active in the court's business and attended most of its sittings:[2] he was clearly discharging the usual duties of a deputy registrar, although he is never so described in terms.

William Barker, occ. 9 February 1585;[3] occ. 30 June 1638.[4]

Thomas Barker, occ. 6 May 1586.[5]

Edward Say, occ. 6 May 1586;[6] occ. 28 June 1586.[7]

Francis Pitman, occ. 15 November 1587;[8] occ. 25 October 1591.[9]

John Plomer, occ. 3 July 1595;[10] occ. 17 May 1602;[11] pr. 2 June 1602.[12]

Edward Peers, occ. 11 July 1638;[13] occ. 8 February 1639.[14]

John Crompton, occ. 22 April 1640;[15] occ. 3 December 1640.[16]

1 *C.P.R.*, 1560–3, p. 256.
2 DEL 4/1/*passim.*
3 DEL 5/1/17.
4 DEL 4/15/357.
5 DEL 5/1/23.
6 DEL 5/1/24.
7 DEL 5/1/34.
8 DEL 5/1/61.
9 DEL 5/1/153.
10 DEL 5/2/33.
11 DEL 5/3/17.
12 DEL 4/2/79.
13 DEL 4/15/357.
14 DEL 4/16/118.
15 DEL 4/16/132.
16 DEL 4/17/81.

John Oughton, occ. 12 May 1641;[1] occ. 29 January 1667.[2]

John Mayer, occ. 22 January 1640;[3] occ. 29 April 1642.[4]

Thomas Oughton, occ. 6 February 1667;[5] app. rev. 21 February 1720.[6]

Thomas Cantrell, occ. 24 May 1690;[7] occ. 19 December 1699.[8]

James Pinfold, app. 21 February 1720;[9] occ. 17 February 1732.[10]

Edward Smith, occ. 14 March 1732;[11] app. rev. 31 March 1741.[12]

Edward Rushworth, app. 31 March 1741;[13] occ. 20 February 1758.[14]

George Bellas, app. 27 February 1758;[15] app. rev. 8 November 1759.[16]

Nathaniel Bishop, app. 8 November 1759;[17] occ. 16 November 1785.[18]

Maurice Swabey, adm. 24 January 1781;[19] res. 26 June 1789.[20]

Robert Jenner, app. 26 June 1789;[21] adm. 10 July 1789;[22] occ. 15 November 1810.[23]

[1] DEL 4/17/136.

[2] DEL 4/21/150.

[3] DEL 4/17/96.

[4] DEL 4/18/1.

[5] DEL 4/21/154.

[6] DEL 9/6/10–11.

[7] DEL 6/25/43. His appointment as deputy was confirmed on 15 August 1695 when Richard Crawley was admitted as principal registrar (DEL 4/27/104).

[8] DEL 6/29/10.

[9] DEL 9/6/12–13.

[10] DEL 6/38/118.

[11] DEL 6/38/125.

[12] DEL 9/7/82–3.

[13] *Ibid.*

[14] DEL 6/44/78.

[15] DEL 6/44/79.

[16] DEL 6/44/117.

[17] *Ibid.*

[18] DEL 6/49/204.

[19] DEL 6/48/36; by the terms of his admission he was to act jointly with Bishop and the entry in the Assignation Book states that he was appointed 'by the Desire and at the Recommendation' of the latter.

[20] DEL 6/49/181; Swabey tendered his resignation formally to Drs Harris and Battine and gave as his reason 'that he intended shortly to take the Degree of Doctor of Law in order to become one of the Advocates of the Arches Court of his Grace the Lord Archbishop of Canterbury'.

[21] DEL 6/49/191.

[22] *Ibid.*

[23] DEL 6/54/77.

James Rivington Wheeler, occ. 14 December 1790;[1] res. 13 December 1810.[2]

He is then described as being the 'Surviving Deputy Registrar', which makes it clear that Jenner must have died or retired between 15 November and 13 December.

James Farquhar, adm. 13 December 1810;[3] occ. 31 January 1829.[4]

James Bush, adm. 13 December 1810;[5] res. 19 January 1815.[6]

Henry Birchfield Swabey, adm. 24 January 1811;[7] occ. 24 January 1829.[8]

William Townsend, adm. 15 May 1820;[9] res. 13 June 1820.[10]

John Benjamin Morgan, adm. 13 June 1820;[11] occ. 2 February 1829.[12]

[1] DEL 6/50/35. [2] DEL 6/54/85. [3] *Ibid.*
[4] DEL 6/56/264. [5] DEL 6/54/85. [6] DEL 6/54/229.
[7] DEL 6/54/87. [8] DEL 6/56/260. [9] DEL 6/55/136.
[10] DEL 6/55/138–9. [11] DEL 6/55/139. [12] DEL 6/56/264.

BIBLIOGRAPHY

I. MANUSCRIPTS

PUBLIC RECORD OFFICE

DEL 1 Processes
DEL 2 Miscellaneous Cause Papers
DEL 3 Depositions and Personal Answers
DEL 4 Act Books
DEL 5 Sentences
DEL 6 Assignation Books
DEL 7 Appeal Case Books
DEL 8 Miscellanea
DEL 9 Muniment Books
DEL 10 Wills etc.
DEL 11 Additional Miscellanea

State Papers, Domestic, Elizabeth I (S.P. 41/11); Charles II (S.P. 29/287)

II. PRINTED BOOKS

(I) PUBLICATIONS OF THE PUBLIC RECORD OFFICE

Calendar of Home Office Papers, 1878–99

Calendar of Letters and Papers, Foreign and Domestic, Henry VIII, 1864–1932

Calendar of Patent Rolls, 1891–

Calendar of State Papers, Domestic, 1856–

(II) PUBLICATIONS OF THE HISTORICAL MANUSCRIPTS COMMISSION

Calendar of the MSS of the Marquess of Downshire, 4 vols., 1924–40

Calendar of the MSS of the Duke of Portland, 10 vols., 1891–1931

Calendar of the MSS of the Marquess of Salisbury, 18 vols., 1883–1940

(III) PARLIAMENTARY PAPERS

Courts of the Archbishop of Canterbury. R. Com. Rep.; 1823 (462) VII, 27

Courts of the Bishop of London. R. Com. Rep.; 1824 (43) IX, 25

Courts of Admiralty, Delegates, and Appeals for Prizes. R. Com. Rep.; 1824 (240) IX, 75

Practice and Jurisdiction of the Ecclesiastical Courts in England and Wales. R. Com. Rep.; 1831–2 (199) XXIV, 1

Return of the Composition of the Court of Delegates...distinguishing Commissions in case of Heresy or unsound Doctrine. H. C. Return, 1850 (565) XLVI, 437

Law of Divorce. R. Com. 1st Rep.; 1852–3, XL, 249

Return of All Appeals in Causes of Doctrine or Discipline made to the High Court of Delegates. H. C. Return, 1867–8, LVII, 75

Public Records. R. Com. 2nd Rep.; 1914 Cmd. 7544 XLVI, 189

(IV) OTHER BOOKS AND ARTICLES

Ackermann, R. *Microcosm of London.* 3 vols. London, 1808–11

Addams, J. *A Catalogue of Processes in the Registry of the High Court of Delegates, from 1609 to 1823.* London, 1823

Reports of Cases...at Doctors' Commons, and in the High Court of Delegates. 2 vols. London, 1823–5

Ayliffe, J. *Parergon Juris Canonici Anglicani.* London, 1734

Bentham, J. *Collected Works.* 11 vols. Edinburgh, 1843

Beven, T. 'The Appellate Jurisdiction of the House of Lords', *Law Quarterly Review*, vol. XVII, 1901

Blackstone, W. *Commentaries on the Laws of England.* 4 vols. London, 1800

Brentano, R. *York Metropolitan Jurisdiction and Papal Judges Delegate (1279–1296).* Berkeley, California, 1959

Brodrick, G. C., and Fremantle, W. H. *A Collection of the Judgments of the Judicial Committee of the Privy Council in Ecclesiastical Cases.* London, 1865

Bromley, P. M. *Family Law.* London, 1962

Browne, A. A. *A Compendion, View of the Civil Law, and of the Law of the Admiralty.* 2 vols. London, 1802

Buckland, W. W. *A Text Book of Roman Law.* Cambridge, 1950

Burn, R. *Ecclesiastical Law.* 4 vols. London, 1781

Cardwell, E. (ed.). *The Reformation of the Ecclesiastical Laws.* Oxford, 1850

Cheney, M. 'The Compromise of Avranches of 1172 and the Spread of Canon Law in England', *English Historical Review*, vol. LVI, 1941

Coke, E. *Institutes of the Laws of England.* 3 vols. London, 1670–1

Cross, A. R. N. *Evidence.* London, 1963

Cunningham, T. A. *A New and Complete Law-Dictionary.* 2 vols. London, 1764–5

Diamond, A. S. 'Some New Thoughts on Legal Procedure', *The Journal of the Society of Public Teachers of Law*, (N.S.), vol. V, 1959–60

Dickens, C. *David Copperfield*

Sketches by Boz

Duck, A. *De Usu et Authoritate Juris Civilis Romanorum.* Leyden, 1654 [London, 1689]

Edwards, E. *A Treatise on the Jurisdiction of the High Court of Admiralty.* London, 1847

Fincham, F. W. X. 'Letters concerning Sir Maurice Eustace, Lord Chancellor of Ireland', *English Historical Review*, vol. XXXV, 1920

Firth, C. H., and Rait, R. S. *Acts and Ordinances of the Interregnum.* 3 vols. London, 1911

Fisher, H. A. L. *The History of England from the Accession of Henry VII to the Death of Henry VIII (1485–1547).* London, 1906

Floyer, P. *The Proctor's Practice in the Ecclesiastical Courts.* London, 1746

Foster, M. *An Examination of the Scheme of Church Power.* London, 1840

Frere, W. H. *The English Church in the Reigns of Elizabeth and James I (1558–1625)*. London, 1904
Gibson, E. *Codex Juris Ecclesiastici Anglicani*. 2 vols. London, 1713
Giffard, H. S. (Earl of Halsbury) and others. *Laws of England*. 31 vols. London, 1907–17
Giuseppi, M. S. *Guide to the Contents of the Public Record Office*. 2 vols. London, 1963
Gwatkin, H. M., and others (ed.). *Cambridge Medieval History*. 9 vols. Cambridge, 1911–36
Hansard, T. C. *Parliamentary Debates* (n.s.). 25 vols. London, 1820–30 [3rd Series, 356 vols. London, 1831–91]
Holdsworth, W. S. *A History of English Law*. 16 vols. London, 1903–66
Inderwick, F. A. *The Interregnum*. London, 1891
Jeaffreson, J. C. (ed.). *Middlesex County Records*. 4 vols. London, 1887–92
Justinian. *Digest*. 2 vols. Berlin, 1870
Langdell, C. C. 'The Development of Equity Pleading from Canon Law Procedure.' *Select Essays in Anglo-American Legal History*. 3 vols. Cambridge, 1907–9
Law, J. T. *Forms of Ecclesiastical Law*. London, 1831
Main Thompson, G. H. *Admiralty Registrars, Some Historical Notes*. London, 1958
Maitland, F. W. *Roman Canon Law in the Church of England*. London, 1898
Marsden, R. G. (ed.). *Select Pleas in the Court of Admiralty*. 2 vols. London, 1894–7
Maxwell-Lyte, H. C. *Historical Notes on the Use of the Great Seal of England*. London, 1926
Morey, A. *Bartholomew of Exeter*. Cambridge, 1937
Mortimer, R. C. *Western Canon Law*. London, 1953
Nys, E. *Le Droit Romain, Le Droit des Gens et le Collège des Docteurs en Droit Civil*. Brussels, 1910
Oughton, T. *Ordo Judiciorum*. 2 vols. London, 1738
Palmer, J. *The Practice in the House of Lords on Appeals etc*. London, 1830
Peek, H. E., and Hall, C. P. *The Archives of the University of Cambridge*. Cambridge, 1962
Phillimore, R. J. *Commentaries upon International Law*. 3 vols. London, 1854–7
Pollard, A. F. *Henry VIII*. London, 1951
Roscoe, E. S. *A History of the English Prize Court*. London, 1924
Lord Stowell. London, 1916
Rymer, T., and Sanderson, R. *Foedera*. 20 vols. London, 1704–35
Sanders, G. W. *Orders of the High Court of Chancery*. London, 1845
Senior, W. *Doctors' Commons and the Old Court of Admiralty*. London, 1922
Squibb, G. D. *The High Court of Chivalry, a Study of the Civil Law in England*. London, 1959
Stow, J. *A Survey of London*. 2 vols. Oxford, 1908

Strype, J. *Memorials of Thomas Cranmer*. 3 vols. Oxford, 1848–54
Trevor-Roper, H. R. *Archbishop Laud 1573–1645*. London, 1962
Usher, R. G. *The Rise and Fall of the High Commission*. Oxford, 1913
Van Espen, Z. B. *Jus Ecclesiasticum Universum*. 2 vols. Cologne, 1729
Viner, C. *A General Abridgment of Law and Equity*. 23 vols. Aldershot, 1742–53
Williams, J. *The Law of the Universities*. London, 1910
Wood, T. *An Institute of the Laws of England*. London, 1772
Woodcock, B. L. *Medieval Ecclesiastical Courts in the Diocese of Canterbury*. Oxford, 1952
Wynne, W. *Life of Sir Leoline Jenkins*. 2 vols. London, 1724.
Yale, D. E. C. (ed.). *Lord Nottingham's Chancery Cases*. 2 vols. London, 1957–61.

INDEX